THE CAMBRIDGE COMPANION TO
CHILDREN'S LITERATURE

Some of the most innovative and spell-binding literature has been written for young people, but only recently has academic study embraced its range and complexity. With discussions ranging from eighteenth-century moral tales to modern fantasies by J. K. Rowling and Philip Pullman, this *Companion* illuminates acknowledged classics and many more neglected works. Written by leading scholars from around the world, it will be essential reading for all students and scholars of children's literature, offering original readings and new research that reflects the latest developments in the field.

A complete list of books in the series at the back of this book

D0148778

THE CAMBRIDGE
COMPANION TO
CHILDREN'S
LITERATURE

EDITED BY

M. O. GRENBY

and

ANDREA IMMEL

CAMBRIDGE
UNIVERSITY PRESS

CAMBRIDGE UNIVERSITY PRESS

Cambridge, New York, Melbourne, Madrid, Cape Town, Singapore,
São Paulo, Delhi, Tokyo, Dubai

Cambridge University Press
The Edinburgh Building, Cambridge CB2 8RU, UK

Published in the United States of America by Cambridge University Press, New York

www.cambridge.org
Information on this title: www.cambridge.org/9780521687829

First published 2009

Printed in the United Kingdom at the University Press, Cambridge

A catalogue record for this publication is available from the British Library

ISBN 978-0-521-86819-8 hardback
ISBN 978-0-521-68782-9 paperback

CONTENTS

CONTENTS

ILLUSTRATIONS

All illustrations reproduced by permission of the Cotsen Children's Library, Department of Rare Books and Special Collections, Princeton University Library, except where noted.

NOTES ON CONTRIBUTORS

BRIAN ALDERSON is an independent scholar. He was children's book editor of *The Times* from 1967 to 1983, and has held visiting appointments at the University of Southern Mississippi, University of California at Los Angeles and the Beinecke Rare Book Library at Yale University. He has curated exhibitions on aspects of children's literature at the British Library, British Museum, National Library of Scotland, Pierpont Morgan Library and elsewhere, and was the founder of the Children's Books History Society and is editor of its *Newsletter*. His books include revisions of F. J. Harvey Darton's *Children's Books in England* (1982), *Sing a Song for Sixpence* (1986), *Looking at Picture Books* (1993), *Ezra Jack Keats* (1994) and *Be Merry and Wise: The Origins of Children's Book Publishing in England 1650–1850* (with Felix de Marez Oyens, 2006).

JULIA BRIGGS was Professor of English Literature and Women's Studies at De Montfort University until her death in 2007. She had formerly been Fellow of Hertford College, Oxford, and Chair of the Oxford University English Faculty, and was awarded an OBE for her services to English literature and education in 2006. Her books include *Night Visitors: The Rise and Fall of the English Ghost Story* (1977), *This Stage-Play World: Texts and Contexts, 1580–1625* (1983, revised 1997), *A Woman of Passion: The Life of E. Nesbit* (1987), *Children and Their Books* (1989, edited with Gillian Avery) and *Virginia Woolf: An Inner Life* (2006).

RICHARD FLYNN is Professor of Literature at Georgia Southern University where he teaches courses in modern and contemporary poetry and children's and adolescent literature. He has been the editor of the *Children's Literature Association Quarterly* since 2004.

M. O. GRENBY is Reader in Children's Literature in the School of English Literature, Language and Linguistics at Newcastle University. He has written widely on eighteenth-century culture and the history of children's literature. His books include *The Anti-Jacobin Novel: British Conservatism and the French Revolution* (2001), *Popular Children's Literature in Britain* (edited with Julia Briggs and Dennis Butts,

2008) and *Children's Literature* (2008). He is currently working on a study of the child reader in the long eighteenth century.

ANDREA IMMEL has been Curator of the Cotsen Children's Library at Princeton University since 1995. She has written widely on the history of illustrated children's books, as well as curated exhibitions, and organised a series of international conferences on various aspects of children's literature. Her descriptive catalogue of the children's books published by the house of Newbery will appear in 2010.

ERIC J. JOHNSON is Assistant Professor and Associate Curator of Rare Books and Manuscripts at The Ohio State University Libraries. He holds a Ph.D. from the University of York (UK) and an MLIS from Rutgers University. His research interests encompass a variety of topics, and he has published articles on medieval literature and theology and military propaganda in children's literature. He is currently working on several projects examining nineteenth-century American story papers and dime novels.

U. C. KNOEPFLMACHER is William and Annie S. Paton Foundation Professor of Ancient and Modern Literature Emeritus at Princeton University. He is the author of seven books on nineteenth-century literature and culture, and the editor or co-editor of ten more. Among the former are *Forbidden Journeys: Fairy Tales and Fantasies by Victorian Women Writers* (1992) and *Ventures Into Childland: Victorians, Fairy Tales and Femininity* (1998).

RODERICK McGILLIS is a professor of English at the University of Calgary. Recent publications include *Les pieds devant* (2007), *George Macdonald: Literary Heritage and Heirs* (2007) and *The Gothic in Children's Literature* (edited with Anna Jackson and Karen Coats, 2007). His next book will be called *He Was Some Kind of a Man: Masculinity in the B Western*.

LISSA PAUL is a professor in the Faculty of Education at Brock University, Ontario. She is the author of numerous articles and essays on children's literature, literary theories and cultural studies, and of several books, including *Growing with Books: Children's Literature in the Formative Years and Beyond* (1988) and *Reading Otherways* (1998). She is an associate general editor of *The Norton Anthology of Children's Literature* (2005) and an editor of the journal *The Lion and the Unicorn*.

MAVIS REIMER is Canada Research Chair in the Culture of Childhood, and Director of the Centre for Research in Young People's Texts and Cultures at the University of Winnipeg, and Associate Professor in the Department of English there. She is the editor of *Home Words: Discourses of Children's Literature in Canada* (2008); co-author, with Perry Nodelman, of the third edition of *The Pleasures of Children's Literature* (2002); and editor of *Such a Simple Little Tale: L. M. Montgomery's*

'*Anne of Green Gables*' (1992). Her current project is a study of Victorian children's literature as a literature of empire.

KIMBERLEY REYNOLDS is Professor of Children's Literature in the School of English Literature, Language and Linguistics at Newcastle University. She has been an active figure in children's literature studies for many years, serving on several national and international boards and committees, including as President of the International Research Society for Children's Literature (2003–7). She played a formative role in the creation of the Children's Laureate, and Seven Stories, the Centre for Children's Books (www.sevenstories.org.uk). She has written numerous books and articles about children's literature and childhood, past and present. Her most recent monograph is *Radical Children's Literature: Future Visions and Aesthetic Transformations* (2007).

DAVID RUDD is Professor of Children's Literature at the University of Bolton, where he runs an MA in Children's Literature and Culture. He has published some 100 articles on children's literature and related areas, and is the author of *Enid Blyton and the Mystery of Children's Literature* (2000). Most recently, he has edited *The Routledge Companion to Children's Literature*.

JUDY SIMONS is Professor of English and Pro Vice Chancellor at De Montfort University, Leicester. She has written widely on gender and women's writing. Among her publications are *Diaries and Journals of Literary Women* (1988), *What Katy Read: Feminist Re-readings of 'Classic' Stories for Girls* (co-authored with Shirley Foster, 1995) and an essay on Angela Brazil and schoolgirl fiction in *Popular Children's Literature in Britain*, ed. M. O. Grenby, J. Briggs and D. Butts (2008).

JOHN STEPHENS is Emeritus Professor of English in the Department of English at Macquarie University, New South Wales. He is the General Editor of *International Research in Children's Literature* and, in 2007, was awarded the International Brothers Grimm Award to mark his contribution to research in children's literature. His publications include *Language and Ideology in Children's Fiction* (1992), *From Picture Book to Literary Theory* (edited with Ken Watson, 1994), *Retelling Stories, Framing Culture: Traditional Story and Metanarratives in Children's Literature* (with Robyn McCallum, 1998), *Ways of Being Male: Representing Masculinities in Children's Literature and Film* (2002) and *New World Orders in Contemporary Children's Literature* (with Clare Bradford, Kerry Mallan and Robyn McCallum, 2008).

DEBORAH STEVENSON is a professor in the Graduate School of Library and Information Science at the University of Illinois, and editor of the *Bulletin of The Center For Children's Books*, one of the major children's literature review periodicals in the USA.

KATIE TRUMPENER is Professor of Comparative Literature, English and Film Studies at Yale. Her essays on children's literature have appeared in *The Cambridge History of Romanticism*, *The Victorian Illustrated Book* (2002) and *The Cambridge Companion to Fiction of the Romantic Period* (which she co-edited with Richard Maxwell, 2008). Her *Bardic Nationalism: The Romantic Novel and the British Empire* (1997) describes Romantic links between childhood and national and imperial memory; her current book project explores the centrality of nurse-maids and nursery memories for European modernism.

LYNNE VALLONE is Professor and Chair of Childhood Studies at Rutgers University. She is an associate general editor of *The Norton Anthology of Children's Literature* (2005) and was the author of *Disciplines of Virtue: Girls' Culture in the Eighteenth and Nineteenth Centuries* (1995) and *Becoming Victoria* (2001), and co-editor of *The Girl's Own: Cultural Histories of the Anglo-American Girl, 1830–1915* (with Claudia Nelson, 1994) and *Virtual Gender: Fantasies of Subjectivity and Embodiment* (with Mary Ann O'Farrell, 1999). She is currently working on a book on the miniature and the gigantic in children's literature and culture.

PREFACE

Most of the volumes in the Cambridge Companions series examine one author, one well-defined historical period or one particular genre. *The Cambridge Companion to Children's Literature* is, by necessity, much broader. Although it deals with only one category of literature, it is a category that has developed over at least 300 years into an entire parallel universe. Children's literature is now almost as large and varied a field as 'adult literature', encompassing not only prose, verse and drama, but fact as well as fiction, and 'texts' that are composed solely of pictures or digital images. It cuts across almost all genres, from myths to manga, humour to horror, science to self-help and religion to romance. It has its own canon of classics, its own radical and controversial experiments, and genres for which there are no precise equivalents for adults. Children's literature now receives considerable critical attention from scholars and students as well as discussion across the popular media. It has become as profitable and exportable as any other cultural commodity. Many of its characters – and even some of its authors and illustrators – are amongst the most celebrated and recognisable international icons.

But in other ways children's literature differs markedly from literature designed for mature readers. Children's literature, uniquely, is defined by its intended audience, but neither childhood nor the child is so easy to define. Overlapping and conflicting cultural constructions of childhood have existed since children's literature began; some persist, while others shift in response to changing values and conditions. Then there are the complications that arise out of the very polymorphous nature of its readership. The 'child' for whom 'children's literature' is intended can range from the infant being read to, to the teenager on the threshold of adulthood, not to mention those adults who delight in picture books, fantasy novels or fondly remembered classics. This 'crossover audience' is by no means a new phenomenon. It is just one of the reasons that the question of audience presents all sorts of knotty problems. Should we, for instance, regard children's literature as produced exclusively for its putative intended audience of children? Or are the adults who (generally) write it, assess it and buy it also to be regarded as important consumers? These grown-ups were all also once children and therefore may be very heavily invested emotionally and intellectually and financially in what children read. In this respect, children's literature is one of the most universal of forms – a truly popular literature – since (unlike most kinds of books for adults) everyone has been part of its target audience. What all this begins to demonstrate is that children's books may be small, short and apparently straightforward, but the study of children's literature is far from simple.

This *Cambridge Companion* confronts this range and complexity directly. No attempt has been made to restrict the subject by imposing artificial limits, whether chronological, generic, thematic or by the intended age of readers. This is not to say that the entirety of children's literature could be covered by this book's sixteen chapters. Some parameters have been inevitable. The focus is on imaginative literature, leaving regrettably little room for the religious, factual and instructive material that has been such an important part of the development of children's books (one important exception being the alphabets that feature in chapter 8). Also largely absent from this volume is detailed consideration of drama, film and some other new media, because they require specialist critical techniques, and certain genres that already have enormous bodies of criticism devoted to them are omitted: fairy tales and comic books for example (although chapter 6, on adaptation, is an exception to both these rules). Finally, only texts first published in English have been included, and particularly those from Britain and America. Concentrating on these traditions, developing in tandem across the last three centuries, has imposed other limits by stealth. It has resulted in a bias towards books written for children who have been understood as highly individual, naturally playful, innocent and malleable, reflecting the dominant cultural construction of childhood in Britain and America since the mid eighteenth century. And because this literature was written for children who were predominantly white, middle-class and heterosexual, this *Cambridge Companion* inevitably reflects these norms, even if it is clearly the case that neither all children, nor all children's literature, can be represented by them. Some discussion of children's books written for different constituencies or with different needs has been possible here. But this *Companion* may serve as a foundation for later studies that will treat in greater depth the more inclusive children's literature of the later twentieth century and today, literature produced for audiences radically different from those of previous generations. To attempt to give multicultural children's literature the attention it deserves, as well as to include discussion of other national traditions, would have broadened the volume's scope, but only at the expense of trivialising these important issues.

What this *Companion* does try to present is a useful sample of the different critical approaches that have been taken to children's literature. Some of the essays focus closely on the texts themselves, often including their illustrations. Others take more historical, sociological, theoretical or materialist approaches, while some concentrate on readers' responses or the contexts of production. This methodological variety is partly a result of the subject itself. Children's books have a strong utilitarian dimension because they are explicitly designed to achieve some goal (this is often as true today as it was in the past) – and, as a result, formalistic or aesthetic analyses may illuminate books for children less fully than books for adults. Particular physical characteristics of children's books – size, format, binding, illustration, decoration, style, paper engineering and so on – also demand what might be called 'extra-literary' approaches, as do the sorts of non-textual responses that children often have (and indeed are encouraged to have) to their books. This explains why chapters focus on the relationship between text and image, the manufacture of books, their adaptation, their origins, and the makings of canons, as well as questions of age, literacy, gender and the cultural construction of childhood.

This critical heterogeneity is one of the most appealing aspects of the study of children's literature, and, it is to be hoped, of this *Companion*. The volume is characterised also by its historical range. Some children's literature criticism has a strong presentist streak, with a tendency to be hostile to works that no longer conform to current models of childhood or judgments about children's capabilities, concerns or best interests. One of the chief goals of this *Companion* is to erase these distinctions, and to offer historical and conceptual frameworks that enable long views of the genre. Even if it is no longer read by its original intended audience, an appreciation of older children's literature is surely essential to our understanding of the children's books of today, and of the future.

M. O. Grenby and Andrea Immel

CHRONOLOGY

ERIC J. JOHNSON

This chronology includes a selection of 'classic' titles, broadly defined as those that have had a significant and lasting effect on the development of children's literature in Britain and North America. The majority of these titles are discussed in this *Companion*. Many of them have had a considerable impact on other media besides the printed book. Other important events in the history of children's literature have been added, with an emphasis on those technological developments that have had a major effect on the appearance, distribution and consumption of books for children.

1475	*The Babees Book, or a 'Lytyl Reporte' of How Young People Should Behave*, an early courtesy book
1484	*Aesop's Fables*, translated and published by William Caxton, an early example of woodcut illustrations
1659	Johann Amos Comenius, *Orbis sensualium pictus ... Visible World, or Picture and Nomenclature of all the chief things in the world*, translated by Charles Hoole, an early use of intaglio engraving alongside a letterpress text
1671–2	James Janeway, *A Token for Children*
1686	John Bunyan, *A Book for Boys and Girls*, subsequently retitled *Divine Emblems*
c. 1690	*The New England Primer*
1693	John Locke, *Some Thoughts Concerning Education*
1694	J. G., *A Play-Book for Children to Allure Them to Read Assoon [sic] As They Can Speak Plain*
1715	Isaac Watts, *Divine Songs Attempted in Easy Language for the Use of Children*, advertised as a reward book for virtuous children

1719   Daniel Defoe, *Robinson Crusoe*

1722   Samuel Croxall, *Fables of Aesop and others*, an early use of
            relief metal engravings

1726   Jonathan Swift, *Gulliver's Travels*

1729   *Histories, or Tales of Past Times*, translated by Robert Samber
            from Charles Perrault's *Histoires, ou contes du temps passé*
            of 1697, retellings of traditional French fairy tales

1730   Thomas Boreman, *Description of Three Hundred Animals*

1740–3   Thomas Boreman publishes by subscription the *Gigantick
            Histories*, a series of miniature guidebooks to London bound
            in 'Dutch gilt paper'

1742   *The Child's New Play-Thing*, a speller with a fold-out plate of
            decorative alphabet cards, published by Thomas Cooper

1744   *Tommy Thumb's Pretty Song Book*, the first collection of
            nursery rhymes, published by Mary Cooper and printed
            throughout in intaglio; *A Little Pretty Pocket-Book* pub-
            lished by John Newbery

1746   *Royal Battledore*, a folded-card alphabet intended as
            an alternative to the hornbook, published by Benjamin
            Collins

1749   Sarah Fielding, *The Governess; or, the Little Female
            Academy*, the first book-length fiction for children

1751–2   *The Lilliputian Magazine*, the first children's periodical, pub-
            lished in numbers by Thomas Carnan, John Newbery's step-son

1753   Wove paper is introduced in England

1762   Jean-Jacques Rousseau, *Émile, or On Education*

1765   *The History of Little Goody Two-Shoes*, published by John
            Newbery

1767   James Greenwood, *The London Vocabulary*, issued in
            'school canvas' binding; *Adam & Eve*, the first in a series of
            harlequinades (a type of 'movable book'), published by
            Robert Sayer in plain and hand-coloured versions

1778–9	Anna Laetitia Barbauld, *Lessons for Children*, an early use of different sizes of type for readers of different ages
1780	*Mother Goose's Melody; or, Sonnets from the Cradle*, a collection of nursery rhymes with illustrations by Thomas Bewick
1782	*The History of Little Goody Two-Shoes* issued by Thomas Carnan in pictorial boards
1783	Noah Webster, *A Grammatical Institute of the English Language*
1783–9	Thomas Day, *The History of Sandford and Merton*
1789	William Blake, *Songs of Innocence*, with text and 'illuminations' both relief etched throughout, and issued in a very limited print-run
1790	Thomas Bewick, *General History of Quadrupeds*, the first major book illustrated with wood engravings
1796	Maria Edgeworth, *The Parent's Assistant; or, Stories for Children*
1798	Alois Senefelder invents lithography; first paper-making machine invented
1799	John Marshall begins publishing his miniature libraries in ornamental boxes; founding of the Religious Tract Society, one of the biggest nineteenth-century publishers of children's books
1800	Development of stereotyping begins; introduction of the Stanhope iron press
1802–6	Sarah Trimmer, *The Guardian of Education*, the first review journal of children's books
1804–5	Ann and Jane Taylor (and others), *Original Poems for Infant Minds*
1805	Sarah Catherine Martin, *The Comic Adventures of Old Mother Hubbard and her Dog*, an early example of a hand-coloured nursery rhyme picture book that became a bestseller

1807	Charles and Mary Lamb, *Tales from Shakespeare for the Use of Young Persons*, the earliest English children's book to have remained in print to the present time
1810	*The History of Little Fanny*, the first in a series of paper-doll books with aquatint illustrations and wallet bindings, published by S. and J. Fuller; introduction of steam-powered rotary printing press
1818–42	Mary Martha Sherwood, *The History of the Fairchild Family*
1820	Hugh Blair's *Precepts*, illustrated with steel engravings
1822	Introduction of mechanical typesetting
1823	The Brothers Grimm, *German Popular Stories*, translated by Edgar Taylor, illustrated by George Cruikshank
1824	Mary Sewell, *Walks with Mamma*, an early example of a book bound in cloth by publisher
1828	Thomas Crofton Croker publishes the first annual produced for children, *The Christmas Box*
1833	Introduction of the printed book jacket
1834	Baxter's 'Polychromatic' printing process introduced in Robert Mudie, *The Feathered Tribes of the British Islands*
1836–57	William Holmes McGuffey, *McGuffey's Eclectic Readers* 1–6
1838	Development of rail delivery services begins to affect book distribution
1839	Catherine Sinclair, *Holiday House*
1840	Dalziel Bros. founded: the firm would establish wood-engraved illustrations as standard commercial practice
1844	Fox Talbot's photographic innovations utilised in book publishing: development of photolithography
1846	Hans Christian Andersen, *Wonderful Stories for Children*, translated by Mary Howitt; Edward Lear, *Book of Nonsense*
1847	Frederick Marryat, *Children of the New Forest*, the earliest work of children's fiction to remain continually in print to the present time

1885	Robert Louis Stevenson, *A Child's Garden of Verses*
1886	Frances Hodgson Burnett, *Little Lord Fauntleroy*
1889–1910	Andrew Lang, 'Colour Fairy Books' series
c. 1890	Ernest Nister, *Nister's Panorama Pictures*, introduction of 'automatic' pop-up books employing die-cut figures raised by paper guides activated as the reader turns each page
1891	E. M. Field, *The Child and His Book*, the first serious attempt at a history of children's literature
1894–5	Rudyard Kipling, *The Jungle Books*
1898	Emma Griffith Lumm, *The Twentieth Century Speaker*, an early use of colour half-tone illustrations in a children's book
1899	Helen Bannerman, *The Story of Little Black Sambo*; E. Nesbit, *The Treasure Seekers*
1900	L. Frank Baum, *The Wonderful Wizard of Oz*; founding of American Library Association section on Library Work with Children
1901	Beatrix Potter, *The Tale of Peter Rabbit*, using three-colour half-tones; Net Book Agreement enacted
1904	First performance of J. M. Barrie, *Peter Pan, or The Boy Who Wouldn't Grow Up*
1905	Washington Irving's *Rip Van Winkle*, illustrated by Arthur Rackham, one of the first so-called 'gift-books'; Stratemeyer Syndicate founded, a book packager specialising in series fiction such as Nancy Drew and the Hardy Boys
1906	Introduction of offset lithography; Hodder and Stoughton and Oxford University Press establish the Joint Venture, the first children's book department headed by its own appointed editor
1908	Kenneth Grahame, *The Wind in the Willows*; Peter Newell, *The Hole Book*, an early novelty book; L. M. Montgomery, *Anne of Green Gables*
1916	Bertha Mahony opens the Bookshop for Boys & Girls in Boston, Massachusetts

1918	Norman Lindsay, *The Magic Pudding*, the first classic Australian children's title
1919	Macmillan, New York, establishes a children's department with Louise Seaman Bechtel as editor
1922	Margery Williams, *The Velveteen Rabbit*; first award of the annual Newbery Medal for the most distinguished contribution to American children's literature
1924	A. A. Milne, *When We Were Very Young*; Bertha Mahony launches *Horn Book Magazine*
1927	Macmillan launches Happy Hour Books, with illustrations printed by Charles Stringer's new four-colour process at Jersey City Printing Company, allowing for a greater range of tones
1930	Arthur Ransome, *Swallows and Amazons*; Dick and Jane readers introduced
1931	Jean de Brunhoff, *The Story of Babar*, an outstanding early example of offset colour lithography
1932–43	Laura Ingalls Wilder, Little House series
1934	P. L. Travers, *Mary Poppins*
1935	*Mickey Mouse Magazine*, the first Disney comic book; Penguin begins publishing mass-market paperbacks
1936	First award of the Carnegie Medal, for the year's most outstanding British children's book
1937	J. R. R. Tolkien, *The Hobbit*
1938	First award of the annual Caldecott Medal for best American picture book; *Action Comics* launched, including earliest appearance of Superman, the first costumed 'superhero'
1940	Dorothy Kunhardt, *Pat the Bunny: A Touch-and-Feel Book*
1941	Penguin begins publishing the Puffin Picture Books children's line
1942	Little Golden Books, a series of high-quality 25-cent picture books, launched by Simon & Schuster

| 1947 | Margaret Wise Brown and Clement Hurd, *Goodnight, Moon* |

1947   Margaret Wise Brown and Clement Hurd, *Goodnight, Moon*

1950–6   C. S. Lewis, *The Chronicles of Narnia*

1952   *The Diary of Anne Frank*; E. B. White, *Charlotte's Web*; *A Child's Book of Horses*, the first book to be entirely film-set

1952–82   Mary Norton, *The Borrowers* quintet

1955   First award of the annual Kate Greenaway Medal for illustration in a British children's book

1956   Dodie Smith, *The Hundred and One Dalmatians*

1957   Dr Seuss, *The Cat in the Hat*

1958   Philippa Pearce, *Tom's Midnight Garden*

1959   John Knowles, *A Separate Peace*

1963   Maurice Sendak, *Where the Wild Things Are*

1964   Roald Dahl, *Charlie and the Chocolate Factory*; Randall Jarrell, *The Bat-Poet*

1967   Russell Hoban, *The Mouse and His Child*

1967–72   Ursula Le Guin, first *Earthsea* trilogy

1970   John Burningham, *Mr Gumpy's Outing*; Maurice Sendak, *In the Night Kitchen*

1972   Richard Adams, *Watership Down*

1973   Rosa Guy, *The Friends*

1974   Robert Cormier, *The Chocolate War*

1975   Judy Blume, *Forever*

1979   Raymond Briggs, *The Snowman*, a wordless picture book

1986   Allan and Janet Ahlberg, *The Jolly Postman: or Other People's Letters*; Michael Palin, *The Mirrorstone*, first use of a hologram in a book

1986–91   Art Spiegelman, *Maus: A Survivor's Tale*, a graphic novel with cross-generational appeal

1989   Picture Me Books launches interactive board books produced using proprietary computer programs to personalise text for individual customers

1990   Ursula Le Guin, *Tehanu*; Salman Rushdie, *Haroun and the Sea of Stories*

1992   Jon Scieszka and Lane Smith, *The Stinky Cheese Man and Other Fairly Stupid Tales*

1994   Robert Sabuda, *The Christmas Alphabet*, an elaborate pop-up book

1995–2000   Philip Pullman, *His Dark Materials* trilogy

1997   Romain Victor Pujebet, *Lulu's Enchanted Book*, an early interactive multi-media children's book published only on CD-ROM

1997–2007   J. K. Rowling, *Harry Potter* novels

2001   Melvin Burgess, *Lady: My Life as a Bitch*

PART I

Contexts and Genres

I

M. O. GRENBY

The origins of children's literature

Many of the most celebrated children's books have a famous origin story attached to them. Lewis Carroll made up 'the interminable fairy-tale of *Alice's Adventures*' (as he called it in his diary) while he was on a boat-trip with Alice, Lorina and Edith Liddell in 1862; *Peter Pan* grew out of J. M. Barrie's intense friendship with the five Llewelyn Davies boys; Salman Rushdie, following the Ayatollah Khomeini's 1989 *fatwa*, wrote *Haroun and the Sea of Stories* for his son, Zafir, for Zafir, like Haroun, had helped his father recover the ability to tell stories.[1] The veracity of these stories, and many others like them, is open to question. But their prevalence and endurance is nevertheless important. We seem to demand such originary myths for our children's classics. What we want, it appears, is the assurance that published children's books have emerged from particular, known circumstances, and, more specifically, from the story told by an individual adult to individual children. C. S. Lewis listed this as one of his 'good ways' of writing for children: 'The printed story grows out of a story told to a particular child with the living voice and perhaps *ex tempore*.' Such a creative method is an antidote to what Lewis thought the very worst way to write for children, striving to 'find out what they want and give them that, however little you like it yourself'.[2] But if we investigate the historical origins of children's books it is clear that Lewis' 'bad way' is precisely how children's literature *did* begin: adults invented a new commodity, deliberately designed to give a newly identified audience what they thought it wanted, or, rather, needed. There are three different kinds of origin to consider in this chapter then, and, on the surface, they can seem incongruent. First, there is the historical genesis of children's literature as a commercial product. Second, there is the idea that children's literature has naturally developed from a culture of adult-to-child storytelling. And third, the biographical accounts surrounding the conception of individual books. What this chapter will argue is that, far from being contradictory, as C. S. Lewis' strictures suggest, all three kinds of origin are importantly interrelated.

Historical origins

Most cultural historians agree that children's literature, as we recognise it today, began in the mid eighteenth century and took hold first in Britain. With its mixture of pictures, rhymes, riddles, stories, alphabets and lessons on moral conduct – its commitment, as its full title puts it, to 'Instruction and Amusement' – *A Little Pretty Pocket-Book*, published by John Newbery in 1744, is often regarded as the most important single point of origin. Newbery's role has been exaggerated, perhaps because of his ostentatious insistence that he was providing education and entertainment fused together – a strategy influentially advocated by John Locke in *Some Thoughts Concerning Education* (1693). Other London author-publishers pre-dated and competed with him, notably Thomas Boreman, whose *Description of Three Hundred Animals* appeared 'for the Entertainment of Children' in 1730, and Mary and Thomas Cooper, under whose names some children's books (such as *The Child's New Play-Thing*, a school book enlivened with alphabets, riddles, dialogues, stories and songs) appeared from 1742. But only Newbery's enterprise endured, the children's publishing dynasty he founded lasting until the nineteenth century. He was the first successfully to commercialise books for children, and he used a simple but durable formula: the encasement of the instructive material that adults thought their children would need within an entertaining format that children might be supposed to want.

What Newbery and his contemporaries did not do was suddenly invent children's literature *ex nihilo*. Instructional books, both secular and religious, had been marketed directly at children for centuries. Among the first British printed books were William Caxton's *Book of Curtesye* (1477) and his translation of *The Book of the Knight of the Tower* (1484), providing boys and girls respectively with instruction on how to behave in a noble household. Francis Seager's verse *Schoole of Vertue, and Booke of Good Nourture for Chyldren, and Youth to Learn Theyr Dutie By* (1557) was one amongst many Renaissance children's courtesy books. By the early eighteenth century a wider audience was being served. George Fisher's *The Instructor; or, the Young Man's Best Companion* (1727) was a frequently reprinted compendium of reading, writing and arithmetic lessons and advice on such things as how to write legal documents, to take accurate measurements, to garden, pickle and dye. Meanwhile, John Foxe had been directly addressing children in his infamous *Book of Martyrs* (1563), and John Bunyan's *A Book for Boys and Girls* (1686, later known as *Divine Emblems*), Thomas Gills' *Instructions for Children* (1707) and Isaac Watts' *Divine Songs* (1715), among many other works, had put religious and moral lessons into verse. James Janeway's *A Token for Children being an Exact Account of the Conversion, Holy and Exemplary*

Lives, and Joyful Deaths, of several young Children (1672) is just the best-known of the many children's books produced by and for Puritans in the late seventeenth century, designed to warn children against worldly temptations and point out the hard path towards salvation. These instructive texts were not suddenly eclipsed in the 1740s. However severe Janeway's accounts of the deaths of pious children might seem in contrast with the milder children's books that subsequently appeared, they remained in print well into the nineteenth century.

Moreover, texts clearly designed to provide entertainment had also been targeted at children before the 1740s. In 1738, Robert Wharton had published *Historiæ pueriles*, an anthology including enjoyable stories such as 'Piramus and Thisbe' alongside more weighty matter. Less miscellaneous, and more thrilling, was the Abbé Fénelon's *Les Avantures de Télémaque fils d'Ulysse* (1699), written as an attempt to instruct readers in politics and morality through an exciting narrative, and so much in demand that it was translated into English within a year of its French publication. And, of course, children read texts that were not necessarily designed exclusively for them. There is evidence from diaries, memoirs and marginalia of their enjoyment of chivalric romances, novels, fairy tales, fables, the *Gesta romanorum* (a medieval collection of legends and biographies), chapbooks and popular ballads. One ballad, *The Friar and the Boy*, first printed in about 1510 though circulating in manuscript beforehand, has sometimes been called (somewhat dubiously) perhaps the first story appealing directly to children, because of its account of a boy's use of a magic amulet to make his cruel step-mother fart uncontrollably. But if this is children's literature, then so too must be many other works published for a mixed audience even earlier. Medievalists have recently argued that children's literature began, in terms of both content and readership, in the Middle Ages. Various manuscript abridgments of *The Canterbury Tales* survive, for instance, that were especially designed for, and used by, children. Other critics have gone further back still, arguing that material was being produced for children to read in early China, classical Rome and Greece, ancient Egypt, and even ancient Sumer in the third millennium BCE.

That all these rival points of origin can compete with one another is because important questions of definition remain unresolved. If we ask what was the first children's book, we are really asking what children's literature is. Do we mean texts designed especially for children, or read only by them, not those intended for adults, or a mixed-age audience, that were also used by children? Should we include only those books that 'give children spontaneous pleasure', as F. J. Harvey Darton maintained?[3] Or should we insist that a true children's book must appeal to today's children, or at least be 'written expressly for children who are recognizably children, with a childhood recognizable today', as Peter Hunt has insisted?[4] The problem with all these attempts at definition is that we can seldom know precisely who used which books, or how they responded to them. We might think of the Puritan texts of the late seventeenth century as so brutally pious that no child could have taken pleasure from them, but what evidence we have argues that they were seen as empowering and enjoyable, relished by children and adults equally. As late as 1821, for instance, one adult reader called Janeway's *Token for Children* 'the most entertaining book that can be', adding that she and her son read it nightly: 'we be never tired of it'.[5]

An alternative strategy might be to define children's literature on the basis of certain qualities of the texts themselves. Perhaps 'proper' children's books are only those which include rounded child characters, not mythical heroes or fairy tale figures, nor the improbable ciphers, like 'Polly Friendly' or 'Francis Fearful', who appear in much eighteenth-century children's literature. Perhaps true children's books are only those which take seriously the child's point of view, and represent it sympathetically. Or, perhaps, we can identify true children's literature because, as Barbara Wall maintains, writers 'speak differently in fiction when they are aware that they are addressing children'. It is, Wall argues, a particular kind of direct 'narrator–narratee relationship' that 'is the distinctive marker of a children's book'.[6] But such generic generalisations invite dissension, for children's literature has become so diverse that it is easy to think of examples that stretch any of these definitions beyond breaking point.

Less tendentious is a means of definition that takes us back to the mid eighteenth century. Beyond questions of readership and response, and of generic textual characteristics, children's literature is a commodity, a product that first became securely commercially and culturally established in the age of Newbery. For the first time, publishers like him began to devote substantial resources to a product that was marketed at children and their guardians. They developed separate publishing lists of children's books. Soon, others, such as John Marshall and William Darton, were able to set up new businesses largely devoted to children's books, while even mainstream publishers found that they could not ignore the profits to be made from this new market. The children's books that they produced were different in appearance, and in cost, from works published for adults. Separate advertisements were placed in newspapers. Reviews began to appear in periodicals. By the end of the eighteenth century, an author could start to think of himself, or more typically herself, as a writer for children only.

The rapidity of this 'invention' of children's literature is remarkable. In 1750 the idea of a separate children's literature was still very novel, but as quickly as 1780 authors were worrying that it might 'seem superfluous to add to the number of Books which have already been written expressly for the use of Children', and by the end of the century commentators could complain that 'real knowledge and real piety ... have suffered ... from the profusion of little, amusing, sentimental books with which the youthful library overflows'.[7] These anxieties prompted Sarah Trimmer to establish the first children's book review journal, *The Guardian of Education* (1802–6), and she found no shortage of books to subject to her careful scrutiny. The question is: how had this proliferation happened? There is no simple answer. What is clear is that a series of factors combined to enable the growth of children's literature as a distinct cultural and commercial entity. Equally obvious is that this process did not happen abruptly, but occurred stutteringly across the course of the seventeenth and eighteenth centuries.

One self-evidently important component of the matrix of factors that generated children's literature was the new status accorded to the child in the early modern period. Philippe Ariès' view (expressed in his 1960 book *Centuries of Childhood*) that modern childhood – recognised as a distinct phase of life, with its own special needs – did not exist until the seventeenth century has been widely contested. But his general observation that children gradually became the object of greater parental and societal solicitude and psychological interest remains convincing. Certainly there were more children around. The English population rose by about 20 per cent between 1720 and 1770. What these demographic and cultural shifts meant was a society increasingly full of, and concerned with, children, and willing to invest in them both emotionally and financially.

Education was closely bound up with this shift. For Ariès, it was a new conviction that children needed religious education that led to the recognition that boys and girls required a period of special treatment before entering the adult world: the period that we now call 'childhood'. Alternatively, we might see the eighteenth century's increased emphasis on education as an effect, not cause, of the new concern for childhood. Certainly, the philosophy of education became a more prestigious subject, with Locke its most celebrated theorist. His call for simple games and books that would engage children, and tempt them to read, has often been cited as an important stimulus for children's literature. But, in fact, Locke's ideas were part of a movement already underway rather than an abrupt innovation. In 1692, a year before the publication of *Some Thoughts Concerning Education*, Sir Roger L'Estrange was already advising that 'Lessons Themselves may be Gilt and Sweeten'd' by incorporating them into pleasant 'Little Stories'.[8] The title of J. G.'s *A Play-Book for Children to Allure Them to Read Assoon [sic] As They Can Speak Plain*, published two years later in 1694, displays the same conviction that entertainment catalyses instruction. Its subtitle – 'Composed of Small Pages On Purpose Not to Tire Children, and Printed with a Fair and Pleasant Letter' – exhibits an awareness that children ought to be provided with distinctive books of their own.

A long succession of pedagogical thinkers and practitioners followed Locke into print, of whom Jean-Jacques Rousseau was probably the most influential. Rousseau may have warned, in *Émile* (1762), against forcing boys to read too early, but the attempt to systematise education that he and many others were embarked on inevitably resulted in the publication of more, and more carefully crafted, children's books. Children in the 1780s should have been congratulating themselves 'on the circumstance of being born in those auspicious times, when children are ... the peculiar objects whose felicity philosophers are studying to promote', wrote the Frenchman Arnaud Berquin in *L'Ami des enfans* (1782–3), a work quickly translated into English, so insistent was the requirement for new children's books.[9] New educational methods were recommended, and many new schools were established. Even if, in many boys' schools, an antiquated classical curriculum remained in place, in many other educational contexts – the girls' school, home education – new books, designed especially for children, were urgently demanded and increasingly supplied.

Equally significant in the establishment of children's literature as a separate entity were developments within the book trade itself. The government ended pre-publication censorship in 1695. An Act of 1710 did much to safeguard literary property, and a 1774 court case ended perpetual copyright in England. All this created a more vibrant publishing industry, with greater commercial security and increased access to established revenue streams, and a wider distribution of risk between printers, publishers and retailers – a climate that encouraged entrepreneurialism and innovation. Technological innovations helped. New printing methods, especially for illustrations, were developed, and new binding techniques pushed down prices and facilitated easier transportation of books.

The professionalisation of literature was also important. A move away from a patronage system to the open market helped authors of low-status, potentially mass-market products such as children's books. Even more crucial was the change in the status of the novel. At the start of the eighteenth century, the novel had been widely seen as a moral form suitable for the whole family. Increasingly though, novelists were declining to act as the guardians of the moral welfare of the nation and its youth, and the didactic element was replaced by greater emphasis on form, style and narrative, amatory and erotic elements, or psychological complexity. These shifts encouraged a new literature for children. In effect, children's literature filled the void which the novel's rise to maturity, and move away from moral didacticism, had left behind.

Perhaps most important of all in the genesis of children's literature is the socio-economic context. Ian Watt's thesis, in his 1957 *The Rise of the Novel*, that the growth of a middle class led to the rise of the novel might have been widely questioned, but the increasing affluence of certain sections of society was certainly a determinant of the expansion of the market for print. The consumption of non-essential commodities increased hugely in the eighteenth century, and children's books were at the centre of this 'consumer revolution'. With handsome type, attractive illustrations, decorative binding and sometimes even gilt-edged pages, many early children's books were evidently designed to appeal to children's wish to possess them. The establishment of a more strongly defined and self-identifying middle class may also have benefited the children's book market by creating demand for a specifically bourgeois children's literature, contaminated with neither plebeian associations (like chapbooks) nor aristocratic tastes (as transmitted in romances or even fairy tales). But just as crucial as any rise in class consciousness or spending power was the growth of the perception that social elevation was actually possible, even purchasable. Education, and educational books for children, were naturally regarded as one possible motor of social mobility – a point succinctly encapsulated in this 1808 title: *The Alphabet of Goody Two-Shoes, by Learning of Which She Soon Got Rich*. To educate a child became an investment, the potential returns of social prestige and prosperity easily outweighing the initial outlay. And social advancement is one of the principal themes of eighteenth-century children's books. John Newbery's original *History of Little Goody Two-Shoes* (1765), for example, dramatises not fairy tale hopes of sudden, random, social elevation, but the possibility of advancement through education and hard work. The characteristics that lead to advancement are not the traditional moral virtues of Cinderella, but the much more commercial qualities of the successful businessman or wise housewife: diligence, thrift, caution, honesty.

Domestic origins

One further cultural shift, important in catalysing the beginnings of children's literature and doing much to shape the way it developed, requires more detailed attention. This is the new understanding of parenthood that emerged in Britain from the early eighteenth century. In particular the proprieties of motherhood were the subject of enormous interest and endorsement, this discourse coming almost to dominate conduct books and medical treatises, as well as portraits and *belles lettres*. 'The Assembly of the Birds', a fable inserted into Sarah Fielding's children's book *The Governess; or, the Little Female Academy* (1749), neatly sums up the principal characteristics of the new, idealised motherhood. In a competition to find the happiest of all birds, it is the dove who wins, even though – in fact precisely because – she does not attend the contest, preferring to remain at her nest, nurturing her brood and awaiting the return of her mate. Such devotion to the home, and especially to children, was increasingly enjoined on men as well, but it was the duties of maternity that were most emphatically stressed. Maternal breast-feeding (as opposed to the use of wet nurses) and the personal supervision of all aspects of infancy were presented as physically and psychologically beneficial to children, but also socially proper, morally virtuous and even patriotic, the surest defence against foreign foes and the best foundation of empire. All this is neatly summed up in the Reverend John Bennett's *Strictures on Female Education* (1787):

> When does she [woman] appear to so much advantage, as when, surrounded, in her nursery, by a train of prattlers, she is holding forth the moral page for the instruction of one, and pouring out the milk of health to invigorate the frame and constitution of another? When is her snowy bosom half so serene, or when thrills it with such an innocent and pleasing rapture, as in these silent moments of domestick attention, or these attitudes of undissembled love?

Worth noting here is the role prescribed for the mother in educating her children. Bennett professes himself shocked that a mother could resign the education of her children to a school or a governess. 'No;' Bennett insisted, 'reason, religion, the thrillings of affection, the voice of nature, and the voice of God, the interests of society, the happiness of private life, the honour, the dignity and *true policy* of woman – all say, that a *mother* should be the *preceptress* of her children'.[10]

The great benefit of maternal education, it was held, was that mothers would be willing to personalise curricula according to the individual needs of their children. Locke's educational philosophy imagined all children to be the same, their blank-slate minds developing only according to how they were taught. But, as Mary Wollstonecraft put it, 'Every child requires a different mode of treatment.'[11] In practice, this meant that mothers were being encouraged not only to design their own lesson plans but also to devise new pedagogical strategies and produce their own educational aids. Instead of 'frequently repeating tiresome Lectures', wrote another commentator, the 'tender Mother successively contrives a thousand new and pleasing Methods to influence her Children'. She will deploy 'little Surprises; Novelties artfully managed; Walks chosen on purpose to introduce new Questions; agreeable Recitals; a Variety of historical Cuts; every thing, in short, is employed to raise the Curiosity, and fill up the Vacuities of that Intelligence which only waits for Ideas'.[12]

Eighteenth-century fiction presents many of these innovating mothers: the eponymous heroine of Samuel Richardson's novel *Pamela, or Virtue Rewarded* (1740–1) is perhaps the classic example, a paragon who, after her marriage to the rakish Mr B, invents educational stories to tell the children. But there is evidence that real-life mothers conformed to this ideal too. Aristocratic and even royal mothers often boasted in their letters of active engagement in their children's education. But the most astonishing evidence of such innovating practices is the collection of educational tools and texts produced during the 1740s by Jane Johnson, wife of an independently wealthy vicar. Johnson manufactured over 400 cards, booklets and sets of tiles, all designed to help her teach her children before the boys were sent away to school aged eight or ten. Perhaps the most remarkable single object is 'A very pretty Story to tell Children when they are about five or six years of age' (1744), a sort of moralised fairy story. In the tradition of home-made stories, Johnson personalised the narrative, naming the two central characters after her two oldest children. What is striking about all Johnson's artefacts is the care with which they were made, and her evidently very substantial investment of time and money. The images are skilfully drawn and coloured; the texts expertly composed or painstakingly transcribed; the cards and booklets are carefully cut and trimmed, and sometimes augmented with commercially available prints or paper. These were exceptionally fine examples, but it seems not unlikely that many of Johnson's contemporaries produced similar materials for their children, even if, regrettably, they have not survived.

Jane Johnson was producing these materials between 1742 and 1747, just after Richardson had described the ideal of maternal education in *Pamela* and at the same time as Thomas Boreman, Mary Cooper and John Newbery were making their experiments with publishing children's books in London. The agreement of dates makes it difficult to resist speculating, as Victor Watson has done, that the commercial ventures should be understood not as 'the "beginning" of children's literature', but as the emergence into the public realm 'of a traditional private and domestic nursery-culture – undervalued, orally transmitted from one generation to the next, responsive to changes in contemporary thinking, making a pragmatic use of available materials, and mostly sustained by mothers'.[13] This is almost to accuse Newbery and others of expropriating somebody else's property, profiting from something that had been available for free, and masculinising something that had previously been produced and controlled by women. But the commodification of home-made products was common in eighteenth-century print culture. Alphabet and picture cards or tiles (common educational aids), 'dissected maps' (geographical jigsaws) and 'harlequinades' (with flaps glued at the edges so that they could be turned up or down to reveal new scenes) were all apparently first made at home before they went into commercial production in the second half of the eighteenth century. And, notably, what was being appropriated by the producers of these new commodities was not only the product itself, but the whole ethos of maternal education. When Ellenor Fenn published *The Art of Teaching in Sport* (1785) to accompany a set of educational toys, she was adamant that the book was to be used only by a mother (or perhaps an elder daughter). We should not regard the commercialisation of domestic education as a kind of piracy, then, but rather as two elements of the same movement.

Nor should we imagine that commercial children's literature suddenly superseded domestic practices and home-made products. Rather, printed and home-made children's texts continued to be produced in tandem. *Fables in Monosyllables* (1783), also by Fenn, gives a nice indication of this symbiotic relationship. Her preface explains 'To My Little Readers' how the book was designed for one little boy:

> One day I met with some nice, clear, large print let-ters; and I cut them out, and stuck them on card; then laid them thus, c-a-t – cat, d-o-g – dog; and he said the words at sight.
> Was this not nice?
> Then it came in mind to print with a pen for him; so I made tales of the dog, and the cat, and such short words – Should you not jump for joy? – He did.[14]

Fenn had apparently taken a commercially available product (the printed letters), stuck them onto card and turned it into an educational game, then written stories based on this game, and then published a book based on these stories. The home-produced and the commercially available were intertwined.

Indeed, the role of the mother as the proper provider of education was continually stressed throughout the first generations of commercial children's literature. She is placed in the most prominent place possible – the frontispiece – in many books, including Newbery's *A Little Pretty Pocket-Book* and Fenn's *Fables in Monosyllables* (fig. 1). In the latter, she hands over a book, doubtless *Fables in Monosyllables* itself, to a child, presumably her own. The symbolism is clear: this mother is giving her child the book as a continuation of her own tuition, and, in more general terms, the book is being identified as an admissible component of domestic education. The book's subtitle – 'Dialogues between a Mother and Children' – confirms how the book should be used, and the preface directly addresses the 'judicious mother' who 'condescends to prattle with her children', and 'thus infuses ideas in their tender

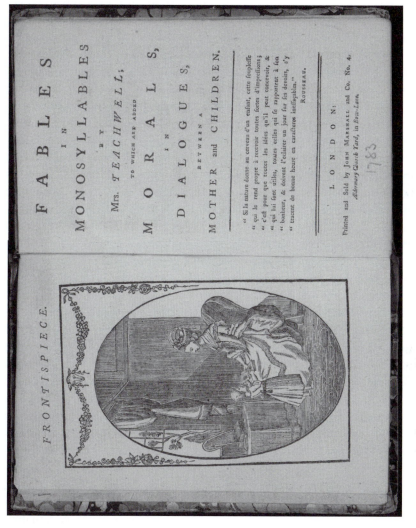

FRONTISPIECE.

FABLES
IN
MONOSYLLABLES
BY
Mrs. *TEACHWELL*;
TO WHICH ARE ADDED
MORALS,
IN
DIALOGUES,
BETWEEN A
MOTHER and CHILDREN.

"Si la nature donne au cerveau d'un enfant, cette souplesse
"qui le rend propre à recevoir toutes sortes d'impressions;
"ce'st pour que toutes les idées qu'il peut concevoir, &
"qui lui sont utiles, toutes celles qui se rapportent à son
"bonheur, & doivent l'éclairer un jour sur ses devoirs, s'y
"tracent de bonne heure en caractères ineffaçables."
ROUSSEAU.

LONDON:

Printed and Sold by JOHN MARSHALL and Co. No. 4:
Aldermary Church Yard, in Bow-Lane.

1783

Figure 1. Lady Ellenor Fenn, *Fables in Monosyllables*. London: J. Marshall, [1783], frontispiece and title-page.

minds, whilst she engages their affections'. Also characteristic of the children's books of this period is the dedication, a carefully choreographed acknowledgement that the book had been written for a particular child (in this case, her adopted son): 'You are now at the same age as my boy was, when I wrote this book for him.'[15]

Stressing that their books were first produced for their own children was a rhetorical act, designed to place the new work in a respectable tradition, linking it with conduct books written for particular children throughout the early modern period, such as Fénelon's *Télémaque* or Lord Chesterfield's *Letters Written to his Son* (1774), and perhaps to such widely known cultural motifs as St Anne teaching the Virgin, or Venus teaching Cupid. It asserted the efficacy of the books, arguing that the text had been trialled by real children and found beneficial. It might be seen as a staking out of territory: 'It seems … a very easy task to write for children', wrote Maria Edgeworth, before adding: 'Those only who have been interested in the education of a family … who have daily watched over their thoughts and feelings … can feel the dangers and difficulties of such an undertaking', effectively disallowing anyone but mothers from producing children's literature.[16] But it also may have acted as an apology for the 'intrusion' into the public sphere by women professedly anxious about transgressing against domestic propriety. Thus in 1785 Dorothy Kilner insisted that she had 'written without the most distant thought of publication' and reluctantly 'consented' to publish only after her friends had convinced her of 'the service in future life, [the book] may possibly afford you, my dear children'.[17] These pre-emptive justifications were placed in the paratextual 'vestibules' of the books – prefaces, dedications, frontispieces – because they were designed to reach parents choosing books for their children to use, not the children themselves. This gives an indication of what was surely the principal purpose of the claim that the books had been designed for, and first used by, actual children: the alleviation of any anxiety that real-world mother–child relations could be destabilised by the new commodity. These paratexts offered the assurance that children's literature was not intended to supplant, but to supplement, the parent.

Specific and symbolic origins

Another way of thinking about the origins of children's literature is to consider what is known about the genesis of individual books. Originary 'myths' have developed around many of the most successful. These are very often accounts of how the book grew from a story told privately by a particular adult to particular children. Carroll's Liddell girls, Barrie's Llewelyn Davies boys and Rushdie's Zafir have already been mentioned, but others are to be found in every period and genre. Robert Louis Stevenson famously based *Treasure Island* (1883) on the map he made for his step-son, and unfolded the story to him every night as it was being written. Frances Hodgson Burnett wrote *Little Lord Fauntleroy* (1886) in response to her son Vivian's questions about the English aristocracy, and modelled the hero on him. G. A. Henty wrote his first adventure story, *Out on the Pampas* (1871), for his own children, whose names he used for the four protagonists. A. A. Milne turned his son's playthings into characters in the Pooh stories. Thomas Hughes wrote *Tom Brown's Schooldays* (1857) to counsel his eight-year-old about school life. It is 'common knowledge' – repeated in biographies, reference books and on countless websites – that *The Wind in the Willows* (1908) and *The Hobbit* (1937) began as bedside stories, that *Watership Down* (1972) was first told to Richard Adams' daughters on long car journeys, that *The BFG* (1982) was for and about Roald Dahl's granddaughter Sophie, that Robert Cormier's son actually did refuse to sell chocolates for his school's annual sale, providing the inspiration for *The Chocolate War* (1974). Although some authors try to repudiate such myths, others have endorsed or even instigated them. Of his prize-winning *The Machine Gunners* (1975), for instance, Robert Westall recalled,

> I ... only intended to read it to my son. It was my gift to him ... I read him the chapters as soon as I had written them, at Sunday teatime. He was the most savage of critics: if a part bored him he'd pick up a magazine and start reading that instead. The parts that left him cold, I crossed out, which is perhaps what gives the book its pace. But I had no thought of trying for publication ... It is, I suppose, ironical that a book written solely for one boy has sold over a million copies.

Echoing C. S. Lewis' views on the 'good ways' of writing for children, Westall has mused: 'Perhaps all the best books start by being written for only one child, and that child very close to you.'[18]

No doubt many of these accounts are perfectly true, but the basic story of a tale told by a parent to a child, with publication only as an afterthought, has been so recurrent that it must often seem more symbolic than biographical. Certainly, these accounts can sometimes appear to be very tightly bound together with the works themselves. Take the complicated though conventional origin story behind William Makepeace Thackeray's *The Rose and the Ring* (1855). First told to the unwell daughter of a friend, the story was based on pictures Thackeray had drawn for his children, and was then finished when his own daughter became ill. Because it is largely concerned with matriarchal power and its absence, U. C. Knoepflmacher reads this fairy tale as an attempt 'to reinstate the maternal femininity' from which

Thackeray 'felt so profoundly cut off' by childhood separation from his own mother and then the insanity of his wife, the mother of his children. By emphasising Thackeray's attempt 'To be father and mother too', as he later put it, the originary story endorses, and almost becomes part of, the literary text.[19] The same is true, more famously, of the 'originary myths' that have grown up around *Alice's Adventures in Wonderland* and *Peter Pan*. Most biographers and critics, and many general readers too, would struggle not to read the texts in the light of, respectively, what is known (and surmised) of Carroll's relationship with Alice Liddell and Barrie's with the Llewelyn Davies boys.

Taking a longer view though, the continued emphasis in these originary myths on individual adults telling stories to individual children can be understood as the persistence of the motif that had been such an important element in the establishment of children's literature in the eighteenth century. The stories remain a sort of paratext, preparing the reader (the child end-user, but more especially the adult purchaser) for the text. One might argue that these originary stories are demeaning, for by rooting children's literature in the domestic they necessarily construct the children's author as an amateur, however gifted. Portraits of children's authors can exhibit this clearly: the images of E. Nesbit and Enid Blyton owned by the UK's National Portrait Gallery, for example, show them with their daughters sitting at their feet. It is difficult to imagine two more professional authors than Nesbit and Blyton, yet their authorial success, the portraits assert, emanates from their motherhood, not their literary prowess or commercial acumen. But these images, like the origin stories in general, are the equivalent of eighteenth-century frontispieces, and, even if they belittle the authors and the genre, they still perform a particular kind of ideological work that requires investigation.

Here, for instance, is another paratext, Rudyard Kipling's invocation of his daughter 'Effie' as the inspiration for some of his early *Just So Stories for Little Children* (1902):

> Some stories are meant to be read quietly and some stories are meant to be told aloud … All the Blue Skalallatoot stories are morning tales (I do not know why, but that is what Effie says). All the stories about Orvin Sylvester Woodsey … are afternoon stories because they were generally told in the shade of the woods. You could alter and change these tales as much as you pleased; but in the evening there were stories meant to put Effie to sleep, and you were not allowed to alter those by one single little word. They had to be told just so; or Effie would wake up and put back the missing sentence.[20]

Kipling presents Effie as his muse, which no doubt she was. But the domestic origin of the stories is very strategically deployed. It frames the stories neatly, and advertises their particular qualities and merits. It enables Kipling to create a hinterland for them, as if they have emerged from a whole mythology (the Blue Skalallatoot and Orvin Sylvester Woodsey stories no longer exist, if they ever did). And it endows Effie, and through her all child readers, with a flattering agency in the creation and conservation of stories. But it also continues to do what those eighteenth-century prefaces and dedications had done. It asserts that the text had been successfully 'road-tested'; it apologises, albeit archly, for presuming to intrude the domestic into the public sphere; it allays any anxieties that a children's book might somehow usurp the role of the parent.

There may be many reasons, then, both specific and general, factual and symbolic, unconscious and contrived, for these biographical accounts of the inceptions of children's books. But these originary stories are at least partly the vestige of the historical origins of children's literature, developed at first within the home, and then as a commercial product that deployed a rhetoric of domesticity to justify and advertise itself. In this sense, all these different kinds of origin – the historical, the domestic and the biographical – coalesce. It seems that, even today, children's literature has not been entirely able to escape the conditions, and anxieties, of its origins.

NOTES

1. 'Lewis Carroll's Diaries', 6 August 1862, in *Alice's Adventures in Wonderland*, ed. Richard Kelly (Peterborough, ON: Broadview, 2000), p. 244; Rosalía Baena, 'Telling a Bath-Time Story: *Haroun and the Sea of Stories* as a Modern Literary Fairy Tale', *The Journal of Commonwealth Literature*, 36 (2001), 65–76.
2. C. S. Lewis, 'On Three Ways of Writing for Children', in *Of This and Other Worlds*, ed. Walter Hooper (London: Fount, 1984), p. 44.
3. F. J. Harvey Darton, *Children's Books in England*, 3rd edn, rev. Brian Alderson (1932; Cambridge: Cambridge University Press, 1982), p. 1.
4. Peter Hunt, *Criticism, Theory and Children's Literature* (Oxford: Blackwell, 1991), p. 67.
5. Gillian Avery, 'The Puritans and their Heirs', in *Children and their Books. A Celebration of the Work of Iona and Peter Opie*, ed. Gillian Avery and Julia Briggs (Oxford: Clarendon Press, 1989), pp. 95–118 (p. 113).
6. Barbara Wall, *The Narrator's Voice. The Dilemma of Children's Fiction* (London: Macmillan, 1991), pp. 2 and 9.
7. Sarah Trimmer, *An Easy Introduction to the Knowledge of Nature* (1780; London: J. Dodsley, 1781), p. v; Hannah More, *Strictures on the Modern System of Female Education* (2 vols., London: Cadell and Davies, 1799), vol. I, p. 170.
8. Roger L'Estrange, *Fables of Æsop and Other Eminent Mythologists with Morals and Reflexions* (London: R. Sare *et al.*, 1692), pp. 2–3.
9. Arnaud Berquin, *The Children's Friend; Consisting of Apt Tales, Short Dialogues, and Moral Dramas*, trans. Mark Anthony Meilan (London: 'for the translator', 1786), p. 36.

10. John Bennett, *Strictures on Female Education; Chiefly as it Relates to the Culture of the Heart* (London: 'for the author', 1787), pp. 95–6 and 151–2.
11. Mary Wollstonecraft, *Original Stories, From Real Life* (London: J. Johnson, 1788), p. vii.
12. Noël-Antoine Pluche, *Spectacle de la Nature: or, Nature Display'd* (6 vols., London: R. Francklin *et al.*, 1763), vol. VI, pp. 38–9.
13. Victor Watson, 'Jane Johnson: A Very Pretty Story to Tell', in *Opening the Nursery Door: Reading, Writing and Childhood 1600–1900*, ed. Mary Hilton, Morag Styles and Victor Watson (London: Routledge, 1997), pp. 31–46 (p. 45).
14. Lady Ellenor Fenn, *Fables in Monosyllables* (London: J. Marshall, [1783]), pp. xi–xii.
15. Fenn, *Fables in Monosyllables*, pp. ix and v.
16. Maria Edgeworth, *The Parent's Assistant; or, Stories for Children*, Part I (London: J. Johnson, 1796), p. iv.
17. [Dorothy Kilner], *Miscellaneous Thoughts in Essays, Dialogues, Epistles, &c.* (London: J. Marshall, 1785), pp. iv–v and ii.
18. Robert Westall, *The Making of Me: A Writer's Childhood*, ed. Lindy McKinnel (London: Catnip, 2006), pp. 186–7; and 'How Real Do You Want Your Realism?', *Signal*, 28 (1979), 34–46.
19. U. C. Knoepflmacher, *Ventures into Childland: Victorians, Fairy Tales, and Femininity* (Chicago: University of Chicago Press, 1998), pp. 75–6.
20. 'Preface' to the 'Just So Stories', *St Nicholas Magazine* (December 1897), rpt in Rudyard Kipling, *Writings on Writing*, ed. Sandra Kemp and Lisa Lewis (Cambridge: Cambridge University Press, 1996), p. 47.

2

ANDREA IMMEL

Children's books and constructions of childhood

What do children know? How do they learn best? What rights should they have? All these fundamental questions about childhood can be contested (and frequently are). The framing of discussions about childhood are therefore influenced by the time and culture, as twentieth-century historians, anthropologists and sociologists have shown. How a person formulates responses to such questions, moreover, is also shaped by his or her perspective as an artist, biologist, economist, parent, philosopher or teacher. The issues at stake are not purely academic: whatever the answers, they are likely to have some impact on the way children are regarded and treated in a particular culture at a given time. A subsistence farmer in thirteenth-century France, a society where childhood mortality was extremely high and Roman Catholicism permeated all of life, would have had quite a different perspective on childhood from an upper middle-class father in Victorian England, whose children were likely to survive into adulthood but would bear the weight of dynastic, national and imperial expectations. Just as conceptions of childhood can differ sharply, so can ideas about children's books. The nursery rhyme anthology that delighted a mother in post-Second World War America might be condemned by an ardent communist in the Soviet Union of the 1920s as laughably deficient for training up the future citizens of the new society. But whatever the circumstances, there is no guarantee that children will accept the books adults press on them.

Ideas about children's books are inextricably bound up with cultural constructs of childhood. But what does 'construct' or 'construction' mean in this context? Derived from psychology, the term is defined by the *Oxford English Dictionary* as 'an object of perception or thought, formed by a combination of present with past sense-impressions'. Since the *Oxford English Dictionary* also equates 'construct' with 'anything constructed, especially by the mind; hence specifically, a concept specially devised to be part of a theory', we might say that a construct is more authoritative than a notion or a belief, because it is an idea based on observation and refined by analysis. A construct can never claim the authority of a model, paradigm or law. But it can exert considerable influence on people's thoughts and actions much like the *habitus*, which French sociologist Pierre Bourdieu defines as: 'necessity internalized and converted into a disposition that generates meaningful practices and meaning-giving perceptions'.[1] Constructs might be thought of as those acquired notions, of which we are generally unaware, that influence our attempts to accommodate larger social and cultural priorities with individual requirements in a given situation.

In this chapter, I will focus on describing ways constructs about childhood can influence the form children's books take, and shape discourse about children's literature. In the first section, I will resort to a fiction about a woman selecting holiday gifts to show how constructs figure in her approach to book selection. In the second section, I will argue that constructs are dynamic concepts that evolve over time but provide a basis for understanding changes in the conception of the children's book. John Locke's famous discussion of reading instruction in *Some Thoughts Concerning Education* (1693) will be the point of departure.

Bookbuying for children: constructs in action

The time is Christmas, a season when, in the West, books are traditionally purchased for children as gifts, and the agent will be Mrs X., a well-educated, affluent white woman living somewhere in the northeastern United States. She plans to visit her local branch of a national chain of bookstores for some items to contribute to a local holiday book drive, but her experiences would be similar anywhere in the developed world. As Mrs X. puzzles over what to buy, she draws – consciously or semi-consciously – upon cultural constructions about childhood and books to make decisions that can be justified as in the child's best interests.

When Mrs X. enters the bookstore, she does not need to ask where the children's section is located because she can take it for granted that it will be readily identifiable from the architecture and décor. It takes her almost no time to spot the semi-enclosed room painted in bright primary colours that announce the existence of a kid space. It never even occurs to Mrs X. that the children's books might be integrated into appropriate adult sections, as that would fly in the face of the near-universal modern practice of assigning merchandise for children to their own spaces. But the practice of putting this particular category of books in a special department is indirectly predicated upon the notion that childhood is a separate stage of life, a cultural construction that may not always have been in place. This construction was the subject of Philippe Ariès' famous study, *Centuries of Childhood* (1960), where Ariès observed that, in early modern Western Europe, it was eventually 'recognized that the child was not ready for life, and that he had to be subjected to a special treatment, a sort of quarantine, before he was allowed to join the adults'.[2]

Segregating the children's books from the rest of the volumes in the store certainly reflects that 'special treatment,' for specialisation – in this case, the differentiation of facilities and products for young people from those for adults – is a form of quarantine. The children's book department where Mrs X. is shopping supposedly provides the same safe and comfortable space that a public library offers young patrons, but with the important difference that all the books are for sale. But, in fact, the concessions made to children, the stated primary users of the space and notional beneficiaries of purchases made there, are relatively minor. It's true all the merchandise is intended for young customers, who can avail themselves of tables and chairs whose proportions are too small for grown-up bodies. But little children can comfortably access only the lower shelves of the book cases. Moreover, the alphabetical filing of books by the author's last name within each section is counterintuitive to all but relatively mature children. If they were consulted about how the books should be organised, they might suggest ways based on different criteria, such as the response a story arouses (fright, laughter or boredom, for example) or favourite characters (Captain Underpants, Olivia the Pig, Harry Potter). It is the adults who can easily navigate the shelves and are therefore invited to locate – and therefore screen and select – any book. Adults will bring the material chosen mostly under their supervision to the cash register, which is also sized for the big people who pay for the books, not for little people who will read them.

Thus far it looks as if the quarantine construct posits an unattainable ideal. Is the most logical conclusion that the needs of children are being overlooked or ignored? Relying on binary oppositions between a construct and reality in discussions about the adult and child is always risky because, as other chapters in this volume demonstrate, they over-simplify an extremely complex relationship. Western constructs of childhood, infused with adult projections, expectations and anxieties about individual fulfilment and society's future, usually point to foundational principles. While the quarantine construct arises from the conviction, based on observation, that enlightened segregation from adults serves children's needs, it does not serve as a formula, blueprint or heuristic. Indeed, the flawed design in the children's section actually underscores a tension inherent in the quarantine construct, for it calls attention to the fact that a child's limited agency means that segregation is rarely total. If adults need to play an active role assisting children in the bookstore, including the all-important one of paying for purchases, they must be accommodated. This tension also bears out observations by sociologists that the tendency in modern Western culture to 'island' children, or to insulate them from experiences for their own benefit, further restricts their agency by making them more, not less, dependent upon adults.[3]

Let's return to Mrs X. She has started to survey the stock. She knows from experience that in a large children's book department a high percentage of the books will be assigned to subject sections by the implied reader's age. The subdivisions also roughly correspond to levels of reading ability: pre-readers (from babies to four- or five-year-olds); beginning readers (four or five to seven or eight years); independent readers (eight to ten or eleven years); and older readers on the cusp of the transition to adult texts (ten or eleven to fourteen or fifteen years). It's easy to see that the arrangement of books within the children's department reflects another application of the quarantine construct. Here children are islanded as readers, by being separated not just from adults, but also from children who belong to other age groups.

Mrs X has never given much thought to the system, however, having found it perfectly straightforward and convenient over the years. She accepts it as natural, partly because it is consistent with a ubiquitous modern cultural construction of childhood: that children develop biologically and mentally as they pass through a series of age-related stages until maturity is attained. Mrs X may not have delved into cognitive psychology, but she has undoubtedly remembered something from her college classes, or, at the least, has been exposed to popular childrearing literature by physicians, such as Doctor Spock or Penelope Leach. The publications about children's books she undoubtedly read when her own children were small are full of iterations of the development construct. While waiting in the paediatrician's office, she might have leafed through a dog-eared copy of *Writer's Digest*'s annual, *You Can Write for Children*, where she would have encountered the construct in articles laying out 'what most children should know and understand, from kindergarten through eighth grade' so that aspiring writers can be 'in tune with what your audience knows at each level in life'.[4] If she ever consulted a book selection guide like Eden Ross Lipson's *New York Times Parent's Guide to the Best Books for Children* or visited its on-line equivalent at Parents.com, she would have picked up various tips for matching the book to the child, based on criteria keyed to competencies at each age-defined developmental phase.

Mrs X. pauses in front of the young adult fiction section, wondering if she is really up to the task of choosing books for this age group. She feels as if she's about to enter a minefield. It's so hard to predict what kids will and won't like even when you know them, she agonises. Then there are the parents to consider. Everybody has different tolerances for the representation of controversial topics like violence, sexuality and race. She would not object to her child receiving a copy of Robert Cormier's *The Chocolate War* (1974) from a stranger, but she would wonder what that person was thinking if the selection were an extreme manga such as Kouta Hirano's *Hellsing* (1997–2008). She would also be pretty offended if her child received a title in Cecila von Ziegesar's Gossip Girl series (2002–7), but neither would she be very comfortable with bestselling Christian young adult fiction like *The Rise of the False Messiahs* (2004) in Left Behind: The Kids series by Jerry B. Jenkins and Tim LaHaye. She decides instead to focus on finding books for younger children, and wanders over to the baby book section to see what there is.

As Mrs X. begins to look through the baby books (untearable and water-proof formats for pre-schoolers), it occurs to her that board books would make a perfect donation. A board book is an excellent way to introduce children to reading as it is designed to be sturdy enough for children to handle from the time they can sit up. A baby book's dimensions (small, square and chunky) and materials (cloth, cardboard, wood, or plastic) are defences against users who cannot be expected to hold a book steady and turn its pages expertly. In the case of the board book, its thick laminated pages can be wiped clean of any marks left by dirty fingers. The rounded corners of pages mini-mise the chance of poking of tender gums at the time of life when browsing a book may mean a certain amount of exploratory chewing. Another thing Mrs X. appreciates about the board book is the way the contents are as carefully calibrated to the pre-reader's mental capabilities as its physical form is strategically adapted to work with his rudimentary motor skills. Unlike many people, she does not dismiss baby books as non-books: they are designed to teach critical skills and schemata that prepare children for reading and therefore precede the introduction of more complex texts and literary works. An early concept book focuses on familiar things the child encounters around his home (apple, ball, shoe, telephone), or introduces concepts such as opposites or colours, letters of the alphabet, ordinal numbers or categories of things (animals, modes of transportation). Photographic illustrations are preferred for the objective and naturalistic representation of the subjects, but illustrators also favour pictographs in bold primary colours. The text is rarely more than a one- or two-word caption per page but it is sufficient to help the child establish the essential connections between the lexeme, the picture and the thing.[5] Mrs X. sees this as a win–win situation: the child can have pride of ownership while absorbing important ideas and learning how to 'operate' a book, the design having significantly reduced the necessity to caution, 'Gentle, gentle! We don't tear our books.' Indeed, it represents the triumph of the development and quarantine constructs.

The selection in this store certainly could be better, Mrs X. thinks crossly, passing over titles like *My First Barbie: Shapes at the Ballet* (2000), the *Motown Baby Love Board Book Number 1: My Girl* (2001), *Super Mario's Adventure: My Very First Nintendo Game Boy* (1997) and heaps of Thomas the Tank Engine and Peter Rabbit spin-offs. What she wants are board books that will help the child acquire age-appropriate concepts without sacrificing high standards of bookmaking. She keeps digging until she finds titles that prove it is possible to be highly creative within the confines of the baby book genre: *Is It Red? Is It Yellow? Is It Blue?* (1987) and *Push Pull Empty Full* (1972) by distinguished American photographer Tana Hoban; *Duck is Dirty* (1997), a quirky comic nineteen-word story by the Japanese-born illustrator Satoshi Kitamura; and *Inside Freight Train* (2001) by African-American artist Donald Crews. Mrs X. also snaps up two finds on the sale table: a very slightly damaged copy of the Ahlbergs' novelty book *The Jolly Postman* (1986), and the *Cheerios Play Book* (2000), touted on the back cover as 'tasty, interactive fun that toddlers will love!'

All in all, Mrs X. is quite pleased with her purchases even though they include an activity book that is a blatant advertisement for an international brand. She has also managed to pick a pretty diverse group of author-illustrators, who succeed in presenting material in an engaging, imaginative fashion that appeals to the child's senses, but is also arresting to the more sophisticated adult. The level of artistry suggests their creators believed that children deserve good writing, good art and good design from the very beginning – and that giving them inferior work could deter them from becoming acquainted with books that will make them lifelong readers. All of her selections should be more than acceptable to give as Christmas gifts. Even though the exchange of books will be anonymous, she hopes her thoughtful choices communicate her affection and regard for the children who will be the recipients of her benefaction.

Mrs X.'s desire to find books for children who have yet to master the letters of the alphabet reflects some interesting discrepancies in the ways she thinks about child readers. On the one hand, she considers herself to have been buying 'for' the child without being aware that the tension about child agency in the quarantine construct is surfacing in another context. Although the child's status entitles him or her to special treatment as a reader, he or she actually has very limited autonomy for years, until a certain level of competency has been achieved. Even though Mrs X. knows from experience that reading is one of those critical gaps in skill that cannot be bridged without adult assistance, she has left the adult mostly out of the equation during the selection process.

Yet the youngest 'readers' depend upon adults to show them how to make sense of their baby books, so reading is not a solitary experience, in which words are silently construed on the page in the order they were printed. Rather it is a social encounter, in which the adult uses an illustration as a point of departure to explain a concept through conversations with the child. The mother may point to the picture, say its name and point to the word, and make up questions (What is this? Do we have one in our house? Is it in this room? No? Where is it?) that allow the child to form eventually the connections between the thing, its visual representation, the word and the concept. With a child who cannot yet speak, the process is one-sided, with the adult asking and answering the questions. In practice, a baby book is used together by a child and an adult, and so is more correctly a cross-written text, or one for a multigenerational audience.

From this perspective, Mrs X's board books are likewise as much a present to the parent as the child because the books offer them the opportunity to bond through reading together. Indeed, it could be argued that the potential for this kind of experience may be the gift's most valuable aspect because of the role it plays in defining relationships within a complex social network with literature at its centre. As an instrument of socialisation, the book establishes connections between the child and the giver, but also the giver, the parent and teacher (when they are different people). With the giver's invitation to read comes the reciprocal obligation to take reading seriously. The gift book also tries to lay the foundation of an alliance between the older and younger generations, but also between the giver and the recipient as members of the community of literate (and ideally civilised) readers.

In this context, the giver's generosity is not measured chiefly by the amount of money spent, but by the aesthetic, moral and cultural values she believes worthy of passing to the next generation. The book may represent the necessity of acquiring cultural capital: learning to read is a critical first step towards mastering skills that will enable the child to earn a living, or, better yet, produce wealth and propel social advancement. Alternatively, the book may promote reading as the disinterested pursuit of self-knowledge and self-control for the individual's psychological, moral or spiritual well-being, and, indirectly, that of society. Whatever the giver's motive, the book is the token of a cultural exchange in which the adult shows the child a road that can (or should) be taken. It is a pledge, not a free gift, and to treat it lightly reflects poorly on the recipient, such as Collodi's Pinocchio, who thoughtlessly treated the primer Gepetto gave him as disposable property when he needed money for admission to a show (fig. 2). Equally ungrateful was Rebecca Sharp upon her departure from Miss Pinkerton's academy in William Thackeray's *Vanity Fair* (1847–8). As the coach drives out of the gates, Becky heaves Johnson's *Dictionary*, a copy of which is presented to all Miss Pinkerton's girls, out of the window. It is the audacious parting shot of a shrewd, ambitious and relatively

Figure 2. Carlo Collodi, *Le avventure di Pinocchio*. Illustrated by Attilio Mussino. 8th edn, Florence: Marzocco, 1943, p. 62.

...quando tornò aveva in mano l'Abbecedario per il figliuolo.

unscrupulous young woman who will not play the hypocrite and pretend to accept the headmistress's value system embodied in the dictionary's definitions.

If asked, Mrs X. would readily admit that she hadn't really thought about all the cultural baggage that can be attached to a gift of books. But she would have to acknowledge that those board books are hardly devoid of that connection. When buying books for strange children, she has thought of them in less personal terms than of the nieces or nephews whose personalities, interests and parents she knows intimately. Of course, she feels herself to be under greater obligation to choose only books that parents from backgrounds different from hers would not find objectionable. To be honest, Mrs X. concedes with a wry grin, it is so much easier to vet baby books. The content is not controversial because it consists of basic information that everybody agrees is necessary for children to learn young.

But suddenly Mrs X realises that, in her attempt to be sensitive, she has not selected any literature per se. And childhood reading is supposed to be all about the discovery of enthralling narratives. In modern Western culture, she remembers, books are given to children for reasons that don't revolve around filling them up with information as if they were empty vessels. Of course, it is difficult to factor the child's potential for philosophical, moral or magical thinking into the equation because it doesn't lend itself to precise measurement or quantification. But how many people, Mrs X. wonders, would side with Mr Gradgrind in the famous schoolroom scene in Charles Dickens' *Hard Times* (1854), in which he calls upon students to define a horse? Who knew more about horses, Sissy Jupe, the supposedly ignorant pupil whose father is an equestrian rider in the circus, or Bitzer, who spits out the zoologically precise answer without having seen one? She recognises Gradgrind's deficiencies as an educator because he cannot see that children have their own ways of seeing and thinking that are valid precisely because they reveal aspects of things that may be overlooked from the more fixed perspective of an adult. Mrs X. doesn't thrill to Wordsworth's figure of the child trailing clouds of glory in the ode 'Intimations of Immortality from Recollections of Early Childhood' (composed 1802–4), but she has certainly been in the position of Wordsworth's narrator in the poem 'We Are Seven' (1798), surprised by the child's naïve but profound response to a question that supposedly had one correct answer. One doesn't have to be a romantic with a capital R, she muses, to agree with Wordsworth in Book v of the 1805 *Prelude* when he characterises the ideal childhood as a time 'when every hour brings palpable access / Of knowledge, when all knowledge is delight, / And sorrow is not there'.[6] Like Wordsworth, she also believes that books ought not to be among the 'engines' that 'confine' the child, but rather wondrous vehicles that transport him out of himself (l. 358). That capacity for complete immersion in

universal truth, but rather a culture-specific formulation. Because a construct may take somewhat different forms, we must be alert to the possibility that the current interpretation of the construct's key terms may not correspond to that of an earlier period. But even when two historical manifestations of a construct may vary significantly in certain respects, others of its terms may serve as common ground for discussion. Understanding when, where and why those shifts occur can be very helpful in understanding the nature of changes to children's books and how those changes are received.

While Locke's vocabulary in *Some Thoughts* might strike us as a bit old-fashioned, the ideas packed into that phrase are not. During the first stage of lessons, Locke argued, it was best if the teacher could motivate the child to concentrate without letting on that the two of them were working on a task. As proof, he offered examples of children he observed who had been eager to settle down and learn the letters of the alphabet when the assignment was presented as a game. If the child wanted to be a proficient player, then he or she would have to be motivated to transfer a previously mastered skill to a new context. At the second stage of reading instruction, when the child begins to put letters into syllables, words and sentences, Locke conceded that it was more difficult to find ways to enliven the process. But if a teacher were to present the pupil with a text that was both understandable and interesting, the chances were certainly increased. 'For what pleasure or encouragement can it be to a child', Locke asked, 'to exercise himself in reading those parts of a book, where he understands nothing? ... none should be proposed to a child but such as are suited to a child's capacity and notions'.[8] The child had to come before the curriculum.

It's easy to see why Locke's ideas are regarded as containing the germs of an enlightened modern attitude towards childhood reading, given their emphasis on accessibility, comprehensibility and entertainment. Still, his formulation of appropriateness must be seen in the context of the seventeenth-century teaching methods, educational politics and market for children's books to comprehend more fully where priorities lay and how they might have shaded the meaning of his key terms. Reading was taught through spelling in the seventeenth century – that is, spelling preceded reading. It was justified on the grounds that complex material was broken down to its smallest parts, the letters, which were then recombined into syllables, words and sentences. Because the method was highly analytic, children were expected to memorise a great deal of material. This approach also required a great deal of the teacher if it were to be done well, but reading instruction was considered a tiresome and unrewarding assignment that was not, consequently, particularly well remunerated. The process of learning to read could take years, depending upon the competence and patience of the instructor (and many were reported by irate parents to be neither). Typically, children could not understand much of what they were able to spell out for some time, especially if instruction began, as was not uncommon, at age two or three.[9]

Locke's remarks on reading instruction in his day were integral to his extended critique of the antiquated Latin curriculum and an equally out-moded pedagogy. Locke thought it unconscionable that so much time was wasted trying to coerce resistant, resentful boys to acquire a little Latin by appealing to their dread of corporal punishment. Why adhere to the bad old method of beating learning into a little child, argued Locke, when it was relatively simple to devise ways to trick him into doing the same thing? Identifying those circumstances where new pastimes might reduce the reliance upon corporal punishment was therefore a high priority. He argued that a readily available toy like dice that could be adapted into effective teaching aids, could, when used in conjunction with more psychologically astute methods of motivation, increase the odds of children learning the letters of the alphabet painlessly and pleasurably.

Locke lays out the potential of educational games with such enthusiasm that it comes as a surprise to encounter what appears to be indifference to the subject of children's books. In fact, he admits to ignorance about the con-temporary market for children's books, almost as if he didn't think it was worth the trouble to become better informed. He does not even seem to have been familiar with Comenius' *Orbis sensualium pictus* (1658), arguably the greatest children's book of the seventeenth century, which had been available in Charles Hoole's English–Latin translation since 1659. Locke's noncha-lance is puzzling. When educational reformers cannot recommend works to their readers, they typically call upon public-spirited men of letters to com-pose new kinds of books for children, but Locke does not do this.

One possible explanation for Locke's apparent lack of interest in the contemporary children's book publishing was that he was confident that traditional texts were perfectly adequate as a child's first reading assignment, provided teachers used them intelligently. The 'easy pleasant book' did not have to be written exclusively for a young audience to be appropriate for them: it merely needed to be appropriate for their abilities at a given time. No book was inherently 'good' for children, including the Bible, in Locke's opinion, unless they were ready for it. He disapproved of the widespread prac-tice of having children read the Old and New Testaments straight through, because they could not be expected to comprehend a text of which so much was at a vast remove from their experience. Suitable passages, such as the story of Joseph or David and Goliath, could be excerpted and adapted for lessons at this stage. Locke recommended instead that new readers start with Aesop's fables, for a variety of reasons, not the least of which was the small child's fascination with animals. Fables were brief and succinct, making them suitable for readers with short attention spans. There were many illustrated editions of Aesop, which facilitated the teaching of new concepts via the senses. When a child found he was capable of reading an entertaining book, he was rewarded for having learned the skill, as well as given an incentive to continue this pleasurable activity. A fable collection also contained many important ideas expressed in ways that might spark a child's curiosity. While fables had the advantage of being simple enough for a young child to comprehend, nevertheless the texts were not disposable, so to speak, once the child could read independently. Their meanings could not be exhausted after repeated exposures, or even during subsequent stages of development. Fables were worth retaining throughout life.

While Locke's concept of the easy, pleasant book certainly does not rule out the possibility of quarantine and specialisation, he himself never ventured very far down that road. The godfather of the modern children's book tried to improve, not supplant, Aesop in the one book he produced for young learners of Latin.[10] His chief priority was to keep children from languishing at the first stage of instruction, where they not only suffered unnecessarily, but lost valuable time that could be spent acquiring the fundamentals of other important new subjects. Perhaps he could not imagine new ways of writing for children – although some of his Restoration contemporaries did, chiefly the Baptists like James Janeway, Thomas White or John Bunyan, who set out to create easy pleasant works suited to the capacities of Puritan children. There are no grounds for inferring from his comments on children's reading that he himself conceived of a semi-autonomous genre of children's literature, much less thought it desirable or necessary to his efforts to reform and modernise the curriculum.

Suppose Locke were to be transported to the children's book department where Mrs X. is. Would they be able to hold a conversation about the 'easy pleasant books' of the early twenty-first century? What would transpire once he became accustomed to the riot of primary colours that increases visual stimulation to a high and not especially comfortable level? He begins by looking for modern editions of what he supposes are still essential works. But there are no stout little leather-bound volumes of Aesop's fables, just tall slim picture books with brief, evocative titles carefully incorporated into the inviting 'posters' for their contents on the front covers. It slowly dawns on him that innovations in printing technologies since the 1690s have made it possible to integrate word and image seamlessly anywhere in a book, including its binding, endpapers and dust jacket. He is having a hard time wrapping his mind around the idea that colour pictures are now commonplace, not fabulous luxuries.

Mrs X. notices that the gentleman seems to be disoriented and comes over to ask if he needs some help. He thanks her and asks where the editions of Aesop's fables might be found? He explains that, while he sees a great many books about animals, there seem to be no Aesops. Mrs X is somewhat taken aback by his request, because she has always considered fables pretty difficult, dry and prescriptive for little children, even if they are classics. Perhaps he is home-schooling his children. Many home-schoolers seem to have very conservative tastes in children's books and Aesop has more than enough morals to go around. 'There's a retelling of *The Tortoise and the Hare* by Janet Stevens in the picture book section, would that do?' she asks. He stares at the cover, perplexed by the athletic shorts and sports shoes, having never seen a set of fable illustrations featuring animals in anything except their fur, feathers, scales or shells. 'Thank you', he says again, 'but I would like a book with more than one fable. Surely there must be some. There are so many books here.' He is still trying to comprehend that everything here is for children to read, but that absolutely nothing looks familiar. 'Well', says Mrs X., pointing across the aisle, 'it would be in this section, but I don't see anything except that Dover Thrift Classic edition. But it's so dull and unattractive, I can't imagine any child would be tempted to look into it. Amazon.com would have a pretty big selection, though. The reviews posted on the site would probably help you find a nice lively version with good illustrations. I think there's a terminal over there.'

Locke feels as if she is speaking to him in a foreign language. The edition she didn't like looked quite good to him: the selection of the fables was unobjectionable and the type large and clear. It was certainly preferable to the one she showed him where the huge colour pictures overwhelmed the brief text. Locke walks over to the sale table and begins looking through the marked-down books, but can't really make sense out of anything. 'I'm sorry to trouble you again, madam, but what are Cheerios?' he asks. 'Oh, it's a brand of cereal', replies Mrs X., wondering just exactly where he comes from. 'It's eaten for breakfast with milk and sugar and fruit.' Now Locke is really confused. 'How exactly is the child supposed to play with this book?' 'Oh', says Mrs X., opening up *The Cheerios Play Book*: 'Cheerios are easy for toddlers to pick up. See the recessed spaces in the pictures? You help them complete the pictures by placing the correct number of Cheerios in the spaces provided. It's an easy way of encouraging little children to develop fine motor skills, learn their numbers, recognise patterns, etc.' Locke can now see certain cleverness in the approach, although he can't refrain from observing to Mrs X. that it is surely a bad idea to encourage children to waste food like this. Mrs X. nods yes, hoping that the gentleman hasn't noticed she is holding a copy. After taking a second look at the book, she can't believe she fell for such a superficial gimmick so unimaginatively executed just because it was 49 cents.

'Now here is a really nice book for young children', she says, showing him a copy of *The Jolly Postman*. He is quite delighted at its ingenuity, but is taken aback to discover that the text is woven around a collection of what he would call old nurse's songs (nursery rhymes to Mrs X). He has never seen this kind of nonsense printed in a book and can't imagine it serving any useful purpose. Mrs X. notices the funny look on his face and takes a deep breath before launching into an explanation. 'Nursery rhymes introduce very young children to poetry', she explains. He tries to keep his expression politely neutral. 'And the Ahlbergs were a very clever and creative husband and wife team. They have won all kinds of awards for their children's books. *The Jolly Postman* is very popular – it was one of my daughter's favourite books when she was little. She loved taking all the letters out of the envelopes and hearing me do all the different characters' voices.' Locke wonders how it is possible for people to make a living writing such things. Sensing his disapproval, Mrs X. hurries on. 'This is a book where all novelty features have an educational purpose. They help the child learn how to "read" their world through the story – everything from decoding written language, to following a narrative, internalising conventions of visual and literary repre- sentation, assimilating information or schemata, participating in literary play … But the child doesn't realise how much he's learning because the story is so much fun to read.' She stops abruptly, sensing that she has lost the gentleman in her enthusiasm to promote what she considers one of the cleverest books to appear in recent memory.

That we could imagine Locke and Mrs X together in a bookstore evalu- ating picture books is due to various constructs providing them with a vocabulary to discuss the perennial concerns of childhood education, such as utility, user-friendliness, ends-versus-means, even though their points of reference diverged quite dramatically. They both recognised childhood as a critical stage of life, but their understandings of what children like and need, as well as what could be expected of them, were shaped by their respective culture's resources and values. Of course, there were many more issues they could have touched upon, had they examined different books. If Mrs X. had tried to explain the concept of young adult fiction to Locke, they might have had quite a contentious discussion, arising out of a fundamental disagree- ment over when childhood ends (Locke would probably be inclined to say maturity begins sooner than would Mrs X. so that children could move on to texts that had not been specially adapted for them). The difficulties Locke and Mrs X. experienced in communication are not merely symptomatic of their holding different constructs of childhood and of children's books.

Rather, the constructions to which they both adhere are pervasive in the analysis of children's books in general, which tend to be designed as much for the use as for the pleasure of their readers. As long as writers try to engage young readers in the present with an eye to influencing their future selves, constructs inevitably come into play in the creation, merchandising and evaluation of children's books. A keen awareness of how constructs can direct our responses to children's books enhances our ability to interpret them intelligently, sensitively and knowledgeably.

NOTES

1. Pierre Bourdieu, *Distinction: A Social Critique of the Judgement of Taste* (Cambridge: Cambridge University Press, 1984), p. 170.
2. Philippe Ariès, *Centuries of Childhood: A Social History of Family Life*, trans. Robert Baldick (New York: Vintage, 1962), p. 412.
3. John R. Gillis, 'Epilogue: The Islanding of Children – Reshaping the Mythical Landscapes of Childhood', in *Designing Modern Childhoods: History, Space, and the Material Culture of Children*, ed. Marta Gutman and Ning de Coninck-Smith (New Brunswick: Rutgers University Press, 2008), pp. 316–30.
4. Alijandra Mogilner and Tayopa Mogliner, 'On the Level', *You Can Write for Children* (December 2006), 16–19.
5. Bettina Kümmerling-Meibauer and Jörg Meibauer, 'First Pictures, Early Concepts: Early Concept Books', *The Lion and the Unicorn*, 29 (2005), 324–47.
6. William Wordsworth, *The Prelude, 1799, 1805, 1850*, ed. Jonathan Wordsworth, M. H. Abrams and Stephen Gill (New York: W. W. Norton, 1979), lines 395–97, p. 80.
7. John Locke, *Some Thoughts Concerning Education* (1693) in *The Educational Writings of John Locke*, ed. James L. Axtell (Cambridge: Cambridge University Press, 1968), p. 259.
8. Locke, *Some Thoughts*, p. 261.
9. Ian Michael, *The Teaching of English from the Sixteenth Century to 1870* (Cambridge: Cambridge University Press, 1987), pp. 14–16.
10. Robert H. Hurwitz and Judith B. Finn, 'Locke's Aesop's Fables', *Locke Newsletter*, 6 (1975), 71–83.

3

BRIAN ALDERSON

The making of children's books

One of the most famous and widely facsimiled letters ever written is that directed to Noel Moore from Eastwood, Dunkeld, on 4 September 1893. In it the sender, who signs herself 'Yours affectionately, Beatrix Potter', writes and illustrates a story about a disobedient rabbit. Several years later, Miss Potter – who had been having some success in selling designs for greeting cards – conceived the idea of converting the story into a book. She borrowed the letter from Noel and worked it up, with more drawings, into a tale of publishable length and despatched it unavailingly to a sequence of at least six publishers.

Having faith in her work (and a little money put by), she determined that, if the trade were not interested, she would publish it herself and so, for Christmas 1901, she had ready for distribution 250 copies of *The Tale of Peter Rabbit*, eighty-six pages, illustrated with electrotypes of her original line drawings, plus a colour-printed frontispiece, the whole bound in pale green paper over boards. Within a month the success of the venture was such that she had another 250 copies run off, while, at the same time, the publishers Frederick Warne began negotiations for an edition that would enter the mainstream book trade. They besought the author to convert her line draw-ings into watercolours (which would, like her earlier frontispiece, be among the earliest book illustrations to be printed by the new 'three colour process') and, with a prudence common to many in the business, they agreed only a modest royalty for this new and unknown author, but with provision for an increase should success attend the project (fig. 3). Thus, in October 1902, two issues of the trade edition appeared on the market, one costing a shilling bound in dark grey or brown paper over boards with a laid-down (that is to say, pasted-on) colour portrait of Peter on the front and with distinctive ornamental lettering for the titling, the second a 'deluxe' edition, bound in green cloth gilt. A year later, with the introduction of pictorial endpapers, four of the colour plates had to be dropped, not to return in standard trade editions until 2002.

Although somewhat truncated, this account of the emergence of a cele-brated children's book provides first-hand evidence of the collaborative

Figure 3. Beatrix Potter, *Peter Rabbit*, front boards of the trade edition (left) and privately printed edition (right).

nature of the creative process.[1] What we are seeing is the conversion of an intimate personal communication (which could even, under other circumstance, have been purely verbal – like a bed-time story) into a public document, and this emerges through the agency of more than just the original storyteller. There is her alter ego, the illustrator (often, of course, an entirely different person from the author, sometimes militating against such a harmonious marrying of work and picture as occurs in *Peter Rabbit*). Then there are the craftsmen: papermakers, typefounders, blockmakers, printers, bookbinders involved in the physical production of both the private and the trade editions. And finally there are the publishers who are not only responsible for co-ordinating the whole production process but who, through their direct relationship with the author, may make, or encourage, many decisions which can have a crucial influence on readers' responses to the finished work. Thus, authors, far from having their divine afflatus conveyed unmediated to their audience, must mostly be seen as executants within a collaborative endeavour – and not always the leading ones or even the originators at that.

For reasons related partly to their production – as seen with *Peter Rabbit* – and partly to the immaturity of many of their readers, children's books have been given a treatment that often differed from what was customary with books for adults. For much of their history they have been regarded primarily as keys to unlock gateways into learning, or proper social comportment, or even reading itself. And from as early as the seventeenth century it was recognised that, if children could see a potential for entertainment on the other side of the gateway, then they would be the more eager to pass through. Thus it was that Johann Amos Comenius' *Orbis sensualium pictus* employed an ingenious design in carrying out its encyclopaedic aim of introducing children to the facts and concepts of the world which they inhabited. First published in Nuremberg in 1658, it divided this world into 150 'classified' subjects, each one of which was presented to the reader in a woodcut picture. Within the picture were cut minuscule numbers which linked items there displayed – animals, objects, even ideas like 'providentia dei' – to a subjoined text, and that text itself was printed in both German and Latin. The book thus became for its readers a most sympathetic guide to both information and language. The importance of the physical presentation of the material was instantly recognised. Within a year the book was translated into English. Finding woodcuts an unsatisfactory medium for conveying the many pictorial details with their accompanying tiny numbers, the English publisher had them converted into engravings on copper, a finer but more expensive process (fig. 7). Printing from copper plates, where images are incised into the surface of the plate, required a separate press from that used for the letterpress text; hence each sheet had to be printed twice. The method was not altogether fool-proof and the subjects of the plates were occasionally misjudged so that the wrong picture accompanied the text, presumably to the confusion of the reader.

As *Peter Rabbit* and the *Orbis pictus* clearly show, it is an over-simplification to regard the making of a children's book as a process of parthenogenesis. There are rare exceptions, such as the 'illuminated books' of William Blake – not only was *Songs of Innocence* (1789) written and illustrated by him but also he etched the words and pictures, printed them on his own press, coloured them by hand according to his intentions for individual copies, and published the books from his home address. Otherwise, though, almost every book is a collaboration. Each possesses a private history of its own, a study of which will reveal its dependence on influences operating outside the control of its origi-nator. This dependence also imposes limitations on authorial creativity, the chief of which relate to the social circumstances prevailing at a given time and the materials and technology then current. Only in exceptional circumstances will production be undertaken without some calculation as to the profitability of the venture and – as was apparent in the case of *The Tale of Peter Rabbit* – it is the publisher rather than the author who is usually foremost in the essential economics of the system – taking profits or suffering losses. It was Miss Potter as publisher rather than writer who was able to finance the reprint of her private edition; Miss Potter as author was beholden to Frederick Warne for the contractual terms of the first, and subsequent, trade editions.

In so far as prospects of profit persuade publishers to a course of action in the choosing and making of their books, their awareness of 'the market' plays a double role. As entrepreneurs, they will see the value of inventiveness and novelty in what they offer to the (frequently adult) purchasers of their wares. Indeed, in the mid eighteenth century, when children's books first became a significant element in mainstream publishing, several imaginative ploys were quickly tried which differentiated them from both contemporary adult books and the workaday manuals and textbooks with which children were usually furnished. Thus the influential *Child's New Play-Thing*, first published by Thomas Cooper in 1742, introduced as a folding frontispiece an alphabet grid designed to be cut up and used as cards in a learning-game. But publishers will also be aware of the customs and mores of their time and will temper experiment with prudence. When the 'Rev'd Mr Cooper' (actually Richard Johnson, a writer who produced many children's books published by the Newbery firms between 1770 and 1793) brought 'the Beauties of the Arabian Nights entertainments' into the nursery in 1791, he called the book *The Oriental Moralist* and assured purchasers that he had 'carefully expunged everything that could give the least offence to the most delicate reader'.[2] A like tenderness for consumers' sensibilities has never gone away. In the 1970s, for instance, Roald Dahl and his illustrator were forced, for now very obvious reasons, to alter their treatment of the Oompa-Loompas in *Charlie and the Chocolate Factory* (1964) (figs. 5–6), while the McGraw Hill Book Company went so far as to issue guidelines to staff members and authors on the equal treatment of the sexes.[3]

It is also necessary to note how the publishers' fear of sanctions from 'the market' arises from an awareness of the constituency they are seeking to serve. For well over 150 years, the print-runs of children's books were governed by expectations of sales to a largely middle-class public, or to schools and Sunday schools, where unthreatening convention prevailed. In the twentieth century, however, beginning in the United States, the public library movement brought children's librarians to the fore as wielders of corporate budgets, and many publishers trimmed their production to tastes and fashions espoused by professional readers of children's books who were inclined to encourage experiment and leave popular appeal to look after itself. (The drastic cutting of library book-budgets in recent decades has had the effect of driving publishers back to fostering popular sales and exploiting the potential of such non-literary ploys as 'character' merchandising.)

There are other reasons too why it is problematic to talk about the author as the sole originator of a children's book. Again the career of Richard Johnson demonstrates this very nicely. Some of his accounts have fortunately been preserved.[4] They reveal that he was an *assembler* of children's books as much as an author, or rather that the two roles can be indistinguishable. He was paid 16 guineas for 'abridging' the *Arabian Nights* stories, and he is also found 'writing', 'translating', 'compiling' other volumes, and authors are still being commissioned to fashion texts to meet the requirements of their publishers. Text may be demanded that fits a particular series, like the Ladybird Books, or to support a body of already-existing illustrations. Walter de la Mare did this on a number of occasions, most notably for Harold Jones' lithographs in *This Year, Next Year* (1937). Likewise, Philippa Pearce, as 'Warrener', supplied texts for some storybooks based on designs used to decorate the 'Bunnikins' children's ceramic ware.

Even when the author seems more *auteur* than hack, the publisher may intrude as a significant partner. Beatrix Potter's second book, *The Tailor of Gloucester* (1902), evolved in a very similar pattern to her first, but with her publisher making more extensive cuts to the privately printed edition, much to the author's chagrin. *Alice's Adventures in Wonderland* (1865) was similarly the product of a long and intricate series of collaborations. Having begun, like *Peter Rabbit*, as a tale told to a child, it was also expanded and turned into a manuscript volume which was illustrated by the author and presented to the girl for whom the story was invented. Then, like Noel Moore's letter, it was borrowed back, and prepared for 'official' publication

with commissioned illustrations. Much of the business and production nego-
tiation was undertaken by the author in association with the 'professional'
publisher Alexander Macmillan, and the surviving correspondence between
the two gives an intimate view of the book's wayward course towards its
ultimate success.[5]

The insights which these detailed examples of copy-preparation give us are
exceptional for books of the distant past. They do confirm though that
authors' experiences may differ widely in their negotiations with publishers,
a contention that can often be supported by detailed modern evidence. For
while in the past it was a matter of routine for many authors and publishers
to tidy their files into the dustbin, recent decades have found institutions
garnering such papers as valuable research materials – a process abetted by
authors' pleased discovery that this can be a remunerative way of clearing
their work-rooms. Collections of working papers, correspondence, manuscripts and original illustrations held by some libraries in Britain and the
United States offer confirmation of the former fragmentary evidence of the
collaborative effort through which individual books are created. The archive
of the celebrated editor Kaye Webb, now held at Seven Stories, the Centre
for Children's Books in Newcastle upon Tyne, is shedding much light on the
collaboration behind so many successful Puffin books; similarly, careful
study of the Ezra Jack Keats archive in the de Grummond Collection of the
University of Southern Mississippi has revealed much about his work.[6]

Whatever the origins of, or the innovations in, the bookmakers' products,
the limitations imposed on them by the physical resources at their disposal are
decisive in determining the appearance and character of each generation's
children's books. Put another way, one cannot overestimate the importance
of technological factors in determining the kind of books produced for
children over the whole history of children's literature. For example, publishing decisions inevitably involve consideration of the paper on which work is
to be printed. In the hand-press period, which lasted from the days of William
Caxton to the early nineteenth century, the limitation on sheet sizes imposed
by the dimensions of the hand-held mould in which the paper was made was
a strong determinant of format. One of the earliest examples of children's
books as an emergent sector of the book trade was the series of *Gigantick
Histories* published and sold by Thomas Boreman at his stall 'near the two
giants in *Guildhall, London*' (1740–3). The series title may have made play
with the stall's location but there was a joke too, since the tiny books were
anything but 'gigantick', measuring only 2¼ x 1¼ inches – a satisfying economic arrangement since they could be printed and made up from a single
paper sheet (of about 15 x 20 inches). Many of the other children's books of
that period, being modest in both scale and creative ambition, were similarly

economical in both the quality of the paper used and its formatting. There was a tendency to treat the sheet in a Procrustean manner, abridging texts to make them fit or adding extraneous verses, fables, homilies and suchlike if spare space needed to be filled. Only where engravings were to be printed – and the picture books that emerged at the start of the nineteenth century were entirely engraved – was it advisable to turn to superior paper stocks.

The advent of the subsequent 'machine-press period' was heralded by, among other things, the arrival of mechanical papermaking, whose operation allowed for a widening, almost to infinity, of the ways in which paper could be employed. (Modern web-fed presses complete the printing of entire books non-stop in a matter of minutes.) This notably increased the options open to the children's book publisher and resulted in the printing of picture books (often called 'toy books' in the nineteenth century) where the kinds of paper and the dimensions of a book's leaves were capable of much variation (see fig. 9). The long-established firm of Dean & Munday (later Thomas Dean, Dean & Son, and many other iterations) was particularly versatile in bringing out series in varying formats and, following their model, other publishers took up the challenge. Two of the most energetic, George Routledge and Frederick Warne, produced over 1,000 different titles before the end of the century. The subjects ranged from alphabet books to traditional tales, to original stories and verses, in varying formats and with prices ranging from a halfpenny to 2 shillings, the books in the latter category having their paper backed with linen to become 'indestructible books'. Up to the late 1850s most toy books were printed on a single paper stock, with coloured-paper wrappers and with the illustrations hand-coloured. After that date, colour printing became customary, with varying requirements demanded of the book's structure. In many instances the text would be printed on one side of the sheet of a light wove paper with the coloured illustrations appearing on one side of a thicker stock (possibly from a different, specialist printer). The two units would be brought together with text facing picture and stitched into colour-printed card wrappers, often with the endleaves of text as pastedowns.[7]

Access to so many paper stocks at manageable prices (especially after paper duty was reduced in 1837 and abolished in 1861) also gave a great stimulus to the production of magazines, which were to be a prominent element in the nineteenth-century children's book trade. Their appeal was manifold. Children liked them for their regular arrival, usually weekly or monthly – an event always to anticipate – and also for their diverse contents, for encouraging readers to send in letters or other contributions, for supplying amusements like competitions and puzzles, and above all for serial stories. The latter were also an asset both for the publisher, since a good serial helped to retain readers, and for the author who could receive payment for each number and then a further payment if the serial was turned into a book. That happened frequently and many classics, such as George MacDonald's *At the Back of the North Wind* (serialised 1868–89; published in book form 1871) or Robert Louis Stevenson's *Treasure Island* (1881; 1883), or most of the stories by E. Nesbit, first appeared in magazines. Only after the Second World War was there a serious falling-away in Britain of magazines (as opposed to that altogether different phenomenon, comics), the last two examples of note both being associated, first, with individual publishers and, second, with the editorial genius of Kaye Webb: *Collins' Magazine* (later *Collins' Young Elizabethan*) and that peerless adjunct to the 'Puffin Club', promoting everything to do with children's books and reading, *Puffin Post*.

Closely associated with magazines were the Christmas annuals that could range from being bound-up versions of the weekly or monthly parts, furnished with additional leaves of colour plates, to wholly new compilations. The latter flourished most notably in the first half of the twentieth century and in many instances owed much to paper resources. A thick, soft paper, sometimes termed 'featherweight antique', bulked out some volumes to an impressive size, while shiny, coated papers could be used for coloured illustrations (some of which might be individually mounted on a different coloured featherweight). Cheerfully decorated or pictorial papers could be used on the board binding which was a decidedly cheaper alternative to cloth. This in its turn could be protected by a paper jacket, an adjunct to book design whose use became universal from the beginning of the twentieth century.[8]

As the now prevalent term 'paper engineer' suggests, it can be argued that the versatility shown by papermakers in the manufacture of tough papers and thin card singles them out as the founders of 'the movable book', a generic term which encompasses the intrusion of modelling processes upon the conventional book-block. Very early examples of this can be found in the use of volvelles – revolving discs mounted on the leaves of manuscripts or printed books, often found in astronomical or astrological treatises – and hinged flaps, used in anatomical works to show the inner workings of body parts. While such might well fascinate children, the first entertaining exploitation of cut paper was in the turn-ups, or 'harlequinades', which were associated with theatrical interludes in the mid eighteenth century and which had a broad popular appeal. These harlequinades were illustrated verse texts printed from two engraved copper plates on two sheets of paper. One sheet was placed on top of the other and they were joined along the top and bottom edges. Then the upper sheet was cut to produce eight flaps which the reader could lift sequentially to reveal a development of the story on the sheet beneath.[9]

Turn-up narratives were almost always preposterous, attracting their readership through the paper mechanisms rather than any intrinsic merit, and that was to be a common factor in the exploitation of paper toys that reached high peaks of popularity in the latter halves of both the nineteenth and the twentieth centuries. Almost always, even in the comic movables of Jan Pieńkowski or the inventive and over-elaborate creations of Robert Sabuda, it is a 'gasp' factor that brings the praises for which a paper engineer or even a team of designers may be chiefly responsible. Such persons were rarely named when the great wave of Victorian novelties began its course, although, round about 1856, the firm of Darton & Co. placed a printed slip in their *Book of Trades, Showing the Mechanical Movements in Each Trade* which announced that 'Mr Griffin, the original inventor of moveable books for children arranges and fixes the whole of [their] Instructive...Books'.[10]

More or less simultaneously with Mr Griffin's efforts a rival firm was producing 'Dean's Moveable Books'. Using a pull-tab within French-folded leaves they offered customers a crude lever through whose agency characters in the pictures could be caused to move certain limbs. From then on movables proliferated, series following series: 'Changing panorama toy books', 'Scenic effect books' (the first pop-ups, activated by pulling a ribbon), 'Pantomime toy books', 'Flexible-face story books', 'Transforming picture books' – thus paper was engineered to create toy books that were indeed primarily toys.[11]

Paper is not, however, only important for its role in the physical make-up of books. There is also its role as a printing surface. In so far as that surface presents a given verbal text to the reader, legibility will depend more on typography and printing than the quality of paper, although the latter's colour and texture will play some part. Demanding or unfamiliar texts are more likely to gain a readership if they have an attractive appearance; conversely, it hardly seems to matter how well or ill works of accepted popularity are presented: street literature, chapbooks, comics, paperback reprints of the adventures of Biggles or the Famous Five feeding cheaply an assured market.

Where the quality of paper does matter, however, is in the printing of illustrations, one of the most prominent among the defining elements of children's literature. As well as being – for adults as well as children – a feature of immediate interest, a book's illustrations can also be the subject of an analytical debate far more complex than that applied to the printing of texts, and one in which questions of illustrative technique are inseparable from those of paper surfaces.

At the heart of this debate is the disjunction between origination and result. Authors may dispatch their manuscripts to publishers hand-written, or typed, or as computer print-outs, or as electronic files on disk or attached to emails, and, although there may be arguments and changes made before the manuscript is finally put into pages, the transfer will have little effect on the substance of the author's discourse. With the illustrator, however, the gap between conception and final appearance is wider and is filled by several incommensurables.

The simplest procedure is that over which the illustrator has most control. This will occur in autographic methods of picture-making, such as etching or lithography, where the artist is not only working on the surface from which the illustration will be printed but overseeing at least some part of the print-run on as hospitable a paper as is obtainable. Thus, the etcher-engravers preparing the plates of text and pictures for the harlequinades of the 1760s, or, as already mentioned, those creating all-engraved picture books at the start of the nineteenth century would be able to proof their plates to their satisfaction and expect to see them printed on a finer-grade 'plate paper' suitable to their graphic detail. We know nothing of how decisions were made as to the choice and positioning of tints in the hand-colouring process, but plate paper was very hospitable to watercolour pigments.

In similar fashion, the lithographic illustrator will work directly on the stone (or equivalent surface) as, say, Edward Lear did in his *Book of Nonsense* of 1846 (fig. 4), or Kathleen Hale in her 'Orlando' books 100 years later.[12] Such work might call for experienced assistance in preparation for publication, but the artist would be far less dependent on the intervention of other parties than the many illustrators who worked on the multitude of illustrated books that were engendered by the stimuli of the machine-press period.

Much of the illustration during the early decades of this period was from engraved wood blocks which could be printed alongside letterpress texts in the same press. As an artistic medium in the hands of its first great exponent, Thomas Bewick, and of the many creative artists who have delighted in it (and still do), it calls for very careful presswork on a responsive paper which usually needs to be damped in order to take a good impression from the block (fig. 13). Yet the adaptability of wood engraving to many illustrative purposes made it a popular medium and publishers of books and magazines put most of the work in the hands of commercial engravers who copied the artist's original drawings. (Some artists drew on the blocks before passing them to the engravers and, from 1861 onwards, their drawings could be photographed on to the blocks, allowing them to retain the originals.) No special provision was made for the paper on which monochrome blocks were to be printed, publishing decisions on that score being determined by the total costing of the book or magazine in question, and illustrators (unprotected by copyright) were apt to suffer various indignities from poor engraving of their drawings, illogical placing of them in the text, poor presswork on unresponsive paper, and the re-use of (sometimes worn) blocks for reprints or for quite other purposes than those intended. Illustrators rarely had much say in these matters but, in one famous instance, John

There was an old Derry down Derry,
Who loved to see little folks merry;
   So he made them a Book,
   And with laughter they shook,
At the fun of that Derry down Derry!

Figure 4. Edward Lear, *A Book of Nonsense*. London: T. McLean, 1846, 'There was an old Derry down Derry'.

CHARLIE AND THE CHOCOLATE FACTORY

"I see him, Charlie!" said Grandpa Joe excitedly.

And now everybody started shouting at once.

"There's *two* of them!"

"My gosh, so there is!"

"There's more than two! There's one, two, three, four, five!"

"What are they *doing?*"

"Where do they *come* from?"

"Who *are* they?"

Children and parents alike rushed down to the edge of the river to get a closer look.

"Aren't they *fantastic!*"

"No higher than my knee!"

"Their skin is almost black!"

"So it is!"

"You know what I think, Grandpa?" cried Charlie, "I think Mr. Wonka has made them himself—out of chocolate!"

The tiny men—they were no larger than medium-sized dolls—had stopped what they were doing, and now they were staring back across the river at the visitors. One of them pointed towards the children, and then he whispered

Figure 5. Roald Dahl, *Charlie and the Chocolate Factory*. Illustrated by Joseph Schindelman. 1st edn. New York: Alfred A. Knopf, 1964, p. 72.

CHARLIE AND THE CHOCOLATE FACTORY

"I see him, Charlie!" said Grandpa Joe excitedly.

And now everybody started shouting at once.

"There's *two* of them!"

"My gosh, so there is!"

"There's more than two! There's one, two, three, four, five!"

"What are they *doing*?"

"Where do they *come* from?"

"Who *are* they?"

Children and parents alike rushed down to the edge of the river to get a closer look.

"Aren't they *fantastic*!"

"No higher than my knee!"

"Look at their funny long hair!"

The tiny men—they were no larger than medium-sized dolls—had stopped what they were doing, and now they were staring back across the river at the visitors. One of them pointed towards the children, and then he whispered something to the other four, and all five of them burst into peals of laughter.

Figure 6. Roald Dahl, *Charlie and the Chocolate Factory*. Illustrated by Schindelman. New York: Alfred A. Knopf, 1973, p. 72. Redrawn and revised text.

Tenniel's complaints to Charles Dodgson over the printing of the blocks in the first edition of *Alice's Adventures in Wonderland* led the tyro author (who was paying for the job) to withdraw the finished copies and have the book done over again by a different printer.

The coming of the camera revolutionised the craft of illustration in more ways than allowing the simple transfer of image to block and thence to page, and it eventuated in the demise of the commercial hand engravers. Photography allied to chemical etching enabled the exact replication of a line drawing as an electrotype block while also permitting reductions or increases in the size of the original, and, with the invention of the half-tone process, it became possible to print photographs and drawings with continuous tone without having to resort to the linear cross-hatching required in wood engravings.

Even more momentous was the role played by photography in colour printing. To begin with, this too had been a hand craft, albeit one subject to various attempted refinements. Essentially, it relied on the printing of separate colours from wood blocks (or, later, the use of lithographic surfaces) in such a way that a range of tints could be achieved by overlaying one colour upon another: blue upon yellow to make green, for instance. Very often a linear key-block was used to lay down the outlines of the illustrations but the mixing of colours depended largely on the skill and experience of the colour-printer. Edmund Evans, probably the most famous representative of that craft, has described his cutting of the colour blocks for Randolph Caldecott's picture books (1878–86) (fig. 8) once the artist had supplied him with models coloured on to a proof of the key-block:

> I would engrave the blocks to be printed in as few colours as necessary. This was settled, the key block in *dark brown*, then a *flesh tint* for the faces, hands and wherever it would bring the other colours as nearly as possible to his painted copy, a *red*, a *blue*, a *yellow*, and a *grey*.[13]

In the hands of craftsmen of Evans' distinction, the procedure was often very impressive, but also laborious. At the end of the century, however, the half-tone process, as applied to black-and-white images, was adapted to colour. With the use of graduated colour screens, it became possible (as noted in the description of *Peter Rabbit*) to photograph coloured drawings so that they could be reproduced by printing in only three colours: yellow, blue and red (although sometimes black was added). The resultant printing demanded careful control of the registration of the three printing plates and a careful selection of ink, but an inescapable drawback was the need to print on a glossy coated paper. Full-colour picture books would be printed entirely on such paper, books with only a selection of colour plates would have them bound or tipped in alongside the standard paper used for the letterpress. Nevertheless, the principle of three-tone photography was adaptable and lent itself happily to more advanced colour-printing methods where sophisticated, electronic colour analysis can occur and where developments in lithographic printing and the production of paper can result in almost perfect reproduction of an artist's work.

Thus it is that, through an ever more complex sequence of technological changes, the physical representation of an author's work makes its way to the reader. A final point to consider though is the outer dress in which it appears, a feature of special interest for the makers of children's books since the look of the book may influence the initial desire of a potential reader to buy and open it.

The importance of the binding was not lost on the early purveyors of children's books and Thomas Boreman and his mid-eighteenth-century contemporaries deserve a place in bibliographical history as perhaps being the first to bind complete editions of their books in a manner designed to attract buyers. Paper again was an essential element, these early traders using a variety of coloured papers, or even wallpapers, to cover their productions and imply (not always very truthfully) the colourful delights within.

That precedent was never relinquished. Throughout the hand-press period, ideas for paper bindings abounded: decorated paper on its own or covering thicker boards, coloured glazed paper with printed or pictorial labels, simple (but often dowdy) sugar-paper covers with full letter-press elaborations of the title descriptions. And with the advent of cloth binding at the start of the machine-press period, children's books were also in the forefront of developments, John Harris publishing cloth-bound books as early as 1824. There were even casings for the casings. John Marshall, followed by a number of competitors, made up wooden boxes with sliding lids (some painted to look like elegant book cases) filled with miniature, but readable, story books or simple instructive books in coloured paper covers, while the firm of S. & J. Fuller, trading at 'The Temple of Fancy', published paper-doll books which were sheathed in printed card wallets with a wrist-ribbon attached. Subsequent technical developments would be exploited by bookbinders and publishers (who gradually established specialist designers or design departments) so that, right up to the Second World War, an immense range of plain, decorative or pictorial covers in various combinations of materials is to be found.

As an adjunct to the attractions possible for the outer covering of children's books came also a playfulness in the transition point formed by the book's endpapers, the double leaves facing each other at its front and nether ends which helped to attach the covers to the text-block. Having these plain, coloured or decorated, and usually of a different paper-stock, was a common occurrence, but, especially in the twentieth century, the endpapers could become part of the narrative contents. They could be symbolic of events in the story: the jungle endpapers of Maurice Sendak's *Where the Wild Things*

Are (1963); they could be maps, either repeated front and back as in Arthur Ransome's *Swallows and Amazons* (1930), or changing in detail as with 'Thror's map' in the front of J. R. R. Tolkien's *The Hobbit* (1937) and 'Wilderland' at the back; they could offer information, as with the simple mechanical definitions in Virginia Lee Burton's *Mike Mulligan and his Steam Shovel* (1938); or they could make a 'before-and-after' joke: the dowdily illustrated 'Wonder Books' of the 1920s and 1930s probably sold beyond their merits because of the endpapers where various homunculi going about practical jobs at the front are shown to meet with cataclysmic events at the back. In *In and Out of Doors* (1937), by the Williams-Ellis family, endpaper overkill takes place: a pictorial grid at the front is brought to life through a 'magic carpet' which is inserted in a pocket cut into the book's back cover.

From 1945 onward, however, staider conventions prevailed in the physical make-up of children's books, partly because of economic and manufacturing constraints and partly because of the dominance of the library market, for whom gimmicks appealing to the public at large took second place to demands related to durability and conservation. (Tiny books, pop-ups, ragbooks and the like found no favour among librarians.) At the same time the irresistible rise of the illustrated book jacket obviated the need for fancy cloth, or cloth substitutes, and the even more irresistible rise of the paperback brought a concomitant shift in publishers' marketing. 'Hardbacks for libraries, paperbacks for bookbuyers' may over-simplify this shift, but it summarises a 'democratisation' of the product – the cheapness, the unformidable nature, the informality of paperbacks encouraging a notable growth in bookshop sales. Kaye Webb's 'Puffin Club' (from 1967) brought soaring printruns for many titles – the Club was arguably the chief motive force behind the popularity of C. S. Lewis' Narnia – and the subsequent rise of 'young adult' fiction was mediated through paperbacks. Indeed, it is said that manufacturers of jeans had to increase the capacity of pockets to accommodate the customary small crown octavo. In recent years shrink-wrapped teenage paperbacks may incorporate samples of lipstick and other fashion products *de rigueur* for the sensitive reader.

Much of this survey has attempted to assert that the form in which authors' works reach their readers is the result of activities of persons beyond the solitary figure crouched over the writing-desk or the keyboard. The rights of authors over their texts may be identified and asserted under the Copyright, Designs and Patents Act, just as copyright protection in one form or another has subsisted since children's books first appeared. But the composition of that text may owe something – much or little – to editorial control by the publisher, while the physical form in which it meets the reader's eye (and hence engenders a distinct response) will owe almost everything to such features as paper, print, illustration or decoration, and binding, which are largely outside the author's competence.

It must also be borne in mind that, within periods of copyright, or in places where copyright has not been asserted or recognised, or where copyright has lapsed, many transmogrifications of text may occur. *The Tale of Peter Rabbit* again supplies a telling example. Beatrix Potter was a shrewd businesswoman and, quite early on in her authorial life, she realised that the popularity of her creations could lead to their exploitation outside the limits of her own authorisation, and in consequence she was at pains to extend her, and her publisher's, control of such varied products as dolls, wallpaper friezes and ceramic ware. Indeed, it may well be that the successful merchandising of Potteriana provided a model for other copyright holders of popular children's book characters who have mightily extended the procedure since the 1980s.[14] But it does not end there. For, owing to what proved to be a culpable oversight, Frederick Warne failed to copyright *Peter Rabbit* in the United States when it was first published. As a result it has been open-season on that book for over a century in that country and nothing could be done to prevent all manner of abridgments, retellings and re-illustration of the original text, including its featuring in school textbooks, miscellaneous compendia, and as a pop-up book. (At almost the same date, the publisher Grant Richards failed to protect his own copyright in Helen Bannerman's *Story of Little Black Sambo* (1899). The mass publication in the United States of editions with illustrations by other artists, with images more blatantly racist than Bannerman's, was a critical factor in the opprobrium which the book met with from the 1960s onwards.[15])

Even where copyright control of a text is maintained, adjustments to both text and production values can be made – a factor again especially noticeable in the passage of texts in one direction or another across the Atlantic. The quality and character of book-papers, bindings and dust jackets will differ. Editors may require changes to spelling, to word-usage or even to the substance of a narrative to meet the different social or educational circumstances of their own market. More often, and more immediately observable, will be the commissioning of new illustrations for the same text.

Books that publishers failed to copyright, or that have survived their period of copyright, become aligned with the works that could never have had such protection: the literature of tradition. Nursery rhymes, with whatever minor alterations, tend to be sacrosanct in their formal patterning (unless adapted for religious, political or advertising purposes); folktales though – existing as recognised clusters of types and motifs – may have a universal presence, but particular formulations or translations of them may well belong to, or be associated with, particular editors, translators and illustrators. In consequence there has developed a barely analysable range of variant treatments which come to be equally applied to the lengthier texts of 'children's classics', those works which have left the territorial waters of copyright protection and, like folktales, are common property for whatever trawlermen or buccaneers they may encounter.

Few authors offer themselves up as examples more obligingly than the hapless Hans Christian Andersen, who is often wrongly thought of as a purveyor of traditional folktales rather than – as is actually the case – works whose conception is entirely original. From the moment when his 'eventyr' first began to appear in English, in January 1846, he has suffered every possible indignity at the hands of the bookmakers. Only rarely was there any formal agreement with him in Britain or the United States over the publication of his stories. No-one, until as late as 1893, was concerned to assess the accuracy with which his storytelling voice was replicated (the tales were often translated from unsatisfactory German editions). Distortions and abridgments abounded. Indeed, the very first translation, Mary Howitt's *Wonderful Stories for Children* (1846), included only an excerpt from 'The Flying Trunk' which was offered without explanation as 'A Night in the Kitchen'. Almost every form of publication for varying quantities of tales was adopted: magazine publication, picture books, illustrated and unillustrated selections and attempts at 'complete works', broadsheet issues, versifications and all kinds of movable book.[16]

The regularity and frequency with which such changes occur in the presentation of an author's and/or an illustrator's work suggest a central role for analytical bibliography in the study of children's literature, harnessing that seemingly dusty subject to the critical process. If it is arguable that the reader – child or adult – responds not to an author's unmediated creation but to 'the word made flesh' as a physical package, then the variant forms that that package may take will affect the response. In what ways will a reader's view of Peter Rabbit, or the Tailor of Gloucester, or Pigling Bland, be affected by the form and the illustrations through which they meet the text? But there then arise wider and more delicate comparative issues: what treatment of the text comes closest to meeting critical demands for 'an ideal copy', the one which has most to offer the reader? Arguments to and fro may not be unduly onerous where *Peter Rabbit* is concerned but they take on an almost insurmountable – but ultimately fruitful – complexity in an analysis of, say, Hans Christian Andersen translations.

The fruitfulness in that and many other instances lies in the stimulus given to critical thought through comparative arguments, which demand a close consideration of texts and their implications. Over the historic span of the making of children's books one cannot help but glory in the evolution of production techniques and in the fluctuating success and ingenuity which has attended their application. On the very day that these words are written, the business commentary of *The Times* leads with an article on 'the slow death of the book', strangled by the digits of electronic publishing. Seemingly authoritative speculation is mounted on the likely transference of all texts to hand-held (and apparently single-format) screens.[17] No doubt the words being floated across the ether will still be formatted in both familiar and new ways by editors and designers. No doubt technological change will continue to be an overriding factor in the way that readers receive and respond to text – the making of texts will remain a collaboration between composers and technicians, between those who imagine the text into being, and those who materialise it into readers' hands. It remains to be seen, though, whether this new technology will encourage, or stifle, the wild diversity that has for centuries attended and illuminated the making of that three-dimensional artefact, the printed book.

NOTES

1. For fuller accounts, see Leslie Linder, *A History of the Writings of Beatrix Potter Including Unpublished Work* (London: Frederick Warne & Co., 1971), pp. 92–110, and Judy Taylor, *That Naughty Rabbit; Beatrix Potter and Peter Rabbit* (London: Frederick Warne & Co., 1987).

2. [Richard Johnson], *The Oriental Moralist or the Beauties of the Arabian Nights Entertainments* (London: E. Newbery, n.d.), pp. [i–ii].

3. The guidelines are repeated in *Sexism in Children's Books: Facts, Figures and Guidelines* (London: Writers and Readers Cooperative, 1976), pp. 45–56.

4. Relevant sections of Johnson's 'day-books' are transcribed in M. J. P. Weedon, 'Richard Johnson and the Successors to John Newbery', *The Library*, 5th series, 4 (1949), 25–63.

5. Morton N. Cohen and Anita Gandolfo (eds.), *Lewis Carroll and the House of Macmillan* (Cambridge: Cambridge University Press, 1987).

6. Brian Alderson, *Ezra Jack Keats: Artist and Picture-Book Maker* (2 vols., Gretna, AL: Pelican Publishing Company, 1994 and 2002).

7. For more detailed analysis, see Tomoko Masaki, *A History of Victorian Popular Picture Books: The Aesthetic, Creative, and Technological Aspects of the Toy Book Through the Publications of the Firm of Routledge 1852–1893* (2 vols., Tokyo: Kazamashobo, 2006).

8. For more on the significance of book jackets (too often neglected), see Alan Powers, *Front Cover: Great Book Jacket and Cover Design* (London: Mitchell Beazley, 2001), and *Children's Book Covers* (London: Mitchell Beazley, 2003).

9. See Jacqueline Reid-Walsh, 'Eighteenth-Century Flap Books for Children: Allegorical Metamorphosis and Spectacular Transformation', *Princeton University Library Chronicle*, 67 (2007), 751–89.

10. Lawrence Darton, *The Dartons: An Annotated Check-List* (London: British Library, 2004), p. 334 (H93e).

11. See Peter Haining, *Movable Books* (London: New English Library, 1979), and Julia and Frederick Hunt, *Peeps into Nisterland* (Chester: Casmelda Publishing, n.d. [2006]), pp. 291–344.
12. See Kathleen Hale's *A Slender Reputation* (London: Frederick Warne, 1994), pp. 211–14, for an account of her experiences with colour lithography.
13. *The Reminiscences of Edmund Evans*, ed. Ruari McLean (Oxford: Clarendon Press, 1967), p. 56.
14. See Brian Alderson, '"All the little side-shows", Beatrix Potter among the Tradesmen', in *'So I Shall Tell You a Story…': Encounters With Beatrix Potter*, ed. Judy Taylor (London: Frederick Warne, 1993), pp. 154–67. Also Elizabeth Booth and Deborah Hayes, 'Authoring the Brand: Literary Licensing', *Young Consumers*, 7 (2005), 43–53.
15. See Elizabeth Hay, *Sambo Sahib: The Story of Little Black Sambo and Helen Bannerman* (Edinburgh: Paul Harris, 1981), pp. 25–8.
16. See Brian Alderson, *Hans Christian Andersen and his Eventyr in England* (Wormley: Five Owls Press, 1982).
17. Antonia Senior, 'Publishers are Braced for the Slow Death of the Book', *The Times*, 13 February 2008, on-line at http://business.timesonline.co.uk/tol/business/columnists/article3359899.ece (accessed 25 February 2008).

4

KATIE TRUMPENER

Picture-book worlds and ways of seeing

The world in images

When adults look back on their lives, Virginia Woolf argues in *The Waves* (1931), they 'turn over these scenes as children turn over the pages of a picture-book'.[1] Memories of childhood may become indelibly linked to early memories – visual, tactile, spatial – of reading picture books, whose 'picture worlds' may permanently shape readers' worldview. Since the Enlightenment, illustrated books have aimed to teach children how to read, apprehend and make sense of the world. This chapter describes how an emerging picture-book tradition developed particular visual conventions, working both to initiate children into this tradition and to push them into autonomous seeing.

Precisely because of its ambitions to represent the world itself, the picture book frequently understands itself as a *Gesamtkunstwerk* (a work integrating multiple art forms and appealing to multiple senses), and hence reflecting more general trends in visual, literary and intellectual culture. Unlike other forms of children's literature, the picture book makes meaning largely through its visual format, the way its images relate to one another, to the verbal text, and to the space on (and physical layout of) the page. This chapter, accordingly, traces the history of several influential and enduring picture-book formats.

In the seventeenth century, Moravian pastor/educator Jan Komensky (who published under the Germanicised and Latinised name of Johann Amos Comenius) developed a highly influential pedagogy through viewing. An advocate of universal education, Comenius believed aspiring learners needed to ascertain objects with their senses – particularly sight – before grasping them in words. His *Orbis sensualium pictus* (Nuremberg, 1658, translated as *Visible World, or Picture and Nomenclature of all the chief things in the world*, 1659) and the many 'Orbis Pictus' books it spawned demonstrated the world's visual and species diversity in the form of educational tableaux, while fostering scientific methods of observing, classifying and recording (fig. 7).

Figure 7. Johann Amos Comenius, *Orbis sensualium pictus … Visible World, or Picture and Nomenclature of all the chief things in the world.* London: J. Kirton, 1659, CXX 'Societas parentalis'.

Nineteenth- and twentieth-century picture-book formats widened to incorporate elements from the naturalist's sketchbook and from the panorama. Meanwhile, parodic cautionary tales began inviting children to savour the complexity and ambiguity of the image itself. And a wide range of experimental picture books (some influenced directly by various forms of visual modernism) worked to forge their own iconic systems or inculcate their own methods of parsing and making sense, their own ways of seeing.

Even more than other forms of children's literature, the picture book is cosmopolitan in both its developmental history and its intended address. Because their appeal is partly non-verbal, picture books have frequently crossed, even challenged, linguistic and cultural barriers. Comenius' *Orbis sensualium pictus* was bilingual, helping German-speaking children learn Latin (still Europe's scholarly *lingua franca*). Pictures themselves functioned here as a universal language which could help students bridge linguistic divides, and align otherwise disparate language systems – a belief vindicated by *Orbis*' rapid translation into English and many additional vernaculars, even as its picture dictionary format was adapted to teach other technical and specialised vocabularies. Forerunners of Denis Diderot's illustrated *Encyclopédie* (Paris, 1751–77), Orbis Pictus books reflected a humanist belief in the transparency of language and universality of human experience; they remained widely popular throughout eighteenth- and nineteenth- century Europe, especially in Central Europe.[2]

Key nineteenth- and early twentieth-century picture books were also distributed and translated internationally. Heinrich Hoffmann's *Struwwelpeter* (Frankfurt, 1845), for instance, was rapidly translated into English, generating many local spin-offs and topical parodies; picture books by Kate Greenaway, Walter Crane, Palmer Cox and Beatrix Potter (and Richard Felton Outcault's *Buster Brown* cartoons) were rapidly translated into French. Thanks partly to such stimuli, distinctive picture-book traditions emerged in several parts of Europe, in many cases spearheaded by masterful renderings of foundational national tales, poems or legends: in England, Walter Crane and Randolph Caldecott's picture-book versions of traditional nursery rhymes; in France, Louis-Maurice Boutet de Monvel's hagiographic *Jeanne d'Arc* (Paris, 1896); in Russia, Ivan Bilibin's renderings of Alexander Pushkin's fairy tales and traditional folktales. Yet Crane and Bilibin's illustrations often show strong influences from Japanese, Persian and Arabic art, an apparently nationalist choice of text thus offset by self-consciously cosmopolitan illustrations. Even outspoken French nationalist 'L'oncle Hansi' (Jean-Jacques Waltz), prosecuted by German authorities in 1913 for his picture books about the contested province of Alsace, derived his anti-German caricatures from Germany's premier satirical journal, *Simplicissimus*.

Early twentieth-century picture books frequently drew on the visual innovations – and shared the internationalism – of the modernist avant-gardes.
Émigré artists facilitated this cross-pollination. Emigrants from the Soviet
Union – most notably Alexandra Exter, Nathalie Parain and Feodor
Rojankovsky – played a critical role in the resurgence of French picture
book art in Paris during the 1930s, as well as in Germany.[3] In the
mid-twentieth-century United States, too, the so-called 'Golden Age' of
picture books was shaped substantially by immigrant artists – including
Rojankovsky, Roger Duvoisin, Ingri and Edgar Parin d'Aulaire, Ludwig
Bemelmans, Miska Petersham and Tibor Gergely – from many parts of
Europe, as by self-consciously 'ethnic' artists like Wanda Gág (raised in a
German-Bohemian immigrant enclave in rural Minnesota).

Some artists were immigrants several times over, their style reflecting international training and publishing careers. Siberian-born Esphyr Slobodkina
emigrated with her family to China during the Russian Revolution; moving
to the United States in 1929, she worked as an abstract painter and published picture books, including many Margaret Wise Brown stories, and
her own *Caps for Sale* (New York, 1940). Alexandra Exter studied art
in Kiev and Paris, and lived in Petersburg, Odessa, Rome and Moscow;
settling in Paris in 1924, she retained close ties to revolutionary Soviet
Constructivists like Kazimir Malevich (and avant-garde Russian theatre
and ballet) as to Picasso, Georges Braque and Fernand Léger. Jean Charlot
was strongly shaped by Mexican modernism; son of a Russian émigré father
and Mexican mother, he grew up in France, moved to Mexico City in 1921
(where he worked with revolutionary muralists like Diego Riviera), then, in
the 1940s, to Hawai'i. Originally from Hamburg, German-Jewish émigré
H. A. Rey lived successively in Rio de Janeiro, Paris (where Gallimard
published his first picture books in the late 1930s) and New York (where
he began publishing his *Curious George* series in 1940). Rey's depictions
of city life thus reflect not only American comics and movies, but also
Berlin urbanism – Walter Trier's illustrations for Erich Kästner's *Emil und
die Detektive* (Berlin, 1929) and 1930s French picture books by Jean de
Brunhoff and Alexandra Exter.

Their visual breadth made migrant and ethnic artists crucial to the
American picture book. Growing up in Brooklyn, in a Polish-Jewish immigrant family, Maurice Sendak was steeped in comics and Anglo-American
picture books, yet his own highly influential work manifests continuing
preoccupation with Central European literary and visual traditions, encompassing Grimms' fairy tales, Isaac Bashevis Singer's Yiddish fiction and
Lothar Meggendorfer's pop-up books. Post-war immigrants to the United
States – including Peter Spier (who emigrated from Holland in the early

1950s), Peter Sís (who defected from Czechoslovakia in 1982) and Gennady Spirin (who emigrated from Russia in 1991) – continue to introduce novel perspectives. Sís' recent work moves between recreating the lost visual world of Prague (*The Three Golden Keys*, New York, 2001), embracing the ethnic and visual diversity of his adoptive city, New York, and meditating on the long histories of global exploration and map-making. In such cases, émigrés' international transits reinforce the picture book's aspirations to create and show a world.

Surveying the world: tableau, sketchbook, panorama

From the outset, picture books attempted a wide purview. From the Reformation through the Enlightenment, Orbis Pictus books demonstrated the world's knowability, by laying out visual realms (from natural history to architecture). Their tableaux arranged collections of representative items, persons or activities, often numbered and labelled. Sometimes they showed items embedded – and being used – in domestic or occupational scenes, sometimes objects already isolated for analysis. In both cases, objects gained further significance from context. With its emphasis on close observation and taxonomic classification, this mode of visualisation dovetailed with juvenile science education. Yet from Comenius onward, the Orbis Pictus genre and its German successor, the eighteenth- and nineteenth-century *Anschauungslehre* book, also diagrammed social life, from occupational milieu to familial relationships. As the designation 'Anschauungslehre' suggested, such picture books offered 'teaching through seeing', not only conveying information but modelling modes of visual analysis.

In Britain, too, the picture book developed from two complementary types of portfolios: natural history engravings, illustrating zoological taxonomies (Thomas Boreman's *Description of Three Hundred Animals*, London, 1730), and the Cries of London, evoking urban complexity and sensory overload. If Renaissance composers like Orlando Gibbons, William Byrd and Clement Jannequin used the Cries of London and Paris as the basis for polyphonic fugues, eighteenth-century Cries portfolios imagined metropolitan economic exchange in proto-symphonic terms. Cataloguing each 'guild' of London peddlers according to their characteristic wares, costumes and sung sales pitch, the Cries appealed simultaneously to multiple sensory and aesthetic registers. By the Romantic period, picture-book versions of the Cries were addressed to child readers. Some, like Ann and Jane Taylor's *New Cries of London or, Itinerant trades of the British metropolis* (London, 1806), emphasised the Cries' tragic undertones: as the metropolis became bigger and more anonymous, the individual peddler's call implicitly articulated a cry for help, a fear of starvation amid plenty.

The Taylors' *City Scenes, or A Peep into London for Good Children* (London, 1806?) teaches political economy more indirectly. The volume's short pieces (alternating poems and prose descriptions) describe different facets of urban life. Each piece is keyed to engravings (by their brother Isaac Taylor the Younger), grouped in threes on the facing page, a format which synchronises image and text, yet allows an autonomy of medium and address. The Taylors' urban survey, indeed, envisions city dwellers bound by continuity, economic exchange and ethical responsibility, but often fated to live past one another. *City Scenes'* principles of juxtaposition and contrast were magnified by the Taylors' companion volume *Rural Scenes, or A Peep into the Countryside for Good Children* (London, 1806?). In their oppositional pairings, experimental relationship between image and text, and account of city and country life, the *Scenes* offer implicit dialogue with William Blake's visionary *Songs of Innocence* and *Songs of Experience* (London, 1789, 1793). Now the most famous illustrated books of the Romantic period, Blake's *Songs* were not meant for child readers (despite many songs written in children's voices, and Blake's stress on children's lives as an index of social morality); conceived as experimental artist's books, the *Songs* circulated as codices inside Blake's small London circle (including the Taylors, children of Blake's fellow copperplate engraver Isaac Taylor the Elder).

Picture books gained a secure market niche in nineteenth-century Europe. Yet amateur artists continued to design private picture-narratives, intended solely for familial or coterie use. Frankfurt psychiatrist Heinrich Hoffman composed *Struwwelpeter* as a Christmas present for his son; Lewis Carroll's *Alice's Adventures in Wonderland* (London, 1865) and some Beatrix Potter books originated, likewise, as hand-illustrated picture-stories written for particular children. Once published, these picture-narratives became children's classics. Others remained, for generations, in private hands.

Two particularly fascinating family compilations were begun in 1859 yet not published until the 1980s. 'Christine's Billedbog' ('Christine's Picture Book'), an elaborate scrapbook compiled by Hans Christian Andersen and Adolph Drewsen for Drewsen's granddaughter, assembled an encyclopaedic cross-section of nineteenth-century print culture (including news headlines, etchings, Danish broadsides, catalogue clippings, zoological and religious images), embellished with hand-cut silhouettes.[4] In its heterogeneity, this multi-media collage parallels nineteenth-century crazy quilts, and anticipates surrealist collage books like E. V. Lucas and George Morrow's *What a Life* (London, 1911) and Max Ernst's *Une semaine de bonté* (Paris, 1934). Yet topical ordering and hand-written annotations also render the scrapbook internally harmonious, section by section.

Drawing on a different range of visual traditions, the autobiographical watercolour album begun, at ages eleven and twelve, by British sisters Louisa and Madalene Pasley offers rare insight into the creative lives of nineteenth-century children. The Pasleys chronicle their comic misadventures as aspiring entomologists: even on vacation at Lake Windermere, they escape their drawing master to gather beetle larvae. Their album parodies key aspects of nineteenth-century visual education, from naturalists' field-notebooks and taxonomising to sketching assignments and watercolour landscape-drawing.[5] Yet it also includes a comic, Orbis Pictus-derived watercolour tableau (complete with numbered key) anatomising the Pasleys' frenzied vacation departure; wry sketches of the doomed sketching party and the girls' struggle with outsize insects; and, finally, the title-page of Madalene's first published field-guide, fruit of their autodidactic field education.

The Pasleys, trained in naturalist recordkeeping, reinvented the sketchbook as autobiography and parody. Randolph Caldecott crosses the sketchbook with the Orbis Pictus, to relativise the tableau as a format for visual information. A new phase of picture-book production began, proverbially, with the mid-nineteenth-century development of new methods of colour printing. Walter Crane's and Caldecott's path-breaking nursery rhyme books were thus anchored by richly coloured, subtly detailed tableaux. Yet the exigencies of picture-book publishing often necessitated colour spreads to be interspersed with black and white pages. Caldecott turns this economic consideration into a structural principle, playing off highly detailed, yet fundamentally static colour tableaux against a running series of brilliantly drafted black-and-white sketches. Later illustrators continued Caldecott's experiments. The colour spreads in Lois Lenski's Mr Small series (New York, 1934–64) involve only one additional colour beyond black and white – yet this only increases their impact; Dahlov Ipcar's *The Cat at Night* (New York, 1969) oscillates between colour and black-and-white to explore the inverse world visible with feline night-vision; Remy Charlip's *Fortunately* (New York, 1964) does so to explore perspectival differences, as his story oscillates between fortunate and unfortunate developments.

Like the Orbis Pictus books, Caldecott's tableaux offer overviews of literary, cultural or historical tradition. The frontispiece of his virtuoso *Sing a Song for Sixpence* (London, 1880) – an old lady beckoning a young audience – echoes the famous frontispiece of Charles Perrault's *Tales of Mother Goose* (*Histoires ou Contes du Temps passé, ou Contes de ma mère l'Oie*, Paris, 1697); *Sing*'s later plates compactly evoke the corpus of traditional stories and chapbooks long central to children's experience of literature. The walls

Figure 8. Randolph Caldecott, *Sing a song of sixpence*. London: Frederick Warne, *c*. 1883. 'Queen was in the parlour counting all her money'.

of the little king's counting-house are lined with murals depicting *Robinson Crusoe* and *Jack the Giant Killer*, while the tile fireplace features the Bremen Town Musicians and animal fables; murals in the little queen's parlour depict Bo Peep, Babes in the Woods, and Red Riding Hood, and on a tiled sideboard, The Three Bears (fig. 8). Yet if such multi-layered tableaux firmly nest Caldecott's book in a long storytelling tradition, his intervening sketches insistently insert the story into the present, capturing transient, singular moments, fleeting movements, expressions and impressions. Some sketches are wordless, opening hitherto unexplored facets of the story. Others animate a tiny phrase, even a single word ('Baked'). Caldecott's sketch aesthetic changes his – and his readers' – relationship to the familiar text he illustrates. Instead of treating it as a single coherent narrative, Caldecott breaks its words into autonomous groups of sound, meaning and visualisation. Lines or verses the reader already knows by heart, as a firm, fixed unit, are given new meaning, as previously subordinate phrases are depicted in their own right.

Early twentieth-century author-illustrators continued Caldecott's experiment with sketchbook elements, along with other visual formats. Using naturalists' observational, watercolour and taxonomic techniques, Walter Crane and Beatrix Potter in England, Sibylle von Olfers and Ernst Kreidolf in Germany and Switzerland, and Elsa Beskow in Sweden created anthropomorphic tales of animal and plant life.

Others adapted the sketchbook itself as a format for expository narratives. Ernst Thompson Seton's *Two Little Savages* (New York, 1903), recounting Canadian boys' woodcraft explorations, is both illustrated by Seton's interpolated plate illustrations and framed, on most page margins, by running sketches and diagrams; Kurt Wiese's circulation novel *The Chinese Ink Stick* (New York, 1929) likewise alternates verbal and visual ethnographic sketches. Orbis Pictus books offered cross-sections of the world; now, slender sketchbook stories began to support almost encyclopaedic apparatuses. Holling Clancy Holling's *Paddle-to-the-Sea* (Boston, 1941) and *Minn of the Mississippi* (Boston, 1951) interlard narrative with tableaux, maps and scientific diagrams.

Virginia Burton's *Katy and the Big Snow* (Boston, 1942) and *Maybelline the Cable Car* (Boston, 1952) explore new technology in relationship to urban planning, visualised as friezes or as stylised communication or transportation networks literally framing individual pictures. The lecture on earth's evolution in Burton's *Life Story* (Boston, 1962) uses multiple pictorial layers and frames to underscore both the complexity of all timelines, and the interconnection of cosmological, geological and biological developments. Antonio Jiménez-Landi and F. Goico Aguirre's *La ciudad* (*A First Look at a City in Spain*, Madrid, 1955) and David Macaulay's popular *Cathedral* (Boston, 1973) and *Pyramid* (Boston, 1975) introduce young readers to urban planning and architectural drawings; Anne Millard and Steve Noon's *A Street Through Time* (London, 1998) adds a temporal dimension to the cross-section.

Peter Sís' *Follow the Dream: The Story of Christopher Columbus* (New York, 1991), *A Small Tale from the Far North* (New York, 1993), *Starry Messenger: Galileo Galilei* (New York, 1996) and *Tibet through the Red Box* (New York, 1998) simultaneously explore the shape of the world (or cosmos) and the long history of attempts to chart or picture its dimensions.

Expeditions and astronomical discoveries are thus chronicled by evoking a huge range of pictorial records, from 'official' navigational and meteorological charts to mythological star maps and ethnographic sketches in the distinctive style of nineteenth-century whalers' and Inuits' whalebone scrimshaw carvings.

Sís' *Madlenka* (New York, 2000) foregrounds the lingering influence of the nineteenth-century panoramas. Gigantic paintings-in-the-round, often displaying landscapes, cityscapes or battles, panoramas were displayed publicly in dedicated circular buildings, which enabled seamless 360-degree viewing. From Lothar Meggendorfer's fold-out, 360-degree paper surround *Im Stadtpark (The City Park*, Munich, 1887) to Clement Hurd's *Town* and *Country* (New York, 1939), children's novelty books replicated this format in miniature and on paper. The late-nineteenth-century 'Emperor's Panorama' (*Kaiserpanorama*) offered the opposite viewing experience of private, stereoscopic views. Seated at intervals around a polygonal pillar (housing a double slide carousel), each visitor looked through specific eyeholes at a three-dimensional photograph. At regular intervals, each scene gave way to the next; sometimes a sequence of photographs cumulatively unfolded a semi-panoramic view, of riverbank or cityscape. In 1930s France, Marie Colmont and Alexandra Exter's influential Panoramas of Père Castor series – *Panorama du fleuve (Down the River*, Paris, 1937); *Panorama de la montagne (Up the Mountain*, Paris, 1938); *Panorama de la côte (Along the Coast*, Paris, 1938) – conjoined both traditions. In each, Exter's series of panorama 'slices', viewed initially as separate double-spreads, could be unfolded to form a full 360-degree paper panorama. Many paper panoramas were wordless; these, like nineteenth-century panorama guides, are explicated, panel for panel, by Colmont's verbal descriptions of the landscape's geographical, geological and economic dimensions.

Exter's tableaux echo specific scenes – balloon view of a tropical coast, dockside view of a port, ski-slope view of an alpine landscape – from Jean de Brunhoff's *Le voyage de Babar (Babar's Travels*, Paris, 1932). Brunhoff's earlier *Histoire de Babar (Story of Babar*, Paris, 1931) offered a more eclectic range of visual pleasures: urban spectacles (Babar riding the elevator, elephants studying store windows, Babar maturing as he acquires a fashionable new look and is photographed); angled urban views; a semi-aerial countryside tableau. Following *Babar*, American illustrators alternated panoramic tableaux with other perspectives. In Robert McCloskey's *Make Way for Ducklings* (New York, 1941) and Don Freeman's *Fly High Fly Low* (New York, 1957), birds raising young in Boston and San Francisco occasion bird's-eye and kerbside urban views.[6] H. A. Rey's *Curious George* (Boston, 1941) moves from a balloonist's aerial perspective to the stylised firehouse map of the same city; *Curious George Takes a Job* (Boston, 1947) juxtaposes urban street scenes with the window-washer's view into the skyscraper's – and the city's – hundred storeys, and stories. Rey's picture book thus inherits both versions of the panorama, combining broad overviews with visual depth, alternating between a tabular and an advent calendar approach to illustration, each picture a window to look through.

Madlenka, likewise, explores a single New York City block using differently scaled visualisations, from an aerial city map to 360-degree circular mapping (adapted from traditional panorama guides) of every building. In the process, Sís reconciles apparently disparate genres within expository picture books: sketchbook experiments in perspective and cross-section; city planning books; panoramas. What enables fresh perception, paradoxically, is an immersion in much older visual conventions, an awareness of the palimpsestic layers of urban spaces.

Twentieth-century picture books offered many ways of locating one's place in the world. Some hewed close to the Orbis Pictus: in E. Boyd Smith's *The Farm Book* (Boston, 1910), *The Seashore Book* (Boston, 1912) and *The Railroad Book* (Boston, 1913), for instance, children's summer visits to farm, boatyard, station became didactic occasions for tableaux depicting eco-spheres, occupational cultures and technology. Other milieu studies, in contrast, stressed the texture of locales, vicissitudes of perception, subjective dimensions of seeing. William Kurelek's *A Prairie Boy's Winter* (Montreal, 1973) recalls farm routines, celebrations and setbacks as indices of Depression-era rural poverty, yet the apparently monotonous prairie landscape proves visually rich, teaching the author to see and to paint. Kurelek's semi-naïve tableaux record striking compositional conjunctures: fresh truck tracks on snowy road; skaters' rigid, asymmetrical legs bisecting flat prairie horizon; snowfall, blizzard or snowplough backdraft changing the quality of light; a woman bent over the fence, calling the pigs; transparent water becoming opaque skating-rink ice. The charged autobiographical tableaux of Carmen Lomas Garza's *Family Pictures / Cuadros de familia* (San Francisco, 1990) and Faith Ringgold's *Tar Beach* (New York, 1991) centre similarly on materially impoverished but visually expansive childhoods; in Texan immigrant communities and New York tenements, Chicano and African-American children sleeping on the roof are empowered by panoramic survey. In such narratives, perspective *is* power.

Angles of seeing: the gospel of modernism

What does it mean to see the world with fresh eyes? Using clearly labelled pictures, Orbis Pictus books initiated children into the world's complexity, teaching them ways of observing, analysing, categorising. Influenced by amateur naturalists, nineteenth- and twentieth-century sketchbook narratives stressed children's growing independence of discernment, judgment and expression. Orbis Pictus books envisioned child readers as learners; sketchbook narratives saw them as observers and future artists.

Both genres depicted the world as stable and knowable. Yet other formats attempted to inculcate scepticism, teaching child readers to question the veracity of text and image. Parodic cautionary tales armed children against didactic pieties and social conventions. Pedagogues expecting children to follow a strict moral and behavioural code, they suggest, have forgotten what it is like to inhabit a child's mind and body; meanwhile, they seem oddly blind to adult failings.

Parodic cautionary tales demonstrate this double standard in their own bifurcation of content and form, using doggerel and comic rhymes to convey strict messages, juxtaposing stern narrative with playful or mocking pictures. Visual hyperbole renders some of *Struwwelpeter*'s pictures funny as well as disturbing. The cat chorus bewailing their self-immolated mistress mocks the conventions of the pious juvenile deathbed; the self-righteous parents angrily bemoaning their lost dinner (while their chair-tipping child lies pinned beneath its wreckage) lack all parental solicitude. In Hillaire Belloc's 'Jim, Who Ran Away from his Nurse, and was Eaten by a Lion' (*Cautionary Tales for Children*, London, 1907), likewise, the narrator's gloating enumeration of the adult world's kindnesses to Jim is undercut by Basil T. Blackwood's illustration showing him snoozing through humdrum 'treats'. At the zoo, the lion's corpulent keeper *almost* bestirs himself to prevent catastrophe; his failure of action dooms Jim. And Jim's parents quickly abandon all pretence at grief for hatchet-faced moralising about the inevitability of their son's violent demise.

In Maurice Sendak's Belloc-inspired *Pierre* (New York, 1962), parents fail to subdue their son's stubbornness and leave him home alone, where a lion eats him. Once again, familial efforts at bribery – if Pierre behaves, he may fold the folding chair – appear pathetic; juvenile misbehaviour stems partly from faulty disciplinary strategies. Given the adult's misjudgment of both child psychology and interests, the joys of acting up exceed those of docility. Yet if rules of decorum seem anachronistic, Sendak suggests slyly, it might be an amusing reversal of expectations to follow them. Cautionary parodies indict such rules as over-regulating childhood, inculcating a literary approach to the world divorced from children's psychology and curiosity. Most unexpectedly, such tales invite child readers to read their pictures as leverage against their texts. While their texts insistently draw moral conclusions, their pictures potentially spring children from the didactic cage.

Crane's late-nineteenth-century nursery books impart a similarly critical perspective on traditional children's literature. His *One, Two, Buckle My Shoe* (London, 1867) consists of ten stately, even static tableaux. Yet, cumulatively, they offer a faceted view of domestic life, contrasting servants' utilitarian basement sleeping and work spaces with their employers' lush upstairs quarters. Alongside such visual and social contrasts, the volume's pictures juxtapose several households. Even where there seems continuity, viewers are actually shown different, differently angled rooms. Reprising the book's title image, Crane's culminating tableau shows a lady dishing up dinner, while a housemaid serves a young child. Surrounding these figures and utterly flattening the picture space is a large screen depicting 'Sing a Song of Sixpence'. Another scene shows a genteel family in their Arts and Crafts living room, viewed from an unusual angle, and emphasising an elaborate Japanese fire screen, whose picture presents its own complex perspectives (fig. 9). Such *japonaiserie* is key to Crane's own experiments with perspective and angle. British Arts and Crafts households offer fascinating new angles of vision to the children growing up there; for them, Crane suggests, the world takes shape under the influence of alternative, Asian ways of seeing.

The breakthroughs in chromoxylography which enabled Crane's and Caldecott's masterpieces spurred the mass printing not only of inexpensive, multi-coloured picture books, but of a new range of paper toys, dolls and board-games. Cut out and assembled by nimble-fingered children, one single printed sheet might produce a fully populated cityscape, castle (with movable drawbridges) or farmhouse (with paper animals and trees for dioramic grouping around semi-attached outbuildings); several such sheets might produce an elaborate paper theatre, with proscenium arches, and multi-layered, differentiated on-stage and back-stage spaces.

Two-dimensional printed pages, children learned, potentially produced complex three-dimensional ensembles. Following related construction principles, pioneering illustrator-designers from Meggendorfer to Tom Seidmann-Freud (Sigmund Freud's niece) developed pop-up and other movable picture books. Apparently flat pages unfolded or unfurled to create semi-panoramic, multi-planed visions, even (in books incorporating volvelles or more complicated 'dissolving pictures') continually moving picture worlds. Such books implicitly 'break the binding'.[7] With their movable parts, their magical ability to add extra dimensions to two-dimensional viewing surfaces, they rupture children's sense of a static, fixed picture plane, metaphorising books' capacity to intervene in everyday life.

Using very different means, the long tradition of children's 'novelty books' and the many picture books shaped by avant-garde art movements reshape

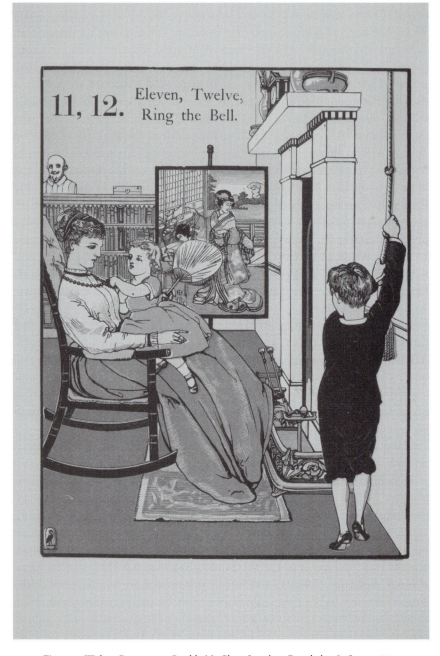

Figure 9. Walter Crane, *1, 2, Buckle My Shoe*. London: Routledge & Sons, 1867.
'11, 12, ring the bell'.

the frame and content of childhood vision. Novelty books frequently collapse distinctions between books' form, content and angle of perception. Peter Newell's *The Hole Book* (New York, 1908) follows a bullet through a series of tableaux; a neat hole is drilled through the middle of the cover, and every page. Newell's *The Slant Book* (New York, 1910), printed on sharply slanted pages, follows the precipitate downhill race of a baby carriage, upsetting all in its path. Eighteenth-century 'harlequinades' – early movable books in which the lifting of flaps created new scenes – challenged readers to anticipate how the image would metamorphose. Newer tactile books grounded stories of animal and human life in digital sensations: the feel of sandpaper adorning the father's stubbly cheek in Dorothy Kunhardt's *Pat the Bunny* (New York, 1940), or of fur binding Margaret Wise Brown and Garth Williams' *Little Fur Family* (New York, 1946).

Other books play with purely visual questions of scale, perspective, vantage point and transparency. Beatrix Potter's *Tale of Two Bad Mice* (London, 1904), Wanda Gág's *Snippy and Snappy* (New York, 1931), Marjorie Flack's *Angus and the Cat* (Garden City, NY, 1931) and William Nicholson's *Clever Bill* (London, 1926) view the human world from the stance of mouse, dog or tin soldier, sometimes bending or refracting perspective in the process. Margaret Wise Brown's *Noisy Books* (New York, 1939–47, illustrated by Leonard Weisgard and Charles R. Shaw, and published by experimental children's publisher William R. Scott) decouple and synaesthetically recombine the senses, as a blindfolded dog hypothesises his environment (fig. 10). Colour washes in Alvin Tresselt and Roger Duvoisin's *Hide and Seek Fog* (New York, 1965), or onionskin overlays in Bruno Munari's *Nella nebbia di Milano* (*Circus in the Fog*, Milan, 1968), simulate fog's visual opacity.

Many early-twentieth-century picture books reduce or compress the visual complexity of the modern world into new kinds of pictorial allegory or vocabulary. In Edward Steichen's *First Picture Book* (New York, 1930), black-and-white photographs of everyday objects and scenes are stylised into exquisite, decontextualised icons; constructivist primers like El Lissitzsky's *Suprematicheskii skaz: pro dva kvadrata* (*A Suprematist Tale of Two Squares*, Berlin, 1922) reduce complex political processes into instantly recognisable geometric shapes, legible to illiterates as to small children.

In Orbis Pictus tableaux, and in many later alphabets and primers, the illustrations are in part determined by the arbitrary rigour of alphabetical order, and startling, even incongruous, groupings of objects rarely found together in real life can emerge. Angela Banner's *Ant and Bee* (1950) provides a good example of the way in which adherence to alphabetic logic creates an unrealistic isolation of visual elements and peculiar narrative juxtapositions. Mid-century American picture books, in contrast, often explore their own

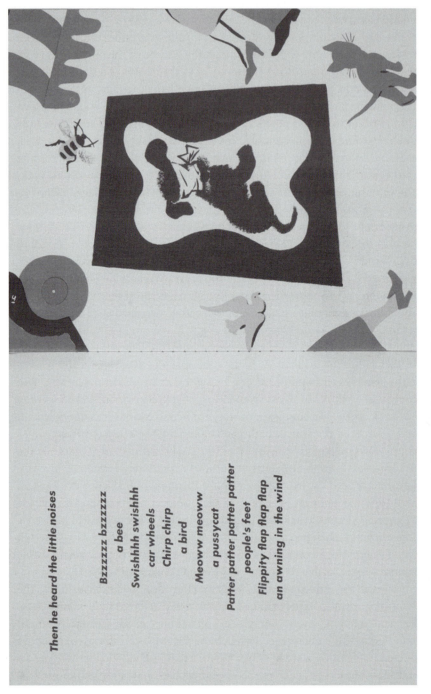

Then he heard the little noises

Bzzzzzz bzzzzzz
   a bee
Swishhh swishhh
   car wheels
Chirp chirp
   a bird
Meoww meoww
   a pussycat
Patter patter patter
   people's feet
Flippity flap flap flap
   an awning in the wind

Figure 10. Margaret Wise Brown. Illustrated by Leonard Weisgard, *The Noisy Book*. New York: Scott, 1939, p. 1. 'Then he heard the little noises'.

ability to generate meaning. Margaret Wise Brown and Leonard Weisgard's *The Important Book* (New York, 1949) insistently stylises objects into essences: a spoon *means* roundness. Posed as one long visual riddle, Charles G. Shaw's *It Looked Like Spilt Milk* (New York, 1947) demonstrates (and implicitly questions) children's propensity for reading the world – even natural phenomena like clouds – as shaped, representational, meaningful. Crockett Johnson's *Harold and the Purple Crayon* (New York, 1955) shows a picture-narrative coming into being out of nothing, as a child's line-drawing, random, accidental or deliberate, shapes a narrative world – and just as easily unmakes or negates it.

As Norman Brosterman has argued, the Froebel kindergarten's craft-centred curriculum, encountered in early childhood, decisively shaped the lifework and aesthetic philosophy of generations of influential modernists, from Frank Lloyd Wright to Paul Klee. Only a few modernist art movements (most famously, Russian Constructivism in the service of the new Soviet state) self-consciously undertook children's visual education. Yet a wide range of picture-book authors (and visionary publishers like William R. Scott) were unofficial promulgators of a gospel of modernism, using a wide range of tactics to inculcate in children a modernist vision of the world.

Many picture books explore the conceptual, perspectival and representational issues raised by modernist art. Against the background of impressionist, Fauvist and Expressionist colour experiments, master watercolourists (Louis-Maurice Boutet de Monvel in France, K. F. von Freyhold in Germany) explored colour's utopian possibilities. Other artists extended William Morris' revival of the illuminated manuscript, envisioning the illustrated book as a multi-layered artisanal object. Conrad Felixmüller's self-referential dedication page to *ABC: ein geschütteltes, geknütteltes Alphabet in Bildern* (*Nonsense ABC*, Dresden, 1925) shows the Expressionist artist carving a wood block to print the book, while his children look on. *Prinz Lennarts A.B.C.-bok* (Stockholm, 1912) and Franz Keim and Carl Otto Czeschka's *Die Nibelungen* (Vienna, 1909) evoke medieval illuminated manuscripts as prototypes for the stylisations of Art Nouveau and of the Wiener Werkstätte. (From 1903, the Viennese Workshops produced distinctive book, textile, furniture and craft designs.)

Some picture books explicitly promulgated Art Nouveau, cubist or Constructivist frames of reference. Von Olfers' anthropomorphised images appear encased in elaborate, stylised frames; W. W. Denslow's lavish illustrations for L. Frank Baum's *The Wonderful Wizard of Oz* (Chicago, 1900) repeatedly overprint text with image; Ivan Bilibin illustrates Russian fairy tales with complex layerings of image and patterning frame.

Many Art Nouveau children's books confront viewers with layer upon layer of design and history. Later picture books refract their vision. Lois Lenski's *The Little Auto* (New York, 1934) and Virginia Burton's *Choo Choo* (Boston, 1937) adapt cubist and futurist techniques to show movement. In the tradition of Crane's *One, Two, Buckle My Shoe*, Esphyr Slobodkina's Constructivist illustrations for Louise Woodcock's *Hiding Places* (New York, 1943) and Clement Hurd and Margaret Wise Brown's *Goodnight Moon* (New York, 1947) push children to a cubistically oriented study of their own surroundings. As its child protagonist searches a room, *Hiding Places* offers different cross-sections of the same space, successively 'panning' across the room, each tableau offering subtly different perspectives on the same scene. *Goodnight Moon*'s repetitive, overlapping scenarios of nightly fare-well, likewise, are attended by subtle shifts in the illustrations' perspective and content; repeat readers are challenged to memorise the lulling story while spotting differences of verbal and visual iteration.

Like Caldecott's and Crane's nursery books, *Goodnight Moon* and its companion volumes, *The Runaway Bunny* (New York, 1942) and *My World* (New York, 1949), delight in self-referential and cross-referential games. The little rabbit in *Goodnight Moon*'s Great Green Room has *Goodnight Moon* on his bedside table. The Three Bears picture above his bed incorporates a tiny black-and-white version of the picture (Cow Jumping Over the Moon) that hangs on the next wall; a miniature black-and-white image from *The Runaway Bunny* decorates the facing wall. In a book preoccupied with restating, rerea-ding and re-seeing, such devices not only promote cross-reading but open shafts into parallel literary worlds.

If Orbis Pictus tableaux proffered apparently unproblematic ways of organi-sing the world, these modernist books emphasise the partial, perspectival, self-generated nature of their views. Yet they are also careful to keep child readers anchored in time, place and domestic routine. Postmodern picture books, in contrast, take pleasure in disorienting child readers temporally, spatially, gener-ically, culturally, metaphysically. Some picture books thus relativise their own narrative and visual worlds as vertiginous meta-fictions. The wordless, quasi-cinematic worlds of Istvan Banyai's *Zoom* and *Re-zoom* (New York, 1995) or Barbara Lehmann's *The Red Book* (Boston, 2004) involve startling shifts of scale; the constant, retroactive calling-into-question of each book's previous pictures; *mise en abîme* or moebius-strip constructions which defy logical parsing in their use of recursion, infinite regress or the mutual imbrication of narrative levels. Many recent picture books reflect, at least implicitly, on the nature of literary history and the visual repertoire – and with them, the future of the book.

Orbis Picti presented scenes full of objects which gained meaning from being collected and categorised together. Twentieth-century picture books recreated seamless, panoramic vision, their intricate, often wordless tableaux inviting detailed, immersive (re-)seeing. Recent novelty books, in contrast, use densely detailed pictures to pose visual scavenger hunts.[8] Judith Cressy's *Can You Find It?* series (New York, 2002–), co-published by and featuring paintings from the Metropolitan Museum, frames such activity as a first step towards appreciating complex artworks. Yet such framings also deny the significance of aesthetics and form, reducing paintings to sheer information, didactically anchored in their wealth of details, yet significant only in aggregate.

Other picture books offer principled challenges to literary and artistic authority, eager to empower child readers and vindicate juvenile taste. Reinventing the eighteenth-century epistolary novel, Allen and Janet Ahlberg's *The Jolly Postman: Or Other People's Letters* (London, 1986) foregrounds its letters' materiality through bound-in envelopes which enclose detachable missives; these letters offer demystifying glimpses into the romantic and economic lives of familiar fairy tale characters. In Chris Van Allsburg's *Bad Day at Riverbend* (Boston, 1995), the stylised, black-and-white world of the Western is unexpectedly infused with sci-fi emanations (as broken streaks of colour appear on the sky) and finally relativised completely; the initial picture-narrative proves to be a colouring book, that lowest form of picture book, now being coloured by avid children in the world above. Van Allsburg's narrative offers unexpected homage to the crayon marks 'decorating' many copies of children's books. Generally read by adults and librarians as a sign that children have 'ruined' their own books, these marks function here as supernatural manifestations (children are the unseen gods of the colouring-book and picture-book worlds), as signs of reception visible inside the text itself, and as children's attempts to collaborate in the picture-making process, infusing creative colour into often lifeless narratives.

In fact, the picture book has always had a close relationship to mass cultural forms of print culture. Eighteenth- and nineteenth-century picture stories often imitated the format of popular chapbooks, and reflected the influence of satirical cartoonists like William Hogarth, James Gillray and Thomas Rowlandson. As picture-narrative and proto-cartoon, Wilhelm Busch's *Max und Moritz* (Munich, 1865) influenced both the story and graphic form of the longest-running American comic-strip, Rudolf Dirks' *The Katzenjammer Kids* (begun 1897 and still in syndication), as well as early Walt Disney cartoons. Sendak's *Where the Wild Things Are* (New York, 1963) and *In the Night Kitchen* (New York, 1970), conversely, jump off from the characteristic closing panels of Windsor McKay's spectacular *Little Nemo* comic strips (USA, 1905–13, 1924–6), yet develop more assertive child protagonists and depict different, Freud-inflected dream work. And while children's librarians long banned comic books from their precincts, picture-book illustrators as divergent as Dr Seuss, Edward Ardizzone and Raymond Briggs adopted various aspects of the cartoon format, from its line drawing and speech bubbles to its narrative blocking.

Many recent picture books celebrate an increasing convergence with comic books, manga and graphic novels. Yet others refute the apparent impending obsolescence of the codex, by reviving 'extinct' forms of book illustration: if illuminating and wood-block printing proved fragile artistic and artisanal forms apparently doomed by Gutenberg's development of movable type, they remain fascinating aesthetic and cultural objects, many centuries later.[9] Still others aspire to disentangle the picture book altogether from the history of bookmaking, to align it instead with alternative picture-narrative and performance traditions: stained-glass windows in Brian Gleeson and Robert Van Nutt's *The Savior is Born* (Westport, CT, 1992); Persian miniatures in Diane Stanley's *Fortune* (New York, 1999); Japanese screen painting in Odds Bodkin and Gennady Spirin's *The Crane Wife* (New York, 1998); Javanese shadow-puppets in David Weitzman's *Rama and Sita* (Boston, 2002); early cinema in Avi and C. B. Mordan's *Silent Movie* (New York, 2003). As a century before, with Walter Crane and Ivan Bilibin, such experiments with alternative pictorial vocabularies announce both a newfound cultural and historical relativism and the attempt to revitalise indigenous picture-book traditions.

In 2008, Brian Selznick's 550-page picture novel *The Invention of Hugo Cabret* (New York, 2007) made headlines, as the first novel ever to win the Randolph Caldecott Medal for most distinguished American picture book. Selznick's *Invention* both enacts and historicises the current sense of epochal medial shift: its plot centres on the interwar rediscovery of Georges Méliès' pioneering trick films, yet its psychological intensity stems from pictorial spreads – many graphic zooms – depicting 1931 Paris in iconography indebted to nineteenth-century images by Edgar Degas, Vincent van Gogh, Gustave Caillebotte and Adolph Menzel. In this latest incarnation, at least, the picture book crosses painting, novel, comic book and film, inhabiting several media and temporalities at once.

NOTES

1. Virginia Woolf, *The Waves* (London: Granada, 1977), p. 161.
2. Warren W. Wooden, *Children's Literature and the English Renaissance*, ed. Jeanie Watson (Lexington: University Press of Kentucky, 1986), pp. 1–22.
3. A. L. de Saint-Rat, 'Children's Books by Russian Émigré Artists: 1921–1940', *Journal of Decorative and Propaganda Arts*, 11 (Winter 1989), 92–105.
4. The book can be viewed online at www2.kb.dk/elib/mss/stampe//index-en.htm (accessed 19 June 2009).

5. Ann Bermingham, *Learning to Draw. Studies in the Cultural History of a Polite and Useful Art* (New Haven: Yale University Press, 2000).
6. McCloskey conceived *Make Way* after working on murals of Boston. Leonard S. Marcus, *Ways of Telling: Conversations on the Art of the Picture Book* (New York: Dutton, 2002), pp. 110–12.
7. 'Breaking the Binding: Printing and the Third Dimension', Beinecke Library exhibit, curated by Timothy Young, Yale University, 2006.
8. See Kit Williams, *Masquerade* (London: Cape, 1979); Martin Handford, *Where's Wally?* series (London: Little, Brown, 1987–), republished as *Where's Waldo?* in North America; Walter Wick and Jean Marzollo, *I Spy* series (New York, 1992–); and Norman Messenger, *Imagine* (London, 2005). Barbara McClintock's *Adéle & Simon* (New York: Farrar, Straus and Giroux, 2006), relatedly, borrows from famous French paintings to construct *fin-de-siècle* Parisian city tableaux, each containing scavenger-hunt clues.
9. See Pauline Baynes (ill.), *The Song of the Three Holy Children* (London: Methuen, 1986); Stephen Krensky and Bonnie Christensen, *Breaking into Print: Before and After the Invention of the Printing Press* (Boston: Little, Brown, 1996), and Gabrielle Gern and Rebecca McBride Tröhler, *Prinz Wolf: Ein Märchen* (Lucerne and Freiburg: Rex Verlag, 2000).

5

RICHARD FLYNN

The fear of poetry

Critics in children's literature studies, by and large, tend to ignore children's poetry, but one can hardly blame them. Exciting and innovative work appears fairly often in fiction, many picture books offer enticing visual and literary pleasures, and there are several non-fiction works for young people that are sophisticated and illuminating. But, with some notable exceptions, the vast bulk of children's poetry published today is goofy, sentimental or recycled from days of yore. As I write, the most recent children's poetry bestseller list from the Poetry Foundation (a spin-off of *Poetry* magazine in Chicago) contains, besides work by Shel Silverstein and Jack Prelutsky, primarily anthologies, such as *Mary Engelbreit's Mother Goose: One Hundred Best-Loved Verses* (2005) and *A Family of Poems: My Favorite Poetry for Children* (2005) edited by Caroline Kennedy. Caroline is, like her mother, a celebrity anthologist, and Mary Engelbreit is a franchise. This is, for the most part, the kind of fare one encounters at the large chain bookstores like Barnes and Noble.

This market-driven narrowing of the genre is a shame because children's poetry is historically an expansive body of work. Until recently, the distinction between poetry for children and poetry for adults has been usefully blurred: prior to the late twentieth century, poetry anthologies for children tended to include verse traditionally considered 'adult', as well as an eclectic mixture of light verse, nonsense verse, narrative verse, along with lyric poetry. Additionally, children's formal encounters with poetry in school tended to place more emphasis on the poem than on the genre itself or the individual poet. Older pedagogies that focused on the memorisation and individual and choral recitations of poetry served to emphasise the sonic and performative aspects of verse over print-based texts geared towards exercises in analysis and comprehension. And, certainly, the poetry generated by children themselves – nursery rhymes, playground rhymes and other performance-based poetry – forms the basis of early and largely positive experiences with poetry, emphasising pleasurable and often interactive experiences with poetic language.

But today, in the United States and to a lesser extent in Great Britain, children's poetry is considered a marginal subset of children's literature, so marginal that the *Cambridge Guide to Children's Books in English* (2001) has no entry for the genre of poetry, despite the fact that the well-known children's poetry scholar Morag Styles is one of its general editors. While poetry plays a larger role in more pedagogically oriented disciplines, such as education, there the traditions of poetry in English are often viewed with hostility. And while poetry is seen as something children might easily learn to write, rarely are they encouraged to enjoy reading it, or memorising it, or performing it. A large part of the problem stems from a reluctance to say what poetry is. According to one well-known college textbook for prospective elementary teachers, 'There is an elusiveness about poetry that makes it defy precise definition. It is not so much what it is that is important, as how it makes us feel.'[1]

Alongside this amorphous definition of poetry is a growing insistence among language arts educators that children's poetry not only exists in a world apart from poetry for adults, but that, for children, a separate poetry is preferable. Perceiving some disdain for poetry for children among those who value 'real' poetry, Glenna Sloan in her 2001 article 'But Is It Poetry?' champions a separate children's poetry, but she poses and answers a rhetorical question that dismisses fundamental aesthetic concerns: 'What *is* poetry? Who's to say?'[2] The defence of a children's poetry that excludes poetry for adults is often couched in arguments for children's preferences. Paradoxically, this respect for children's preferences is often disregarded in pedagogical settings. Sylvia Vardell cites studies from 1974, 1982 and 1993 that show that children prefer narrative verse and verse with rhyme and metre. These studies also conclude that children dislike free verse and haiku; nevertheless, free verse and haiku are the very kinds of poetry preferred by teachers, if not by children.[3] At a presentation I gave at an American national teachers' organisation in 2003, in which I advocated musicality as the salient quality of the best contemporary children's verse, an audience member seemed almost offended by that notion and insisted that she did not permit her elementary students to use rhyme in the poetry she asked them to write. It became clear from several responses that poetry pedagogy in schools almost always involves creative writing instruction and very seldom advocates reading or performing poetry for pleasure.

The aforementioned teacher forbade her students to use rhyme, she said, because it 'gets in the way of their self-expression'. Such attitudes seem to substitute immediate gratification (the teacher's more than the child's) for the responsible attitude advocated by poet John Mole: 'a notion of poetry for children which puts poetry first – for the sake of the children and the adults they will become'.[4] Mole, who is a gifted poet for children, advances an argument that seems to be more prevalent in Great Britain than in the USA. Perhaps because of the longer history and greater institutional support for poetry in Britain, Mole's argument that children's poetry should not be separated off from the world of poetry in general is more persuasive than it would be to an American audience. Nevertheless, the question remains as to why contemporary scholars and readers actively ignore poetry, to the point where it seems to have been consigned to the margins of children's literature.

Several answers suggest themselves. First, the definition of poetry compounds the problem of defining children's literature itself in that so much of what might be considered 'children's' poetry, from nursery rhymes to Robert Frost, was never composed specifically for a child audience. Second, notions about the elevated status of poetry as a genre have tended to foster a view of poetry as the preserve of the expert, or even as inherently elitist. Finally, because poetry is the genre where language itself is foregrounded, its potential power can be frightening. Paradoxically, that fear is based on the very versatility of language and its potential to multiply rather than foreclose meanings.

The fear of poetry in the twenty-first century, then, is intimately connected with the fear of play, particularly the fear of serious language play. Language as it is being learned by children (or at least as it is being taught to them) has increasingly been circumscribed by insisting that it should serve primarily to steer the youngsters towards approved modes of consumption and 'competency'. While we devalue serious language play, we overvalue serious business. Linguistic competency is measured by the achievement of 'functional' literacy, which is 'mastered' for narrowly utilitarian ends, and that 'mastery' is measured by increasingly standardised tests in schools that have, for the most part, jettisoned poetic language, along with the rest of the arts, from their curricula. Contemporary culture reacts as the 'other bats' do to the protagonist of Randall Jarrell's *The Bat-Poet* (1964). When the Bat-Poet discovers poetry and then tries to interest the other bats in it, they say to him, 'When you say things like that, we don't know what you mean.'[5]

More often than not, it is the 'other bats' who define curricula that either ignore poetry or relegate it to the periphery, disregarding its potential for encouraging linguistic growth and fostering interpretive skills. I don't mean to dismiss or disregard the pedagogical function of poetry for the young. The history of children's poetry, like the history of children's literature, is inextricable from its pedagogical context. But our pedagogies are at odds with poetry's potential to encourage language as exploration. Poet Lyn Hejinian writes of the child's relationship to language:

> We discover the limits of language early, as children ... Children objectify language when they render it their plaything, in jokes, puns, and riddles, or in

glossolaliac chants and rhymes. They discover that words are not equal to the world, that a shift, analogous to parallax in photography, occurs between things (events, ideas, objects) and the words for them – a displacement that leaves a gap.[6]

This passage is from Hejinian's well-known essay 'The Rejection of Closure', in which she argues for a poetics aimed at generating multiple meanings as opposed to a poetics aimed at foreclosing meaning. In pedagogical terms, this means the resistance to a pedagogy directed towards a single correct answer. That 'single answer' pedagogy holds sway today might well be traced to the influence of the New Critical reading strategies that have trickled down to our schools. The New Criticism was a mid-twentieth-century formalist critical theory that insisted on the autonomy of the text in order to reveal its complexities, without recourse to extratextual considerations such as biography, historical contexts and reader response. As early as 1949, in her prescient book-length meditation *The Life of Poetry*, poet Muriel Rukeyser attributed the fear of and resistance to poetry to the New Critics' 'treatment of language' that

gives away their habit of expecting units (words, images, arguments) in which, originating from certain premises, the conclusion is inevitable. The treatment of correspondence (metaphor, analogy) is always that of a two-part equilibrium in which the parts are self-contained.

'The critics of the "New" group', she writes, carry the 'rigid consequences' of Emerson's theory of language as 'fossil poetry' to absurd extremes, seeing 'poetry itself as fossil poetry'.[7]

In 'The Fear of Poetry', the opening section of *The Life of Poetry*, Rukeyser writes, 'In speaking about poetry, I must say at the beginning that the subject has no acknowledged place in American life today':

Poetry is foreign to us, we do not let it enter our daily lives.
Do you remember the poems of your early childhood – the far rhymes and games of the beginning to which you called the rhythms, the little songs to which you woke and went to sleep?
Yes, we remember them.
But since childhood, to many of us poetry has become a matter of distaste.[8]

This passage from Rukeyser spells out a paradox, a seemingly impossible contradiction that remains as true now, early in the twenty-first century, as it did in the middle of the twentieth: we *do* remember, however atavistically, 'the far rhymes and games of the beginning', the rhythms and little songs that were part and parcel of our earliest embodied experience with language as it is being learned. And yet, argues Rukeyser, the ways in which our bodily beginnings were once allied with our nimble intelligence have been elided, erased, reduced to the simple. We might say it is as simple as child's play, if only the linguistic and physical play of children weren't complex. In his fascinating study *From Two to Five* (1925), Kornei Chukovsky argues that children between those ages are 'linguistic geniuses'. Although he indicates that, as the heightened cognitive activity associated with language acquisition fades, the intense need for 'creative activity with words' passes, he nevertheless spells out a connection between the imaginative activity of children 'from two to five' and the potential richness of adult imaginations. The job of children's poets, he writes, is to 'adapt our writing to the needs of the young' while at the same time to 'bring the children within reach of our adult perceptions'.[9]

In most accounts of the history of children's poetry we find a narrative of 'progress', in which, sometime during the nineteenth century, children's poetry moves from instruction to delight, 'from the garden to the street', from the 'adult-centred' to the 'child-centred', from the bad old days of memorising and reciting poems to the good new days of free children and free verse. Typically, this narrative insists, children's poetry (to an even greater extent than children's fiction) changes as Puritan (and puritanical) constructions of childhood are 'liberated' by Romantic and post-Romantic constructions of the child. Coexisting alongside this progress narrative is a nostalgic narrative of decline: people, including children, used to read and recite and enjoy poetry which, in its more popular manifestations, both served a civic function and provided emotional and intellectual sustenance.

While the better accounts of this progress narrative, such as Morag Styles' *From the Garden to the Street* (1998), are relatively nuanced, there is nevertheless an aesthetic assumption that 'moral instruction' – even that allied with a tender rather than severe view of children, such as in many of Isaac Watts' *Divine Songs* (1715) – was replaced (fortunately) by more child-centred and child-friendly poetry, beginning with the Romantics. In addition to the growing popularity of narrative verse, humour and nonsense by the end of the nineteenth century, the supposedly child-centred lyricism practised with great skill by Robert Louis Stevenson in *A Child's Garden of Verses* (1885) may be seen as ushering in a strain of sentimental nostalgia, circumscribing children's lyric poetry in a way that represents a diminution rather than an expansion of its range and possibilities.

In any event, by the late twentieth and early twenty-first centuries, as critic Angela Sorby argues in her book *Schoolroom Poets* (2005), nineteenth-century equations of poetry as natural to childhood, with 'poetry as a form of childhood' (along with the powerful institutions that promoted and perpetuated those notions), helped bring about the 'infantilization' of the genre itself. 'In the splintered, niche-driven world of middle-class popular culture', writes Sorby, 'poetry has maintained a toehold in America as a children's genre, supported by the institutions of children's publishing, elementary schools, and libraries'.[10] The forms of children's poetry that dominate today are cute and sentimental picture-book poetry aimed at the parents of babies, humorous verse often written by lesser practitioners, or the institutionally manufactured and apparently highly marketable novel-in-verse. For every able poet who has worked in these contemporary genres – a Valerie Worth, a Dr Seuss, a Karen Hesse – there are annually scores turning out volumes of derivative junk.

An expansive view of children's poetry could serve to counteract the institutionalised status quo. Such a view that recognises the value of both the serious and the whimsical, that recognises poetry as a social as well as a solitary pleasure, seems best designed to promote a lifelong love of poetry. Calling for a more expansive anthology of children's poetry, Joseph Thomas observes that such an anthology 'would be one in which various and sometimes incommensurate poetries exist in dialog with one another. This arrangement would allow a child – a beginning reader – to start her reading experiences with as heterogeneous a conception of poetry as possible.'[11] This expansive view of poetry is intimately related to a view of children that recognises them as capable of enjoying a wide range of literature. Of course children enjoy what Seuss' Cat in the Hat calls 'lots of good fun that is funny', but that isn't all there is to poetry. The most meaningful experiences with poems come from living with them for a long time, internalising their rhythms and music, and pondering the conundrums they often pose. So, although it is counterintuitive, many of today's teachers, anthologists and even some children's poets insist that children's poetry must be instantly accessible and confined to subjects that adults have decided are 'relevant'. While anthologies for children have traditionally included poetry intended for adults, there is, at least in the United States, a kind of separatist movement regarding poetry for the young. Perhaps this movement is a reaction to 'prestige' anthologies such as Elizabeth Sword's A Child's Anthology of Poetry (1995) and Gillian Avery's The Everyman Anthology of Poetry for Children (1994), in which the selection criteria for poets seem to be that they are canonical poets for adults. These anthologies are well intended in their desire to avoid condescending to children, but they risk boring the child reader just as much as a steady diet of easily accessible and 'relevant' verse.

Anthologies may be inherently conservative, but they may also serve to broaden the aesthetic range of children's poetry, or even to open up the canon to previously excluded voices. Great anthologies like Walter de la Mare's Come Hither (1923) or Ted Hughes and Seamus Heaney's The Rattle Bag

(1982) allow poems from a wide aesthetic range, from nursery verse to poems one might not expect to be within the range of children, to bump up against one another in unexpected ways. While those particular anthologies may be justly charged with ethnocentrism, they avoid the aesthetic sameness of anthologies like Jack Prelutsky's *Random House Book of Poetry for Children* (1983). The anthology's function as an agent of canon formation may well be conservative, but it can aim at broadness and inclusiveness in more than token ways. The truly inclusive anthology, one that practises neither cultural partition, nor what poet Harryette Mullen terms 'aesthetic apartheid', remains to be made. Anthologies of African-American poetry, such as those by Arnold Adoff or Ashley Bryan, British-Caribbean anthologies, such as those by Grace Nichols and John Agard, or Naomi Shihab Nye's anthologies of poems from the Middle East are all necessary steps in moving towards a culturally inclusive canon or in developing counter-canons. Nevertheless, such canons need to be constructed in tandem with one that refuses easy distinctions between poetry for children and poetry for adults. While we don't need any more 'Hoary Chestnuts: Poems Adults Think are Good For You', neither do we need any more 'Because I Could Not Pick My Nose: Poems Guaranteed to Gross Out Your Parents'. What we need and don't yet have is a way for poems of varying registers to bump up against one another: the formal alongside the experimental, the tender alongside the humorous, the elegant argument alongside nonsense, the Anglo-American canon alongside traditionally excluded poetries, the child alongside the adult.

Thus, is it all the more unfortunate that the Peter Pan-ish children's poetry celebrity dominates the contemporary scene. Recently, the Poetry Foundation used some of the pharmaceutical money it received from Ruth Lilly to establish a US Children's Poet Laureateship. According to the press release, 'The new award aims to raise awareness that children have a natural receptivity to poetry and are its most appreciative audience, especially when poems are written specifically for them.'[12] The first Laureate, to no-one's surprise, was Jack Prelutsky, and now the Poetry Foundation's website is graced by such work as Prelutsky's 'Be Glad Your Nose Is on Your Face', which warns the reader that if the nose were placed 'between your toes / that clearly would not be a treat, / for you'd be forced to smell your feet'.[13] From there one can go on to read more work in the same vein by Prelutsky or even more trivial work by his acolytes such as Dave Hawley's 'My Doggy Ate My Homework'.

Since the death of Shel Silverstein, Jack Prelutsky is unquestionably the chief celebrity in the world of children's poetry in the USA. Like the celebrity 'children's laureates' of the nineteenth and early twentieth centuries Sorby discusses in *Schoolroom Poets* – 'Longfellow, Whittier, Riley, and Field' – Prelutsky and his compatriots manufacture a child's perspective that adult readers can easily adopt as their own perspective on childhood. And like those former children's laureates, they cultivate their fame and celebrity by performing the same *shtick* for their adoring audiences. Such performances carry a lot of power in creating, perpetuating and reinforcing contemporary views of childhood. Karen Glenn, in her Poetry Foundation feature on Prelutsky (entitled 'Never Poke Your Uncle with a Fork') cites a list of adjectives that have been used to describe Prelutsky's poetry, but these adjectives might just as well describe the nature of children and childhood assumed by readers of the poems:

> consider some of the actual words that critics have used to describe his (almost countless) poetry books for children: zany, charming, irreverent, gothic, tongue-in-cheek, surreal, rich, varied, rib-tickling, silly, playful, wacky, inventive, whimsical, preposterous, frivolous, hilarious, and pure fun. Not to mention WEIRD and BIZARRE!
>
> Then think about the ways that reviewers and interviewers have described the 66-year-old Prelutsky himself: a child in an adult's body, a boy who never grew up, a daydreamer.[14]

The mythology of the childish adult (most often a boy-man) as uniquely able to address the literary needs of children has, of course, a long history. And the importance of nursery rhymes, nonsense and verse from the oral tradition for children's poetry cannot be overestimated. But Prelutsky is the leading practitioner of what Joseph Thomas has termed 'domesticated playground poetry', in which the subversive, anarchic energy of children's oral tradition is tamed and endlessly recycled by a series of entrepreneurs from Longfellow to Prelutsky.

The preponderance of lightweight (as opposed to light) verse wouldn't be so troubling if it were not for the distinguished and honourable tradition of humorous and nonsense verse read by children. The best comic verse, from the work of Edward Lear and Lewis Carroll to more recent work by poets such as Edward Gorey, Roald Dahl or Margaret Mahy, is always aware of the darkness that gives nonsense its power. Grappling as it does with serious subject matter – mortality, authoritarianism, vanity and, most of all, with the arbitrary nature of language – poets in the tradition of Carroll and Lear tend to risk more than the Prelutskys of the world. While the latter play it safe, the masters of nonsense tend to go out on a limb, as it were, as in Lear's 'There Was an Old Person of Slough',

> Who danced at the end of a bough;
> But they said, 'If you sneeze,
> You might damage the trees,
> You imprudent Old Person of Slough.'[15]

Lear's use of understatement serves to defuse and emphasise the Person of Slough's precarious predicament. The very word 'slough' itself suggests both that the Person will find himself in the swamp, perhaps even in the 'Slough of Despond', and also that the Person has cast caution to the wind by sloughing off prudence so that he himself has become dispensable. It would certainly seem so to 'they', whose main concern is the damage to the trees.

Less indeterminate than 'purer' forms of nonsense, cautionary verse is often seemingly subversive in the service of inculcating conventional morality and proper behaviour. When this conservative aim – the 'moral', if you will – is most obvious, potentially powerful verse becomes tame. When I was growing up, a particular favourite in my family was Gelett Burgess' 1900 etiquette manual, *Goops and How to Be Them: A Manual of Manners for Polite Infants*. The children in my family, of course, delighted in the transgressions of these miscreants, but we were not fond of the heavy-handed closure of the poems soliciting our good behaviour:

> The Goops they lick their fingers,
> And the Goops they lick their knives,
> They spill their broth on the table-cloth –
> Oh they lead disgusting lives!
> The Goops they talk while eating
> And loud and fast they chew;
> And that is why I'm glad that I
> Am not a Goop – are you?[16]

Poems in which children's misdeeds are celebrated and punished extravagantly, as in Heinrich Hoffman's *Struwwelpeter* (1845) or the cautionary verses of Hilaire Belloc, proved to be preferable to tamer offerings such as those of Ogden Nash. Sometimes, however, we loved the quieter ironies of a poem like A. A. Milne's 'Disobedience' (from *When We Were Very Young*, 1924) because the adult–child role reversal appealed to us in relatively unthreatening ways, and it was liltingly musical at the same time. While we were too old to have enjoyed Maurice Sendak's *Pierre* (1962) as children, we certainly found ourselves enjoying it with our children, either in a call-and-response reading of the Nutshell Library book, in which the child would supply the 'I don't care!' refrain, or in the delightful Carole King musical settings.

Nevertheless, I suspect that children are remarkably adept at detecting that the subversiveness of certain poems is the sugar that helps the medicine go down. Ever since the brilliant parodies of didactic verse by Lewis Carroll in the *Alice* books (1865 and 1871), critics have perpetuated a reductive opposition between 'bad old' moralistic verse and the liberating subversiveness of nonsense, but poetry really isn't an either/or game. The verse we encourage children to read has more to do with our constructions of childhood than it does with actual children's needs and preferences.

Whatever else you might say about it, didactic poetry, in which an adult poet overtly rather than covertly aims at instruction, was certainly intended to foster the well-being of children and was concerned with the adults they would become, as well as for their immortal souls. At its best, as in Watts' *Divine Songs* or the early nineteenth-century work of Ann and Jane Taylor, it respects children's capacity for negotiating the sonic and figurative pleasures of language. While clearly subject to divine ordinance and the authority of adults, the child addressed in these poems is capable. In the opening poem in Watts' *Divine Songs*, 'A General Song of Praise to God', the speaker poses the question:

> How glorious is our Heavenly King,
> Who reigns above the Sky!
> How shall a Child presume to sing
> His dreadful Majesty?[17]

The poem concludes that the child's 'first offerings' are no more presumptuous than those of men or angels: 'Th' eternal God will not disdain / To hear an infant sing':

> My Heart resolves, my Tongue obeys,
> And Angels shall rejoice
> To hear their mighty Maker's praise
> Sound from a feeble voice.[18]

After Watts, we find in the poems of Ann and Jane Taylor the bodily rhythms of 'Baby's Dance' ('Dance little baby, dance up high, / Never mind baby, mother is by') that later poets such as Christina Rossetti would develop with great skill, or cautionary tales delivered with panache and humour.[19] The linguistic inventiveness of Anna Laetitia Barbauld's *Hymns in Prose for Children* (1781) demonstrates a wide range of poetic language (despite her questioning the appropriateness of poetry for the young) that extends beyond the regular metres of previous male practitioners.

Though it sometimes adopted a child's voice, poetry before the middle of the nineteenth century spoke, for the most part, *to* the child. After the first half of the century, poets more and more spoke *for* the child, seeking 'authenticity' through a form of ventriloquism. They concerned themselves more with capturing the child's perspective than with the way poems work. A poem, as William Carlos Williams famously noted, is a 'small (or large) machine made of words':

> When a man makes a poem, makes it, mind you, he takes words as he finds them interrelated about him and composes them – without distortion which would mar their exact significances – into an intense expression of his perceptions and ardors that they may constitute a revelation in the speech that he uses. It isn't what he says that counts as a work of art, it's what he makes.[20]

Notably, 'significances' is plural in this formulation, but in children's poetry the notion of the authenticity of the child's voice or experience is directed towards a single significance. Language plays second fiddle to the attempt by the poet to masquerade as a child or the child's closest ally. Thus, it is typically considered a 'breakthrough' in the progress narrative that Robert Louis Stevenson's chief innovation in children's poetry was the creation of an 'authentic' child's voice. But on what basis is the judgment of authenticity made? Stevenson's child in *A Child's Garden of Verses*, in the words of the valedictory poem, 'To Any Reader', 'is but a child of air / That lingers in the garden there'.[21] Sickly, pampered, occasionally naughty but too docile to throw even so much as a temper tantrum, Stevenson's child speakers reinforce a regulatory adult agenda more insidiously than the overtly didactic *Divine Songs* of Watts. While Stevenson insists on the importance of imaginative play, stories and flights of fancy, there is something a little too pleasant about it all – something just a little treacly. Rudyard Kipling's wicked parody of Stevenson, 'A Child's Garden' (from *The Muse Among the Motors* (1919)) targets Stevenson's excesses brilliantly (though it must be noted that Kipling was quite fond of Stevenson's work):

> Now there is nothing wrong with me
> Except – I think it's called T.B.
> And that is why I have to lay
> Out in the garden all the day.[22]

While Stevenson may leave us only halfway down the treacle well, if not well in, his primary address is to the spectral child that has grown up and gone away. The reader can't lure this child outside the book.

Compare Stevenson's speaker in 'The Land of Counterpane' with the child who speaks Randall Jarrell's 1949 poem for adults 'A Sick Child'. (It seems likely to me that Jarrell, who undoubtedly grew up with Stevenson's poems, mounts a critique of Stevenson's brand of sick child in his poem.) Stevenson's child revels in the power his sickness confers upon him:

> When I was sick and lay a-bed,
> I had two pillows at my head,
> And all my toys beside me lay,
> To keep me happy all the day.

> And sometimes for an hour or so
> I watched my leaden soldiers go,
> With different uniforms and drills,
> Among the bed-clothes, through the hills;
>
> And sometimes sent my ships in fleets
> All up and down among the sheets;
> Or brought my trees and houses out,
> And planted cities all about.
>
> I was the giant great and still
> That sits upon the pillow-hill,
> And sees before him, dale and plain,
> The pleasant land of counterpane.[23]

In Jarrell's 'A Sick Child', a similar child speaker entertains a more philosophical view of the imagination's power, one which is more disturbing than pleasant:

> The postman comes while I am still in bed.
> 'Postman, I say, what do you have for me today?'
> I say to him. (But really I'm in bed.)
> Then he says – what shall I have him say?
>
> 'This letter says that you are president
> Of – this word here; it's a republic.'
> Tell them I can't answer right away.
> 'It's your duty.' No, I'd rather just be sick.
>
> Then he tells me there are letters saying everything
> That I can think of that I want for them to say.
> I say, 'Well, thank you very much. Good-bye.'
> He is ashamed and walks away.
>
> If I can think of it, it isn't what I want.
> I want … I want a ship from some near star
> To land in the yard, and beings to come out
> And think to me: 'So this is where you are!
>
> Come.' Except that they won't do,
> I thought of them … And yet somewhere there must be
> Something that's different from everything.
> All that I've never thought of – think of me![24]

Stevenson's sick child, like Jarrell's, would 'rather just be sick' and uses his imaginative play to confirm his position as an invalid, his egocentrism transforming him into 'a giant' who is 'great' but nevertheless 'still'. Indeed, invalidism is equated with pleasure, or, rather, with the 'pleasant'. Jarrell's sick child is ultimately confronted with the limitations of his passivity and egocentrism, and wishes to be imagined by something outside the self. That Jarrell's poem was not originally written for children doesn't preclude the possibility that it may speak to children in more meaningful ways. It poses metaphysical questions about the nature and power of the imagination that go beyond Stevenson's more limited assertion that imaginative play can make being sick in bed more enjoyable.

While there's undoubtedly some inherent sentimentality in the trope of the sick yet imaginative child, in the nostalgic appeal of recreating a child that has 'grown up and gone away', there is also in contemporary poetry a narrowing of what is permissible in terms of poetry's emotional range. For late twentieth- and early twenty-first-century children, light comedy is all the rage, but tenderness and genuine sentiment are often in short supply. One thing that can be done to broaden the range of poetry available is to establish a high level of critical discourse surrounding children's poetry. That children's poetry has greater status in the UK may be attributed not only to greater institutional support, but to the ongoing critical conversation about children's poetry that took place in the journal *Signal* (1970–2003). The provocative essays that appeared as part of the *Signal* Award for Poetry sparked interest and debate about the neglected genre. The *Lion and the Unicorn* Award for excellence in North American poetry (for which I have served as a judge for three years) is an attempt to begin an analogous conversation on this side of the Atlantic. Recently, there have also been a number of important books that discuss poetry and its relation to children, including Angela Sorby's *Schoolroom Poets* (2005), Joseph Thomas' *Poetry's Playground* (2007) and cultural historian Joan Shelley Rubin's *Songs of Ourselves: The Uses of Poetry in America* (2007). While there are a number of awards among the education-oriented disciplines that call attention to excellent books, these are not usually accompanied by a body of literary criticism that attempts to articulate excellence in children's poetry.

There is also the perennial rhetoric bemoaning the absence of serious engagement with poetry and, for that matter, serious literature, in the age of mass media and the internet. Again, the discourse in the USA is generally more alarmist and sensationalist than it is in the UK. In an interview with Lara Saguisag, poet Michael Rosen notes that he has been able to use the mass media successfully to promote poetry, proposing the concept of an 'inter-*media*-ated world', made possible by state-run rather than corporate-sponsored media: 'I know in the States, they sort of feel that TV is this foul, commercial, gutter-stuff. In this country there's a slightly different attitude. TV isn't the enemy. I think it's possible in Britain to live in an intermediate world without compromising yourself.'[25]

But in order to use contemporary technologies to aid in the dissemination of poetry, it takes poets who are adept at performance, while also remaining vigilant in detecting the uses and misuses of the media with which they hope to interact. Television shows such as *Sesame Street*, or children's singers like Raffi, present songs and nursery rhymes in ways that are very appealing. The internet has potential for presenting poetry in attractive formats, though it does not seem to have begun to fulfil that potential. And no matter how useful various technologies may be, they are no substitute for the embodied experience that characterises the young child's first encounter with poetry. Children can only have a valuable 'inter-media-ated' experience if they are media literate, and media literacy can only be learned if there is a foundation of meaningful literacy to build on. Poems that challenge beyond their surface appeal, that will inhabit children and encourage them to inhabit language, are indispensable, if only we can see and hear them.

NOTES

1. Barbara Z. Kiefer, with Susan Helper and Janet Hickman, *Charlotte Huck's Children's Literature*, 9th edn (New York: McGraw-Hill, 2007), p. 409.
2. Glenna Sloan, 'But Is It Poetry?' *Children's Literature in Education*, 32 (2001), 45–56 (p. 56).
3. Sylvia Vardell, *Poetry Aloud Here! Sharing Poetry with Children in the Library* (Chicago: American Library Association, 2006), p. 75.
4. John Mole, 'Tune, Argument, Colour, Truth', *Signal*, 98 (2002), 79–90 (p. 85).
5. Randall Jarrell, *The Bat-Poet* (New York: Macmillan, 1964), p. 6.
6. Lyn Hejinian, 'The Rejection of Closure', in *Writing/Talks*, ed. Bob Perelman (Carbondale: Southern Illinois University Press, 1985), p. 278.
7. Muriel Rukeyser, *The Life of Poetry* (1949; Ashfield, MA: Paris Press, 1996), pp. 166–7.
8. Rukeyser, *Life of Poetry*, pp. 9–10.
9. Kornei Chukovsky, *From Two to Five*, trans. Miriam Morton (Berkeley: University of California Press, 1966), pp. 7 and 154.
10. Angela Sorby, *Schoolroom Poets: Childhood and the Place of American Poetry, 1865–1917* (Durham, NH: University of New Hampshire Press, 2005), pp. 187 and 189.
11. Joseph Thomas Jr, *Poetry's Playground: The Culture of Contemporary American Children's Poetry* (Detroit, MI: Wayne State University Press, 2007), p. 114.
12. 'Poetry Foundation to Name First Children's Poet Laureate', 18 September 2006, on-line at www.poetryfoundation.org/foundation/release_091806.html (accessed 20 February 2008).
13. Jack Prelutsky, 'Be Glad Your Nose Is on Your Face', *Poetry Foundation Archive*, on-line at www.poetryfoundation.org/archive/poem.html?id=177537 (accessed 20 February 2008).
14. Karen Glenn, 'Never Poke Your Uncle with a Fork', *Poetry Foundation Online Journal*, on-line at www.poetryfoundation.org/archive/feature.html?id=178694 (accessed 20 February 2008).

15. Edward Lear, *Nonsense Books: More Nonsense Pictures* (Boston: Little Brown, 1904), p. 41.
16. Gelett Burgess, *Goops and How to Be Them* (New York: Frederick A. Stokes, 1900), unpaginated.
17. Isaac Watts, *Divine and Moral Songs, attempted in easy language for the use of children*, ed. J. H. Pafford (Oxford: Oxford University Press, 1971), p. 149.
18. Watts, *Divine Songs*, p. 150.
19. Ann and Jane Taylor, *Rhymes for the Nursery* (1806; Philadelphia: George Appleton, 1849), p. 51.
20. William Carlos Williams, *Selected Essays* (New York: New Directions, 1954), p. 256.
21. *Robert Louis Stevenson: Collected Poems*, ed. Janet Adam Smith (London: Rupert Hart-Davis, 1950), p. 411.
22. Rudyard Kipling, *The Muse Among the Motors* (1919), on-line at whitewolf. newcastle.edu.au/words/authors/K/KiplingRudyard/verse/musemotors/child-sgarden.html (accessed 20 February 2008).
23. *Robert Louis Stevenson: Collected Poems*, p. 370.
24. Randall Jarrell, *The Complete Poems* (New York: Farrar, Straus, 1969), p. 53. Copyright renewed 1997 by Mary von S. Jarrell. Reprinted by permission of Farrar, Straus and Giroux, LLC.
25. Lara Saguisag, 'Performance, Politics and Poetry for Children: Interviews with Michael Rosen and Benjamin Zephaniah', *Children's Literature Association Quarterly*, 32 (2007), 3–28 (p. 11).

6

JOHN STEPHENS

Retelling stories across time and cultures

Throughout the world, literature for children originates with retelling and adapting the familiar stories of a culture – folktales, legends and stories about historical and fictional individuals memorialised for their heroism or holiness, adventurousness or mischief. When English-language children's literature emerged as a visible entity from the seventeenth century, it followed this route, with the publication of various fairy (or folk) tale collections and religious texts. Subsequently, the principal domains of retold stories in children's literature expanded to include myths and mythologies; medieval and quasi-medieval romance, especially tales of King Arthur's knights; stories about legendary heroes such as Robin Hood; oriental tales, usually linked with *The Arabian Nights*; and modern classics, from Shakespeare to Kenneth Grahame and L. Frank Baum.

A story retold for children serves important literary and social functions, inducting its audience into the social, ethical and aesthetic values of the producing culture. Retellings are thus marked by a strong sense that there is a distinct canon within any of the domains. The tendency for children's literature to evolve as both separate and specialised is very pertinent here: its dominant concerns, especially social issues and personal maturation, make retellings for children a special area, which cannot be simply covered by implication in studies which do not explicitly discuss writing for children. Only a couple of the principal domains of retellings can boast a study dedicated to this writing, however.[1] Most research has focused on retellings for adults and on fairy tales, which are implicitly treated as a special case, perhaps because feminist criticism has focused on them rather than on other kinds of retelling.

To be a retelling, a text must of course exist in relationship to some kind of source, or 'pre-text', although this is only sometimes identifiable as a specific work, and stories may lose or accrete elements as they are refashioned over time. A new retelling may therefore include elements and motifs from multiple stages of a text's tradition, may draw more widely on the genre with which

a text is associated, or shape the text in the light of contemporary reinter-
pretations. Retellings of old tales are thus shaped by interaction amongst
three elements: first, the already-known story, in whatever versions are circulating at the time of production, together with other stories of similar type
or including similar motifs; second, the current social preoccupations and
values (that is, metanarratives, or the larger cultural accounts which order
and explain individual narratives) which constitute its top-down framing and
ideology (and these may be mediated by current interpretations of the known
story); and third, the textual forms through which the story is expressed
(narrative modes, genres and so on).

A substantial change to a story can quite quickly become naturalised. An
example is the introduction of a Saracen/Muslim character as one of Robin
Hood's companions in the highly influential British TV series *Robin of
Sherwood* (1984–6): the character subsequently seems to have become part
of the story's fabric, at least in film and television retellings. An obvious
precedent is the evolution of the figure of Maid Marian, especially over the
past two centuries, from shadowy companion to feminist heroine. A second
example, also rapidly developing in the late twentieth century, is the mutation
of the story of Aladdin under the influence of the Western folktale motif
whereby someone is granted three wishes. Introduced to the story in the early
1980s and made pivotal in the Disney film of 1992, the motif, and the
metanarrative of social responsibility and altruism which lies behind it, is
now the only version of the story known to many people. Such a change can
have a deep impact on what a story is generally thought to signify.

Few retellings are simple replications, even when they appear to reproduce the story and narrative point of view of the source. In such cases, the
purpose is generally cultural reproduction, in the sense of transmitting
desired knowledge about society and the self, modes of learning and forms
of authority. Myths, legends and folktales function as stories with tangible
links to a larger system or pattern of narratives, and this relational network
guarantees that any specific story has a significance over and above mere
story outcome: its meaning is determined by its relationship to a presumed
whole. In other words, any particular example is always already interpre-
table as a moral fable or allegory whose significance is shaped by a powerful,
sometimes indefinable, emotional supplement and by its articulation within
culture. Already existing stories thus offer children privileged patterns of
thinking, believing and behaving which explain or suggest ways in which the
self might relate to the surrounding world.

Retellings may therefore have several kinds of significance, in addition to
transmitting literary heritage, but three are of particular importance. First, a
traditional story is invested with value as *story* itself. That is, as a narrative

which audiences may recognise as similar to other such narratives because it is patterned by archetypal situations and characterisations, a story transmits its latent value as a particular working-out of perennial human desires and destinies. The structural pattern itself signifies without needing to be interpreted, because the meaning lies in the repeatability and the deeply laid similarity amongst otherwise apparently diverse stories. All traditional stories are liable to be subjected to such a story-only focus, but the principle also underlies numerous abridged retellings of substantial pre-texts. Well-known fairy tales, for example, may be reduced to a bare outline in mass-market picture books in which texts and illustrations merely reproduce the same abbreviated information. More subtle abridgments, such as Lucy Meredith's 1988 retelling of the Grimms' *Dornröschen*, may narrow the possibilities of reader response by eliminating material extraneous to story but rich in implication. Meredith renders the moment at which the princess pricks her finger as follows:

> She climbed the stairs and came to a little door with a golden key in the lock.
> She turned the key, the door flew open, and she saw a tiny room and an old woman spinning flax. The old woman welcomed her and showed her how to spin. But she hardly touched the spindle when she pricked herself and at once fell down in a deep sleep.[2]

This narration has focused on the moment at which the curse is fulfilled and the implication that the old woman is part of a trap. Meredith accentuates the latter possibility by substituting an inviting golden key for the rusty key (*ein verrosteter Schlüssel*) of the Grimms' pre-text. A strong influence on interpretation of this moment in 'Sleeping Beauty' retellings has been Disney's 1959 identification of the old woman with the fairy who cast the spell, and readers may readily instantiate this connection. The princess's curiosity is pivotal to the curse in Grimm, but Meredith's abridgment minimises this by omitting the question-and-answer exchange between princess and old woman which expresses that curiosity. Even a careful and competent abridgment is thus apt to limit the narrative, and an examination of the process will call into question the notion that story has latent value.

The second significance attributed to retellings lies in an assumption that traditional stories embody timeless and universal significances. Such an assumption underlies Freudian readings of fairy tales, or Jungian readings of hero stories and folktales. From seventeenth-century stories of childhood piety to Gregory Maguire's inventive reworking of modern tooth fairy legends in *What-the-Dickens: The Story of a Rogue Tooth Fairy* (2007), stories have pivoted on quests for identity. In *What-the-Dickens*, for example, the eponymous fairy begins life as an orphan and is clumsy and ignorant, but as his understanding grows so does his courage and compassion, and by the end of the story he is poised to transform his world. That the story of *What-the Dickens* is narrated to three children by a young adult striving to get through a stormy night in an end-of-the-world scenario well illustrates how narratives about social behaviour are framed by interpretative protocols: the frame story and the embedded story stand in a relationship of mutual interpretation, and demonstrate how the quest for identity may permeate story structure.

Third, traditional stories are thought to facilitate intercultural communication by bringing out the similarities between various world cultures, and hence to affirm the common humanity of the world's peoples. This assumption is often linked with folktales and the retelling of analogues from apparently unconnected cultures. As a grounding assumption of folktale collections, internationalism emerged strongly as the impetus for Andrew Lang's colour fairy books, published between 1889 and 1910: individual volumes drew widely on European and Asian folktale traditions, and included a sprinkling of stories from Africa and the New World. The practice remains widespread, although the range represented by Lang's series is now largely an untapped resource and only a few canonical tales dominate retellings. A popular example in the USA is Rafe Martin and David Shannon's *The Rough-Face Girl* (1992), a retelling of a Native American story belonging to the Algonquin people. A quick surf of the internet will yield several teaching units working on comparisons between *The Rough-Face Girl* and a version of *Cinderella* from the Perrault–Grimm traditions. Such a strategy has a strong appeal because it affirms a common humanity shared by people of diverse cultures, and seems to suggest that all people have similar desires and emotions.

A different impulse for retelling stories stems from a desire to challenge the cultural hegemony attributable to the metanarratives that shape notions of heritage and universality (metanarratives employ a society's ideologies, systems and assumptions to generate narrative forms that explain knowledge and experience). To retell a story from familiar pre-texts can be somewhat akin to reproducing 'facts' (the already known), and the process was long grounded on third-person narration told from the singular point of view of an all-seeing narrator. For most genres – mythology, folk and fairy tales, Arthurian retellings, stories of Robin Hood – actions were described as reported by the narrator, characters were seen from outside, and their reactions and responses to events were narrated rather than focalised by the characters themselves. This narrative mode does not entirely preclude inventiveness or innovation, but does tend to leave a text's assumed core values unaddressed and hence unchallenged.

To some extent, a retelling may be enabled to interrogate the tradition simply through changes in the mode of discourse entailed in any retelling, since the language and style of pre-texts are usually not then reproduced. This is clearly seen in the numerous retellings of Shakespeare's plays as factual prose. The following, from Bernard Miles' retelling of *Macbeth* (1976), refashions the play as commented information:

> Now that he [Macbeth] knew the worst he became desperate and resolved to carry his wickedness to the very end. He would kill everyone who stood in his way. First of all he sent the two men who had killed Banquo to kill Macduff. But Macduff had already begun to suspect that Macbeth had murdered both Duncan and Banquo and that he might be next on the list. So, when the murderers arrived at his castle he was already on his way to England, to join Malcolm. In their fury the murderers killed his wife and little children instead. And that was the worst crime Macbeth ever committed, even worse than killing Duncan.[3]

The story is presented as already interpreted, with clear cause-and-effect relationships ('Now that ... he became'; 'In their fury ... killed') and temporal framing ('Now ... when ... already'). The retelling is at pains to explain motivation, and hence incorporate an interpretation of the story, but it does not depict motivation from the character's perspective. The fleeting attribution of thought to Macbeth in the second sentence is outweighed by the authorial comment of the final sentence.

Such strategies contrast strongly with the sparer narrative cultivated by Charles and Mary Lamb in their classic 1807 retelling: 'Macbeth, stung with rage, set upon the castle of Macduff and put his wife and children, whom the thane had left behind, to the sword, and extended the slaughter to all who claimed the least relationship to Macduff ... These and such-like deeds alienated the minds of all his chief nobility from him.'[4] The Lambs rely more on a story-only focus which includes a brief reference to motivation and a moral judgment implied by adduced public consensus rather than narrator opinion. In this version, the core values are presumed and taken for granted rather than aggressively asserted.

A retelling is better facilitated to interrogate its story by two significant changes in predominating narrative strategy that occurred in the middle of the twentieth century: an increased tendency to tell the story from the point of view of one (or more) of the characters; and an increase in first-person narrated fiction, to the extent that it has become the dominant narrative form. Both developments also introduced the possibility of a range of voices, as a text might also have more than one narrator, several focalising characters, or even a mixture of both. From about 1970, these developments in narrative strategy coincided with a heightened attention to social issues pertaining to the representation of gender, ethnicity and class, and became extensively employed by feminist writers, in particular.

First-person narration situates point of view very specifically, enabling a perspective that is both personalised and restricted. Readers will normally align their sympathies with the narrator, but are also positioned to know no more than can be deduced from his or her telling. Access to story events and to the minds of other characters may thus be limited, encouraging readers to speculate about motivations and power relations amongst the characters. Gary D. Schmidt's Rumpelstiltskin narrative, *Straw into Gold* (2001), places its readers in a speculative position because its narrator, an orphan child given seven days to find the answer to a riddle, lacks access to any crucial information. Having grown up in an isolated place, and knowing little of the world, Tousle cannot understand that his quest to solve the riddle embodies a quest to uncover the Rumpelstiltskin story (already retold in the peritext before the novel proper begins), his own place within it, and the wider significances of the story.

The effect of such positioning can be very strong when the narrator-focaliser is a character who has the role of Other or Villain in the pre-texts. Donna Jo Napoli's multifocalised *Zel* (1996), for example, not only represents Rapunzel and her aristocratic lover as focalising characters, but frames the novel as the Witch's first-person narration. The capacity to present other or multiple perspectives dismantles simplistic good–evil dichotomies and foregrounds the conflicting desires of the characters. Such narrative strategies enable a text to rework relationships grounded on gendered or other hierarchies and to renegotiate the ideologies and values inherent in those hierarchies.

As a wider range of narrative strategies has appeared in retold stories, the processes of retelling seem to have consequently become more self-reflexive, as narratives ponder their own telling. They may do this, for example, by foregrounding the storyteller's function, by embedding subsidiary stories, or by incorporating discussion of interpretative practices. Perhaps the most brilliant of modern retellings of the Robin Hood story, Michael Cadnum's *In a Dark Wood* (1998), places such issues of interpretation at the centre of his retelling of one of the story's most often retold incidents, the night spent by the Sheriff of Nottingham in the forest as Robin Hood's 'guest'. As the Sheriff enters the forest with Robin, he rehearses protocols for interpreting the natural world as a sign system that reinforces social and religious beliefs. But when he is presented with an extempore story composed by Little John, and asked by Robin to interpret the story according to his previously demonstrated method, he cannot. He protests that, having never heard the story before, he cannot guess its meaning.[5] The meaning of the story thus inheres in the audience's reading competence, and Robin is depicted as using the Sheriff's interpretative failure as a way to explicate his limiting enculturation. Readers are then left with a problem of interpretation that sits very well with

Cadnum's overall reframing of the traditional story by presenting it from the point of view of the Sheriff and thematising thereby problems of political power, social responsibility and human agency within social and political systems.

Cadnum's move to a radical, against-the-grain point of view raises questions of how far retold stories can depart from models of interpretation exemplified by *What-the-Dickens*. The only study that attempts to formulate a general theory of retellings for children, *Retelling Stories, Framing Culture* (1998), argues that the processes of retelling are subject to a limited number of metanarratives.[6] Considered from this perspective, the Sheriff's bafflement may be seen to stem from an inability to identify an appropriate metanarrative, and hence an inability to identify which represented behaviours are desirable and which undesirable, and how the story is oriented towards his culture's ideologies, systems and institutions. *In a Dark Wood* exemplifies a desire in many modern retellings to suspend a reader's regular protocols in order to think about the focus story in a different way.

An opportunity to challenge regular protocols is also available in stories which have moved to the periphery of the canon because they fail to conform to the dominant metanarratives. A useful example is the story of *Rumpelstiltskin*, which is widely familiar as a (slightly peripheral) story in the most widely discussed area of retold story – the literary fairy tale. In the version collected by the Grimms, a miller boasts that his daughter can spin gold out of straw. To test this, the King locks her in a roomful of straw with a spinning wheel. She is saved from failure by the appearance of a little man who does spin the straw into gold in return for her necklace. This is repeated on a second night (in return for her ring), and on the third, when the girl has been promised marriage to the King if she succeeds. But to recompense the little man, she thoughtlessly agrees to give up her first child to him. In due course, then, he arrives to claim the new Queen's child. When she protests, he tells her that she may keep the child if she can guess his name within three days. All attempts are fruitless until one of her messengers encounters the man dancing round a fire, singing his name. When the Queen correctly calls him 'Rumpelstiltskin', he is vanquished.

Rumpelstiltskin is shaped by a bundle of familiar story conventions, but they are conventions which fail to yield up determinable meanings and are therefore subject to slippage in retelling. Further, the tale has no clear moral direction, in that none of the characters can be said to behave ethically. The ethical question places demands on any reteller to impart some kind of moral shape to the retelling – this is most likely to pivot on depicting the miller's daughter as victimised by all three men in the story, and depicting Rumpelstiltskin as non-human and alien: *other*.

One approach to these problems is seen in William J. Brooke's *Teller of Tales* (1994), where, having been told an abbreviated version of the Grimms' rendering, the teller ponders the tale's gaps and lack of convincing motivation, tells a tale which addresses some of these problems, and imagines a happier ending for Rumpelstiltskin himself. Another is when Vivian Vande Velde poses the same bundle of problems in her collection *The Rumpelstiltskin Problem* (2000), and writes six different versions within that frame. Brooke and Vande Velde make explicit the dialogue within which retold stories unfold: the already-known story is shaped by the metanarratives pertaining at the time, or times, of its production; and subsequent retellings, sometimes consciously and sometimes implicitly, are likewise informed and shaped by whatever social preoccupations and values are current when subsequent versions are produced.

Rumpelstiltskin is also somewhat problematical as a retold story because its pre-texts are uncertain and variable. Retellings in English are occasionally influenced by English folktale analogues such as *Tom Tit Tot*, but most retellings derive from the Grimms' 1819 version, probably mediated through Andrew Lang's *The Blue Fairy Book* (1889), clearly identifiable by the fate of the mysterious little man, who 'in his rage drove his right foot so far into the ground that it sank in up to his waist; then in a passion he seized the left foot with both hands and tore himself in two'.[7] Many versions, however, prefer a less violent ending in which Rumpelstiltskin's stamping opens a crevasse into which he falls and disappears (presumably falling into Hell where he belongs).

Retellings may depart more comprehensively from what an audience might think of as the 'original' story. An urge to interrogate the androcentrism and class-centrism underpinning the pre-text and the cultural heritage of which it is part may foreground a detail which modern audiences often find problematic: the female character is so much a disposable object that the King seems to be quite indifferent as to whether he kills or marries her. This indifference may be used to foreground social ideologies pertaining to gender, class, materialist and economic assumptions in relation to (and in reaction to) the mores of current society. Schmidt's *Straw into Gold* resolves the problem as an issue in the politics of succession, whereby, in a borrowing of a motif from the story of patient Griselda, Rumpelstiltskin removes the baby to protect him from the lords of the realm who will not accept the son of a peasant as their king. This novel overtly affirms a teleology shaping the story, a 'design' lying deeper than mere chance.

Aspects of retelling evident in these versions foreground the major questions to be asked about the process. What do the metanarratives that structure the texts indicate about the assumed social values that inform them? How are social and personal development framed? What is the nature of intersubjective relationships? What assumptions are being made about class and gender?

What material and spiritual aspirations inspire the characters? What ethical and moral paradigms are implied? What teleology shapes the story?

The metanarratival domains implicit in these questions are invoked by Donna Jo Napoli and Richard Tchen in their novelisation *Spinners* (1999), through the personal items that the miller's daughter can offer Rumpelstiltskin. These items prove a logical irritant for many readers, since Rumpelstiltskin can have no interest in their small material value. His interest must instead lie in their symbolic value, culminating in possession of the child, as representations of love and marriage. The girl (named 'Saskia') is here identified as Rumpelstiltskin's daughter, a fact known only to him. When, on the third night, she says she has nothing more to offer other than her body, the situation instantiates some specific responses within the metanarratival domains pointed to above. First, humanistic paradigms of social and personal development are threatened by the likely consequences of her offer; second, power inequality perverts an intersubjective relationship; third, appropriate gender relationships – father/daughter, old/young, ugly/beautiful – are being violated; fourth, the material necessity to preserve life forecloses 'higher' aspirations; and fifth, although culturally accepted ethical and moral paradigms are being breached, moral judgment is compromised by the shadow of another metanarrative which decrees that Saskia's reluctant self-prostitution is its own moral compromise.

Traditional stories, especially fairy tales, are frequently retold in picture-book form. A subtle picture book uses its interaction of words and pictures to engage with the possible meaning or meanings conveyed by a particular motif. In Paul O. Zelinsky's 1986 Caldecott Honor Book *Rumpelstiltskin*, for example, the young woman's third encounter with Rumpelstiltskin clearly positions her as victim: the King's power and the enormity of the task demanded of her are emphasised by an illustration dominated by the sheer abundance of straw and the multitude and ornateness of the columns in the room, and her helpless, defensive posture is accentuated as she appears to shrink away from Rumpelstiltskin, who leans over her like a bird of prey. Illustration is thus pivotal in framing character interactions and audience response. In contrast, her subsequent victory depicts her dressed as befits a queen, in red and gold, leaning towards and looking down at Rumpelstiltskin, whose otherness is emphasised through his caricatured face and his possession of a large cooking ladle, the latter a phallic motif elided by the Grimms although collected in their first manuscript version of the tale (fig. 11). The Queen's servant enacts joy at the extreme left of the scene, contrasting with the anger on the right. Finally, the contrast between realistic portrait (Queen) and caricature (Rumpelstiltskin as a small grotesque) weighs the balance of power heavily in the Queen's favour. Further, Zelinsky's use of an Italian Renaissance setting allows him to invoke a discourse and body of work

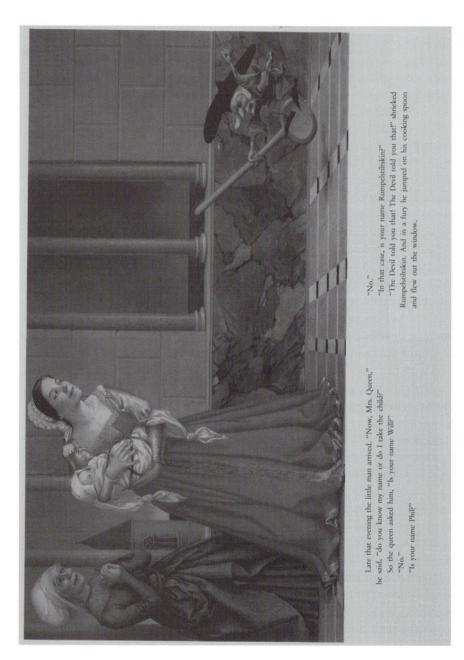

Late that evening the little man arrived. "Now, Mrs. Queen," he said, "do you know my name or do I take the child?"
So the queen asked him, "Is your name Will?"
"No."
"Is your name Phil?"
"No."
"In that case, is your name Rumpelstiltskin?"
"The Devil told you that! The Devil told you that!" shrieked Rumpelstiltskin. And in a fury he jumped on his cooking spoon and flew out the window.

Figure 11. Paul O. Zelinsky, *Rumpelstiltskin.* New York: Dutton's Children's Books, 1986, pp. [35] and [36].

which adds authority and cultural capital both to the story he is retelling and to the text itself.

Illustrations themselves may function as retold stories. This example plays a game with isomorphism, in that it quotes and inverts the positioning of the Virgin Mary and the Angel Gabriel in Fra Filippo Lippi's *The Annunciation* (c. 1442), which is already a playful reworking of a familiar scene and subject: Lippi's Angel Gabriel has possessed himself of the iconic lilies of purity usually found in a vase in this genre scene, so that the vase, prominent in the foreground, is now empty; Zelinsky then replaces the lilies with the astonishingly phallic ladle on which Rumpelstilstkin rides. The long tradition whereby paintings are retold stories is likewise wittily exploited in Diane Stanley's *Rumpelstiltskin's Daughter* (1997), where they feature as backgrounds to a narrative which blatantly imposes a utopian democracy on an autocratic social system: the most notable is a dialogue established between a reworking of Sandro Botticelli's *Birth of Venus* (c. 1482), Hans Andersen's *The Emperor's New Clothes* (1836) and the narcissistic arrogance of the King in the *Rumpelstiltskin* story.

In the Zelinsky illustration, the contrast between the victorious Queen and the more or less monstrously other Rumpelstiltskin is a trope in visual texts, although this is not a matter of cross-influences, but of the underlying meta-narrative of struggle and victory. Zelinsky's portrayal of the Queen's triumph over those who have victimised her is clinched by the final page, when she rejoices in her baby as her husband, the King, strays in from the background apparently wondering if he has missed something. Zelinsky has conflated a couple of the Grimm versions to produce his text, but the outcome illustrates how a retelling will be more than a simple replication of the story and point of view of its source(s).

When a familiar classic is retold in another era and in an unexpected genre, the impact on its significance can be very striking. For example, Kenneth Grahame's *The Wind in the Willows* (1908), which is narrated in linguistic and social discourses that may today seem as inaccessible as Shakespeare, has been repackaged in several ways. A conservative approach has been to update the appearance of the book by replacing the older illustrations of Arthur Rackham and Ernest Shepard with illustrations by eminent modern picture-book artists, including John Burningham (1983), Eric Kincaid (1986), Michael Foreman (2001) and Robert Ingpen (2007), amongst many others. While the text remains unchanged, the illustrations place it in a new context and invest it with new values and new intertexts: Burningham's depiction of Toad standing beside his first car is very reminiscent of the first opening of his earlier *Mr Gumpy's Outing* (1970), for example. *The Wind in the Willows*, or sections of it, has been retold as a play, film, and television series, and in the late 1990s French illustrator Michel Plessix turned the story into a four-part comic book series.

Grahame's text consists of omniscient narration and character direct speech, whereas Plessix's text, in accord with European comic book conventions, consists predominantly of pictures (incorporating extralinguistic typographical signs suggesting emotion, such as a thought bubble containing '???') and an embedded verbal text that mixes narrative (often character focalised) and direct speech. The result is not only faster-moving, less introspective and more humorous, but its attitudes and social concepts belong to a different era from the pre-text. While it cultivates affectionate parody rather than the trenchant social revisioning of Jan Needle's *Wild Wood* (1981), the comics series does make fun of the class and gender assumptions of *The Wind in the Willows*. The comic book genre itself produces meaning in a unique way, as comparison of the following narrative segments, describing Toad's relationship with the daughter of his jailer, makes clear. Here is Grahame:

> Toad, of course, in his vanity, thought that her interest in him proceeded from a growing tenderness; and he could not help half regretting that the social gulf between them was very wide, for she was a comely lass, and evidently admired him very much.[8]

And here is Plessix:

> The Toad was convinced that his warm charm wasn't leaving the young woman indifferent. But too many differences separated them – there was a social gulf between them that nothing could ever span. Baron Tadpole with some jailer's daughter ... what a ridiculous idea![9]

The pivotal difference here is that the focus for Grahame's irony is, explicitly, Toad's egocentric vanity, and 'the social gulf' – apparently taken for granted – has been elided by an earlier comment that the girl 'was fond of animals as *pets*'. In contrast, the emphatic and exclamatory style pertaining to comic book discourse, the shift into free indirect speech at the second sentence, and the transfer of 'comely lass' into a larger-than-life close-up of the woman's eyes and curly hair shifts the focus to Toad's internalised classist thinking.

It is very apparent that the genre itself is playing a major role in the production of meaning. Some genres more obviously than others bring with them a metanarratival overburden, which may in turn be dealt with consciously and playfully. Diana Wynne Jones' *Howl's Moving Castle* (1986) uses folktale in such a way. The novel is not a retelling of a particular story, but rather draws inventively on numerous folktale motifs. Hence a fairy tale conjuncture of setting and cultural conditions dominates the opening of the novel:

In the land of Ingary, where such things as seven-league boots and cloaks of invisibility really exist, it is quite a misfortune to be born the eldest of three. Everyone knows you are the one who will fail first, and worst, if the three of you set out to seek your fortunes.

Sophie Hatter was the eldest of three sisters. She was not even the child of a poor woodcutter, which might have given her some chance of success.[10]

The assertion that magical objects such as seven-league boots and cloaks of invisibility exist here, and the reference to how the rule of three conventionally functions in fairy tales, asserts a fairy tale discourse. On the other hand, the retrospective narration and the taken-for-granted tone of the narrating voice invoke a realist mode. The discourse thereby hovers between the narrative conventions of everyday realism and those of fairy tale.

The oscillation between realism and fairy tale focuses attention on conventional and figurative elements likely to be central for the novel's significance, especially the references to appearances and beauty, which evoke the common fairy tale theme of the gap between surface appearance and reality. Once Sophie is transformed into an old crone, her role in the novel focuses on the struggle to recuperate a fallen world, that is, to retrieve a state of being which has been lost. Sophie's subjectivity has already been diminished because of her withdrawn introspection, and, in Howl's case, because of the displacement of his heart and fragmentation of selfhood. Once they learn to connect Self to Other and Self to world, they can achieve the personal and moral growth necessary for reunification of the self.

When in 2004 Hayao Miyazaki transformed the novel into an animated film, he worked within a different genre. The difference is not simply that one is a novel – an entirely verbal medium – and the other a film – a multimodal text which, in this case, subordinates narrative to visual representation, while also making use of words and music. Rather, the film illustrates how Japanese anime has its own forms and styles, and characteristically hybridises its common genres. Thus, while we can identify various story elements that derive from Jones' novel, and a continuation of the theme of fragmented or lost subjectivities, the anime might also be said to have rather little to do with that novel.

For this reason, and because when film retellings are concerned modern stories may also be retold, it is important to observe that a particular set of principles governs the retelling of books as films, namely a selection from the three modes of adaptation identified by Geoffrey Wagner: transposition, commentary and analogy. The first of these, transposition, in which a novel is transferred to the screen with the minimum of apparent interference, applies to the *Harry Potter* films. The other two modes apply to Miyazaki's film, however. On the one hand, it functions as 'commentary' in so far as it is a narrative which has taken apart its pre-text and reassembled it as a version which is a new textual and ideological configuration. On the other hand, it also functions as an analogy – that is, as a departure from its pre-text for the sake of making *another* work of art. It is primarily an analogy, in that the anime genres which underpin it, its foregrounding of a story about war which is only a background threat in the novel, and its very different characterisation of Sophie and Howl make it a very different production. Hence audiences need to take notice of Wagner's argument that an analogy 'cannot be indicted as a violation of a literary original since the director has not attempted (or has only minimally attempted) to reproduce the original'.[11]

Anime characteristically combines elements from several different genres; to some it may seem to be underplotted, although this aspect is largely because Japanese narrative is apt to be more interested in character than in events, so if audiences are used to the event-driven narratives of Disney films they may think anime seems disconnected. Reviews of *Howl's Moving Castle* have tended to find the ending too abrupt, although it is effectively enabled in two main ways: the romance element; and the shift of the underlying fairy tale more towards a version of *Beauty and the Beast*, underpinned by the motif of the kiss that breaks a magic spell and by the overt articulation of theme in Sophie's remark to Howl that 'A heart is a heavy burden.' Hence the sudden, astonishingly happy ending to a story of destruction, betrayal, malice, alienation and the threats to subjective wholeness posed by an irrational war and by the inner dangers of depression, despair and loss of identity, may suggest that human intersubjectivity is the only resource we have for keeping disorder and entropy at bay.

The intertextual fabric evident in both novel and film of *Howl's Moving Castle* is taken a stage further in Terry Pratchett's reworking of the Pied Piper of Hamelin story, *The Amazing Maurice and his Educated Rodents* (2001). The presence of intertexts and allusions in this novel constitutes an overt signalling that various characters, motifs, registers and so on are borrowings from other texts, but it also reminds us that, as a corollary of the self-reflexive turn in processes of retelling, many stories are now retold as parodic and iconoclastic versions. Iconoclasm is most familiar in the form of the fractured fairy tale, in which the roles of major participants may be reversed, expected outcomes deflected or subverted, and point of view transferred from heroes to villains. An outcome is that the authority of tradition and of familiar story conventions are challenged. But fractured fairy tale is only the best-known site of such subversions, and none of the domains of twice-told tale have been immune. Bible story is wittily parodied in Pratchett's *Truckers* (1989), and Tony Robinson's zany, feminist retellings of the Robin Hood story in the BBC TV series *Maid Marian and her Merry Men* (1989–94) raised calculated anachronism to an art form as it laid bare the cherished ideological presuppositions of traditional retellings.

As its frame story, *The Amazing Maurice* retells Robert Browning's well-known *The Pied Piper of Hamelin* (1842), but accords with numerous modern retellings in concluding that Browning's poem masks an underlying story of fraud and deceit, and so constructs a story about how the cat Maurice exploits a tribe of rats and a naïve young musician to enact a 'plague of rats' scam in small towns. The novel goes further than other *Pied Piper* retellings, though, in presenting much of the narrative from the point of view of the rats and enriching the story with borrowings from numerous other texts and discourses.

Like *Howl's Moving Castle*, *The Amazing Maurice* extends its referencing beyond traditional folktale or myth to invest modern texts with a similar value to that attributed to older narratives. It is thus a fitting culmination for a discussion of retold tales because it incorporates the complete range of pre-texts found in retellings. It alludes to specific earlier texts by direct quotation or indirect citation – for example, Beatrix Potter's *Peter Rabbit* stories and Browning's *Pied Piper* are invoked on the opening page; oblique reference is made to Kenneth Grahame's *The Wind in the Willows*; and the familiar discourse of Enid Blyton's Famous Five novels appears frequently, as in, 'it would be more ... satisfying if we were four children and a dog, which is the right number for an adventure'. Common archetypal narrative motifs are deployed, such as the orphan of unknown parentage who restores the waste land to fertility, along with motifs from well-known stories, such as the folktale and pantomime of *Dick Whittington and his Cat* – 'a young man with a smart cat can go a long way', points out one character, Malicia (granddaughter of the 'Sisters Grim'). In Pratchett's retelling, Whittington has become 'Dick Livingstone', Mayor of Übergurgl, but the joke also extends to our own world and time, the allusion being to Ken Livingstone, just elected Mayor of London when *The Amazing Maurice* was published.[12]

The overtly eclectic mixing of genres and conventions is one of Pratchett's key strategies in his flaunting of the novel's intertextuality – the references include fairy tales and folktales, adventure stories, romances, as well as Hollywood Westerns and arthouse films. A very effective example of this occurs when Malicia, who persists in reshaping everyday life into the form of a familiar story, is introducing herself to Keith as a Cinderella figure: Sardines, the dancing rat, comes abseiling down the kitchen wall behind her, and Maurice thinks to himself, 'Of all the kitchens in all the town he could turn up in, he's turned up in this one.' Maurice's thought is obviously a (mis-) quotation of a famous line spoken by Humphrey Bogart in *Casablanca* (1942). We now have a kind of dialogue between misquoted texts:

Malicia's misappropriation of Cinderella, and Maurice's misquotation of *Casablanca*. The potential for such references to be arcane is epitomised by a psychoanalytic joke referring to Lacan's version of the mirror stage in infant development: '[Maurice had] realized something was odd that day, just after lunch, when he'd looked into a reflection in a puddle and thought *that's me*. He'd never been *aware* of himself before.'[13]

One feature which most of these intertextual references have in common is a more or less parodic relation between the focused text and the pre-text. A parody is a comic imitation of something. While the purpose of parody is in general the production of humour of some kind, whether it be of a light-hearted or satirical nature, the object of that humour is not necessarily the parodied pre-text or narrative form. Instead, the object of humour will often be particular sentiments or values evoked via the mockery of a pre-text. Thus, Pratchett's parodic allusions to *The Wind in the Willows* mocks not so much the pre-text itself, as the socially privileged, idyllic rural ideologies under-pinning such narratives.

Any story deemed traditional or 'classic' may be retold. The processes involved in retelling are rich and varied, but characteristically begin with raw material that is usually unstable, and usually unfixed in its origins. The metanarratives which have shaped the story over time are themselves subject to change, and the story may be transposed from one genre to another. There may be a dialogue amongst various retellings, but this dialogue may also turn out to be coloured by ways of reading earlier versions of the focus tale.

NOTES

1. Ruth Bottigheimer, *The Bible for Children: From the Age of Gutenberg to the Present* (New Haven: Yale University Press, 1996); *Adapting the Arthurian Legends for Children*, ed. Barbara Tepa Lupack (New York: Palgrave Macmillan, 2004).
2. Lucy Meredith, 'Thorn Rose, the Sleeping Beauty', in *The Faber Book of Favourite Fairy Tales*, ed. Sara and Stephen Corrin (London: Guild Publishing, 1988), p. 139.
3. Bernard Miles, *Favourite Tales from Shakespeare* (London: Hamlyn, 1976), p. 30.
4. Charles and Mary Lamb, *Tales from Shakespeare Designed for the Use of Young Persons* (2 vols., London: Thomas Hodgkins, 1807), vol. I, pp. 229–30.
5. Michael Cadnum, *In a Dark Wood* (London: Orchard Books, 1998), p. 140.
6. John Stephens and Robyn McCallum, *Retelling Stories, Framing Culture: Traditional Story and Metanarratives in Children's Literature* (New York: Garland Publishing, 1998).
7. Andrew Lang, *The Blue Fairy Book* (New York: Dover Publications, 1965), p. 99.
8. Kenneth Grahame, *The Wind in the Willows* (1908; London: Puffin, 1994), p. 136.
9. Michel Plessix, *The Wind in the Willows*, vol. III: *The Gates of Dawn*, trans. Joe Johnson (New York: NBM Publishing, 1999), p. 15.

10. Diana Wynne Jones, *Howl's Moving Castle* (London: Methuen, 1986), p. 1.
11. Geoffrey Wagner, *The Novel and the Cinema* (Rutherford, NJ: Fairleigh Dickinson University Press, 1975), p. 227.
12. Terry Pratchett, *The Amazing Maurice and his Educated Rodents* (London: Doubleday, 2001), pp. 87 and 182.
13. Pratchett, *Amazing Maurice*, pp. 69 and 17.

7

DEBORAH STEVENSON

Classics and canons

Most readers of American and British children's literature can easily offer examples of children's literature classics, readily agreeing that, say, Lewis Carroll's *Alice's Adventures in Wonderland* (1865) would belong in that category. As its front-line representatives, classics publicly define the genre – but how does the genre define its classics? In order to answer this question, one must explore the unique forces and processes that affect children's literature and its reception. Children's literature operates differently from adult literature, for the latter offers a consistency of creators and audience: an adult book is written by adults, read by adults, judged by adults and passed on to adults; the people in the position of gatekeepers, selecting and championing particular texts for admission to the canon and lionisation as classics, are themselves inarguably members of those texts' official and intended audiences. The forces behind the approval and canonisation of children's literature constitute a complex Venn diagram, with categories defined by profession (academic literary critic or hands-on practitioner in libraries or schools), fields of study (English department, education department or school of library science), professional status (professional user of children's literature or lay reader of books as parent or interested adult) and age (child or adult), all in dynamic relationship to one another, with categories sometimes overlapping, sometimes acting complementarily, sometimes operating antagonistically. The conscious if complicated canon selection of professional practitioners and academics is a world away from the popular anointing of classic texts; most people making popular judgments about children's literature – parents and other caring adults seeking to transmit an important literary experience to children – have little access to, and even less interest in, academic judgments of children's literature when it comes to choosing the works they believe to be the best.

Although children themselves are the ostensible audience for this literature, their position in this configuration is perhaps the most complicated of all. In name, the genre belongs to children, but in actual fact their direct influence is limited. They can have some effect on a text's status through purchasing, but they are likely to exercise their limited financial power on books that aren't otherwise available to them through adult-run institutions and adult-funded shopping; their word of mouth can contribute to the reading popularity of a title, but that influence is more notable in connection with otherwise obscure or adult-unfriendly texts (author Judy Blume owed her great popularity in the late twentieth century to child support more than to adult approval) than with the known quantity of a prospective classic. Young people's influence is heavily mediated and shaped by adults, as in the many book awards labelled 'children's choice' that almost invariably start the judging process with an adult-selected list of titles, from which the child judges then select a winner; even when young readers are given what looks like free choice, there is an adult control at an early level of selection, be it collection development, funding provision or publishing. This adult mediation tends to treat books and reading on the nutritional model, operating on the theory that children, left to their own devices, will tend to consume junk, but that tactful adult assistance will lead them to partake of equally enjoyable and much more healthful fodder. This mediation is justified by the conviction that books affect young readers, that children cannot always judge what is and isn't good for them, and that adults have not just a right, but a duty, to ensure children's lack of judgment does not result in harm. (This protective impulse is now literarily unique; we have lost previous eras' concern that poor-quality literature may harm adult readers and have concentrated all our efforts on uplifting child readers.) Yet children are still necessary to the literature, and competing adult claims of childish knowledge play a significant part in struggles for authority over the genre. Often, however, these children are theoretical, drawn from either adult ideals of childhood or memories of childhood. Ultimately, the literature's most powerful children are ex-children.

History of critical assessment

The tradition of adult critical interest in children's reading goes back several centuries, in logical concert with the production of materials for children to read. Even as early as Richard Steele's 1709 article in the *Tatler*, wherein his persona Mr Bickerstaff fondly recounts his young godson's literary commentary, we have an adult revelling in a child's pleasure reading.[1] For genuine reviews of children's books, however, we must wait for the nineteenth century and Sarah Trimmer, whose periodical the *Guardian of Education*, published in Britain from 1802 to 1806, offered the first regular reviews of children's literature. Its aim was to assist parents and teachers 'in their selection of safe and good' reading matter, since, as Trimmer put it, 'There is not a bad principle inimical to religion and virtue which can be named, that is not to be found in books for children.' Reviews carefully warned against books that might offer poor moral examples. Yet Trimmer herself had clearly been susceptible, as a child, to the charms of literature more geared to the pleasures of imagination than to the guidance of morals, and was initially unwilling to condemn such joys as *Mother Goose's Fairy Tales*, a collection still well established as canonical material; Trimmer had loved books with a sentiment that allowed her to term several 'the delight of [her] childish days'. Trimmer, in fact, obligingly plays out in her writing the forces that have influenced the genre of children's literature for centuries, and the popularity of her periodical (and the vigour of her readers' correspondence) offers a solid early indication that one didn't have to be a prominent professional to care strongly about what children would read and to believe firmly that it was worth identifying the books that were truly superior.[2]

Other writers soon picked up Trimmer's baton. *The Juvenile Review; or, Moral and Critical Observations on Children's Books* was published in London in 1817, and in America – even before the development of children's librarianship in the latter part of the nineteenth century, and its attendant assessment of children's books – children's literature was reviewed in numerous periodicals. Richard Darling has identified over thirty that regularly reviewed children's books, from broadly popular journals such as the *Nation* and *Atlantic Monthly* and literary periodicals such as the *Dial*, to educational journals such as the *New England Journal of Education*, industry magazines such as *Publisher's Weekly*, and children's periodicals themselves such as *Our Young Folks* and, best-known of them all, *St Nicholas*.[3] The twentieth century saw the further creation of review journals for the emerging field of librarianship, and the publication of children's books in ever-growing numbers in the USA and the UK; Trimmer, overwhelmed by the enormity of assessing the children's books in 1806, could hardly have borne the magnitude of the task that assessment was quickly to become.

Academics and canon creation

Despite the long history of interest in evaluation of children's literature, the academy of scholars came late to the genre. As a result, in the strict academic sense, the children's literature canon is a recent invention. The teaching of children's literature at university level is a practice that became established only in the twentieth century, and the English department only in the last quarter thereof; the dominant critical journals were all founded in the 1970s, decades after the establishment of book-review periodicals for practitioners rather than scholars. This growth of interest in literature departments, where earlier there had been essential silence on this genre, is key to the issue of canonicity. It is this field that has the most enduring efficient machinery for establishing an academic canon, and that consequently, of all the main academic disciplines involved with the study of children's literature, has been at the forefront of exploring its nature. In the struggle to establish children's literature as a scholarly field, children's literature studies turned to the traditional tools of legitimation and professionalisation, the creation of specialised critical journals, the production of critical anthologies, the generation of academic experts and the development of a rising profile within the literary community, all of which have resulted in an increasing investment in selectivity. As a result, there are increasing numbers of students in higher education learning about children's literature; if one might cynically define a canon as 'the books that you're told in school are important', an increasingly large number of people are now learning the children's literature canon.

Canon creation, however, is never a simple and uncontroversial matter. In children's literature, this drive towards canon creation came, ironically, just as English departments were reconsidering and dismantling canons, making children's literature an old-fashioned field of study even as it newly arrived; the Children's Literature Association's canon-declarative *Touchstones: Reflections on the Best in Children's Literature* (1985–9) appeared at a time when such 'great books' approaches were falling precipitately out of favour. There is also a quiet paradox, or at least a tension, between the tendency to exclude the literature of institutional education from children's literature, focusing instead on texts designed to be read for pleasure, and the desire to have those texts authoritatively judged not by the pleasure readers but by institutions of education. Even more than children's literature in the popular sphere, children's literature in the academy is an indirect literature, read by an audience explicitly excluded by the literature's own name. Library science and education classes tend to teach the literature in expectation that its students will use the works directly with children, returning the books to their official audience, but in literature departments the teaching continues the tradition of indirectness: students read the works as an end, as a way that they as adults can understand the genre, rather than as texts they will be bringing to children. Another growing movement since the 1980s, however, removes the child from even the theoretical picture in the teaching of young people's texts; some educators are including children's or young adult texts alongside adult texts in high school and university classes, subjecting all the texts to the same scholarly puzzling (and/or bored resentment) and treating the adult, rather than the child, as the intended reader.

The community of scholars with an investment in canon creation therefore expands, but at the same time it grows increasingly heterogeneous and increasingly varied in its requirements, making it less and less likely that one single canon will suffice to encapsulate significance for all comers. The traditional academic markers of canonicity have never really been disinterested roll-calls of the pantheon, uninflected judgments of significance, anyway; anthologies and syllabi develop out of a variety of needs, including taste, expediency and availability, either of books or of affordable reprint rights, and they are called upon to meet many different needs. The literature draws from several centuries and several countries (it is interesting that the 2005 *Norton Anthology of Children's Literature* carefully employs the plural in its subtitle, *The Traditions in English*), and it contains a multitude of subgenres, ranging from fantasy and historical fiction through non-fiction genres such as biography to the illustratively significant picture books. Often a text achieves significance within the scope of its subgenre and then acts as a delegate for its kind within the larger literature, so that a syllabus or anthology will include representative poetry, representative fantasy, representative history, not even claiming to include the best books of the genre as a whole.

It is interesting to see how some specific texts, each of which has embodied a fair degree of critical and/or popular success, fare in a quick look at current on-line syllabi. Virginia Euwer Wolff's *True Believer* (2001) is a critically acclaimed winner of the prestigious National Book Award, while Louis Sachar's *Holes* (1998) won both the National Book Award and the Newbery Medal (all in the USA); K. A. Applegate's Animorphs series (1997–2001) is a mass-market paperback fantasy series, wildly popular and profitable in recent years but dwindling rapidly in status since the conclusion of the series, while J. K. Rowling's *Harry Potter* novels (1997–2007) is a bestselling fantasy series whose popularity continues unabated. A limited Google internet search for these texts in university syllabi (in 2007, and predominantly American, but any Anglophone syllabus was counted) reveals some intriguing patterns. In a limited sampling, *True Believer* was featured in thirteen syllabi, roughly equally divided between Education, English, and Library rubrics, while *Holes* was featured in forty syllabi, twenty-one of which were English (it turned up, intriguingly, on Ecology, Theatre, and 'Corrections' or Criminal Justice syllabi as well). Animorphs was mentioned in six syllabi, in all cases as an example of a mass-market series assignment rather than as a specific assignment; Harry Potter appeared in sixteen syllabi, twelve of which were English literature (this number is deceptively low, since the high rate of hits on 'Harry Potter' meant that a considerably higher proportion of hits within the limits were false), as well as being the subject of two courses in their entirety. The mere fact that all of these texts turned up in syllabi is significant in its own right, indicating that critical acclaim and popular prominence have ensured that they are considered worthy of academic notice, but already some differences between the pairings are apparent. With only the single data set, it is impossible to rely on these figures as indications of future academic status, but the different fates are suggestive; despite similar award status, *Holes* and *True Believer* are faring quite differently in the classroom; despite both being the subject of popular frenzies, the Animorphs and the *Harry Potter* novels are hardly equally represented in the academy.

Popular audiences and classic creation

Yet children's literature, like other popular genres, can never be wholly assessed within the academy, and academic status means little to the popular audience (it is unlikely, for instance, that the news of Harry Potter's inclusion in syllabi has drawn a single new child reader to the books, outside the classroom). Since such audiences rarely feel like invested participants in disputes about the relative merits of *King Lear* and *Hamlet*, they are generally uninterested in challenging the academy's judgment on such questions. Children's literature, however, is a different matter, offering considerable ground for challenge to the notion of special academic authority. Children may have limited influence even in the popular sphere – indeed, it is the power vacuum left by the audience's weakness that enables the adult factions' claims of authority – but they are completely excluded from the academic sphere, an exclusion that often results in other audiences' privileging their viewpoints on the grounds that they are more informed by child response. Even practitioners have more impact on lay adult enthusiasts than do academics, with library associations offering the highest-profile recognition for texts in the form of awards such as the Newbery Medal in the United States and the Carnegie Medal in Great Britain.

By the genre's very nature, it should be accessible to and appreciable by non-professionals, and we all started out as the named audience for this literature, so we all have insiders' credentials; in fact, for many people, childhood is the time of their greatest literary involvement. As a consequence, popular adult audiences feel an ownership of this genre. Children's books are part of the family, not part of the academy; popular readership isn't seeking a canon of anthology inclusion but a collection of classics that are cherished legacies from previous generations and gifts of love to the next, a transmission that is the genesis of classic status. Such texts are still discriminatingly selected and celebrated – popular audiences merely assess based on different criteria from the academic world, and the popular sphere offers different indications of status. While the academic audience looks to scholarly anthologies such as the *Norton Anthology of Children's Literature* for a compilation of the important, popular audiences turn to books whose titles prominently feature the word 'treasury', whether it be in controversial conservative William Bennett's *The Children's Treasury of Virtues* (2000), which argues for its own criteria for classic children's literature, or in the venerable *World Treasury of Children's Literature* (1984) by Clifton Fadiman, an associate of Mortimer Adler, founder of the mid-century Great Books movement. Inclusion in such treasuries can certainly indicate popular regard and likely classic status; more significant indications include library circulation figures, sales numbers, the creation of multiple editions and reprintings (especially significant in regard to a text still in copyright, because of the greater financial investment on the part of the publisher). Sometimes generations do not so much interpret a work anew as celebrate it anew: sale value of memorabilia can indicate popular value, as can references in current popular culture. It has been a long time since Louisa May Alcott's *Little Women* (1868) was a cultural rite of passage for young female bookworms, but only a few years ago it played a key role, in a plotline that depended on the book's actual storyline, in an episode of the television series *Friends* (1994–2004). The internet again offers some informative indications: returning to our four sample texts, we find the following numbers in a series of Google searches, conducted in 2007, for author and title or title equivalent: Wolff's *True Believer* received 73,900 hits, Sachar's *Holes* 439,000; K. A. Applegate's Animorphs elicited 119,900 hits, while Rowling's Harry Potter produced 4,280,000 hits, leaving no doubt as to which texts elicit the most interest. On the Amazon.com website, all four texts are qualitatively equal, each receiving a rating of four and one-half stars, but *True Believer* had 49 reviews and *Holes* 3,161; the bestselling Animorphs title (no. 2) had 52 reviews, while *Harry Potter and the Sorcerer's Stone* had 5,241, demonstrating that interest levels may vary considerably even when judgments of quality are equivalent.

More traditional venues still play their parts in the delineation of classic status: while bookstores seem to have largely abandoned classics sections for adults, such sections remain staunchly entrenched in children's areas, conferring quasi-official status on the titles on their shelves. Such sections are fairly consistent in their type of offerings, whether the store in question is a chain store or an independent, and they are conservative and exclusive clubs: the cut-off publication date tends to be the mid twentieth century (later revisions and reillustrations of earlier publications are allowed, with the idea of a particular work rather than the specific edition or full version being the important consideration); there is no apparent concern for representation, with authors included almost uniformly white, and the non-Anglophone authors being old standards of the nineteenth century and earlier

(Hans Christian Andersen, the Brothers Grimm, Jules Verne, Johann Wyss). There is no informational non-fiction, poetry tends to be limited to A. A. Milne, and very few picture books creep in: Margery Williams' *The Velveteen Rabbit* (1922) or the facsimile reprint of the American edition of Helen Bannerman's *The Story of Little Black Sambo* (1899).

These titles weren't chosen for this section merely on those characteristics, however. Classic status accrues from writerly qualities as well, with the makers of such sections and the readers and buyers who haunt them evincing a firm belief that classic status must mean something about the text itself, not just its history. 'High literary quality' is a commonly proffered criterion for classic status – a classic has to be *classy*. Classics are books expected to give readers a real literary experience – books where the writing alone has the capacity to bring kids something important. (It is somewhat ironic, then, that the classic status accrues sufficiently to a book's title or idea to allow for abridgments and adaptations to count as classics as well as the original work.) The idea is that the classics are the best representatives of the genre of children's literature – books published to respect and acclaim (most of them were, indeed, well received and well reviewed on their first appearance) as well as popularity; subsequently, their fine qualities have been proven by these texts' continued prominence. Ultimately, they are classics because they are still here, just as much as they are still here because they are classics.

Their subject matter varies, and they are not relentlessly cheerful – there is certainly death and illness in *Little Women* and savagery in Robert Louis Stevenson's *Treasure Island* (1883) – but these darker notes tend to occur in the service of a glorious and fantastical adventure, to cast subtle shadows in a way younger readers might miss, or to operate as events in a larger story whose ultimate message is upbeat and hopeful. That ultimately positive nature is important to their inclusion in the classic family, because classics need to be loved, not just respected, and their textual story needs to fit into the popular audience's story of childhood. These are not, as a rule, books to help their readers deal with pressing contemporary issues; instead, these are books that could support Isaac Bashevis Singer's 1969 view of the child as 'a last refuge from a literature gone berserk and ready for suicide'.[4] Regardless of what these books may have brought in their day, today they are definitely agents of refuge and escape.

That difference between their day and this day is significant, since time clearly plays an important part in easing entry to classic status. The youngest books in these sections are nearly 50 years old, and most are closer to 100. Classic status seems to be subject to a mandatory waiting period, which helps soften the sharper edges of immediacy and grant a text a requisite patina. 'New classic' is, functionally speaking, oxymoronic; a classic has to be old.

The age of these books also means that they entered popular consciousness in a different era of book evaluation; these are all texts that were published and popular before the dismantling of 'Western Civilisation' courses and the challenging of the very notion of canonicity in the late twentieth century. The titles on the classic shelf are great books from a time when being a great book meant something important; the very collecting of these classics rejects the last quarter-century's challenges to such hierarchical privileging and proudly stands firm on the notion of concrete and non-relativist excellence.

This classics section is therefore more anachronistic than reflective of contemporary realities, possessed as it is of the very narrowness that elicited the anti-canonical ferment of the late twentieth century. Contemporary children's literature may not be a perfect distillation of global or even national cultural diversity (and it is worth remembering that notions of diversity are culturally and chronologically conditioned, so books of the past were diverse in their way and contemporary literature may appear shockingly uniform to future generations), but it is far from monolithic; no longer are its most celebrated authors or annual award winners a relentless parade of whiteness and straightness. Children's literature has become as consciously aware of inclusion as the children's classics shelves are, like the canons of the past, unconscious of their exclusivity. The boom in multicultural literature hasn't been reflected in the pantheon of classics, and the classics section may now be the whitest spot in the bookstore.

That restrictiveness could simply be an artefact of the age requirement for a classic. Classic titles come from an era when the genre's subjects and authors were rarely identifiable as anything other than white and heterosexual, so a contemporary re-examination of earlier texts finds few works that could be added to increase the diversity of the classics collection. Even for those rare exceptions, such as the works of prominent mid-century African-American authors such as Jesse Jackson or Lorenz Graham, it is unlikely that popular regard would manage to claim them as classics alongside *Little Women* and *Treasure Island*, since there is no mechanism for such popular recovery. If one were to name classic authors or books from the latter part of the twentieth century, however, few would exclude luminaries such as Virginia Hamilton, a gifted novelist and recipient of a MacArthur 'genius' grant along with too many awards to list, or John Steptoe, legendary prodigy whose *Stevie* (1969) was one of the first picture books to feature a child narrator speaking in everyday, colloquially informal African-American English. Even if the chronological threshold for classic status moves up as the years go by, however, it is possible that the extant classics are too definitive to allow for broader inclusion; that the very diversity of recent literature is enough to mark it as too recent, too contemporary, insufficiently long ago and far away to be considered for classic status. Classic-ness would seem to be recursive, defining itself by what's already there and thereby favouring not the groundbreaking but the traditional. Harry Potter's chance at classic status is thereby enhanced by the series' operating in a recognisable, beloved convention. A classic must look like a classic.

On the other hand, classics may demonstrate more linguistic diversity than the genre as a whole. While translated works such as *Heidi* (1881) and *The Swiss Family Robinson* (1812–13), by Swiss authors Johanna Spyri and Johann Wyss, respectively, are comfortably naturalised alongside born Anglophone classics, translated contemporary books face a rough ride in publishing or promotion, with Cornelia Funke's *The Thief Lord* (2002), originally written in German, a rare contemporary import in its achievement of genuine popularity in the USA and the UK. The genre is even farther from true multilingualism; even in the USA, bilingualism is largely limited to a handful of picture books, and only a few publishers regularly offer second-language publications for young people, most of them translations into Spanish rather than original non-Anglophone texts. Internet specialist publications such as the periodical *Críticas* (sister journal to professional publications *Library Journal* and *School Library Journal*) and distribution services such as Libros Sin Fronteras (now owned by major American distributor Baker and Taylor), are increasingly making available tools for disseminating such works, but the American classics are still largely an Anglophone phenomenon.

Unlike texts in the academic canon, a children's classic must also retain an association with children. This association can come from actual young readership, and there are certainly young readers fixed on the idea of reading classics; the cachet of reading certain books is not a phenomenon limited to adult books. Most children, however, are not as concerned with a text's classic status as their elders are; the test of living, trusted, peer readers or their own experience is far more important than the test of time. C. S. Lewis' *Chronicles of Narnia* (1950–6) continues to win numerous readers not merely because of its classic status but because it continues to please a large number of the young people who take the time to read it. This current generation of young people includes countless numbers of adults-to-be who will joyfully transmit those titles to a subsequent generation, supporting the retention of the Narnia books in the family of classics. However, a text can survive for some time on the classics shelf without a large child audience; *Little Women*, for instance, has a diminished readership these days and also, quite likely, a fairly high put-down percentage, a large number of readers who did not find the book rewarding enough to finish. More important than actual children is the *idea* of a child audience; as long as adults can remember themselves as children reading that title (or even intending to read that title), a classic has the children's imprimatur it needs for current status. The break in the chain comes when the young generation that eschewed a classic text grows up and passes on passing it on, leaving formerly popular favourites such as Thomas Bailey Aldrich's *The Story of a Bad Boy* (1870) or Mary Mapes Dodge's *Hans Brinker, or the Silver Skates* (1865) to turn into quaint relics, recognised vaguely if at all.

Texts can also have their status heightened or re-energised from external factors, accelerants that fuel the fire of their popularity. Such accelerants may be film versions, televisual incarnations, appearance on book-themed educational television programmes such as the venerable *Reading Rainbow*, line-extension merchandising in general, and the winning of well-known awards. (It is fascinating to contemplate what might happen should Oprah Winfrey turn to children's books in her book club, since an Oprah pick is not so much an accelerant as an immediate conflagration.) Accelerants can operate directly on the popular audience – individuals may as a consequence say 'Oh, now I really want to read that book' – or such phenomena can operate to enhance availability – an editor with a particular interest can deliberately choose to champion and reprint older texts (as Sharyn November does in her Firebird imprint at the Penguin publishing company), or a series imprimatur such as the *Reading Rainbow* logo can help keep titles in print. In Britain, the declaration by the bestselling contemporary children's author Jacqueline Wilson that Eve Garnett's once-lauded but now rather old-fashioned *The Family From One End Street* (1937) was one of her favourite books was enough to make Penguin rush it back into print as one of their Puffin Modern Classics. Customer reviews on Amazon.co.uk confirm that this is good business: 'I bought this book after hearing the author Jacqueline Wilson recommend it on T.V., up till then I'd never heard of it', writes 'A Customer', adding an emphatic 'Let me tell you I'm so glad that I did!'[5] Accelerants act as a text's unofficial public relations department.

Though such enhancements help keep a text alive, they aren't likely to pull a book from comparative obscurity into classic status; the movies, television series and pop-culture references to *Little Women* help it retain its status, but Dodie Smith's *The Hundred and One Dalmatians* (1956), a charming book inherently very suitable to classic status, wasn't suddenly catapulted into the canon as a consequence of being the source of two highly popular films, one of them a minor animated classic. Cross-media popularity increases chances of a title's availability – the films play a key role in keeping Smith's title in print – but it's the cinematic Dalmatian wagging the literary tail, with the books operating as a line extension for the movie, complete with covers taken from publicity stills that suggest that Smith's work is another novelisation of the film. Canonically, accelerants can only perpetuate an already burning fire – Harry Potter books were internationally famous even before the film series became monumentally successful – otherwise their own popularity will consume the very title that sparked them. This fate is particularly likely if, as with *One Hundred and One Dalmatians*, the accelerant is a film from the Disney studios; Disney's unstoppable combination of child-appealing storytelling and powerhouse marketing almost invariably results in its version of a text becoming the definitive one to its audiences.

It is tempting to try to reduce predictions of classic status to a formula: degree of initial critical regard plus degree of initial popularity times nature of contents times x generations of audience plus y accelerants equals likely classic status. Returning to the four sample texts, *True Believer* would seem to score poorly; despite critical acclaim, it never reached wide general popularity, it has no boosts from other media and its National Book Award hasn't been enough to keep its profile high; its verse-novel artistry and contemporary themes helped its critical reception but militate against its being taken to the loving bosom of the popular audience. *Holes* has a better chance; it was widely popular as well as critically regarded, and it was made into a modestly successful film; its quirky and slightly distorted reality gives it a fairy tale quality that may allow it to be embraced despite the serious elements of its story. On the two series, Animorphs generated few respectful reviews but tremendous popularity, including a spin-off television show; it lost considerable interest, however, upon the cessation of its publication, and its mass-market status makes its embrace unlikely. Harry Potter, on the other hand, has scored well in awards, reviews, popularity and film accelerants; if the sentimental canon continues to adopt members as it has in the past, Rowling's series is the likeliest not just of these texts, but of all contemporary texts, to achieve classic status.

Changing times

Even if such a formula could be created to explain the category's current inclusions, however, it may fail in predicting future additions. Since the sentimental canon's main tendencies are retrospective and static, change is not a common occurrence; nor does there seem to be much serious interest in an activist approach on the front lines or championing particular titles for broad acceptance as classics. (The recent changes on one bookstore's classic shelves were the inclusion of Robert McCloskey's *Homer Price* (1943) and Laura Ingalls Wilder's Little House series (1932–43), both of those well-loved and high-profile favourites.) Cultural transformation, however, comes not so much from individuals changing their ideas as from the changing of the cultural guard as generations that held particular ideas die off, retire, stop publishing, become technologically obsolescent, to be replaced by those with different approaches. So it will be with children's literature. There have been changes in the collection of classics, both deletions and additions, and the creation of an academic canon for children's literature is in itself a change. What the future seems likeliest to bring, however, is not future additions to the category of 'classic' but instead the creation of new categories; the changes in the way we interact with information and text will change the approach to the family of classics and to academic canons as well.

The number of children's books produced is substantial; while numbers vary depending on how measurements are taken (and few are exact), there are easily over 4,000 new trade books published for young people in the USA each year, and recent reports suggest British numbers may be even higher. The overwhelming number of children's texts leaves consumers of the literature burdened with what social theorist Barry Schwartz calls 'the paradox of choice', a situation where the multitude of options means more work for, possibly, no more reward on the part of the consumer.[6] The popularity of children's literature and the establishment of the internet as a mouthpiece as well as marketplace also means that there are more people publicly interacting with and commenting on the literature, more places to turn to for critical judgment.

Even in the old established reviewing journals for practitioners, pluralism has become the norm. Unsigned reviews, formerly the rule, are now a rarity in review periodicals, so individual critical voices are known; it is also unusual for a publication to have one sole vehicle for communicating with readers, with most journals possessing both websites and a number of specialised publications with original content. What is more, critical assessments are increasingly licensed into compilations and databases, so review consumers may encounter a journal's reviews on Amazon.com, in the Children's Literature Comprehensive Database, or in the electronic academic-journal service Project Muse in addition to the source journal. Awards too are increasingly pluralistic; the American Library Association, which bestows the most prestigious awards in American literature for young people, now gives awards not only for the best book, but for best book in various categories (picture book, informational book, the best African-American titles of several types, and the best Latino titles). Such recognition is, as always, a double-edged sword, bringing titles to prominence but enhancing the separatism of the literary strands and emphasising the marginalisation of those topics and subgenres not featured in any such awards. Yet increasingly such foci provide a useful entry point for audiences seeking excellence in a particular area of children's literature: for, to be blunt, the readers and parents of readers untempted by the consistent middle-class whiteness of the popular pantheon and who seek a different kind of prospective classic. At the same time, children's literature continues to broaden as an academic subject in fields such as cultural studies, area studies, sociology and history; if univocality of academic opinion ever existed, it is certainly gone now. Even syllabi are frequently turning to a more pluralistic approach, opting for a choose-your-own-title syllabus within each of several specified subgenres and emphasising the impact and significance of the genre rather than the importance of individual titles, a practice that militates against the creation or support of a canon.

This diversification is part of a larger cultural trend whose impact on books is still in its infancy. New technology for information ranging from the internet to the iPod are triumphs not only of breadth but of pluralism, diversification but on a global scale. As a consequence, specialisation can paradoxically occur in larger and more viable groups, or 'mega-niches', as Clay Shirky discusses in *Wired Magazine*; Chris Anderson writes of 'The Long Tail', the increasing viability of small-audience merchandise in a world where physical costs and limitations are eroding, and the consequent disappearance of truly common culture.[7] Specialised audiences are no longer the small groups of pre-internet days, since the ability to reach audiences globally and instantaneously means that a specialised niche that might formerly have included only a handful of people can contain millions of people. Issues of translation, of convention (both cultural and linguistic) and of marketing mean that children's literature currently still falters at true cultural internationalism, but it too is increasingly able to support what might be considered to be niche audiences because the global connections allow for broader knowledge and availability. One early demonstration of the global effect was the American release of the second Harry Potter title, *Harry Potter and the Chamber of Secrets* (1999), which lagged sufficiently behind the British publication for eager North American readers simply to place web orders in the UK and receive their copy prior to US publication. This trend further complicates the notion of literary authority; ratings of trust for reviewers on websites create and define authorities on the most specialised topics, and lists provided by such experts are gratefully received and referred to with respect.

Another change is the appearance of new literary categories that allow for the celebration of additional titles without requiring any change in the definition of a classic. We are seeing the development of the concept of 'modern classics', for instance, a term that appears in the title of two different reprint series (Oxford University Press and Puffin), which both feature a number of books written by still-living authors. Bookstores have prominent sections labelled 'award books', a category that centralises the location for celebrated but not-yet-ready-for-true-classic-status titles. Series books are subject to reconsideration as well (in fact, those very classics shelves are teeming with series, many of them mass-market); the visual cues differentiating mass-market series from respectable trade series are beginning to lose their reliable meaning, and the contemporary celebration of popular culture is beginning to allow less highbrow pleasures into the family of cherished literature. The Nancy Drew mystery series has re-emerged in a number of forms, for example, with retrospective catalogues offering a facsimile of her first adventure, *The Secret of the Old Clock* (1930), for sale alongside the nostalgic lures of Nut Goodies, old-fashioned candy and hot-dog roasting skewers. Nancy has her own titled section in some bookstores, with reprints of her 1970s classics (considered upstart additions in their day) right alongside the 1990s paperback series and the brand new adventures of eight-year-old Nancy. In the true tradition of the classics section, it is the idea rather than the edition that matters, with the various incarnations of Nancy all allomorphs of the Nancy Drew morpheme.

Ultimately, the future seems to promise a chorus of canons: old classics hanging on where they are still cherished, new family classics satisfying a wider variety of families – not all of them white or straight – and a variety of texts that reach the top of the standard for their particular section of the children's literature audience. Similarly, academic children's literature canons will move more towards a pluralistic approach to representation rather than identification of touchstone texts. It is a long way from Sarah Trimmer, but she would recognise the work of adults determinedly mixed-up in children's business and irretrievably entangled with children's literature.

NOTES

1. Richard Steele, *The Tatler*, 95 (15–17 November 1709) (2 vols., London: H. Hills, 1710), vol. I, p. 533.
2. Trimmer, *The Guardian of Education* (5 vols., London: J. Hatchard, 1802–6), vol. I (1802), pp. 65 and 62. See M. O. Grenby, '"A Conservative Woman Doing Radical Things": Sarah Trimmer and the Guardian of Education', in *Culturing the Child 1690–1914: Essays in Memory of Mitzi Myers*, ed. Donelle Ruwe (Lanham, MD: Scarecrow Press, 2005), pp. 137–61.
3. Richard L. Darling, *The Rise of Children's Book Reviewing in America, 1865–1881* (New York: Bowker, 1968), p. 19.
4. Isaac Bashevis Singer, 'I See the Child as a Last Refuge', *The New York Times Book Review*, Children's Book Section (9 November 1969), pp. 1 and 66, reprinted in Robert Bator, ed., *Signposts to Criticism of Children's Literature* (Chicago: American Library Association, 1983), p. 50.
5. On-line at www.amazon.co.uk (accessed 22 February 2008).

6. Barry Schwartz, *The Paradox of Choice: Why More Is Less* (New York: Ecco, 2004).
7. Clay Shirky, 'Tiny Slice, Big Market', *Wired* 14.11, on-line at www.wired.com/wired/archive/14.11/meganiche_pr.html (accessed 22 February 2008); Chris Anderson, *The Long Tail: Why the Future of Business Is Selling Less of More* (New York: Hyperion, 2006).

PART II

Audiences

8

LISSA PAUL

Learning to be literate

In all of children's literature, the character with the surest sense of the vital importance of being literate is the spider Charlotte from E. B. White's classic 1952 novel, *Charlotte's Web*. Charlotte knows, as does everyone else on the farm, that pigs like her friend Wilbur are slated from birth for violent, unnatural deaths. In order to save his life Charlotte must take heroic measures. Her plan of attack? A war of words.

In the context of the life-and-death seriousness of the situation, it may seem odd that the first words Charlotte chooses to write in her web, 'Some Pig', are colloquial, rural, grammatically dubious and puzzling. Yet the phrase invites speculation. After reading Charlotte's carefully woven sign, the likely wielders of the knife, the farmer Zuckerman and his henchman Lurvy, discuss their pig seriously. They try to figure out why Wilbur is not just any old pig. They wonder what makes him 'Some Pig'. That's what saves him. If, instead of 'Some Pig', Charlotte had written the clichéd commandment 'Thou Shalt Not Kill' into her web, would it have had the same effect? Not likely.

In using her words to save Wilbur from the Christmas slaughter, Charlotte participates in the historical tradition that equates reading with intellectual accomplishment and the ability to save a life. In early modern Britain, convicted felons sentenced to death by hanging could claim what was called 'benefit of the clergy'. If they could read 'the neck verse', the beginning of Psalm 51, they would be reprieved. They usually did not escape completely, but might be branded: 'M' for murder and 'T' for theft. Reading could not save them a second time. Though the sense of life itself being at stake in learning to read has long since receded, the legacy of literacy as fundamental to civility and humanity remains – despite even the disturbing twenty-first-century fashion for oppressive, large-scale, high-stakes literacy testing.

In order to tell the long and often twisted history of literacy education I take my direction from Charlotte's author, E. B. White. Besides being a writer of children's books, White (1899–1985) was a *New Yorker* essayist and a consummate prose stylist. In 1958, he also revised and rewrote a major guide to composition, William Strunk's *Elements of Style* (1918), in which he makes the case for the vital importance of good writing – and the dangers of the bad. 'Muddiness', he cautions, 'is not merely a disturber of prose, it is also a destroyer of life, of hope'. White was a defender of good style and good prose. Above all, as he emphatically put it, he championed 'Clarity. Clarity. Clarity.'[1]

The instructional materials and methods used in literacy education over the centuries range from the peaks of clarity to the troughs of muddiness, from the miracle of the invention of the phonetic alphabet to the murky depths of literacy test scores. The cultural emphasis has careened between religious and secular; between pretty, engaging texts for the elite, and banal texts for the masses; between individualised, loving instruction by caring, often maternal, tutors, and factory-model instruction driven by cost-efficient bureaucrats. Littering the rocky road to literacy education are piles of discarded teaching materials – which reveal that even the most disarmingly simple texts reflect changing socio-economic priorities and that learning to read is as much of an ideological process as a means of individuation and personal growth. Over time, the value of being literate has decreased from being important enough to save a life to being merely another bean to be counted by bean-counting statisticians.

At the heart of this chapter is the phonetic alphabet. Though I do not travel from A to Z, from the beginning to the end of literacy education, my chapter starts with – and is structured by – the alphabet.

A is for Alphabet

The Christmas Alphabet (1994) by paper engineering artist Robert Sabuda, is a pop-up book. Each letter is printed neatly in a corner of a piece of heavy coloured paper, folded like a Christmas card, to conceal the predominantly white pop-up inside. The blank cover of each card turns the letter on its face into a potential present, a puzzle for readers who instantly become participants in a 'guess-the-Christmas-image' game. What does A stand for? 'Apple' is not Christmasy enough. A pop-up 'Angel' flies whitely out of the card. 'Tree' is not, as one might expect, under T, but under E for 'Evergreen'. And P is 'Poinsettia', with 'Presents' popping up under G (for 'Gifts') and U (for 'Unwrap'). L, fittingly, is a 'Letter' to Santa.[2] *The Christmas Alphabet* is a perfect modern example of the way letters, sounds and images transform magically into symphonies of cultural associations. The process is not as transparent as it looks. Every time we say that 'A' is 'for' something, we attribute to the letter a meaning beyond a phonetic sound. Each letter stands metonymically for a word and when the word is associated with an image, a little cultural narrative is created, saturating the lessons on learning to read words with lessons on learning to read culture.

Everyone knows that learning to be literate begins with ABCs. The phrase itself often stands for the beginning of a task. Yet the sheer elegant brilliance of conveying any word by putting together the appropriate combination of just twenty-six letters is so normal, we tend to forget how deeply that invention changed human thought. The Sumerians are credited with the oldest writing systems, dating from around 3500 BCE. These were ideographs, based on the principle that a sign represented an idea. Chinese writing systems still work that way: individual symbols often representing whole words. The Egyptians, beginning around 3000 BCE, used a mix of hieroglyphs and syllabic signs. The first Hebrew alphabet, developed around 1700 BCE, had signs only for consonants, so the Greeks, by including vowels, developed the first completely phonetic alphabet, sometimes called the first technology. With the phonetic alphabet was born the possibility of keeping track of spoken words and so, ultimately, the record keeping, classification systems, abstractions and law-making principles that became the foundations for civilised societies – which depend, of course, on laws, accounting and abstract codes of behaviour. Literacy instruction, however, only became a cultural imperative when, in Judeo-Christian and Islamic traditions, it was linked to the words in holy books – words that outlined the group's defining beliefs and behaviours. The alphabet made manifest the words of God.

R is for Religion

Before the invention of the printing press in the middle of the fifteenth century, the words attributed to God had to be laboriously hand-written. The first book printed with movable type, tellingly, was a bible printed in Germany by Gutenberg. Once multiple copies of a text could be quickly reproduced mechanically, profound changes to religion became inevitable.

But the new mechanical printing press soon revealed itself able to do more than spread the word of God. Secular texts started to appear: ballads, gossipy broadsheets and political pamphlets. As the sheer volume of printed material started silting up the world in the fifteenth and sixteenth centuries, the cultural landscape changed. The printed text became a fixture of workaday life. There was a change in scale too. The books that had been hand-copied in medieval scriptoria were large, heavy tomes, meant to be read on a table or lectern. The reader was required to come to the book. Because the mechanical press could produce smaller, lighter books more efficiently than scribes, the character of texts in the world changed. Instead of going to books, people could take books with them. Like the internet today, the technology did more than just

provide a new medium with which to convey the same message. To adapt
Marshall McLuhan's famous 1964 dictum, the new medium enabled new
messages. With the spread of printed texts came the spread of literacy – and
the need for effective methods for teaching people to read. Once the two
Rs – Reading and Religion – were linked, the need for pedagogical methods
and materials to teach reading accelerated, particularly in Jewish, Islamic
and, later, Christian cultures. But because mass literacy instruction in English
is so entwined with Protestantism that is where the story of 'R for Religion'
begins.

For children in late medieval England, learning to read meant learning to
read the bible. The first forms of programmed literacy instruction (hornbooks
and primers) directly linked reading with religion by printing the sign of the
cross before the letter A. The alphabet itself became known as the 'criss-cross
row' or the 'Christ-cross-row', with the cross becoming something of a copyright sign, formally linking the graphemic representation of word sounds with
the idea of a holy voice and sacred authorship. For many, learning to read
became synonymous with learning to be a Christian.

As anyone who has attempted to learn a list by heart knows, brute-force
repetition is not a particularly enticing, or effective, technique. Yet that was,
as John Locke says in *Some Thoughts Concerning Education* (1693), the
'ordinary Road' to literacy education: a straight linear sequence 'of the Horn-
Book, Primer, Psalter, Testament, and Bible'. As a result, Locke deadpans, it
was 'usually long before learners found any use or pleasure in reading'.[3]
'Pleasurable' might not seem a particularly apt way to describe the contents
of the Puritan *New England Primer* (1690?), but the book was a significant
marker in the history of literacy education because it deliberately engaged
the attention of children by using pictures and rhymes as *aides-mémoire*.
The rhyming couplet 'In Adam's Fall, / We Sinned All' made the connection
explicit between the story of Adam and Eve eating from the Tree of Knowledge
and learning the alphabet. Although the pedagogical principle of enticing
children into reading with pictures was not new – Johann Amos Comenius
used it to teach Latin in his 1658 *Orbis sensualium pictus* – the widespread
adoption of the *New England Primer* in colonial America meant that its
illustrated rhyming alphabet became standard pedagogical practice, though
still associated with sober Christian obedience.

Islam and Judaism offer other instructive takes on induction into literacy.
In Islam, the complete memorisation of all the verses in the Qur'an is regarded
as an act of great spiritual significance, a sign of full inclusion into Islam, a rite
of passage and a cause for celebration – often with kheer (sweet rice pudding)
and baklava (pastry with nuts and honey). The rationale is the wish to ensure
that the texts survive – even if the material books that contained the texts

don't. The Qur'an lives as long as there are people who hold its words in their memories.

In Judaism children are also 'admitted into the communal memory by way of books', says Alberto Manguel, and their entrance sweetly celebrated. He describes a medieval initiation rite in which eating letters, eating words, becomes a symbolic entry into Jewish life: a boy was wrapped in a prayer shawl and carried by his father to the teacher who then sat the boy on his lap and gave him a slate on which was written 'the Hebrew alphabet, a passage from the Scriptures and the words "May the Torah be your occupation"'. The teacher read the words, the child repeated them, then 'the slate was covered with honey and the child licked it, thereby bodily assimilating the holy words'.[4]

That sense of the embodied pleasure in learning to read English occurs too, but not until a little later, as an alternative to the ordinary scriptural road. Locke suggested imaginative pleasures (Aesop's fables) and gambling pleasures (dice with letters pasted on each face), but by the second half of the eighteenth century books had appeared that, if not honey-coated, were at least yummier than previous primers. In *The History of Little Goody Two-Shoes* (1765), Goody teaches children to read by pulling letters made of wood out of her basket: 'plum-pudding' is one of the words. Giles Gingerbread, another character from the same period, is taught to read by his father 'who pulled out of his pocket an alphabet which he made out of gingerbread as he was a gingerbread maker'.[5]

C is for Communities

The idea of taking pleasure from a text is familiar to readers of Roland Barthes's *The Pleasure of the Text* (1973). He celebrates the bliss (*jouissance*) of certain kinds of reading. People who grow up to the thrill of being literate understand the pleasure. As a young child in a book-loving family, I remember learning to read *The Cat in the Hat* by Dr Seuss while lying on the carpet in our living room under a framed poster by Arthur Szyk that recalled an illuminated manuscript: 'Books shall be thy companions; book cases and shelves, thy pleasure-nooks and gardens' (fig. 12). The passage is by the twelfth-century Jewish philosopher, doctor and translator, Judah ibn Tibbon, and the words are in English, Hebrew and Yiddish. Even as a young child I recognised that the figures in the poster were oblivious to everything outside their reading. I understood, though could not have expressed it, that reading rewarded concentration. Yet the recognition that some texts reward attention while others do not is a rarely discussed feature in debates about the best methods of induction into a literate community.

Figure 12. Arthur Szyk, poster for Jewish Book Month.

In a 1973 essay, Leonard Mendelsohn, English professor and teacher at a Montreal rabbinical college, recounts a lovely story about asking his own six-year-old son to translate from Hebrew to English, extemporaneously, a passage from Genesis for the benefit of a visitor. The child reads the passage and provides a fluent translation – at which point the visitor asks if the boy had perhaps been 'stealing an occasional glance at the English' in the bilingual edition that unintentionally had been used. Mendelsohn is embarrassed and asks his son to read the English. The boy 'stumbled pathetically over the phonics, and with a grimace exclaimed, "I can't."'.[6] Although Mendelsohn's little story about the trials and tribulations of translation is sad, the consequences are relatively insignificant. Other stories about the tribulations of translation do not end so happily. A tragic feature of the colonisation of Africa, the Americas, Asia and Australasia centres on the ways Europeans deliberately imposed foreign language and culture on indigenous peoples. In *Unsettling Narratives*, Australian critic Clare Bradford explains that 'relations of colonial power were constructed through language'. 'Colonizers', she explains, imposed 'Old World' names on new landscapes, used language to create zones where none had existed, and used the languages of anthropology and ethnography 'to objectify and classify colonized peoples'.[7]

M is for Mothers and Mentorias

Typically, the journey to literacy in Western culture moves away from the intimacy of a loving, maternal, domestic space into the cold, communal, patriarchal space of school. An emphasis on maternal pedagogical instruction briefly disrupted this general pattern in the later eighteenth century. Mitzi Myers explains that Georgian women writers 'fished in a common pool of educational ideas … reading motherhood as social opportunity and valorizing heroines as rational educators'.[8] Lady Ellenor Fenn, for example, in her cunningly titled *Cobwebs to Catch Flies: Dialogues in Short Sentences* (1783), recognises the value of enticement and entrapment in winning willing converts to literature. Charlotte the spider used exactly the same tactic to engage Zuckerman and Lurvy in their life-saving conversation about Wilbur. The first commercial primers for children were by women for women teaching children in their care to read. Most famous was Anna Laetitia Barbauld's *Lessons for Children* (1778–9) which became the model for the published books of instruction that followed. Although books for children had been sized for small hands since the mid eighteenth century, Barbauld is credited with insisting on wide margins and big, clear print. Her books for mothers teaching children to read focus on pleasure, conversation and the happy acquisition of knowledge for living in the world. The very first lesson begins with an invitation to the child

Charles 'to sit in mamma's lap'. 'Now read your book', she continues. Though Barbauld moves in the traditional way from letters to syllables to words, she invites Charles to see these lessons as stepping stones into the world:

> Once papa could not read, nor tell his letters.
> If you learn a little every day you will soon know a great deal.
> Mamma, shall I ever have learned all that there is to be learned?
> No, never, if you were to live longer than the oldest man, but you may learn something every day.[9]

The lesson is cosy, inviting, yet extends the idea that reading is not just for little children, but directly linked to a grown-up life. The text, composed in the cadences of everyday speech, holds out the bright future of a lifetime of pleasurable reading. The same sentiments occur repeatedly in the texts by women of the late eighteenth and early nineteenth centuries. Surviving copies of their educational books often provide evidence that teaching children to read was private and personal even if it was conducted using commercially produced texts published in bulk. Some copies show alterations designed for a particular child. Sometimes there are tender inscriptions bridging the gap between a generic commercial publication and a private, domestic gift. Some 'mentorias' certainly manufactured their own teaching aids, but once a child had learned to read there would have been little reason to keep the materials. That is why the survival of the little handmade alphabet cards, mobiles and story cards constructed by Jane Johnson (1708–59) for her own children is so rare and astonishing.[10]

Although there are relatively few extant examples of the handmade texts that linked maternal teachers and their pupils, there are some records of the pedagogical principles that informed them. One famous eighteenth-century political radical, Mary Wollstonecraft, was deeply committed to the advancement of education. Besides her political tracts and reviews, Wollstonecraft wrote fiction for children, including *Original Stories from Real Life* (1788). Of her 'Lessons', intended for children just learning to read, only a few survive, for Wollstonecraft died before they could be completed. They still ring with the quick spirit of lively conversation between a mother and toddler. In the fourth lesson, for example, Wollstonecraft writes: 'Drink milk, if you are dry. Play on the floor with the ball. Do not touch the ink; you will black your hands.'[11] Even in this brief text, refreshment (drink milk), play (with a ball) and literacy (the reference to the ink) are intimately entwined in an inspired flash of what appears ordinary domestic conversation.

But Wollstonecraft's mode of literacy instruction did not become the dominant one. As the necessity of universal literacy became increasingly important through the nineteenth century, the emphasis in reading instruction became more narrowly focused on mechanics, especially when teaching lower-class children. Generally, well into the nineteenth century, reading instruction meant proceeding from letters to syllables to words (conventionally called 'phonics' instruction, though more precisely defining the links between the graphemic symbols, the letters, and the phonemic sounds). There were, however, also attempts at instructional methods favouring an introduction to reading via a limited vocabulary of sight words, what we might call the 'look–say' method. In support of that method was 'Mrs Felix Summerly', a pseudonym for Marian Fairman Cole, wife of Henry Cole, a prominent Victorian advocate for a new and delicate grace in the graphic design of children's books. Mrs Summerly's *Mother's Primer* (1844) is a beautiful example. It is printed in blue, red and ochre. In the preface, the author explains that traditional methods of reading instruction were often 'accomplished at the cost of many tears and much grief to the poor child' who was 'scolded for not knowing that the sounds of letters are no guide to the sounds of the words'. Mrs Summerly suggests an alternative:

> My experience with children is that learning to read may be a pleasant instead of a painful task. The child who is made first to learn its alphabet, and then to spell over syllables such as ba, be, bo, &c. often gets a distaste for learning to read, before any reading in fact has been begun. It has appeared to me best to begin reading at once with short easy sentences, even before learning the alphabet perfectly. The child must repeat the words after you, pointing to each one as it is said. Then he may read the words in irregular order: he will soon know them at sight, and will recognize them in other reading lessons.[12]

Even though the sentences are short in *The Mother's Primer*, the rhythms work and the text makes sense. One early lesson, for example, is 'To bed I go. / To my bed I do not go', a perfect glyph on a child's resistance to the tyranny of bedtime.

F is for Factory

Through the nineteenth century, class distinctions in literacy education became more pronounced. The cosy, individualised reading instruction that Anna Barbauld designed for well-loved, financially advantaged children existed in contrast to the growing demand for utilitarian materials that could be used to teach poor children to read, cheaply and quickly.

If Charlotte from *Charlotte's Web* has her antecedents in Lady Fenn's 1783 *Cobwebs to Catch Flies*, then late-twentieth-century developments such as DISTAR (Direct Instructional System for Teaching and Remediation) and DIBELS (Dynamic Indicators for Basic Early Literacy Skills) have their antecedents in Joseph Lancaster's 1803 *Improvements in Education as It Respects the Industrious Classes of the Community*, a factory-model system based on instant order and obedience. Children respond, in unison, to direct instructions:

> A number of commands, trifling in appearance, but conducive to good order, are given by the monitors. When a new scholar is first admitted, he is pleased with the uniformity, novelty and simplicity of the motions made by the class he is in. Under the influence of this pleasure he readily obeys, the same as the other boys do.

Lancaster offers minutely detailed accounts for teaching each step of reading, writing and arithmetic, with a teacher signalling a command and monitors enforcing its execution. The beauty of the method, as Lancaster explains, is that 'if seven hundred boys were all in one room, as one class, learning the same thing, they could all write and spell by this method, at the dictation of one monitor':

> The commands that a monitor usually gives to his class, are of a simple nature: as, to go in or out of their seats: 'In'–'Out.' The whole class do this at one motion – they learn to front, or go to the right or left, either single or double. They 'show slates', at the word of command; take them up, or lay them gently down on the desk, in the same manner.

Lancaster's factory model was admirably cost-efficient, and, because he had to do more with less, he developed inspired pedagogical practices. Rather than insist that children purchase expensive books, pens and ink – which had to be replaced when used up – Lancaster focused on renewable materials. Beginners learned to write their letters in small sandboxes set at a child's table height. After each attempt at writing a letter with a pointed stick, the sand was smoothed over. As the children progressed in the Lancastrian system, they wrote with soft slate pencils on the hard sheets of slate – wiping the slate clean at the end of each exercise. Lancaster also developed a cheap alternative to the one-book-per-child model of reading instruction. By printing each leaf of a book at three times its normal size and suspending it from string or a nail on the wall, groups of children could move around the room reciting the lessons as they went from sheet to sheet. That way, Lancaster explains, '*two hundred boys* may all repeat their lessons from *one* card, in the space of *three hours*'.[13]

Despite Lancaster's pedagogical creativity, his instructional techniques look and sound eerily similar to the DISTAR method, developed by Siegfried Engelmann in the 1960s. The Direct Instruction website offers a series of training demonstration films. Under the 'Mastery of Reading' title is a model which, like the Lancastrian method, involves a series of oral and visual cues given by a teacher, to which children respond in unison. A teacher holds a big book in her hand, raises her free hand in a fist, and issues the verbal cue, 'Get ready.' Then she points to a letter, M for example, and the children make the sound – 'mmm' – holding it for at least two seconds. In the American film clips, the teachers and the children are predominantly African-American or Hispanic.[14] The lesson sounds almost identical to one Lancaster described in 1805:

> They are required to read every word slowly and deliberately, pausing between each. They read long words in the same manner, only by syllables; thus in reading the word, Composition, they would not read it at once, but by syllables: thus, Com-po-si-tion; making a pause at every syllable.[15]

The tediousness – and the tyranny – of the Lancastrian process persists. In 'Slow Reader', from Allan Ahlberg's 1983 poetry collection *Please Mrs Butler*, this kind of instructional oppression is poignantly manifest:

> I-am-in-the-slow
> read-ers-group-that-is
> all-I-am-in-I
> hate-it.[16]

As literacy instruction increasingly focused on how to teach rather than what to teach or why, it became disconnected from anything important – such as saving a life or being inducted into a cultural community. As the mass-market factory model came to dominate, literacy instruction increasingly narrowed into regimented, tyrannical modes.

T is for Textbook and Test

The search for the very best methodology for literacy instruction contributed to the rise of an entire industry. The story of American educational publishing makes the general pattern clear. The *New England Primer* probably stands as the first bestselling textbook, although it was about teaching religion as much as reading. The pedagogical emphasis changed from religious to political with Noah Webster's eighteenth-century 'blue-back speller', as the 1829 edition was called (the original version was published in 1783 as the first part of *A Grammatical Institute of the English Language*). Webster believed that his instructional textbooks would serve to galvanise and unify Americans, 'to implant, in the minds of the American youth, the principles of virtue and liberty'.[17] In the nineteenth century, the Eclectic Readers created by William Holmes McGuffey (first published in 1836) marked the change from 'speller' to 'reader' as the term used to identify an introductory textbook of literacy instruction. The McGuffey Readers also gave voice to American culture, as they featured the developing genre of American poetry. Henry Wadsworth Longfellow's *Hiawatha*, for example, appeared in McGuffey's sixth Reader and was recited by generations of school-children across the country. By the 1930s, however, an increasingly industrialised approach was being used and the Elson-Gray Dick and Jane readers, with their controlled vocabulary lists and look–say methods of instruction, came to dominate literacy instruction.

By the late 1950s a backlash against the look–say model was in full swing. In *Why Johnny Can't Read?* (1955), Rudolf Flesch produced a scathing, influential critique on the use of a sight vocabulary to teach reading. His central point is that the flexible technology of the phonetic alphabet provides complete access to a literate community – while static words do not. According to Flesch, every 'Johnny' force-fed on basal readers (that is to say, this kind of reading textbooks series) was doomed:

> He gets those series of horrible, stupid, emasculated, pointless, tasteless little readers, the stuff and guff about Dick and Jane or Alice and Jerry visiting the farm and having birthday parties and seeing animals in the zoo and going through dozens and dozens of totally unexciting middle-class, middle-income, middle-I.Q. children's activities that offer opportunities for reading 'Look, look' or 'Yes, yes' or 'Come, come' or 'See the funny, funny animal'.

Besides being disgusted with the prose, Flesch is also disgusted with the profit motive fuelling the production and adoption of commercial reading programmes. 'There are', he says with despair, 'millions of dollars of profit in these little books'.[18] Fifty years later, billions of dollars are now at stake – as the George W. Bush administration's 'Read First' and 'No Child Left Behind' initiatives made abundantly clear.

The spectre of Flesch's barely reading Johnny still haunts us – though the methodology battles have not changed much. In the 1960s and 1970s they see-sawed between look–say and phonics, and in the 1970s and 1980s between phonics and whole language. The key point here is that the public discussions rarely addressed the idea of matching methodology to child – as advocated by the maternal pedagogues at the end of the eighteenth century. The twentieth century saw competition for a single 'best' instructional methodology. Lost from view were the reasons for reading: the religious reasons of the seventeenth-century *New England Primer*, the political reasons of Webster's eighteenth-century speller, and the cultural reasons of the nineteenth-century McGuffey Reader. Perhaps as a response to the loss of reasons for learning to read, British author Pat Hutchins composed *The Tale of Thomas Mead* (1980) about a boy who refuses to learn to read. 'Why should I?' he keeps asking, intelligently. Hutchins demonstrates the dangers of illiteracy. Thomas ignores the warning about workmen on ladders and ends up with paint spilled on his head. He pushes the pull door and knocks people over, then enters the women's washroom instead of the men's. He is eventually arrested for jaywalking and thrown into prison where:

> His cellmates thought it was a crime
> that Thomas Mead was doing time,
> and all because he couldn't read.
> 'Please help me to!' cried Thomas Mead.
> They taught him words he ought to know
> Like UP and DOWN and STOP and GO,
> IN and OUT, EMPTY, FULL,
> EXIT, ENTRANCE, PUSH and PULL,
> and BATHROOM, LADIES, GENTLEMEN,
> and DANGER, WET PAINT, WALK, DON'T RUN
> and then they said they'd better get
> him started on the alphabet.[19]

Hutchins plays the look–say / phonemic awareness debate diplomatically, by engaging both sides.

Battles about reading methodologies, however, pale in comparison to battles about reading assessment. In the late twentieth and early twenty-first centuries, across the Western world, the emphasis on a 'best' method has been replaced by a focus on keeping score. The medium has shifted from books of reading instruction to instruments of assessment – otherwise known as 'tests'. These testing regimes, often mandated by local or national governments, are fundamentally driven by a need to produce high literacy scores, and are the result of a perceived need for data which can be compared across political and geographical boundaries. The tests, generally, are designed to examine a child's understanding of narrowly defined rules of literacy with little regard for literacy's chief benefits and purposes (fostering cultural, religious or political awareness – as well as developing facility with language).[20] And because entire testing edifices have been built only on rigidly constricted scoring rubrics, the prose to which school-children might be exposed has too often descended from the heights of Charlotte's clarity into the muddy troughs of assessment.

In opposition to the recent fixation with testing and ranking of literacy scores are the findings of a team of American researchers who studied the induction into literacy of eighty children over a two-year period in 1985. Their findings emphasised the relationship between reading and interpretation. In stark contrast to the tightly controlled ranking of literacy skills in large-scale assessment exercises, their longitudinal studies demonstrated that learning to read is not so much about skill as about interpretation and knowledge.[21]

Despite my attention to methodology in this chapter, it would be wrong to conclude without attention to the literature which inducts children into a literate community. For children learning to read in the middle of the twentieth century, Dr Seuss, a pseudonym for Theodore Geisel, was a kind of magician, a saviour from the tyranny of basal readers, a writer able to negotiate the precarious balance between reading instruction and reading pleasure. The Cat in the Hat may well subtly make that point himself when he says in his eponymous book:

> I can hold up the cup
> And the milk and the cake!
> I can hold up these books! And the fish on a rake![22]

Other examples of compelling inductions into a literate community include Allan Ahlberg and Colin McNaughton's Red Nose Readers (from 1985), Arnold Lobel's Frog and Toad stories (from 1970) and Brian Wildsmith's Cat on the Mat books (from 1982). A final example of the kind of book that begins with the assumption of the intelligence of children and their desire to learn, and is engaging to even the newest of young readers, is Mommy? (2006), drawn by Maurice Sendak around a scenario by Arthur Yorinks, and with paper engineering by Matthew Reinhart. The book has only two words and two punctuation marks: 'Mommy?' and 'Baby!' Sendak's round, sleep-suited baby looks for his Mommy in a haunted house of pop-up monsters: 'Mommy?' he asks on each page, as he searches for her. At each page-turn, a monster pops up to threaten him. And each time, the baby provides the consolation – popping a soother into a vampire's mouth, pulling a painful bolt out of Frankenstein's neck, unwrapping bandages from a mummy – until he is reunited with his bride-of-Frankenstein Mommy – who smiles happily as she reaches to her 'Baby!' In Sendak's story, the 'Baby' is a competent person, able to assess and resolve tricky situations. The child reader is invited into the story, becoming a participant, a member of a network of readers who belong to a literate community. If there is any hope for a literate future, it is found with the authors who care about clarity and communicating something that new readers want to know. Texts in a large-scale assessment exercise have little hope of doing that.

The last words in this chapter go to Ted Hughes. In his introduction to Poetry in the Making, a book about reading and writing poetry for school-children, Hughes explains that 'All falsities in writing – and the consequent dry-rot that spreads into the whole fabric – come from the notion that there is a stylistic ideal which exists in the abstract.' Teachers, he explains, 'should have nothing to do with that'. Instead, he says, their 'words should not be "How to write" but "How to try to say what you really mean" which is part of the search for self-knowledge and perhaps, in one form or another, grace'.[23] Unlike the advocates of assessment tests, Ted Hughes, E. B. White, Charlotte and the felons who were spared because they could read the 'neck verse' all aspire to clarity, and to grace.

NOTES

1. William Strunk, *The Elements of Style with Revisions, An Introduction and a Chapter on Writing by E. B. White*, 3rd edn (New York: Macmillan, 1972), p. 79.
2. Robert Sabuda, *The Christmas Alphabet* (New York: Orchard Books, 1994).
3. John Locke, *Some Thoughts Concerning Education*, ed. John W. Yolton and Jean S. Yolton (Oxford: Clarendon Press, 1989), p. 213.
4. Alberto Manguel, *A History of Reading* (Toronto: Alfred Knopf, 1996), p. 71.
5. *The History of Little Goody Two-Shoes*, a facsimile reproduction of the 1766 edition (Tokyo: Holp Shuppan, 1981), and *The History of Giles Gingerbread: A Little Boy Who Lived Upon Learning* (York: Kendrew, 1820), p. 19.
6. Leonard R. Mendelsohn, 'Sophisticated Reading for Children: The Experience of the Classical Jewish Academy', *Children's Literature*, 2 (1973), 35–9 (p. 37).
7. Clare Bradford, *Unsettling Narratives: Postcolonial Readings of Children's Literature* (Waterloo, ON: Wilfred Laurier University Press, 2007), p. 19.
8. Mitzi Myers, 'Impeccable Governesses, Rational Dames, and Moral Mothers: Mary Wollstonecraft and the Female Traditions in Georgian Children's Books', *Children's Literature*, 14 (1986), 31–59 (p. 34). Myers deployed the term 'mentoria' to refer to these 'rational dames', playing on Ann Murry's book *Mentoria: or The Young Ladies Instructor* (1782).
9. Anna Laetitia Barbauld, *Lessons for Children* (London: Baldwin, Cradock *et al.*, 1834), pp. 3–4. This passage was first introduced in the 1808 edition.
10. See Evelyn Arizpe and Morag Styles, with Shirley Brice Heath, *Reading Lessons from the Eighteenth Century: Mothers, Children and Texts* (Lichfield: Pied Piper, 2006).
11. Mary Wollstonecraft, 'Lessons', in *The Works of Mary Wollstonecraft*, ed. Janet Todd and Marilyn Butler (7 vols., London: Pickering, 1989), vol. IV, p. 469.
12. Mrs Felix Summerly, *The Mother's Primer: A Little Child's First Steps in Many Ways* (London: Longman, Brown, Green and Longmans, 1844), p. 4.
13. Joseph Lancaster, *Improvements in Education as it Respects the Industrious Classes of the Community*, 3rd edn (1805; rpt with an introduction by Francesco Cordasco, Clifton: Augustus M. Kelley, 1973), pp. 108–9.
14. Association for Direct Instruction website, 'Tips on Signalling': http://adihome. org/index.php?option=com_content&task=view&id=19&Itemid=40 (accessed 21 March 2008).
15. Lancaster, *Improvements in Education*, p. 21.
16. Allan Ahlberg, *Please Mrs Butler* (London: Puffin, 1983), p. 13.
17. Quoted in E. Jennifer Monaghan, *A Common Heritage: Noah Webster's Blue-Back Speller* (Hamden, CN: Archon Books, 1983), p. 13.
18. Rudolf Flesch, *Why Johnny Can't Read?* (New York: Harper and Row, 1955), pp. 6–7.
19. Pat Hutchins, *The Tale of Thomas Mead* (New York: Greenwillow, 1980), pp. 6–7.

20. In Ontario, Canada, for example, several school districts mandated the use of 'Comprehension, Attitudes, Strategies and Interests' (CASI) packages: reading booklets, test booklets, a teacher guide and anchor booklet (containing grading rubrics). In the tests, children are scored on a 1–4 scale on several categories, including reasoning, communication, organisation of ideas, and application of language conventions. The texts on which literacy skills are tested are distinguished by their banality.

21. Edward Chittenden and Terry Salinger with Anne M. Bussis, *Inquiry into Meaning: An Investigation of Learning to Read*, revised edn (New York: Teacher's College Press, 2001), p. 38.

22. Dr Seuss, *The Cat in the Hat* (New York: Random House, 1957), p. 18.

23. Ted Hughes, *Poetry in the Making: An Anthology of Poems and Programmes from 'Listening and Writing'* (London: Faber, 1969), p. 12.

9

JUDY SIMONS

Gender roles in children's fiction

Girlhood and boyhood, at least until quite recently, have often been treated as separate, different and unequal in children's literature. Eighteenth-, nineteenth- and twentieth-century children's books are full of strong, active boy charac- ters, and much more submissive, domestic and introspective girls. But equally prevalent, even if sometimes less immediately obvious, has been a recurrent expression of the flimsiness and artificiality of the division between boys and girls, and of the desire of many protagonists to contravene the gender iden- tities enjoined on them. Many favourite characters from children's books either long to defy the simple gender categorisation imposed on them as members of the Anglo-American middle classes, or actually actively transgress the roles assigned to them. Here, for instance, is Georgina, speaking out in the first of Enid Blyton's Famous Five books:

> 'I'm George', said the girl. 'I shall only answer if you call me George. I hate being a girl. I won't be. I don't like doing the things that girls do. I like doing the things that boys do. I can climb better than any boy, and swim faster too. I can sail a boat as well as any fisher-boy on the coast. You're to call me George. Then I'll speak to you. But I shan't if you don't.'[1]

George epitomises both the sharp division between the social construction of girls and boys and the longing to cross the divide. Wearing shorts, with cropped curly hair and refusing to answer to her given name, this dogged eleven-year-old is determined to dodge the female role in which biology has cast her. She is also by far the most popular of the Famous Five, becoming, by the end of the twentieth century, an iconic figure. In frequent newspaper articles written to welcome the reissue of the books, or a new television adaptation, it is always George who is remembered most fondly. Her tom- boyishness is the object of sometimes lurid speculation, her resistance to the stereotype of docile girlhood the subject of often hilarious parody. Blyton's George is a compelling portrayal of liminality, embodying the differences between gender conventions at the same time as defying those traditional boundaries. She may be 'awfully funny' in the eyes of her conservative cousins, but by the same token she is awfully 'exciting'.[2]

However, the kind of liminality, or 'queerness', that George embodies must be seen in the context of the orthodox gender conventions that the characterisation of boys and girls has reflected ever since child, rather than adult, characters became the norm in children's literature. Writing in 1886, the literary critic Edward Salmon pronounced that 'Boys' literature of a sound kind ought to help build up men' and 'Girls' literature ought to help to build up women.'[3] This was a summary of how things had always been, he thought, and how things should continue to be. Salmon would probably have been surprised to learn that some of the very first recognisably modern children's books had been addressed to boys *and* girls. John Newbery's *A Little Pretty Pocket-Book* (1744), for instance, included 'A Letter From Jack the Giant-Killer, to Little Master Tommy' and another, 'To Pretty Miss Polly', that were identical save for the pronouns and words of address.[4] By the end of the eighteenth century, though, there was increased stratification of texts along gender lines that Salmon largely took for granted at the end of the nineteenth. The publisher William Darton produced companion volumes, *A Present for a Little Girl* (1797) and *A Present for a Little Boy* (1798). Some of the lessons these two books taught were similar; others were, as Salmon would have hoped, distinctly gendered. *A Present for a Little Girl* includes a story pertinent to the situation of young well-bred ladies about two tame geese who wander away from their farm to live with the wild fowl. When a fox approaches, the wild birds fly off but the tame geese, unfamiliar with the threat and hardly able to fly, are soon caught and devoured. 'From this short tale we may learn', the narrator tells the intended female reader, 'that those who forsake the state for which they are fitted by nature, will be in danger of sharing a like fate to that of the poor tame geese'. Indeed, the narrator continues, the two geese 'remind me of two little girls which I once heard of, who, walking by a canal, saw a boat being rowed by men'. Thinking they 'could do so too', the girls attempt to man a craft themselves. Naturally, they lose control and have to be rescued by the gardener, learning 'that it was not proper for little girls to row in a boat'.[5]

By the mid to late nineteenth century, the separate fictional worlds of boys and girls were being demarcated with great clarity, each with its own internal laws and its own territory, from which the other sex was outlawed. This development was perhaps especially noticeable in the lucrative market in children's periodicals between 1850 and 1900, probably the most widespread and accessible form of reading for boys and girls. The *Boy's Own Paper* (1855–1967) encouraged the development of specifically 'manly' attributes, for instance. The articles, editorials, stories and advertisements all laid a heavy emphasis on adventure, service to empire, science and sport, and also endorsed the gender-specific ideas of useful recreation, such as stamp collecting or taxidermy. The fiction encouraged a pursuit of an emphatic masculinity, whether in stories about the daredevil pranks of mischievous schoolboys or ones about acts of crime, violence or unruly individualism committed by near-mythic characters on the very margins of society, such as pirates, highwaymen, bandits and smugglers.

Jack Harkaway, the invention of the prolific nineteenth-century writer Bracebridge Hemyng, was the archetypal boy hero. He made his first appearance in *Boys of England* in 1871, pushing the paper's circulation figures to 250,000 copies a week. Courageous, daring, athletic, strong, yet also moral despite his tendency to challenge authority, Jack combined a number of classic traits. As a schoolboy he was a wayward scamp, who played tricks on masters and was always in trouble. Incidents like this foreshadowed his future as the fierce advocate of British racial supremacy: '"You're not a true Englishman"', says Jack as justification for fighting a schoolboy comrade; '"There's a touch of the tar-brush about you which shows you are not a white man."'[6] As his adventures became more extravagant, he ran away to sea and travelled around the world, facing danger in increasingly exotic locations. The Harkaway formula, once implanted, remained predictable: travel, fighting, torture, danger, escape and victory. As has often been noted, not the hero but the scenery changes. His bravery and ingenuity when threatened or trapped in apparently inescapable situations merely served to underline his independence and honour. Harkaway marketed a powerful nationalist ethic at a time when young men were encouraged to take pride in, expand and protect the empire, 'sustaining and sustained by a dream of a fertile wilderness' as Claudia Marquis observes.[7] His stories gripped the attention of young readers, even if it was much to the disapproval of their parents. 'My mother forbade me to read these things', recalled Havelock Ellis in his autobiography; 'Though I usually obeyed her, in this matter I was disobedient without compunction … If this is the literature a boy needs, nothing will keep him away from it.'[8]

During the same period, the *Girl's Own Paper* (from 1880) was instrumental in establishing the girls' story, celebrating family and home as a genre in its own right when it featured domestic fiction by L. T. Meade and Evelyn Everett-Green, among others. The girls' stories show a greater respect for authority and conformity – however reluctant – to adult control than those for boys; young women must learn to do as they are told and the naughtiness, whilst endearing, is represented as a phase they must outgrow. Yet Edward Salmon criticised the dreariness of this exemplary fare for girls, contrasting it unfavourably with the literary diet served up for boys:

Girls' literature would be much more successful than it is … if it were less good-goody. Girls will tolerate preaching just as little as boys … Girls' literature, properly so called, contains much really good writing, much that is beautiful and ennobling. It appeals in the main to the highest instincts of honour and truth of which humanity is capable. But with all its merits, it frequently lacks the peculiar qualities which can alone make girls' books as palatable to girls as boys' books are to boys.[9]

Salmon laid the blame for the insipidity of girls' literature on its subject matter: the domestic tedium of the adult lives for which its readership was destined. Girls might yearn for excitement as much as boys, he noted sympathetically. But real-life heroines like Grace Darling, who, in an open rowing-boat with her father, rescued nine people when the steamship *Forfarshire* broke up off the Northumberland coast in 1838, were few and far between compared with all the male heroes whom boys might be inspired to emulate. While writers for children after 1850 may have moved away from the overt didacticism characteristic of previous decades, many were nevertheless highly conscious of their obligations to edify the audience, whether composed of solitary child readers or family groups. Children's fiction was supposed to prepare youthful readers to enter a society where strict, even unforgiving, codes governed male and female conduct, and to influence their outlooks in ways that would be conducive to a better society in the future.

But Salmon's assertion that Victorian children's literature persistently failed to satisfy both sides of the gender divide equally well should be qualified. In fact, many works, including domestic fiction for girls, when read closely, reveal that it was not uncommon for authors to set up tensions between prescribed and desired gender roles as a means of engaging readers' interest in the narrative. The construction (or rather reconstruction) of masculinity is one of the concerns driving the plot of Rudyard Kipling's *Captains Courageous* (1897). Will the arrogant but effeminate Harold Cheyne Jr, the son of an American railroad tycoon who has been coddled by his mother, grow up to be a man capable of competing in his father's world? The opportunity to prove himself one way or the other presents itself when, en route to Europe, he is washed overboard and rescued by the captain of a fishing boat for whom he must work until the end of the season. The conflict over 'proper' masculinity not only drives the plot here, but is instrumental in setting the moral compass for the story.

While late Victorian and Edwardian juvenile audiences may have absorbed conformist messages reaffirming orthodox gender distinctions from some works, they were also exposed to memorable characters who chafed against authority and deviated from the prescribed path for their gender. What is remarkable is that the characters who abided by, and helped to enforce, traditional gender roles – the boys' own heroes and girls' own heroines – coexisted in children's books with other characters who sought to overturn these same proprieties. Most noticeably, this period saw the rise of the literary tomboy, who, like Enid Blyton's George, fought against the confines of her feminine role, whose clothes got torn and dirty, and who wanted nothing more than to share her brothers' adventures. Perhaps the most celebrated of all is the passionate Jo March in Louisa May Alcott's *Little Women* (1868). Struggling against her fate as one of her mother's four little women, Jo became an emblem of independent girlhood for generations of readers, to whom it hardly seems to matter that Alcott 'cheats' in the novel's second volume (added in response to her publisher's demands) by making Jo relinquish her career as an author in favour of a spectacularly dull husband. Rather, the lasting image in the collective audience memory is the figure of the defiant tomboy chopping off her 'abundant hair' to sell in a magnificent gesture to help pay her father's medical expenses. What we should also note from *Little Women* is that dissatisfaction with assigned gender roles is not restricted to the female characters. Laurie, the Marches' neighbour, envies the harmonious, all-female world, which Meg, Jo, Beth and Amy March inhabit and from which he is excluded. As he gazes wistfully at the March sisters from the window of his house opposite, Laurie yearns to share their camaraderie, suffused with fun, laughter and intimacy.

The tomboy archetype whom Jo personifies can be interpreted in different ways, among them as a girl's aversion towards her own body, an example of what some psychoanalysts call 'abjection'. Viewed in this light, Jo March rejects her femininity when bridling at female ways of dressing, or acting in non-feminine ways. At fifteen, Jo is at that transitional moment when childhood and adolescence collide. Her gangling body and flyaway hair refuse to remain under control. Impatient with her sex, she longs to be a boy. Frustrated in her desire to fight in the American Civil War, she resolves to take over the role of breadwinner for the household. It is her aching need to prove herself and to realise her own identity as an independent being that has made her such a mesmerising figure. Her recognition of self, which is primarily constructed in terms of gender, has been interpreted ever since the novel's publication as a thinly disguised portrait of the author. Entries in Alcott's journals contain much to confirm this autobiographical reading. She thought that she had been 'born with a boys spirit under my "bib and tucker"', and that 'people think I'm wild and queer'.[10] 'Louisa's was an isolated struggle', one biographer has written, 'and the only terms in which she could understand herself were that she was a freak, a girl-boy'.[11] Yet in *Little Women*, as in so many other tomboy stories, the reader is not left with an impression of freakishness, or abjection, or even very severe gender confusion.

It is no coincidence that one of Jo March's favourite authors was Charlotte Yonge. *Little Women* owes a considerable debt to Yonge's most celebrated novel, *The Daisy Chain* (1856), 'an overgrown book of a nondescript class, neither the "tale" for the young, nor the novel for their elders, but a mixture of both',[12] which was an enormous success, appealing to both male and female readers, children and adults, from its first appearance. *The Daisy Chain* provides another good example, in the character of Ethel, of the way in which conflict between the gender role yearned for and that assigned to a character powers a text. But here these tensions simultaneously retail a conformist view of the probity of strictly demarcated roles for men and women. Yonge's was an extremely conservative voice in the later nineteenth-century debate on the place of women in society. Her *Womankind* (1874–7) endorsed the status quo of separate cultures for boys and girls, bluntly asserting that women were inferior to men and that, whatever their intellectual capacity, the exemplary woman is one 'whose affections have been a law to her, and have trained her in self-denial, patience, meekness, pity, and modesty'.[13] *The Daisy Chain* nevertheless explores the appropriateness of discrete behavioural models for boys and for girls, whether consciously or unconsciously on Yonge's part.

Yonge's family chronicle tracks the fortunes of the eleven May children, who span the age range from babyhood to late adolescence, after the sudden death of their mother in a carriage accident. That same accident results in the spinal injury of the eldest daughter, Margaret, who is subsequently confined first to bed and then to a sofa, where she takes her mother's place as the household's spiritual guide until her premature death seven years later. Like other models of female saintliness in Victorian literature, such as Helen Burns in *Jane Eyre*, Margaret's fate also reflects key elements of the ideology of female self-sacrifice in an uncertain world. It is also worth comparing Margaret's position with that of Katy Carr, the eponymous heroine of Susan Coolidge's somewhat cruder American version of this formula in *What Katy Did* (1872). Katy's injury can be interpreted as punishment for her hoydenish antic of flying too high on a home-made swing when expressly forbidden to do so. Her ultimate recovery shows her reverting to a placid femininity, patient, compassionate and nurturing.

Much of *The Daisy Chain*'s appeal, however, lies in its depiction of growing up as a natural and often imperfect process, with youthful high-spiritedness the norm rather than the exception. It is likewise remarkable for its fraught portrayal of another gender misfit, the third daughter of the family, Ethel. Her very name, a diminutive of Etheldred, a name more usually given to boys, hints at her ambivalent status. Exuberant and lively, Ethel is heavily criticised for being 'just like one of the boys'. She is physically gawky, and has inherited her father's academic bent in an age when to be 'a regular learned lady' is to 'be good for nothing'. The family governess echoes the mantra of mid-nineteenth-century views of female education when she bluntly asserts that she considers 'good needlework far more important than accomplishments'. Whereas in her favourite brother, Norman, intellectual brilliance, ambition and love of action are all traits to be admired, in Ethel they are shortcomings, because they deflect from her cultivating womanliness. Ethel's obsession with books is rapidly ruining her eyesight and even though she is allowed only occasionally to use spectacles, wearing them at all makes her a freak in a society that values unspoiled feminine beauty. Yet she is sensitive and compassionate, always conscious of the fact that her energy and ardour are somehow letting down the side. As she incurs her father's rebuke yet again when she returns from a brisk country walk with the hem of her dress encrusted with mud, she explodes with the typical anguish of the misunderstood teenager. 'I am good for nothing!' she wails to Margaret, 'Oh! If mamma was but here!'[14]

While Yonge's portrait of the tomboy Ethel's frustration in mid-nineteenth-century society is authentic, it is also resolutely pragmatic. The siblings who love and support her also voice the limits she should abide by. Yonge gives her young heroine the brainpower to keep pace with her brother's lessons, but she sets out clearly through Margaret's voice the social inequalities that make Ethel's aspirations unattainable. Often compared with George Eliot's Maggie Tulliver, Ethel's determination to keep up with Norman as he advances academically en route to Oxford University is depicted as comically heart-rending but unbecoming. Advised to renounce her classical studies, she breaks down.

> 'Oh Margaret! Margaret!' and her eyes filled with tears. 'We have hardly missed doing the same every day since the first Latin grammar was put into his hands! ... From hic haec hoc up to Alcaics and beta Thukididou we have gone on together, and I can't bear to give it up.'

Just as *The Mill on the Floss* depicts a heroine's struggle with prevailing concepts of female intellectual frailty, so Ethel has to be reminded by Margaret that: 'we all know that men have more power than women, and I suppose the time has come for Norman to pass beyond you'. As Margaret says, 'if you could get all the honours in the University – what would it come to? You can't take a first class.' In a society where women were barred from graduation, Ethel must buckle down and accept that her prime responsibilities should be domestic and that to be 'a useful, steady daughter at home ... and a comfort to papa' should be the pinnacle of her ambition.[15] By the novel's end, Ethel has succeeded to Margaret's place as her father's most trusted daughter and has learned how to administer effectively a school for local poor children. And she has the satisfaction of having found that service to others is a more than adequate compensation for the sacrifice of her intellectual ambitions. Ultimately, the kind of challenge to orthodox gender roles that Ethel represents may be defeated in *The Daisy Chain*, but her resistance wins her the respect and affections of readers, regardless of Yonge's personal views on feminine behaviour.

Both fifteen years old, Ethel and Alcott's Jo clearly share many characteristics, but the differences between *Little Women* and *The Daisy Chain* are critical. Part of the originality of Alcott's narrative is that it was aimed quite specifically at a young female readership rather than at the whole family, unlike *The Daisy Chain*. Overcoming her initial reluctance to undertake the task of writing 'a girls' story', Alcott created a fictional world that celebrates female culture and values. With all the able-bodied adult males away at war, the women are left to cope on their own, and in the liberated society of New England, in striking contrast to the hidebound English class system, they are furthermore allowed to earn their own living without shame. As *Little Women* takes the four sisters and their flawless mother, Marmee, through a calendar year, the story becomes a battle against the odds, with each of the four girls having to wrestle with her own personal demons in order to achieve a standard of behaviour that might meet with their absent father's approval. Above all, as each of the March sisters tries to improve herself, together Meg, Jo, Beth and Amy form a group that validates girlhood. The values of their domestic world are markedly differentiated from those of their neighbours, the wealthy Lawrences. In that all-male household, the crotchety grandfather, the lonely boy and the reserved tutor, John Brooke, live in a world of material affluence but spiritual deprivation. The March sisters may be poor but their lives have an emotional richness that is transformative. Their artistic talents provide them with an inner sustenance that Laurie can only envy. In *Little Women*, femininity performs the traditional civilising function assigned to it in a number of nineteenth-century mainstream fictions.

What Alcott conveyed most emphatically is that girlhood creativity could serve as the basis of a new role model for fictional female characters. The act of creation – whether by sewing, writing, acting or dancing – would continue to feature prominently as a means of agency in late Victorian and Edwardian girls' stories. In novels by Frances Hodgson Burnett, innate artistry helps to carry isolated girls beyond the mundane lives they actually inhabit. In *A Little Princess* (1887), for instance, Sara blocks out the harsh realities of having lost her favoured status within Miss Minchin's seminary through clandestine storytelling to her fellow schoolgirls, and in the process carries them with her. Likewise, Mary Lennox in Burnett's *The Secret Garden* (1911) rescues the sickly, self-absorbed Colin Craven through Scheherazade-like tales that soothe his pain and restore his self-confidence and health. It is not difficult to see the creativity of characters like Sara or Mary as a means of coping with the constraints imposed by gender, especially given their status as orphaned girls dependent upon the charity of others. It is just as easy to read this female creativity as Burnett's attempt to reconcile two conflicting impulses, the desire to remain a 'proper' girl who accepts her place, and the desire to be free from all such restraints that place imposes. Creativity gives Sara and Mary an alternative means of self-actualisation through the exercise of their gifts, but without disrupting ideological and social orthodoxies. Thus, even if these characters seemingly learn to accept the limitations their gender imposes, just like the girls in *A Present for a Little Girl* who learned why it was not suitable for them to mess about in boats, their stories are not invariably accounts of abjection, nor even of subjection. Whatever moulds the heroines are eventually forced into, they still are represented as having triumphed against the odds.

After the First World War, the rigidity of gender roles became more relaxed in children's fiction, at least for girls. Authors writing girls' stories in the interwar years continued to rely on the tension between societal expectations of proper female behaviour and their characters' creative aspirations to drive their novels. One striking change is the portrayal of a network of women who support the girls in their dreams. Noel Streatfeild's *Ballet Shoes* (1936), for example, features three orphan children, Pauline, Petrova and Posy Fossil, who are adopted by an eccentric palaeontologist, 'Uncle Matthew', from whose occupation they derive their surname. With Uncle Matthew absent for the bulk of the narrative, the three Fossils grow up, not unlike the March sisters, in an almost entirely female household, and *Ballet Shoes* shows the survival strategies women adopt in a male-oriented society. In order to pay the household expenses, the children's guardian Sylvia takes in lodgers, and sends the three little girls to stage school, where even as children they can earn a living and learn how to be self-sufficient. Vowing to make names for themselves, the Fossil girls explicitly discard any debt to the past and carve out lives as independent modern individuals. Pauline and Posy prove to be naturally gifted at acting and dancing respectively, while Petrova turns to the profession of an aviator, one that perhaps most dramatically defines the new age. Another of those misfits so beloved by authors of girls' stories, Petrova is never happier than when she is donning overalls at an airfield, where she can follow her bent for engineering and indulge her passion for flight, both metaphorical and literal.

A cast of unmarried women provide them with strong role models. Two of the lodgers are retired teachers, spinsters, who tutor the young Fossils in mathematics and English. Sylvia herself is resourceful in finding ways to meet the rising household costs and she is supported by Nana, her old nanny, who becomes the girls' moral protector. The Principal of the ballet school, Madame, is a refugee from Imperial Russia who exploits the commercial opportunities of her émigré status and her talents. Just as with Alcott's March sisters, the heart of the novel's appeal rests in its celebration of the imaginative expression of female creativity. Alternatively, the tradition of books featuring precocious girls who take starring roles on stage can be regarded as fantasies of female autonomy, most popular in an age when traditional models of femininity were being re-imposed. The Second World War, and the return of men from the armed services at its conclusion, led to a re-validation of traditional familial roles. Novels such as Pamela Brown's *The Swish of the Curtain* (1941) and Lorna Hill's 1950s series of fourteen books about Sadler's Wells ballet school provided an escape. On stage, whether acting, dancing or painting scenery, children are allowed a platform (literally) for self-expression. They can legitimately be the centre of attention and display their hitherto unnoticed talents as they hold audiences enraptured with skilled performances, astonishing parents and friends. These theatrical narratives were followed by Streatfeild's bestselling tales of sporting celebrity, such as *Tennis Shoes* (1937) and *White Boots* (1951). More recent children's novels have heroines who share these kinds of artistic aspirations but do not encounter similar obstacles to satisfying their drive for self-expression, as in Louise Fitzhugh's *Harriet the Spy* (1964) for instance. But the fact that Streatfeild's artistic tomboy stories, like those by Alcott, Ingalls Wilder and Montgomery, are still in print alongside their descendants both confirms the enduring appeal of the literary tomboy and suggests that there remains a need for stories which posit creativity as an alternative means of fulfilment for girls denied, by the limitations of gender propriety, full freedom to express themselves in society at large.

There is no direct equivalent of the word 'tomboy' for boys who behave like girls, or at least no equivalent that is not much more pejorative. This may be taken as an indication that the proprieties of gender roles have been even more rigidly enforced for boys than for girls (certainly it has taken longer for non-boyish boy readers to find sympathetic portraits of themselves in children's books). Perhaps the archetypal retailer of the quick-thinking, noble masculinity so vigorously advanced in the later nineteenth century was G. A. Henty, author of almost 100 classic historical novels for boys. Whether set in Roman or Saxon times or in the more recent conflicts of the American Civil War, Henty's fictions engaged their audience with accounts of action in the wider world rather than interior worlds. They were also acclaimed for both their accuracy and their educational content, providing detailed, compelling accounts of battles, weaponry and events. Featuring boys or young men living in turbulent times who are determined to take full advantage of the excitement the age had to offer, boredom is an anathema and war exhilarating. 'Well, I would give anything to be a soldier, instead of having to settle down and be a banker – it's disgusting!', declares the young Etonian, Tom Scudamore, 'for the twentieth time', in the opening chapter of *The Young Buglers* (1881), one of Henty's most popular works.[16] Naturally his wish is soon to be granted. Henty takes the orphaned Scudamore brothers, aged fourteen and fifteen, off to the 1808 Peninsular War. They are 'regular young pickles', 'up to all kinds of mischief' and 'the pluckiest and most straightforward youngsters imaginable'. They run away from their guardian, a maiden aunt whose sensibilities are particularly ill adapted to cope with boyish exuberance, defeat a highwayman, rescue a black sailor from drowning (who becomes their devoted servant), survive three days on an open raft, successfully spy for the British by attaching themselves to the Spanish guerrilla forces and, after a year of continual adventure, are restored to their lost fortunes and ultimately settle down to lives as conventional English country gentlemen. As cool as they are plucky, resourceful as they are courageous, the Scudamores win the admiration of their commanding officer, not coincidentally named Captain Manley, who, like the author, adopts a language of paternal affection in describing the exploits of these quintessential young English heroes.

The Scudamores' combination of virtues was to live on in the heroes of the continuous, complicated tales of action and audacity featured in comic books, which, in the years just before and after the Second World War, began competing with the periodicals as the dominant mode of cheap reading for children from all classes and age groups. The quality of publications like *Marvel* (launched in 1893), the *Rover* and *Wizard* (both first published in 1922) and the *Eagle* (which first appeared in 1950) was widely disparaged, but the comic book had a profound effect on the development of mainstream children's literature by popularising enduring juvenile literary typologies including the adventure story, the school story, the science-fiction narrative and the historical novel, all of which had already proved their appeal to boy readers in books by Captain Marryat, R. M. Ballantyne and the mass-market periodicals in the latter part of the nineteenth century. Whilst books often appealed to both sexes, periodicals generally remained firmly separatist in the gendered behavioural models they advanced and the discrete genres they offered their readers.

Anthony Horowitz' series about Alex Rider, a fourteen-year-old recruited as a spy, continues this tradition. Starting with *Stormbreaker* (2000), these books send Alex on a series of dangerous missions. A James Bond in miniature, he has had a special-forces training, carries lethal weapons and all sorts of high-tech gadgetry, but his chief characteristics are still the pluck and intrepidity of Jack Harkaway or the Scudamores. He has even inherited their derision for foreigners. The climax of *Stormbreaker*, for example, shows Alex saving the life of the British Prime Minister. 'How did you do it?', howls his Russian opponent; 'How did you trick me? I'd have beaten you if you'd been a man! But they had to send a boy! A bliddy schoolboy! Well it isn't over yet!'[17] The appearance of the Alex Rider books is regarded by some contemporary commentators as particularly timely. In a 2007 speech to the Fabian Society, Alan Johnson, the then British Secretary of State for Education, commended the series and upheld the view that 'Boys like books which depict them in a powerful role, often as sporting, spying or fighting heroes.'[18] Charlotte Yonge had said much the same thing in 1888: 'boys especially should not have childish tales with weak morality or "washy" piety, but should have heroism and nobleness kept before their eyes'.[19] The views of Johnson and Yonge may well reflect political circumstances of their times, but they both implicitly harken back to an earlier age when, supposedly, boys' books had had a more straightforwardly masculine agenda, with the implication that this agenda has somehow become compromised.

But, in fact, neither Johnson nor Yonge took into account the sophistication and complexity of representations of masculinity in children's literature. Certainly many interesting and enduring children's books since the late nineteenth century have not represented any one simple model of masculinity. Neither the hero of Twain's *Adventures of Huckleberry Finn* (1884) nor Jim Hawkins in Robert Louis Stevenson's *Treasure Island* (1883) can be described as 'sporting, spying or fighting heroes', even though they may sport, spy or fight during the course of their adventures. In *Peter Pan*, J. M. Barrie did not represent physical ability, pluck, self-assurance as the major constituents of boyish heroism. Male protagonists, even of the muscular Christian persuasion, have not suppressed their feminine side. Thomas Hughes' campaigning *Tom Brown's Schooldays* (1857) attacked the raw brutality of the masculine ethic endemic in the English boys' public school, for instance. Tom notably resists the temptation of indulging in the aggressive violence of the schoolboy bullies and instead protects the weak and innocent young Arthur, whom he has taken under his wing. And when Arthur dies, Tom, the model of a young Christian gentleman, is allowed to shed copious tears. Cedric Erroll, Burnett's *Little Lord Fauntleroy* (1886), offers another compelling illustration of a popular boy hero who displays the traditionally feminine qualities of compassion and emotional generosity. Intriguingly, theatrical and screen adaptations of the novel tended to cast actresses in the title role, most famously the golden-ringleted Mary Pickford, who played both Fauntleroy and his mother in the 1921 film version. Cedric also plays the role more usually ascribed to women in mainstream nineteenth-century fictions, that of softening a male heart, in this case Cedric's grandfather's, and reintroducing the crusty male to a value system governed by feeling rather than by dogma.

Even twentieth-century authors of epic fantasy have played with readers' expectations of masculinity in their choice of protagonists. In *The Hobbit* (1937), Tolkien (himself a veteran of the First World War's disastrously bloody Battle of the Somme) casts an unlikely character as the unwitting hero of this quest: the hobbit Bilbo – portly, timorous, diffident and wedded to the comforts of home – but who goes adventuring with Thorin and Company anyhow. While readers may suspect that Bilbo will prove to have the pluck and cunning to prevail, no matter what tight corner he finds himself in, just like a more conventional hero, it is in fact his inherent domesticity that triumphs. If Henty's Tom Scudamore would have given anything to be a soldier, instead of settling down to be a banker, Bilbo is happier sitting at home in front of the fire. After having been tested to the full extent of his resources, 'the sound of the kettle on the hearth was ever after more musical than it had been even in the quiet days before the Unexpected Party'. His sword and armour are given to a museum, his magic ring of invisibility is used chiefly 'when unpleasant callers came'. When told by Gandalf that he is 'only quite a little fellow in a wide world', he responds '"Thank goodness!" … and handed him the tobacco-jar' – an emphatic renunciation of the heroic impulse.[20] Indeed, Tolkien makes it plain that Bilbo would have become enthralled to the ring if he had been possessed of a more fiery, restless and 'masculine' temperament.

Bilbo is not unique among heroes of twentieth-century fantasy. When Ursula Le Guin decided to add the fourth volume, *Tehanu* (1990), to her *Earthsea* trilogy (1967–72), she consciously tried to show her hero, Ged, recognising the institutional sexism of his world, and determining to embrace the feminine side of his nature.[21] But it might be said that, while many other boy heroes in twentieth-century children's literature had already exhibited this kind of cross-gender identity, it was not until quite late in the century that this blurring of gender roles became the focus of whole novels, rather than being immersed more deeply in the text. In Anne Fine's *Flour Babies* (1992), to take another example, the ursine Simon Martin discovers through participation in a psychology experiment his capacity for caring and nurturing, and, even more importantly, the necessity for accepting the drudgery of responsibility.

After the Second World War (and especially in the United States), young adult novels have also presented boys who are tested in circumstances where acting like a man in the mould of a Jack Harkaway or Tom Scudamore does not guarantee their triumph over genuinely evil antagonists. In Robert

Cormier's *The Chocolate War* (1974), for instance, Jerry Renault is caught up in the competitive, aggressive and conventionally masculine world of a Catholic all-boys school, where its code is rigidly enforced by the Vigils, a not-so-secret society of boys headed up by the Machiavellian Archie Costello. The boys usually capitulate to the Vigils' demands because resistance seems calculated only to invite more trouble for anyone reckless enough to refuse to co-operate. During the school-wide sale of chocolates, Jerry defies the Vigils, and indirectly the administration, in whose interests it is to raise as much money as possible. The enemies he makes realise that the best way to provoke Jerry is to question his masculinity: 'you're a fairy. A queer. Living in the closet, hiding away.' It seems to Jerry that the only proper response is to play the lone hero standing tall and participate in a fight that will be staged so that he cannot possibly win, in a way that makes a mockery of his principled refusal to play along. Only after he has thrown his punches does he realise that, by having done so, he has submitted to the very system of aggression and competition that he hates: 'A new sickness invaded Jerry, the sickness of knowing what he had become, another animal, another beast, another violent person in a violent world, inflicting damage, not disturbing the universe but damaging it.'[22] Dramatising Jerry's persecution, capitulation and defeat, Cormier 'successfully demonstrates the violent and dark side of masculinity and provides readers with a powerful indictment of conventional manhood', as one critic has put it.[23]

But despite such modern complications of masculinity, a feminine boyishness is still not widely countenanced in male characters, as it is still perceived as sissiness. Neither Tom Brown, Little Lord Fauntleroy, Bilbo Baggins, Jerry Renault or Ged are quite the male equivalent of the tomboy, a boy who behaves like a girl. For Blyton to have included in her Famous Five a boy in a dress who demanded to be called 'Georgina' would have been unthinkable in the 1940s, and even today such a novel would probably be difficult to place with a mainstream trade publisher. There has been much more freedom in the ways in which girlhood has been constructed in recent children's literature. Heroines who openly take on the best qualities of a Jack Harkaway (without his colonial prejudices) do not necessarily arouse hostility or provoke controversy, nor are they characterised two-dimensionally as tomboys or as somehow queer. In fact, brave, smart, resourceful girl protagonists are by no means unusual in recent children's novels – if anything, the portrayal of a traditionally feminine girl may be regarded by some critics as requiring a word of explanation or apology from the author. On the other hand, strong girl characters who may be the superior, in important respects, of a novel's male protagonist, like Hermione Granger in J. K. Rowling's *Harry Potter* novels or a woman warrior like Aerin in Robin McKinley's *The Hero and the*

Crown (1984), are not necessarily allowed to upstage the male hero or the man they love. Likewise Dicey Tillerman, in Cynthia Voigt's *Homecoming*, who displays a degree of courage, resourcefulness and determination far beyond her age in caring for her siblings after abandonment by a mentally ill mother, may seem to some like an updated version of the self-sacrificing May sisters in *The Daisy Chain*.

The deliberate disordering of gender identities in modern children's literature has not, of course, rendered more traditional representations of gender obsolete. C. S. Lewis' Narnia books, for instance, remain popular at the start of the twenty-first century despite the very conservative gender roles that they endorse. It might in fact be argued that some of their popularity comes precisely from this social conservatism. Nor does the modern disordering of gender necessarily mean that child readers are absorbing and abiding by any new proprieties of gender. It is possible that these books should best be understood as a kind of fairy tale of adolescence, enabling children to satisfy an urge to experiment with gender without the need to destabilise their real-life identities. In other words, young girls may always have enjoyed reading about tomboys, but they don't want to grow up in that image. If anything, the fantasy of tomboyhood provides not a challenge to but a necessary preparatory stage for their adult roles as wives and mothers. Readers may like it when gender is destabilised because it offers the usual gratifications of the carnivalesque, just as the tradition of blackface minstrelsy plays with colour but actually only enforces old divisions. Here then is an explanation of why George has remained easily the most popular character from Blyton's Famous Five, and why Alcott's Jo and Montgomery's Anne are among the most iconic characters in all children's literature. It is the depiction of gender dissidence of these characters and the rigidly gendered society in which they operate that readers appreciate. Unambiguous and inflexibly enforced gender boundaries can provide the reassurance and stability which young readers crave, while at the same time offering a delightful opportunity for transgression and socio-cultural adventure.

NOTES

1. Enid Blyton, *Five on a Treasure Island* (London: Hodder and Stoughton, 1942; rpt 1997), p. 19.
2. Blyton, *Five on a Treasure Island*, pp. 21 and 14.
3. Edward Salmon, 'What Girls Read', *Nineteenth Century*, 20 (November 1886), 515–29.
4. *A Little Pretty Pocket-Book, Intended for the Instruction and Amusement of little Master Tommy, and Pretty Miss Polly*, 10th edn (1744; London: J. Newbery, 1760), pp. 13–20.

5. William Darton, *A Present for a Little Girl* (London: Darton and Harvey, 1798), pp. 45–9.
6. Quoted in E. S. Turner, *Boys Will be Boys: The Story of Sweeney Todd, Deadwood Dick, Sexton Blake, Billy Bunter, Dick Barton et al.* (1948; Harmondsworth: Penguin Books, 1978), p. 84.
7. Claudia Marquis, 'Romancing the Home', in *Girls, Boys, Books, Toys: Gender in Children's Literature and Culture*, ed. Beverly Lyon Clark and Margaret R. Higonnet (Baltimore, MD: Johns Hopkins University Press, 1999), pp. 53–67 (p. 57).
8. Quoted in Turner, *Boys Will be Boys*, pp. 68–9.
9. Salmon, 'What Girls Read'.
10. *The Journals of Louisa May Alcott*, ed. Madeline B. Stern (Boston: Little, 1989), pp. 59 and 79.
11. Martha Saxton, *Louisa May* (Boston: Houghton, 1977), p. 165.
12. Charlotte M. Yonge, *The Daisy Chain, or Aspirations*, vol. 1 (1856; Virginia: IndyPublish.com, 2002), 'Preface'.
13. Charlotte M. Yonge, *Womankind*, serialised 1874–7; published in book form, 1887 (new edn, New York: Macmillan and Co., 1890), p. 6.
14. Yonge, *Daisy Chain*, pp. 227 and 221–2.
15. Yonge, *Daisy Chain*, p. 225.
16. G. A. Henty, *The Young Buglers* (1881).
17. Anthony Horowitz, *Stormbreaker* (London: Walker Books, 2006), p. 235.
18. Reported in the *Daily Telegraph*, Thursday 15 March 2007, p. 4.
19. Charlotte M. Yonge, *What Books to Lend and What to Give* (1888), quoted in Kimberley Reynolds, *Girls Only? Gender and Popular Fiction in Britain 1880–1910* (Philadelphia: Temple University Press, 1990), pp. 36–7.
20. J. R. R. Tolkien, *The Hobbit* (1937; London: Collins, 1988), pp. 363 and 365.
21. See Ursula Le Guin, *Earthsea Revisioned: A Lecture Delivered Under the Title 'Children, Women, Men and Dragons'* (Cambridge, MA: Children's Literature New England in association with Green Bay Publications, 1993).
22. Robert Cormier, *The Chocolate War* (1974; London: Puffin, 2001), pp. 168 and 201.
23. Yoshida Junko, 'The Quest for Masculinity in *The Chocolate War*: Changing Conceptions of Masculinity in the 1970s', *Children's Literature*, 26 (1998), 105–22 (p. 113).

10

U. C. KNOEPFLMACHER

Children's texts and the grown-up reader

It is a truth still insufficiently acknowledged that our finest children's books are hybrid constructs that combine a child's perspective with the guarded perspective of the former child we call 'adult'. Pliable and elastic, such mixed texts allow both perspectives to coexist. They may rely on a fictional child/ adult amalgam, or an animal/human composite, such as a Sendakian Wild Thing, as a mediating agent. Or they may require a transformative space that is both mundane and fantastic, as ordinary as a smelly barn and as magical as the mysterious advertising slogans that a tiny spider called Charlotte has spun on her threshold web.

Since it has become routine for critics to scrutinise adult values embedded in juvenile texts, we may no longer need Jacqueline Rose to remind us that children's literature is not 'something self-contained' or exclusively self-referential.[1] Nonetheless, our scrupulous attention to cultural and political frames has hardly moved us beyond Rose's dialectical emphasis on generational binaries. The overlaps and frictions that make most children's books such an interactive meeting ground for readers of different ages still require a much closer attention.

In 1997, Mitzi Myers and I edited a collection of essays devoted to what she called 'Cross-Writing the Child and the Adult'. In our preface, we tried to refine ideas I had posited in a 1983 discussion of Victorian texts 'balancing' generational opposites.[2] The topic continued to intrigue Professor Myers, as it has other critics such as Sandra Beckett and Marah Gubar, who have fruitfully extended it. Convinced that we had unduly homogenised the generational dynamics of texts substantially different in genre and form, Professor Myers wanted us to take a closer look at the variable layerings involved in 'cross-writing'. We had also paid scant attention to the historical role of folktales and fairy tales as prime models for the traffic between child and adult. It was their trans-generational and trans-gendered fluidity, after all, that allowed fairy tales to evolve and spread into other discursive forms.[3] When Charles Perrault and the Grimms infantilised and masculinised texts (which later women writers then re-feminised and eventually reclaimed for adult audiences), they set off trans-generic changes that have continued to flourish in theatre, opera, film and television.

But unasked questions remained even about those texts we had highlighted. What kinds of overlaps exist between a child's constructions of reality and their later reappropriation by adult authors and adult readers? How do different age gaps affect a text's multigenerational appeal? Might books targeted for smaller children – Kipling's *Just So Stories* (1902), say – possibly offer a richer interplay between younger listeners and older readers than narratives designed for the so-called 'young adult', such as Kipling's own *Jungle Books* (1894–5)? And, if so, would picture books for pre-literate children perhaps offer a more successful 'mix' of adult and child interests than books with few or no illustrations? Might comic narratives that rely on shared jokes or that mock plots familiar to both children and grown-ups offer both constituencies a stronger sense of partnership or joint tenancy than texts dominated by a narrator's recognisable adult voice? After all, the repetition and variation of narratives familiar to both children and grown-ups may well result in the communal pleasure of those 'twice-told tales' that John Stephens so valuably highlights elsewhere in this volume.

If our finest child-texts are adult/child hybrids, greater attention must be paid to the triangulating processes through which such hybrids dissolve, reshape and yet also reinstate the divisions between child and adult. In 1983, I used 'See-Saw', a brief tale by the Victorian writer Margaret Scott Gatty, as a crude paradigm for such a process. I aligned Gatty's creation of a mediating third entity, a hermaphroditic snail, with hybrid figurations of the 'childlike adult or adult-seeming child' so frequently found in other Victorian fantasies. Yet my anatomy of these more complex texts was over-simplified, for it depended on an ideal equipoise I represented by drawing a balanced see-saw. Decidedly tilting towards one extreme or the other, mixed texts rarely balance their adult/child components. The Victorian fantasies I considered should thus have been assessed according to the varying proportions of those components. And they should also have been contrasted with the intricate mixtures created by later writers such as Mary Norton or E. B. White, or by artists such as Maurice Sendak and Dr Seuss, the creators of so-called 'icono-texts' (graphic texts in which word and picture are so enmeshed that neither can be understood without the other).

Sendak's case as writer-illustrator is instructive. The rich verbal and pictorial equilibrium of *Where the Wild Things Are* (1963) certainly makes this masterpiece one of the finest specimens of adult/child (or child/adult) interaction that children's literature can offer. Yet the uniqueness of the book's

'mixy' nature also becomes apparent when it is set beside its 1957 forerunners, *Kenny's Window* (1956) and *Very Far Away* (1957). Despite their
thematic kinship with *Wild Things*, these first attempts at illustrated narratives which Sendak wrote himself seem flatter and feebler as bi-textual com-
positions. Why? Without his later confidence in balancing word and image,
Sendak had yet to find the means for injecting an adult presence into a child-
text and thus may have tilted too much towards the child's interests. Conversely, later Sendakian texts, still marketed as children's books, tilt in exactly
the opposite direction. The idiosyncratic pictorial inscriptions of brilliant
works such as *Higglety Pigglety Pop! Or There Must Be More to Life*
(1967) may delight adult critics; yet, by excluding a major segment of the
book's intended audience, they also threaten to diminish the interaction
between younger and older readers.

Facing the title-page of *Higglety Pigglety Pop!* is a full-page drawing of
Jennie, the feisty terrier whom Sendak places against the backdrop of
Leonardo da Vinci's 'Mona Lisa'. By posing two mortals in parallel pictorial
planes that hold them in an ever-frozen moment, Sendak not only aligns his
own canine Mona (whom he had renamed 'Jennie' in real life) with the human
Mona whom Leonardo immortalised as *La Gioconda* but also identifies
himself with the Renaissance artist whose masterpiece Freud and Walter
Pater had analysed as an act of self-projection. He, too, is determined to
combat mutability by 'eternising' a female subject. For Jennie's comic odyssey
can transfigure, through the timelessness of art, the mother-nurtured secu-
rities of childhood that both the artist and his subject must cede to a world of
change and death. Sendak's absurdist elegy is rich in witty verbal and visual
delights. But its pleasures are far less accessible and less universal than those
he had previously produced in the iconotext of *Wild Things*. The exclusivity
of the private meanings we are asked to decode has the effect of barring too
many child readers and can even alienate adult readers who may expect – and
miss – the richly interactive cohesion of the earlier book.

I shall take a closer look at the cohesive artistry of *Where the Wild Things
Are* in the final section of this chapter. But I first want to consider a very
different type of hybrid text, Mary Norton's *The Borrowers* (1952). Like
Sendak's *Higglety Pigglety Pop!*, Norton's fiction tries to defuse adult anxieties about the threat of death. Her anxieties, like Sendak's, are rooted in the
insecurities and compensatory imaginings of a vividly remembered childhood
past. But unlike Sendak's handling of Jennie's surrealist march towards Castle
Yonder, Norton's own exodus narrative interrogates her text's child/adult
mixture. The primarily linguistic hybridity of her novel thus needs to be
carefully examined before we can return to the visual/verbal hybridity offered
in *Wild Things*.

Mary Norton: the problematics of 'bilingualism'

A 1966 letter that Mary Norton wrote to a friend who wanted to know how she came to invent her tiny race of Borrowers wonderfully documents the multiple 'layerings' that shape a hybrid child/adult text.[4] Norton traces her fiction back to 'an early fantasy in the life of a very short-sighted child, before it was known that she needed glasses'. The little girl she describes in the third person is recalled as 'an inveterate lingerer' who lagged behind her older brothers during their country walks: 'she was a gazer into banks and hedge-rows, a rapt investigator of shallow pools, a lier-down by stream-like teeming ditches' (xv). The child's acute myopia, Norton suggests, became an asset rather than a handicap. For she soon transformed the minutiae she saw: a 'small toad', struggling to survive on a piece of bark, turned into 'little people' as 'vulnerable' as this amphibian creature or as her own small self (xvi).

Norton credits that child-self with having begun a layering process that she complicated and refined as an adult writer. For, soon, this most vulnerable of three siblings took 'her small people indoors' and retained them as secret companions unknown to her brothers and 'unguessed at by the adult human beings, who were living so close but so dangerously [by]' (xviii). Yet a new phase began, Norton suggests, after the 'maturing demands of boarding school' displaced the sheltered life of her 'nursery years' (xviii). The provision of a pair of spectacles and the advent of adolescence had opened other realities: 'In the midst of such diversions there was little time for the Borrowers who, denied even humble attention, slid quietly back into the past.' Still, although she had shelved this imaginary band of survivors, what still persisted into adolescence and, eventually, into maturity was her continuing apprehension of the fragility and precariousness that had led to their invention. The fantasies that Mary and her friends traded at their 'convent school' were still defensive. For the teenagers needed to escape their acute awareness of 'the 1914–18 war and the mud and blood across the Channel which engaged our elder brothers' (xix–xx).

It took another world war, however, and the fully matured awareness of a woman who had become a mother-in-exile, to bring back into consciousness a near-sighted child's early imaginings. By then, however, these had accrued new meanings:

> It was only just before the 1940 war, when a change was creeping over the world as we had known it, that one thought again about the Borrowers. There were human men and women who were being forced to live (by stark and tragic necessity) the kinds of lives a child had once envisaged for a race of mythical creatures. One could not help but realize (without any thought of conscious symbolism) that the world at any time could produce its Mrs Drivers who in their turn would summon their Rich Williams. And there we would be. (xx)

'I hope this answers your question', Norton tells her correspondent before finishing the 1966 letter she copyrighted in 1991, a year before her death. By using this epistle as an 'adult' introduction to a children's book, Norton can be said to have added, towards the end of her long life, still another layer to the text she had published, almost forty years earlier, in its 1952 British and 1953 American versions. She seemed eager to alert her public to the idea that a text that opened a privately cherished mythical core to younger readers could also be read by an older audience as a post-Holocaust parable. The year 1952, it may be well worth remembering, was the one in which two other major narratives about the precariousness of survival, *Charlotte's Web* and *The Diary of Anne Frank*, first appeared in the United States. Like each of these texts, *The Borrowers* engages fears of extinction shared by the young and the old.

Norton's reference to future 'Mrs Drivers' who might summon killers like Rich Williams to exterminate undesirable and parasitic creatures had acquired a special poignancy by 1952. Aware of past atrocities, Western nations were resolved to shun the legacy of the Führer, a German word that means 'Leader' as well as 'Driver'. The sadistic housekeeper whom Norton describes as having a moustache was even drawn with a bristly over-lip by Beth and Joe Krutch, the illustrators of the American edition. But the discovery of Stalin's own massacres, sudden fears about subversives, the Korean conflict and, above all, the threat of an atomic war provided a new framework for Mrs Driver's paranoid compulsion to eradicate the last of the Borrowers with poison gas. In her 1966 letter, Norton recalled how, as a child, she had pondered what it would be like to live among the unsafe Borrowers: 'What would one live on? Where make one's home? Which would be one's enemies and which one's friends?' (xvi).

The oppressiveness of the Borrowers' underground quarters is stressed far more in the sombre, *chiaroscuro* drawings by the English illustrator Diana Stanley than in the airily kinetic American illustrations of Beth and Joe Krutch. Indeed, Stanley's depiction of the Clock family's final escape from their hiding place hardly seems liberating. Weighted down by their possessions and hindered by barriers they must traverse, the trio staggers towards an uncertain safety. Stanley's artwork apparently influenced the 1993 BBC television series, with its emphasis on the claustrophobia triggered by cramped spaces and jarring sounds. Cast as a debilitated and worried *paterfamilias*, the actor Ian Holm bears little resemblance to his buoyant, younger counterpart, Eddie Albert, in the rambunctious 1977 American film. Whether as illustrations or in films, the British representations thus seem far more reality-oriented, history-conscious and 'adult' than their light-hearted, escapist and 'child-friendly' American counterparts.

This split harks back to the verbal text's intricate criss-crossing of opposing perspectives. Norton immediately erects barriers that delay our access to the book's fantasy core. Not until the second chapter are we introduced to the points of view of Arrietty Clock and her Borrower parents. The resisting thicket that meets us at the outset resembles the obstacles Perrault had strewn in 'Sleeping Beauty', where a young prince as well as the reader had to sift competing narratives about what a bramble-covered palace might conceal. Norton employs an aged narrator, Mrs May, to adapt the story of the tiny Clock family to a child listener's comprehension. She is a throwback to the storytellers of the traditional *contes de veilles* or 'old wives' tales'. Yet in telling her story to little Kate, this relic from an Edwardian or Victorian past also invokes a child teller as her prime source. It was her 'little brother', Mrs May asserts, who was privileged to see the 'frightened' creatures whom credulous 'ancestors' had still identified as fairies or 'the "little people"'.[5]

But Mrs May also calls into question the trustworthiness of her younger brother's account. He was a 'tease', she explains, who often told his older sisters 'impossible things':

> 'He was jealous, I think, because we were older – and because we could read better. He wanted to impress us; he wanted, perhaps, to shock us. And yet'– she looked into the fire – 'there was something about him – perhaps because we were brought up in India among mystery and magic and legend – something that made us think that he saw things that other people could not see; sometimes we'd know he was teasing, but at other times – well, we were not so sure ...' (6–7)

The multigenerational narrative Norton introduces here thus depends on the uncertain testimony of a sickly and lonely Anglo-Indian boy sent to England to recover from 'rheumatic fever' at the country-house of still another ancient transplant from an earlier era, his bed-ridden and slightly addled 'great-aunt' Sophy. The nameless boy, whose untrustworthiness Mrs May will again stress at the very end of her narrative, is a crucial witness. Unlike Mrs Driver, the housekeeper who reports having seen hundreds of squeaking 'little people like ... mice dressed up' (142), he has held extended conversations with Arrietty before meeting her parents, Pod and Homily Clock. But the boy cannot be recalled in a maturer incarnation to testify about the veracity of his encounters. 'He was killed', Mrs May informs Kate, 'many years ago now, on the North-West Frontier ... He died what they call "a hero's death"' (6).

Like Kate, all readers of Norton's novel thus must depend on Mrs May's guarded translation of a story told long ago by a pre-literate boy whose early fantasy-life had been shaped, much like that of a near-sighted Rudyard Kipling, by the magical tales of his native India. Yet Kate and the child-reader are extricated from adult scepticism as soon as the story adopts the Clock family's point of view. Although the adult reader cannot wholly displace a guardedness now associated with the over-protectiveness of Arrietty's cautious parents, the child reader can embrace the girl's fearless defiance of grown-up constrictions. Only in the last chapter, when Mrs May reappears as narrator, will Kate and the child reader once again have to contend with the book's opening questions about the veracity of its contents.

The layers which structure Norton's novel thus replicate those which she isolated for the recipient of her 1966 letter. The finished novel both retains and complicates her childish belief in the Borrowers. In a significant reversal, the little girl with two older brothers who later went off to war has been transformed into a little boy with two older sisters, one of whom now so cautiously transmits his child-fantasy to a receptive Kate. Yet just as Mrs May distances herself from the boy teller who was a 'tease', so did Norton originally try to distance her readers from that eager believer. Instead of opening the book with a sentence about Mrs May, as all American editions of *The Borrowers* have done until recently, the British edition focused on Mrs May's prime listener: 'It was Mrs. May who first told me about them. No, not me. How could it have been me – a wild, untidy, self-willed little girl who stared with angry eyes and was said to crunch her teeth? Kate, she should have been called. Yes, that was it – Kate. Not that the name matters much either way: she barely comes into the story.'[6]

Why does this authorial 'I' question the identity of Mrs May's interlocutor? Is this a further distancing device? Or is the act of naming a character whose name supposedly matters so little 'either way' meant to be read ironically? The story relayed by a woman called 'Mrs. *May*' *may* or *may not* be founded on fact. But its focus on a feisty teenager called Arrietty should appeal to any 'self-willed little girl' who opposes the adults who try to will her future. As a teenager who is older than the giant boy who becomes her accomplice, Arrietty refuses to be shielded from truths she likes to process on her own. She is what I earlier called a 'third entity', an intermediary who can help the author negotiate between contrary perspectives. It is hardly a coincidence that Arriety's first words in this text should come in the form of a question: '"What," Arrietty would ask, "what did happen to Egglentina?" But no one would say' (13).

Arrietty's parents want to prevent her from knowing the grisly fate of a young cousin who was killed in the house, just as presumably was her Aunt Lupy Hendreary, the emigrant who foolishly tried to return to the vacated living quarters. But by failing to answer an inquisitive child's question, Pod and Homily become her inferiors. It is Arrietty, and not these timid, infantile elders, who brings about the family's emigration. After she confesses to having met the boy she has enlisted to communicate with the surviving Hendrearys, Arrietty begins to take charge. She urges her reluctant parents to join her uncle and her boy cousins in their outdoor habitat, 'a badger's set, two fields away':

> 'Do understand,' pleaded Arrietty, 'please understand! I'm trying to save the race!'
> 'The expressions she uses!' said Homily to Pod under her breath, not without pride.
> But Pod was not listening. 'Save the race!' he repeated grimly. 'It's people like you, my girl, who do things suddenly with no respect for tradition, who'll finish us Borrowers once and for all. Don't you see what you've done?
> Arrietty met his accusing eyes. 'Yes,' she said falteringly. 'I've – I've got in touch with the only other ones still alive. So that,' she went on bravely, 'from now on we can all stick together...' (116)

By 'bravely' contesting her father's authority, Arrietty here resembles little Fern in the opening pages of *Charlotte's Web*, that other 1952 adult/child classic. The child-reader who sutures with such feisty agents can easily set aside any of the qualifications that an ironic narrator may inject. Indeed, unlike Fern, Arrietty has already earned the child-reader's respect by the fearlessness she displayed in her earlier encounter with the boy.

That encounter, however, is also marked by complications that wary older readers cannot quite as easily dismiss. In chapter 9, when Arrietty meets the boy in the garden, she first perceives a huge eye, a 'glaring eye' much 'like her own but enormous'. The voice that addresses her, 'like the eye, … enormous', is threatening. She is ordered not to come any closer, nor to try scrabbling 'at me with your nasty little hands'. 'Or', the voice twice warns, 'I'll hit you with my ash stick'. But Arrietty quickly senses that the owner of this disembodied voice is as frightened as she is. The boy admits that he has previously been scared by tiny 'things' like her: 'I've seen them. In India.' Arrietty quickly capitalises on this opportunity. Remembering her *Tom Thumb's Gazetteer of the World*, a miniature geography book her father 'borrowed' for her, this girl reader calmly points out: 'You're not in India now' (71–4).

As the ensuing exchange makes clear, Arrietty's literacy enables her to rise above the boy who towers over her:

> So this was 'the boy'! Breathless, she felt, and light with fear. 'I guessed you were about nine,' she gasped after a moment.
> He flushed. 'Well, you're wrong. I'm ten.' He looked down at her, breathing deeply. 'How old are you?'
> 'Fourteen,' said Arrietty. 'Next June,' she added, watching him.
> There was a silence while Arrietty waited, trembling a little. 'Can you read?' the boy said at last.

'Of course,' said Arrietty. 'Can't you?'

'No,' he stammered. 'I mean – yes. I mean I've just come from India.'

'What's that got to do with it?' asked Arrietty.

'Well, if you're born in India, you're bilingual. And if you are bilingual, you can't read. Not so well.'

Arrietty stared at him: what a monster, she thought, dark against the sky.

'Do you grow out of it?' she asked.

He moved a bit and she felt the cold flick of his shadow.

'Oh yes,' he said, 'it wears off. My sisters were bilingual; now they aren't a bit. They could read any of those books upstairs in the schoolroom.'

'So could I,' said Arrietty quickly, 'if someone could hold them, and turn the pages. I'm not a bit bilingual. I can read anything.' (74–5)

There are some delicious ironies embedded in this exchange. The boy has defensively exaggerated his age. As Mrs May later informs Kate, 'He was not … a very strong little boy and he was only nine (not ten as he had boasted to Arrietty)' (171). The boy's exposure to Hindi in an oral culture has apparently delayed his development as a reader of English texts even more than it slowed down the seven-year-old Kipling. The undefined scary 'things' he claims to have seen may well be 'scrabbling' insects or even small mammals as deadly as Kipling's cobra-killer, Rikki-Tikki-Tavi. But they may also have been sprites that an imaginative boy exposed to Indian folklore might conjure in his reveries or dreams. The nameless boy tries to justify himself to the girl whose own name has been deformed by her semi-literate parents. He insists that one 'can't read' when one is 'bilingual'. But what he really seems to mean is that, though nine, he does not yet *want* to read. He has resisted the print culture his sisters have accepted. He therefore feels inferior to these older sisters, whose bilingualism has worn off, as well as to the older Arrietty, whose bookishness so greatly impresses her illiterate mother.

Both Arrietty and this defensive boy seem to regard 'bilingualism' as a decided handicap. But what about Mary Norton and the sly Mrs May, her fellow practitioner of indirection? Might they be implying that the boy's retardation could be regarded as an asset? Arrietty has, after all, reached the age of puberty at which Mary Norton shelved her childhood imaginings. Rather than his fourteen-year-old interlocutor, it is the boy who thus acts as the double of the myopic child creator of a pigmy race. Could he, then, actually be Arrietty Clock's creator? In the novel's conclusion, Mrs May hints that Arrietty's memoranda book, which she found outdoors, may well have been a forgery, the handiwork of a boyish 'tease'. Yet this elderly ironist also encourages an alternative speculation. Given her unlettered brother's limited skills and her authorial circumspections, she may simply be masking the invention of an 'old wives' tale' of her very own.

The hybrid text of *The Borrowers* refuses to resolve this conundrum. Instead, the narrative invites the young and the old to participate in a reading process that steadily alternates between affiliation and disaffiliation. We are invited to partake of the pairings on which the novel is structured – the oppositions and alliances between old Mrs May and young Kate, between a Mrs May and the boy who was her younger brother, between that sickly boy and the later 'hero' who died on some 'North-West Frontier', between Arrietty and her parents. All these, and pairings I have not discussed – such as the opposition between Pod and Homily or the alliance Pod forms with great-aunt Sophy, the tipsy matriarch who assumes that he is merely an alcohol-induced figment of her imagination – can seduce us into a suspension of belief that Norton allows her younger readers to maintain but also encourages her older readers to relinquish.

Child readers, as I have suggested, can identify with Arrietty as the novel's heroine. Betty, a nine-year-old from Hong Kong, who enthusiastically recommends this book, singles out Arrietty because, though small, 'she is adventurous and does brave things like being seen by a [huge] boy'. Kelkel, a boy who is also nine and also from Hong Kong, likes the alliance that the boy forms with Arrietty and stresses his helpfulness to the Clocks. Yet he, too, declares Arrietty to be 'my favourite character. She is cute. She is a kind girl. She loves to have company.' He vows to recommend this book to current second graders 'so that next year' they can form a company of fellow-readers. By way of contrast, the eleven-year-old from New Orleans who hides behind the pseudonym of 'Monkey' and protests that 'i am not small like the borrowers in the book' is more guarded. She notes that there are different audiences and different versions of the plot: 'the book is not like the movie that i have seen and is not as exciting'. Still, the possibility of 'different endings and beginnings' entices her to consider sequels with 'a lot more adventures for Arriety'.[7]

The instability that 'Monkey' senses is something Norton asks her older readers not to forget. She is herself a 'borrower' of sorts, not only by reframing her childhood imaginings but also by enlisting the constructs of earlier writers such as Lewis Carroll, Frances Hodgson Burnett and Kipling. Her self-conscious hindsight alerts us to the precariousness of all pre-existing constructs. Children's books, Norton suggests, are innately 'bilingual' in their quasi-elegiac preservation of a receding and diminishing childhood world. The Borrowers cling to decorations and artefacts that have become outdated: 'On the walls, repeated in various colours, hung several portraits of Queen Victoria as a girl; these were postage stamps borrowed by Pod some years ago from the stamp box on the desk in the morning room' (15). Norton insists on the importance of a historical awareness. Yet she also makes it extremely difficult for her readers to affix a precise temporal framework to the story she has Mrs May tell.

When the boy examines the interior of the Clocks' main room, he sees a 'Victorian chair' and proposes to replace the effigies of a young Victoria with 'some better stamps than those', notably 'some jubilee stamps with the Taj Mahal' (126–7). Ostensibly, Norton here refers to either Victoria's golden or diamond jubilees of 1887 and 1897. Yet none of the jubilee stamps issued in 1887 featured the Taj Mahal. They merely reproduced the Queen's profile, as does the spurious 2-pence stamp that Norton's American illustrators, the Krutches, placed on the walls of the Clocks' living room. The boy's postage stamp thus must be an Indian, 2½-anna, brown-and-orange stamp of a 1935 set issued for the silver jubilee of George V. But if so, how could this ten-year-old have been killed 'many years ago' on the North-West Frontier that Kipling's Kim protected as far back as 1888? Even if he were to have died in the carnage of the First World War, in 'the mud and blood across the Channel' where Norton's older brothers fought, the young officer could hardly have availed himself of a 1935 stamp.

Mary Norton here goes beyond the anachronisms she has Mrs May implant. She deliberately undermines the historical veracity of a story that demands that its adult readers be hyper-conscious of mid-twentieth-century events. She wants such readers to understand that her narrative of persecution and survival is meant to evoke both the fall of a Victorian empire and the rise of the darker empires that succeeded it. At the same time, however, she also suggests that the entropy that has winnowed the race of Borrowers is not limited to any one historical period. Their illusory belief in their superiority over human 'Beans' will surely be adopted by others; and the mass-migrations and mass-exterminations to which they are subjected will surely recur.

Is this sombre retrospective narrative at odds with the child-reader's empathy with a forward-looking Arriety? I do not think so. Norton's book is open-ended and self-renewing. As her invocation of a multicultural India as a land of 'mystery and magic and legend' suggests, she is determined to create her own repository for the generational, sexual and cultural binaries that she juggles. Mrs May (whose name is vernal as well as a reminder of the wishfulness that binds young and old alike) shrewdly avails herself of a bilingualism that can traduce the Imaginary into the Symbolic. She resurrects the allure of a myopic child's fantasy-world by translating it into a memorable, self-knowing, printed text.

Maurice Sendak: the bitextuality of word and image

It may seem incongruous to jump from the verbal self-consciousness of Norton's sparsely illustrated text to a colourful picture book composed of ten sentences and 339 words. But Sendak's *Where the Wild Things Are* is a hybrid that blends some of the same polarities that Norton juggles in *The Borrowers*. Norton was a skilled artist who could well have illustrated her own text. She provided a model for both Diana Stanley and the Krutches in a 1951 drawing reproduced as the frontispiece for her novel's 2003 reprint. The drawing contrasts a squatting, book-engrossed, Arrietty, whom Norton prominently places in the foreground, with a thin and distant Homily, the mother, who stands, bent over her dishes, in the background. Norton here presents a conflict that Sendak dramatises in his representations of Max in the first three drawings of his picture book.

Arrietty's egress from a domestic space into the lush outdoors where she will tame a potentially scary giant is quite similar to Max's escape from confinement into a realm of roaring Wild Things. Neither child is intimidated by huge creatures that might so easily have terrified it. But if Arrietty relies on her literacy to assert herself over the younger boy she calls a 'monster', Max subdues monstrosities produced by his own aggressive imagination. The tiny Borrowers were originally invented by a small vulnerable girl; the outsized Wild Things are pseudo-adults created by a little boy who covets greater powers. Max's wolf-suit frees him from his mother's definition of a child and enables him to rule over creatures much taller than himself. Like Arrietty or like that other wolf-boy, Kipling's Mowgli, this fearless child moves between contrary states of being. Yet, as his own drawing of a rudimentary hybrid attests, what has given Max a taste of mastery is wordless art rather than an older child's reading skills. The nesting place that he and Sendak jointly construct in the narrative's first picture-frame distinctly upholds the visual over the verbal.

Conversely, by representing Arrietty as a reader, Norton's drawing calls attention to the power of literacy. Sheets of hand-written letters are plastered on the walls behind the girl. The vertical lines of script complement the printed books piled to the left of the child who is shown totally engrossed by the huge tome she is reading. The postage stamps (indistinct enough to suggest the effigies of either Victoria or George V) glued on the wall-paper also validate the importance of written communication. Bent over her stove, the figure in the back suggests a diminished future for non-readers like Homily. Here, the rapt child reader is mother of the illiterate woman. Arrietty's wider knowledge will persuade Homily to emigrate.

Sendak, on the other hand, celebrates the creativity of the little boy who vows to 'eat up' his mother.[8] Max is not a reader. He steps on two tomes as thick as those which Norton placed near Arrietty in order to reach the nail that will complete his creation of a private fantasy space. The contents of those books matter little to him. Sendak here celebrates a creativity that adults might easily misread as destructive. The adult reader who looks at the incomplete first sentence on the left-hand page of this iconotext will pause on 'mischief', the only two-syllable word among those gliding monosyllables: 'The night that Max wore his wolf suit and made *mischief* of one kind...' Whereas a parent may be horrified by the damage Max's hammer has done, the child viewer who lingers on this picture is attracted to the activity it depicts. The scar on the wall matters less than Max's successful demarcation of a child-space.

Yet even before the first and second drawings establish Max's creative powers, the child viewer who has already seen the book's double title-page will have noticed a size-reversal that is more startling than Norton's drawing of a mother dwarfed by her reading child. The huge Wild Things depicted there cower before the little boy they will later hail as 'the most wild thing of all'. Sendak's child viewer thus meets none of the obstacles that Norton strewed at the outset of a narrative designed for her child readers. The story's plot can be anticipated from the title-page. Already wearing his crown, Max is shown taming oversized monsters with his Mowgli-like 'trick of staring into their yellow eyes without blinking once'. The horned male is scared rather than scary, as is the long-haired, female-looking creature, a grotesque translation of a Jewish mother who called her child a *vilde chayeh* or 'wild thing'.

The juxtaposition presented in these double pages equally alerts the pre-literate child and the adult reader to the reversals that lie ahead. The next double-page spread opposes the minimalist verbal text to the left with the graphic text to the right. Yet this opposition will soon give way to a visual equivalent of the verbal criss-crossings I have discussed in *The Borrowers*. By juggling word and image, by erasing all words from the four double pages that show Max regressively cavorting with his subjects, and by reinstating the verbal text at the end, Sendak toys with the contraries of child and adult. And, like Norton, he challenges our notions of authorial control. The book's last illustration returns Max from a bedroom he may never have left. The older reader of *Wild Things* may well assume that Max's voyage has been a mere day-dream, a reverie cut by the provision of a tangible supper. There are no traces left of the forest that grew and grew before Max's flight into a fantasyland. And yet some changes are apparent. The crescent moon that blossomed at the time of the silent Rumpus is still full. Max's lowered hood reveals a head that is as round; a grin has replaced all his earlier scowls.

If an invisible mother has intervened to nourish her child, so has an invisible artist left his mark on this final picture. The full moon not only matches a domesticated boy's exposed head but also restores the orb greeted by a howling wolf-boy. Did Max's fantasy voyage truly take up a year or weeks or a day? In a text in which wordless drawings gradually displace the verbal narrative, temporality might seem unimportant. And yet time *has* passed here as much as in *The Borrowers* or in that famous adult novel that converts an aborted child-voyage into a voyage for grown-ups, Virginia Woolf's *To the Lighthouse* (1927). The sentence facing Sendak's last drawing must still be completed. Only after turning one more page will the adult reader stumble onto the five words that conclude a navigation that has already ended for Max and the child viewer: 'and it was still hot'.

Where the Wild Things Are has remained 'hot' as a child-classic because generations of ex-children, Mrs Mays and Mr Mays, can recall their own involvement in a story they pass on to their young. Yet Sendak's 'twice-told' text remains as slippery as *The Borrowers*. Although devoid of a self-conscious closure such as Norton's, the book relies on similar co-ordinates and is similarly open-ended. In his story of a wolf-boy who stares down wild things, Sendak invokes Kipling even more directly than Norton did through her creation of an Anglo-Indian boy. But as a writer-illustrator, he also is indebted to the precedent of the *Just So Stories*, that richly interactive text, for his own balancing of image and text, child and adult, the feminine and the masculine. The two hefty books on which little Max stands when he constructs a child-space may well represent Sendak's own earlier child-texts, *Kenny's Window* and *Very Far Away*. Yet they could just as easily stand for the two *Jungle Books* that he learned to read from Randall Jarrell, or even the *Just So Stories* and *The Jungle Book*.

Be that as it may, *Wild Things* is as much preoccupied with overcoming anxieties about the child's vulnerability as are Norton's and Kipling's fables about death and survival. The first-graders of Princeton's Riverside School who wrote to Maurice Sendak in 1997 with suggestions about alternative endings for his book had not quite exorcised their discomfort about the conflict between childish Wild Things and Momma's adult authority. How could this conflict be resolved? Some of the letter-writers wanted Max to retain his island freedom, but they worried that he might either be eaten up by Wild Things or be forced to cut off their heads before returning home.[9] And there was the dilemma posed by his broken symbiosis with the mother who wants him back. Here, in the children's own words, are three alternative possibilities for a happy ending:

(1) Momma got worried about Max and came to pick him up. When she arrived, the wild things ate her up and Max and the wild things lived forever.

(2) When Momma came, she tried to bring Max home, but the wild things said, 'Please don't take our king away!' But Momma ate up the wild things and brought Max home.

(3) Max and the wild things went on a trip around the world. Momma was sad ... On his trip, Max smelled good things and followed the smell home. And the wild things ate *with* him. And they were a happy family ever after.

The most complicated closure, however, was devised by another anonymous first-grader. Whether a girl like the little Mary Norton or a boy like Sendak's Max, this reconciler of opposites may well produce a future masterpiece of hybridity:

(4) Max decided to remain king of the wild things until someone could come to take his place. Momma wanted Max back so she got into her own boat. The wild things tried to eat her, but Max said, 'No! Eat yourselves, but don't eat my Momma!' Momma and Max got back in Momma's boat and sailed home. And into the night of his very own room where their supper was waiting for them ... But it was cold.

NOTES

1. Jacqueline Rose, *The Case of Peter Pan or the Impossibility of Children's Fiction* (London: Macmillan, 1984), p. 143.
2. Mitzi Myers and U. C. Knoepflmacher, eds., 'Cross-Writing the Child and the Adult', special issue, *Children's Literature*, 25 (1997); Knoepflmacher, 'The Balancing of Child and Adult: An Approach to Victorian Fantasies for Children', *Nineteenth-Century Fiction*, 37 (1983), 497–530.
3. Knoepflmacher, 'Introduction: Fairy Tales and the Value of Impurity', in *Marvels and Tales*, special issue, ed. Andrea Immel and Jan Susina, 17 (2003), 15–36.
4. The letter is printed in Mary Norton, *The Borrowers*, Fiftieth Anniversary Edition, foreword by Leonard S. Marcus (Orlando: Harcourt, 2003). References to the pages of this letter will appear in parentheses in the main text.
5. Norton, *The Borrowers* (San Diego: Harcourt Brace Jovanovich, 1986), p. 9. Unless otherwise noted, further references to the novel will be to this edition and will appear in parentheses in the main text.
6. Norton, *The Borrowers* (London: Puffin, 1958), p. 7.
7. These responses are from an international website, *Reading Matters*: www.read ingmatters.co.uk/book2.php?id=108 (accessed 13 March 2008).
8. Maurice Sendak, *Where the Wild Things Are* (New York: Harper and Row, 1963), unpaginated.
9. The children had seen a video of the Sendak/Knussen Glyndebourne Festival Opera in which Max (the soprano Karen Beardsley) swings a sword that accidentally decapitates one of the huge Wild Things created by Jim Hensen. I am grateful to Mr Paul Chapin for sharing these student responses with me.

LYNNE VALLONE

Ideas of difference in children's literature

The rather obvious observation that children are 'different' – from adults, from each other – stands as the point of departure for this chapter on the foundational nature of discourses of difference in the development of 300 years of Anglo-American children's literature. Simply put, without a powerful guiding belief in essential differences between adult and child, there would be no 'children's literature'. Awareness of 'differences', or acknowledgement of the presence of 'others', has been noted and explored in children's literature from its earliest inception: consider one of the tales from John Aikin and Anna Laetitia Barbauld's widely read *Evenings At Home* (1792–6), 'Travellers' Wonders'. In this tale about cultural perspectives, Captain Compass' children – whose imaginations have been stirred by the marvellous sights and people described in *Gulliver's Travels* and stories about Sinbad the sailor – implore him to recount adventures from his own voyages. The fond father replies with a long description of a remarkable people whose habitations, clothes, diet and customs all appear to be perfectly strange to the children – for example the inhabitants fill their mouths with noxious smoke, uncover their heads as a salutation, and spread a delicious grease upon virtually all of their food – until one of them realises with a start that their father has been describing Britain all along. Responding to their surprise, the Captain states, 'But I meant to shew you, that a foreigner might easily represent every thing as equally strange and wonderful among us, as we could do with respect to his country.'[1] The guessing game provides the amusement for the reader, and the recognition and tolerance of different cultural perspectives provides the moral instruction in the tale, twin goals of most eighteenth- and early nineteenth-century literature for children.

This chapter will begin by discussing the 'natural' differences between adults and children that undergird the creation of a literature meant to bridge or mark that difference, and then turns to a consideration of changing categories of difference expressed within children's literature over time – including gender, race, disability and sexuality – and concludes with a brief consideration of size, given that size represents a significant distinction informing the interactions between adult and child in lived, as well as in literary, child experience. I trace two general responses to difference – what might be called 'conversion' and 'resistance', the one dedicated to the erasure of difference between adult and child, the other predicated upon an acceptance and celebration of the differences between children. Didactic 'conversion' narratives lead the child character (and encourage the child reader) out of the vulnerable, incomplete state of childhood and into maturity or proto-adulthood. 'Resistant' narratives, by contrast, reject the politics of conversion that universalise children as well as reify the hierarchical relationship of adult over child, in order to embrace the particular child, the 'differentiated' child. I intend these broad categories to be suggestive and illustrative of general trends, while at the same time I will suggest ways to problematise and historicise each shift. In general, the first of these is dominant in early children's literature of the seventeenth, eighteenth and early nineteenth centuries, in which the difference between adulthood and childhood was typically viewed as both natural (arising from biological and physiological causes) and troubling, while the second, more child-centred view of difference essentially reflects an acceptance of the special nature of childhood as distinct from adulthood and focuses on the differences within children and between different childhoods.

For the last 300 years or so, children have been considered a distinct social category (though what this meant in the seventeenth century is quite different from what it means today, of course), and a clear separation has existed between the child and the adult. The child's perceived difference from adults requires unique responses within legal, economic, educational and family systems. Within the marketplace, too, the child functions both as a separate audience for sellers and as a significant consumer of goods. Clearly, children are also markedly different from adults in both physiological and psychological ways. Children look, sound and act in ways that are distinctly 'childlike' even when they are engaging in the same activities that adults enjoy – playing sport, for example, watching television or even sleeping.

Although children are easily recognisable when we see them, asleep or awake, determining the definition of 'children' and drawing the boundaries of 'childhood' are less obvious. The fuzzy liminality of adolescence intrudes, as do the sober realities of many children's lives. Can child soldiers forced to kill be said to inhabit childhood, for example? Literary characters can reflect this confusion. Characters as varied as Kipling's Kim, Collodi's Pinocchio, Ursula Le Guin's Ged and Louise Fitzhugh's Harriet the Spy are all 'children' of one kind or another in the act of 'becoming', of maturing. Yet they all remain very different both from adult characters and from each other. But even if 'the Child' does not actually exist, this fantasy creature is often invoked, exhibited or manipulated in the intersecting realms of politics, education and social policy.

Literature written specifically for children provides a particularly clear window through which theories of the child can be viewed, and theories of difference explored. In early children's literature, works for children attempted to supply the needs of incomplete, impressionable and ignorant children by offering them religious guidance, moral lessons and/or reading instruction, 'converting' them from childish ways and guiding them away from childhood. In seventeenth-century Protestant religious beliefs (particularly the Puritan strains), the child's soul was considered to be the equal of the adult's soul, and so even the youngest babe was at risk of eternal damnation. Yet, although the same assumptions about the sinful nature of all humans, adult and child, informed the creation of children's books, early religious children's literature adopted a particular learning model suited to young readers, featuring child characters as positive or negative examples for child readers to emulate or to reject. James Janeway's *A Token For Children* (1671–2) functions in just this way. Janeway's conversational preface, 'containing directions to children', identifies and describes sensitive child readers ideally suited to receive his exhortations and directly addresses his audience in mock 'dialogue' in which only the adult actually speaks:

> Methinks that little Boy looks as if he had a mind to learn good things. Methinks I hear one say, well, I will never tell a lye more, I will never keep any naughty Boy company more, they will teach me to swear, and they will speak naughty words, they do not love God. I'le [*sic*] learn my Catechism, and get my Mother to teach me to pray, and I will go to weep and cry to Christ, and will not be quiet till the Lord hath given me Grace. O that's my brave Child indeed![2]

In Janeway's popular work, life-stories of pious children – 'just like you'! – and their inevitable deaths create a persuasive rhetoric of the pleasures of repentance and conversion.

More secular works, such as John Locke's comprehensive and generally humane *Some Thoughts Concerning Education* (1693) aimed at an adult readership looking for guidance in child-rearing, similarly adopted the stance that children must be encouraged to 'convert' from lawless and ignorant childish ways to embrace properly civilised adult modes of behaviour and knowledge. In discussing such varied topics as health and nutrition, play, right and wrong conduct, discipline, social relations and character flaws, as well as curriculum and educational theory and practice, Locke stresses the rational nature of the child as the key to successful education in its broadest sense. By appealing to reason adapted to the child's abilities at different ages, Locke argues, the parent may unlock or 'turn' his child to good effect: '[Children] understand [reasoning] as early as they do language; and, if I misobserve not, they love to be treated as rational creatures sooner than is imagined. 'Tis a pride should be cherished in them and, as much as can be, made the *great instrument to turn them by*.'[3] The treatise's best-known idea, of the child as white paper or formless wax, makes the adult the agent of inscribing or moulding the child, or 'converting' childhood to adulthood.

Jean-Jacques Rousseau's theories about child-rearing are also intelligible only if viewed through the lens of difference. In *Émile: or On Education* (1762), Rousseau argues that a truly healthy, moral, vigorous and dutiful man can be raised only in isolation from the corruption of society and under the firm guidance of an authoritarian tutor who will eventually lead him to enter civil society. Rousseau bases his influential treatise on the premise that differences between adult and child are innate and should be respected. To act otherwise is to encourage social disorder: 'Nature wants children to be children before being men. If we want to pervert this order, we shall produce precious fruits which will be immature and insipid and will not be long in rotting ... Childhood has its ways of seeing, thinking, and feeling which are proper to it.'[4] Yet, the repeated argument that children ought not to be treated as junior adults – indeed, Rousseau vehemently disagrees with Locke's maxim that the child be reasoned with from an early age – must be read in conjunction with the overall purposes of his work: a diagnosis of modern society and psychology by way of an educational experiment designed to produce the ideal Man from the incomplete – even if organically so – child.

Inspired by both Locke and Rousseau, as well as by the practical experience she gained in helping to raise her many younger siblings, Maria Edgeworth's works for children emphasise the natural faults to which children fall prey – laziness, love of attention, frivolousness and selfishness – and either the means by which these faults can be overcome or the devastating consequences of indulging them. For example, Edgeworth uses dialogue between the lively child Rosamond and her parents both to underscore Rosamond's childish misunderstandings about character, conduct and self-control and to highlight her parents' exemplary opinions to which she should aspire. The resolution of these misunderstandings by each tale's end demonstrates her growing maturity. 'The Birth-day Present', a moral tale in *The Parent's Assistant* (1796), opens with a dialogue between Rosamond and her (to modern readers) rather preternaturally even-tempered and rational mother. Rosamond wishes to know why her birthday is not celebrated as is her cousin Bell's. Rosamond's honest question comes from her child's heart, yet the training she requires necessitates that the 'right' answer be given from her mother's *head*, as she mimics Rosamond's speech pattern and emphasises dispassionate thinking:

> 'And will you, Rosamond – not now, but when you have time to think about it – tell me why I should make any difference between your birth-day and any other day?'
> Rosamond thought – but she could not find out any reason.[5]

Government by reason, however, does not preclude affection. Rosamond's parents, while unsentimental, demonstrate their deep regard for their daughters through attentiveness and compliments when deserved. Although Rosamond is often set upon the path in search of rational behaviour and parental approval through such conversations with her elders and betters, Edgeworth's moral tales demonstrate that lessons are best learned through experience rather than lecture. Rosamond remains inexperienced – inherently so – but her stories ably show how a child can be gradually socialised and educated in logical reasoning within a loving family (as opposed to Rousseau's child of nature, Émile, who is raised in isolation from society), and become, by her actions or through observation and conversation, more adult-like and worthy of respect.

For influential authors such as Janeway, Locke, Rousseau, Edgeworth and their inheritors, differences between adult and child are both noted as natural *and* found to be intolerable. As I have suggested, the reliance upon difference as philosophical, biological and ideological underpinnings to the construction of the child, and the concomitant desire to mitigate and mediate those differences in literature, parenting manuals and moral tales, result in texts that stress the importance of leading the child out of vulnerable childhood and into productive citizenship. This conversion narrative, a genre I have been gesturing towards in this history of a certain fixation found in Anglo-American children's literature, was especially skilfully adapted by nineteenth-century Evangelical writers for children through inversion of the typical roles of adult and child. Accessing Romantic-era ideologies about the exceptional wisdom of childhood in addition to scriptural (that is, New Testament) messages about the special nature of childhood, child characters in the sentimental religious novels of popular and prolific authors such as Hesba Stretton function as innocent and saintly correctives to the fallen adults around them, converting them from some of the weaknesses of adulthood – worldliness, greed, self-consciousness and rigidity – to a childish acceptance of God's love. In her hunger and rags, Stretton's 'street arab' Jessica, in *Jessica's First Prayer* (1867) may at first appear to be an unlikely child hero. However, Jessica's suffering and deep yearning to learn about God make her an ideal ambassador for the text's messages about Christian charity, selflessness and true faith, both for characters within the text (such as the minister's daughters and Mr Daniel, the somewhat miserly and status-conscious coffee-stall owner and chapel-keeper) and for the child readers outside of the text. In making her first prayer asking God to send money to repay for donated coffee as well as to learn about Him, Jessica reveals her profound innocence: both in misunderstanding the nature of God's bounty and in embodying the spiritual ideal of a penitent empty vessel before God. This ill-favoured child's prayer helps to deepen the faith of her listeners – especially the adults, Mr Daniel and the minister – who are all moved by Jessica's sincere and selfless supplication to God.

Jessica's First Prayer and other works for children by popular authors such as George MacDonald and Frances Hodgson Burnett build upon powerful, Romantic-era notions of childhood innocence and influence. However, these sentimental reflections of the superlative qualities of the child in relation to the fallen adult give way, in part, to literary representations of adult conceptions of the (middle-class) carefree and protected child's world. The child characters in 'children's world' fiction, among them some of the most beloved creations in children's fiction – Tom Sawyer, Pippi Longstocking, E. Nesbit's Bastables, Arthur Ransome's Blacketts and Walkers and so on – reflect an ideology of difference that recognises the child as valuable as such, rather than only when measured against adults.

A comparison between a late Victorian example of a sentimentally elevated child character whose 'exotic' nature and extreme difference from flawed adulthood is emphasised – Lewis Carroll's Bruno in *Sylvie and Bruno* (1889) – and the mutually respectful adult and child characters (though idealised in another way) in Arthur Ransome's *Swallows and Amazons* (1930) helps to demonstrate both the patronising nature of childhood 'innocence' as a dominant construction of childhood and the growing emphasis within children's literature on an appreciation of childhood interdependence and independence from adults. Although quite different in form and purpose, both *Sylvie and Bruno* and *Swallows and Amazons* represent essentially utopic visions of a childhood set apart from adulthood. In the preface to *Sylvie and Bruno*, Carroll specifically states his particular view of the nature of childhood as hours composed of 'innocent merriment'. *Sylvie and Bruno*, he went on:

> is written, not for money, and not for fame, but in the hope of supplying, for the children whom I love, some thoughts that may suit those hours of which are the very life of Childhood; and also in the hope of suggesting, to them and to others, some thoughts that may prove, I would fain hope, not wholly out of harmony with the graver cadences of Life.[6]

Sylvie and Bruno is a complicated and chaotic dream-vision that, through the experiences of an ailing adult narrator who steps in and out of 'real' life into another world, confronts issues of death, suffering, religious faith and the nature of childhood. The superlative purity, simplicity, frailty and beauty of Carroll's child characters cannot be contained in ordinary childhood – the children are fairies, dream-presences idealised into concentrated and minia-turised representations of Innocence. Carroll's baby-talking Bruno and sweetness-and-light Sylvie may grate on modern ears, yet the interactions between adult and child characters offer a good look at the patronising attitude of this ideology of innocence. During one of the narrator's dream-visions, he joins the fairy Sylvie just as she rushes to comfort a distraught Bruno, whose indignation at a bee sting and a stubbed toe cause Sylvie to kiss away his tears and the narrator to defend Bruno's innocence in the onslaught:

> 'That Bee should be ashamed of itself!' I said severely, and Sylvie hugged and kissed the wounded hero till all tears were dried.
> 'My finger's quite unstung now!' said Bruno. 'Why doos there be stones? Mister Sir, does oo know?'
> 'They're good for *something*,' I said: 'even if we don't know *what*.'[7]

For the nostalgic Carroll, Sylvie (especially, since for Carroll the female retains a connection to innocence unavailable to males) and Bruno do not in the least require conversion to adulthood; indeed, adulthood can represent corruption, worldliness and loss of faith. Their eternal childhood, supplied by their fairy nature, safely protects them from adult corruption. The narrator's hastening journey to another status and sphere – presumably, death and Heaven – is eased by the interaction with child figures that represent child-hood writ large, closer, by far, to God. While no actual children act or speak as do Carroll's creations, realism is not his object.

For Arthur Ransome, however, who based his child characters on actual children, the childhood idyll does not rely upon fairyland or sentimentalised portraits of childhood to make the distinction between childhood's freedoms and adulthood's cares. The two British writers share a nostalgia for the past, to be sure, and a belief in the importance of childhood, yet for Ransome childhood's past can be located in the imagination of ordinary and more realistic child characters.

The Blackett and Walker children of the first book in Ransome's popular Swallows and Amazons series (1930–47) together create an idyllic summer's world of seafaring adventure complete with pirates, natives and 'savages' (various adults). The four Swallows (the Walker children) make a treaty with the two Amazons (the Blackett girls) in order to unite against a common enemy, the Blacketts' Uncle Jim, renamed Captain Flint, who has banished the children from his houseboat in an effort to complete a book manuscript without distraction. Though adult and child are seemingly set against each other, the game is good fun for all parties as the adults participate in the game the children construct. Most importantly, the children camp alone on an island and work together as a team. Within the child-centred social world they create, although the older children wield greater authority, each child plays an important role and, ultimately, pirate and seaman / adult and child unite in the search for Captain Flint's stolen treasure (his typewriter, diaries and manuscript). At the conclusion of the novel, after a great storm that the brave and practical children successfully ride out alone, all of the anxious adults converge upon the children's camp but ultimately let them return to ordinary life in their own time:

> After they were gone the Swallows and Amazons looked at each other. They were rather glum.
> 'It's the natives,' said Nancy. 'Too many of them. They turn everything into a picnic.'
> 'Mother doesn't,' said Titty.
> 'Nor does ours when she's alone,' said Nancy.
> 'And Captain Flint's not a bit like a native when he's by himself,' said Titty.
> 'It's when they all get together,' said Nancy. 'They can't help themselves, poor things.'[8]

For the children, the nature of adulthood is found to be, not surprisingly, limited and even a bit disappointingly 'childlike'. The view that children are 'better' – cleverer, more sophisticated – than adults is a mainstay of contemporary popular culture (including, especially, television and film comedies in which the wise-cracking kids outsmart the dim-witted or preoccupied parents). Many late twentieth- and twenty-first-century children's books feature comic and cynical views of the failures of adulthood in nurturing, educating or even conversing with contemporary youth. In these books the difference between adult and child favours the child not because of any greater intrinsic worth of childhood so much as because the adult values depicted are limited to consumerism, competition and social-climbing.

As this quick sketch has shown, children's literature emerged from perceived differences between adult and child that developed over time, in conjunction with changing constructions of childhood. When difference reads as 'problematic', the focus becomes helping the child character (and child-reader) convert from childhood to adulthood. Or the belief in the child's special status as innocent and wise results in a nostalgic view encouraging adults to fantasise about childhood and, in so doing, become themselves more open to childlikeness. The self-conscious and adventuresome child characters of later fiction tend to remain apart from the adult, and the idyllic child world represents a coherent choice in favour of separation and independence. But these 'macro' level differences between adult and child (or wondrous child-ishness in competition with its opposite, stultifying and rigid 'adultness') fail to tell the whole story: on the 'micro' level, multiple differences – in social class, ability, race, gender or sexual preference, for example – between children or youth may also create plot lines and problems to be solved within the text. In 'resistant' narratives, the universal child becomes the particular child – raced, classed, gendered and so on.

A quick look at the representation of race and class in two influential children's books of the late eighteenth and early nineteenth centuries – Thomas Day's *The History of Sandford and Merton* (1783–9) and Mary Martha Sherwood's *The History of the Fairchild Family* (Part 1, 1818) – both supports and interrupts the conversion narrative that I have been discussing. The target child character (usually a faulty child of the middle or upper class) is instructed in piety and selflessness, industry and manliness, through the actions of a lower-class or 'foreign' character. This type of relationship is most clearly seen in terms of class: in both *Sandford and Merton* and *The Fairchild Family*, lower-class children function as exemplars of higher-class religious, social and behavioural codes. For example, little Henry Fairchild learns the value of Christian submission, gratitude and patience in conversation with young Charles Trueman whose physical circumstances are dire: he is both poverty-stricken and in failing health. Yet Charles' 'good death' – he is eager to die and does so surrounded by friends and family – functions especially effectively because his faith sustains him even in the face of his extreme poverty and privation. Charles' goodness sets the stage for Henry, whose life is much easier, to become a more charitable, helpful and conscientious gentleman's son. Like Jessica, in *Jessica's First Prayer*, the poor child acts as an agent of social and religious conversion within a narrow compass that does not affect the political or social strata at all.

Thomas Day bases his didactic work *Sandford and Merton* on the idea that the hard-working, sober and steady farming class, represented by his ideal boy, Harry Sandford, offers a virtuous model for the middle and upper classes to follow, and in this he underscores a discourse of conversion. Young Tommy Merton, indulged, ignorant and inflated by self-importance, learns much from Harry, the unsophisticated yet noble rustic companion of his youth. Tommy's ultimate gratitude towards Harry makes the book's lesson explicit: 'You have taught me how much better it is to be useful than rich or fine; how much more amiable to be good than to be great.'[9] Yet Day goes further in exploring class difference than this concluding comment might suggest. Harry questions the validity of a system that would seem to prefer the idle over the industrious and the sophisticated over the sensible:

> Surely ... there cannot be so much difference between one human being and another; or if there is, I should think that part of them the most valuable, which cultivates the ground and provides necessaries for all the rest: not those, who understand nothing but dress, walking with their toes out, staring modest people out of countenance, and jabbering a few words of a foreign language.[10]

Similarly, Tommy's feeling of superiority over the black servants in his household is directly interrogated in the text, as is the very notion of a hierarchy of skin colour. In the aftermath of a near tragedy in which Tommy is saved from a rampaging bull by the combined brave efforts of Harry and a poor African man, the African muses, 'Is a black horse thought to be inferior to a white one, in speed, or strength, or courage? Is a white cow thought to give more milk or a white dog to have an acuter scent in pursuing the game? ... Why then should a certain race of men imagine themselves superior to the rest...?'[11] However, although Day's didactic story promotes tolerance and acceptance between races and classes, deep divisions are maintained in the text. In the case of the deserving African man, who refers to the white characters as 'master', the place in the Sandford household that is found for him as a reward for his thankfulness and industry – the stable – suggests that demarcations of differences between race and class have not been entirely overcome or successfully negotiated away from notions of hierarchy.

Within children's literature, the impulse to confront notions of difference cannot be separated from questions of identity – figuring out who the protagonist (and child-reader) might become both in relation to others and in the surrounding world. Early children's fiction tends to use difference in others to highlight the 'normative' (or white, middle-class) character's identity; more recent children's books offer multiple perspectives. In early children's fiction, difference is often used to demonstrate positive qualities in the 'other' child (the 'industrious lower-class child', the 'grateful Negro'), or intolerable distinctions that must be transcended or erased (the black child who 'acts white', the disabled child who overcomes an injury). An 'ethics of resistance' argues that difference should neither be effaced nor explained away, but celebrated, rejecting and resisting the narrative of conversion that holds that the girlish boy or tomboy must become conventionally gender-normed, or that black characters will be successful only in rejecting or ignoring their racial and cultural heritage, or that disabled characters can be miraculously cured of their disability. Many contemporary children's books – this is especially true in terms of gender and race – no longer feel the need to take up the challenge of educating the reader (who is not always assumed to be white or male) about race and gender relations in every narrative. Not every book that includes a protagonist of colour has to be about race relations with a white majority. Some recent children's books resist the essentialising impulse that turns every children's story that includes non-whites into narratives of 'black and white' (for instance, Norton Juster's joyous picture book *The Hello Goodbye Window* (2005), illustrated by Chris Raschka, tells the story of a little girl's relationship with her grandparents, one of whom is black and the other white). In order briefly to touch upon some of the shifts in the politics and discourse of difference in gender, social class, ability and sexuality, and to show some of the ways in which these differences have come to be celebrated and sustained in children's literature, I will pair texts from early and late periods.

Many classic works of Victorian and Edwardian Anglo-American children's literature featured androgynous boys or tomboy girls. From George Arthur in Thomas Hughes' *Tom Brown's Schooldays* (1857) and Colin Craven in Frances Hodgson Burnett's *The Secret Garden* (1911) to Louisa May Alcott's famous Jo March in *Little Women* (1868–9) or Katy Carr in Susan Coolidge's *What Katy Did* (1872), the feminine boy and the boyish girl are 'converted' from gender confusion to conventional gender norms. Fifteen-year-old Jo March, for example, proclaims that she 'can't get over [her] disappointment in not being a boy, and it's worse than ever now, for I'm dying to go and fight with papa, and I can only stay at home and knit like a poky old woman'; ten years later, a chastened Jo gives up her boyish dreams to see the world and remain independent when she admits her loneliness and accepts a husband.[12] Jo's happy ending requires that she modify her desires to reflect more selfless and attainable feminine goals, assisting needy children rather than indulging fantasies of adventure and fame. In late twentieth- and twenty-first-century novels, not surprisingly, female characters, especially in teen fiction, are more likely to be given polymorphous gender identities while male characters develop nurturing qualities. In Anne Fine's comic *Flour Babies* (1992), for example, tough underachiever Simon Martin falls in love with his science experiment, a burlap bag 'infant', and learns not only the effort it takes to care for the helpless, but also how to begin to understand and forgive his own father's abandonment of him when he was a baby. Simon's masculine identity 'improves' through greater flexibility in conventional gender roles. Francesca Lia Block's fiction for teens in the Weetzie Bat series and other works blends gender-bending, punk sensibilities and appealing heterosexual, homosexual and transgendered characters in a utopic, highly mannered vision of a magical Los Angeles in which the evils of intolerance, oppression and disease can be mitigated by sexual expression and loving friendships.

The friendships between lower-class characters and those of more privileged status, in beloved books such as *The Secret Garden* and L. M. Montgomery's *Anne of Green Gables* (1908), are key ingredients in the 'conversions' of others from illness to health, or from loneliness to sociability. The peasant boy Dickon Sowerby in *The Secret Garden* and penniless Anne Shirley in Montgomery's novel both function as agents healing others. Inextricably linked with their low social status to which 'magical' healing properties accrue, these characters' natural childish goodness – Dickon's special qualities derive directly from his close relationship with the soil and all living things, while Anne's charming sense of self is similarly 'simple' and unaffected – transforms the sickly and lonely around them to health and happiness. The abuses and difficulties faced by the Mexican farm-worker population in Depression-era California, as well as the resilience of their close-knit community, explored in Pam Muñoz Ryan's *Esperanza Rising* (2000), by contrast, offers a view of a socio-economic underclass untouched by nostalgia for an agrarian past that relied upon an exploitative labour system. Young Esperanza Ortega's story of growth and maturation, while inspiring, illustrates the shift in children's literature I have been describing. Esperanza's 'difference' (she was born to a wealthy Mexican family, but her father's murder, a devastating fire and political corruption in her town force her to flee with her remaining family members to America) functions solely within her segregated community without 'converting' white characters to a greater social awareness, or without converting her into a white character. 'Outside' of the text, however, a clear message of tolerance and appreciation for the differences of others is promoted.

When differences between children are identified as problems to be solved, rather than something to be tolerated or celebrated, the constructions of childhood that undergird them are exposed. For example, the belief that children are best raised within a family took hold in the nineteenth century (and remains powerful today). In texts from this period, the solitariness of a child without a family often requires a solution. In Charles Dickens' *Oliver Twist* (1837–8), Oliver is a singular orphan. His feminine appearance and desire to be good mark him as special, but his orphan status itself also readjusts once his family history and remaining family are discovered. Oliver represents the orphan who is not really orphaned, or who is without relatives only temporarily. Similarly, in another popular orphan tale, Johanna Spyri's *Heidi* (1881), a change in atmosphere cures a seemingly intractable form of difference: physical disability. The crippled, wealthy Clara Sesemann turns out to be healthy and 'normal' after all. Clara's new-found sociability, her stint in the restorative Alpine air, her diet of delicious goat's milk and the beauty of the mountain views all contribute to her ability to walk. These faux-orphan/faux-'cripple' stories stress a shifting politics of conversion that transforms the incomplete child – without a family, without mobility – into the happy child: 'whole' and social. Again, these categories do not remain entirely fixed over time as the number of children's books that include differently configured families (step-families, single-parent families, bi-racial families, same-sex-parented families) makes clear.

Children's literature has never been free of images of the body. 'Healthiness' and disability have been long-standing concerns, as we have seen. Physical desires have also been a constant presence – appetite, for instance, as appealed to in marvellous long passages about food in Kenneth Grahame's *The Wind in the Willows* (1908), and even passionate, though usually platonic, same-sex friendships such as those described in innumerable school stories of the nineteenth and early twentieth centuries. (Erotic aspects of the child's body or desires have tended to be sublimated into heated descriptions of religious ecstasy.) In modern children's books, however, sex acts, sexual feelings (hetero- and homo-), sexual abuse and sexual identity are no longer entirely taboo subjects. In the 1960s, heterosexual sex entered the Young Adult canon by way of cautionary tales about premarital intercourse leading to unwanted pregnancy (in Paul Zindel's 1969 *My Darling, My Hamburger*, for example). Yet just a few years later, female sexual desire was celebrated in the still notorious *Forever* (1975) by Judy Blume, and artificial insemination (for a lesbian couple desiring a child) in Lesléa Newman's *Heather Has Two Mommies* (1989). Neither Heather, nor her mommies, demonstrate any difference from their neighbours or co-workers: they work inside and outside of the home, care for each other, own a dog; only Heather's birth-story is unusual (and a bit beyond the understanding of the picture book's target audience). In the first brave books for teenagers that tackled issues of homosexual desire and homophobia, such as Sandra Scoppetone's *Trying Hard to Hear You* (1974), the gay characters tended to be a doomed group: first, the very presence of gay characters educated the non-gay characters and readers in the spirit of 'we're all the same, underneath, after all' – but ultimately these characters are generally sacrificed to some kind of accident or trauma that facilitated the non-gay characters learning a lesson. This trend has been slowed with the advent of books by authors such as Nancy Garden and Francesca Lia Block. Although sometimes marred by stereotypes and comic excess, gay characters typically appear more often in television programmes and feature films than in fiction for the young. When the issue of difference is sexual preference or sexuality, the celebration of difference and gay identity has not entirely entered the arena of literature for children.

I began this chapter by historicising the ways ideologies of differences between adult and child were reflected in early children's literature and educational works and then discussed some examples of children's texts that negotiate difference between children via conversion, or suggested some examples in which conversion is resisted. These categories are meant to offer broad strokes only and they can and should be interrogated further. One important way to interrogate the history of difference in children's literature is by an examination of size difference in children's books. The history of size-difference narratives exists alongside the politics of conversion so prevalent in early children's literature and articulates a complementary view of the complex relationships between adult and child or between different children. Often, the extreme difference represented by figures out of scale – giants or thumblings, for example – emphasises similarities rather than antipathies between characters. For example, Mary Norton's *The Borrowers* (1952) explores the sympathies between lonely and imaginative children of wildly different sizes (the large Boy and tiny Borrower, Arrietty). Indeed, when viewed together, conversion, resistance and size offer a more nuanced history of difference in children's literature. Size difference, an essential element in children's literature from folk narratives to various forms of fantasy literature, throws the complicated relationship between adult and child into high relief. The delightful big child / small adult dynamic explored in many children's books, for example, not only indulges a powerful and comic fantasy of power inversion, but also guides the child reader towards serious considerations of the position of the Other, whether adult or another child.

Big and small often function metaphorically as representations of adult and child, or the experienced and innocent, or the powerful and powerless. But, just as often, negotiations between the power imbalance between big and small weighs in favour of the wily small; and sometimes big and small co-operate and form a super-being of superlative size and extraordinary intelligence or empathy in books such as Rodman Philbrick's *Freak the Mighty* (1993), Melvin Burgess' *The Earth Giant* (1995) or the 1999 animated film version of Ted Hughes' *The Iron Giant*. I mention here just a few examples of recent children's literature that use the relationship between big and small to explore questions of ethical conduct and illuminate an ethics of resistance. In particular, a subset of the discourse on size, stories that explore the inverted relationship between miniature adults and 'large' (conventionally sized) children, highlights power relations so that the child figure functions as both the cultural and physical norm. The crisis that ensues as a result of the comic wish-fulfilment fantasy – the child as 'master' and the adult as toy – focuses attention on an exaggerated Otherness the child confronts.

In children's books in which miniature adult characters are typed as vulnerable, their caretakers are often children, thereby inverting the conventional paradigm in which adults protect children. These children's books are written from the perspective of the (large) child, the holders of the normative scale in the books. This combination of big and small combined in the child character helps to highlight lessons about recognising subjectivity in others. These books are particularly well suited to promote an ethics of big and small that emphasise the identities and personhood of the small, and the child's responsibility in understanding and respecting difference. A number of twentieth-century children's books rise to this challenge, among them T. H. White's *Mistress Masham's Repose* (1947), Pauline Clarke's *The Twelve and the Genii* (*The Return of the Twelves* in the US, 1962) and Raymond Briggs' picture book *The Man* (1992).

All three books speak directly to the potential for violent conflict when size difference erases the more important affinities that humans share. They centre on the relationship between a big child and small adults. In *The Man*, the child holds power over a tiny, hairy, naked man, but in this picture book, the Man, unlike the Lilliputians or the Twelve, plays up his helplessness to John, the boy who accepts, somewhat reluctantly, a parenting and nurturing relationship. Their relationship is fraught not only because Man's endless demands require John to lie and dissemble to his parents, to spend his pocket money, and to entertain Man, but also because Man's adult maleness throws into relief John's youth and 'feminine' sensibilities (he likes art and hates sport, to Man's disgust). Man takes advantage of his size, and inability to feed and clothe himself, in order to manipulate John into providing his favourite foods, drink and needs (conversation and cuddles on demand), yet he also shrewdly confronts John by exposing the fascination John feels at Man's strangeness, his otherness. When John attempts to guess Man's origin, he hits upon a likely identity for Man: he must be a Borrower. Not aware of Borrowers, Man reacts badly to the comparison with creatures who live under floorboards and calls John 'prejudiced'.[13] Man and John, by honestly revealing their distrust and resentments, begin to breach the wide divide that separates big and small, adult and child, and even different children. Man wants to be understood for who he is. 'I am ME', he repeats over and over. This is the cry that both adults and children make. Man refutes a discourse of conversion: to be loved, respected, valued, you must act, look and believe more like me.

We continue to believe that children are different from adults – and they are biologically, physically and psychologically 'other'. And the pleasure and pain of human existence contains the impossibility of bridging that difference between self and other. We are always individuals, alone together. The child functions as a unique Other to the adult – each adult carries the memory of childhood within. But these 'children of air', in Robert Louis Stevenson's phrase, haunt and tease with their elusive nearness, their traces of the past.[14] On the one hand, narratives of conversion ask children to leave childhood behind, or to become 'better' children – either more like adults or more like a nostalgic view of childhood that never was. Resistant texts, on the other hand, predicated on more fluid constructions of childhoods that tend to celebrate difference, offer additional identity positions for the child within and without the text. To return to Aikin and Barbauld's 'Traveller's Wonders', the child characters' amazement that the customs of their own people could seem so foreign enlarges their ability, through narrative, to imagine other cultural perspectives. This late eighteenth-century 'voyage' of ethical discovery contains valuable implications for the modern world and for the place of children's literature within it.

NOTES

1. John Aikin and Anna Laetitia Barbauld, 'Travellers' Wonders', in *Evenings at Home; or The Juvenile Budget Opened* (6 vols., London: J. Johnson, 1792–6), vol. I, p. 31.
2. James Janeway, *A Token for Children Being an Exact Account of the Conversion, Holy and Exemplary Lives and Joyful Deaths of Several Young Children* (1671–2; London: Dorman Newman, 1676), p. [xviii].
3. John Locke, *Some Thoughts Concerning Education*, ed. Ruth W. Grant and Nathan Tarcov (1693; Indianapolis: Hackett, 1996), p. 58. Emphasis added.
4. Jean-Jacques Rousseau, *Émile: or On Education*, trans. Allan Bloom (1762; London: Penguin Books, 1991), p. 90.
5. Maria Edgeworth, *The Parent's Assistant; or, Stories for Children, Part II* (3 vols., London: J. Johnson, 1796), vol. II, p. 5.
6. Lewis Carroll, *Sylvie and Bruno* (London: Macmillan and Company, 1889), p. xiii.
7. Carroll, *Sylvie and Bruno*, pp. 308–9.
8. Arthur Ransome, *Swallows and Amazons* (1930; Harmondsworth: Puffin, 1962), pp. 354–5.
9. Thomas Day, *The History of Sandford and Merton* (3 vols., London: John Stockdale, 1783–9), vol. III, p. 308.
10. Day, *History of Sandford and Merton*, vol. II, p. 261.
11. Day, *History of Sandford and Merton*, vol. III, pp. 277–8.
12. Louisa May Alcott, *Little Women* (1868; London: Puffin, 1994), p. 4.
13. Raymond Briggs, *The Man* (London: Red Fox, 1992), unpaginated.
14. Robert Louis Stevenson, 'To Any Reader', in *A Child's Garden of Verses* (London: Longmans, Green and Co., 1885), p. 101.

PART III

Forms and Themes

12

KIMBERLEY REYNOLDS

Changing families in children's fiction

Families, like schools – and for many of the same reasons – have been a constant presence in children's literature, but the way they have been represented has changed considerably over time in line with shifts in cultural needs and expectations about both families and children. The following discussion traces these changes by examining the way the nuclear family is introduced in early children's fiction, consolidated and repositioned during the nineteenth and early twentieth centuries, falls into disrepute in the mid to late twentieth century, and is tested for obsolescence at the start of the new millennium.

Meet the family: families and children in early children's literature

Other contributors to this volume discuss parent–child relationships before the eighteenth century, providing glimpses of the way families were organised in the pre-modern period. In *Centuries of Childhood* (1960), the French historian Philippe Ariès describes this as a movement from the communal model, in which the 'family' incorporated networks of dependants who were not always linked by blood, which prevailed from the Middle Ages to the end of the seventeenth century, to the small, intimate nuclear family familiar today.

The movement towards more intimate family groups gathered speed in the eighteenth century, at about the same time as commercial publishing for children was taking off. Some of these early children's books register this transition by focusing on child characters' relationships within families that consist only of parents and siblings. However, the attitudes to such families that these books convey vary considerably, reflecting conflicting views both about how children should behave and about what kind of training they needed in order to become effective adults. This pattern is typical of the way the family is thereafter treated in children's books: there is a tenacious loyalty to the idea of the nuclear family on the one hand, but a series of challenges and adjustments to it on the other. Early children's books, for instance, include both tales that point to the importance of cultivating independence and entrepreneurial skills in the young by depriving them of their families (so families are viewed as dispensable and potentially enfeebling), and those that stress the importance not only of having a family, but also of high levels of parental intervention intended to create self-controlled individuals dedicated to the principles of ratiocination and self-improvement.

The History of Little Goody Two-Shoes, published by John Newbery in 1765, typifies stories about children who thrive despite losing their families. It tells the story of Margery Meanwell, whose parents die, leaving her and her younger brother Tommy 'to the wide World' with 'nothing, poor Things, to support them … but what they picked from the Hedges, or got from the poor People'. Readers might expect this to signal that their lives will be tragic and short; in fact, Tommy is sent off to sea and returns a rich man while Margery – soon to acquire her better-known soubriquet 'Goody Two-Shoes' – rapidly rises from ragged child to respected teacher to woman of fortune. *Goody Two-Shoes*, then, is among the first children's books to take up the fairy tale motif of the child whose deprivation of or separation from the family initiates a series of adventures that culminates in success of various kinds.

Goody Two-Shoes inaugurated a rags-to-riches structure that became the stock-in-trade of self-help stories such as those of the influential nineteenth-century American writer, Horatio Alger Jr. Beginning with *Ragged Dick; or, Street Life in New York* (1867), his stories generally feature destitute boys who achieve financial security and respectability through their own efforts and abilities. Not all stories about children who grow up outside families focus on financial success, however. In *Children of the New Forest* (1847), for instance, Captain Marryat has the Beverley children learn survival skills in the forest against the backdrop of the English Civil War, while Kipling's Kimball O'Hara (*Kim*, 1901) learns both about himself and how to play the 'Great Game' (spying for the British Secret Service) while moving between the worlds of white and native India. In the nineteenth and early twentieth centuries, orphan girls acquire loving surrogate families and learn to become admirable women through the vicissitudes of their family-less childhoods. This pattern is typified by L. M. Montgomery's *Anne of Green Gables* (1908) in which the orphan Anne Shirley arrives at the farm of aging brother and sister Matthew and Marilla Cuthbert full of potential but lacking in love and self-control. By the end of the first book in the series she has become a much-loved daughter-figure, supporting Marilla after her brother's death and achieving academic and social success in the community.

The tradition of children who succeed outside conventional families con-tinues to the present day in bestselling series such as Philip Pullman's *His Dark Materials* trilogy (1995–2000), J. K. Rowling's *Harry Potter* novels

(1997–2007) and Anthony Horowitz' books about Alex Rider (2000–). A notable change is that many of these new stories about lone children focus on messianic figures: children charged not with learning to survive and become responsible citizens but with saving the world, whether this be from the faulty philosophy and totalitarian machinations of the 'Magisterium' (Pullman), Armageddon (Rowling) or super-villains wanting world dominance (Horowitz).

Although heroic family-less children are plentiful in writing for children, more common by far are stories in which the family makes up the child's world. The first books for children show families that are loving and committed to caring for their offspring, but they do not assume that this is a natural state of affairs or that parents invariably know what is best for their individual progeny. Many of the best-known writers and books of the eighteenth and nineteenth centuries contain instructions for parents about how to raise and teach their children, alongside lessons to children about the proper way to behave, learn and think. The implication that parenting of this kind is a relatively new art can be seen as evidence that the nuclear family is a recent concept and that ideas about parenting and childhood are in transition.

A good example of such a work is Maria Edgeworth's *The Parent's Assistant*, first published in 1796. It begins with a preface outlining the aims and responsibilities that parents should keep in mind when educating their children. There follows a series of stories in which child characters find themselves in difficult practical and ethical situations. While the focus is on the children's responses, that they *do* learn is shown to be a result of good parenting – a task which Edgeworth views as being fraught with 'dangers and difficulties'.[1]

Edgeworth's model parents are vigilant – always looking for concrete ways of encouraging their children to learn from their experiences, even if these result in uncomfortable or embarrassing mistakes in the short term. One of her best-known stories is 'The Purple Jar', about seven-year-old Rosamond, whose mother gives her the opportunity to choose between a pair of shoes that she needs and a beautiful purple jar she has seen in a shop window. At the beginning of the story her mother had set an example by not being tempted to purchase pretty things of which she had no need, but Rosamond chooses the seductive jar, only to find when it is delivered to her home that the colour she had admired came from a liquid that was not part of the purchase. Meanwhile, her shoes are so worn that she cannot walk comfortably in them and her father will not be seen in public while she is wearing them so she misses an outing to a place she had particularly wanted to visit. In this way Rosamond learns to be more judicious in her decision-making.

During the eighteenth and early nineteenth centuries, good parents and successful families are frequently contrasted to those in which children are spoiled through indulgence, neglect, bad servants, unhealthy lifestyles and lack of education in all its forms. For instance, in the anonymous 'Francis Fearful', one of the *Entertaining Memoirs of Little Personages, or, Moral Amusements for Young Gentlemen* (*c.* 1775), the parents of the eponymous Francis have paid insufficient attention to his upbringing, leaving him to the care of servants before he is of school age. Because of this, Francis' head is full of superstitions and misinformation that incapacitate him with fearful fantasies about all kinds of creatures and phenomena. By contrast, in Mary Martha Sherwood's *The History of the Fairchild Family* (1818), Mr and Mrs Fairchild take great pains in raising their children, in one instance by telling them in some detail about the death of Augusta Noble, daughter of the local gentry. Augusta, whose parents have left her upbringing to inadequate servants, dies horribly when she uses a forbidden candle (indicating that she has not been taught obedience) to look at herself in the mirror (she has not learned about the sin of vanity) while her parents are away playing cards (highly disapproved of). As these examples show, the inference in many of the best-known early works for children is that creating a successful family is an acquired skill: parents must be taught to parent effectively and must be prepared to work at it tirelessly.

The force with which this message is driven home is probably not unrelated to the fact that it helped create and sustain two branches of publishing that flourish to this day: books containing advice for parents and books that teach children about acceptable and unacceptable behaviour. The family being understood as a fundamentally bourgeois social unit (even if the royal family increasingly presented its most conspicuous model), the increased emphasis in early children's literature on the child's place in the family may also have been bound up with attempts by the middle classes to exert greater ideological influence on society. But children's books did not simply reflect social changes; they were clearly involved in advancing new ideas about how the family, and society more generally, should function.[2]

The child in the family

While the first books for children tended to emphasise the responsibilities of parents as educators and role models, by the middle decades of the nineteenth century attention began to shift to the role of the child in the family and the need to pay attention to children's emotional needs and social potential. Middle-class bias is still evident in that exemplary families tend to be middle-class even if, as in the case of Louisa May Alcott's March family (*Little Women*, 1868), they live in reduced financial circumstances. Problem parents belong either to the upper classes who fail to value their children, or to the dissolute poor. Typical examples include the widowed Member of Parliament in Florence Montgomery's tragic novel *Misunderstood* (1869), who fails to realise that his sturdy older son is deeply grieving the loss of his mother until the boy is fatally injured while attempting to save his frail little brother, with whom his father has been preoccupied. Montgomery is at pains to highlight the father's inadequacies, especially the fact that he is unaware of the boy's inner world and feelings, reading only the outward appearance. Montgomery gives this erring parent a chance to learn from his faults and let his son know he is loved before he dies. The alcoholic actress mother in Hesba Stretton's *Jessica's First Prayer* (1867) is not so fortunate. Jessica is given a new home and a new start in life before, as the text would have it, she is contaminated by her defective biological parent.

Not all penurious parents are vilified in Victorian children's books. *Jessica's First Prayer* belongs to the genre of waif stories that came to prominence in mid to late nineteenth-century Britain. Concerned with the trials and tribulations of children who are orphaned, abandoned, abused, neglected or separated from their parents or entire families, waif tales take quite a different view of the lone and destitute child from that found in *The History of Little Goody Two-Shoes*. Set against the Victorian ethos of the loving family, they were intended to rouse pity for the many poor children who were living precariously in Britain's metropolises, sometimes with ne'er-do-well parents, sometimes on their own after losing their parents. Their authors hoped to stimulate the levels of concern needed to create the organisations, agencies and social reforms necessary to provide for them. A popular example in which poor parents are also shown as loving and trying to do well by their children is *Froggy's Little Brother* (1875), by 'Brenda' (Mrs G. Castle Smith), in which two young boys are orphaned after their mother succumbs to a wasting illness and their father is run over by a wealthy group who are driving their carriage recklessly after drinking too much at the races. Because they have been well raised, the little boys are kind, courteous and moral; the older brother, Froggy, struggles to support young Benny by sweeping crossings but eventually Benny dies and Froggy is taken into care. The book ends with an exhortation for readers to send 'pennies and shillings to help schools, and Homes, and Kindergartens' and 'respon[d] liberally to ... appeals' to help poor children.[3] This appeal for money underscores one of the principal roles of the family: to support its members financially.

It is important not to overlook the pressures exerted by economic forces on the family unit, both in life and on the page. In *Postmodernism: or the Cultural Logic of Late Capitalism* (1991), the critic and theorist Fredric Jameson identifies three distinct phases in capitalism to date, and these phases map very neatly onto changes in the way families are represented in children's

literature. He begins with what he calls 'market capitalism', characteristic of
the late eighteenth to early nineteenth centuries, when commercial publishing
for children was in its infancy. Market capitalism he sees as being driven
by the Industrial Revolution in tandem with Romantic philosophy and
aesthetics – precisely the forces at work in the depiction of family life by
early writers for children like Edgeworth and her contemporaries. These texts
assume an audience of 'masters' – the class who will run the government and
own/manage the workplaces. Central to this agenda is the avoidance of social
unrest: the stories carefully instil principles of justice, democracy and *noblesse
oblige*.

While many of the first children's books foreground the importance of the
everyday life of families living together at home in moulding good men and
women for the future, it has to be said that the family life depicted is deeply
controlling and, despite occasional sensational incidents (one of the best-
known stories in *The Fairchild Family*, for instance, is when the children
are taken to see two corpses on a gibbet), far from exciting. It is not surprising,
then, that once the idea of the nuclear family was well established, books in
which families are put to more dramatic and exotic tests achieved great
popularity. Just as *Goody Two-Shoes* ushered in the tale of the child who
thrives without a family, so the Swiss pastor and author Johann Wyss' 1814
Robinsonnade, *The Swiss Family Robinson*, was the progenitor of tales about
families who undertake adventures together.

The Swiss Family Robinson is typical of market capitalism in that it shows
the central family as tightly bound by economic necessity, which resulted in
many families travelling long distances to work or to take up new opportunities, sometimes migrating permanently as the Robinson family do, though
in this case the land they reach is a remote island where they are shipwrecked
and forced to survive. *The Swiss Family Robinson* shows how firmly entrenched
ideas about the nuclear family had become in the nearly two decades that
separate it from *The Parent's Assistant*. It takes for granted that the family
will function well, including by looking to their future economic security,
whatever the circumstances.

The Robinsons are indeed a very able and adaptable unit in which each
member contributes to the family's survival and comfort, though always
learning to do better and praise God for their successes under the omniscient
gaze and ever-ready guidance of father Robinson. Wyss is more overt than
Edgeworth in the parallels he draws between children, family and the state.
For instance, the father, whose journal purportedly forms the basis of the
novel, has a clear idea of the role of the family in rearing the kind of children
needed by a nation and seeks to draw readers into the family project: '[M]y
great wish is that young people who read this record of our lives and

adventures should learn from it how admirably suited is the perfect, industrious, and pious life of a cheerful, united family to the formation of strong, pure, and manly character'.[4] That he refers exclusively to the 'manly' character reflects both the fact that the Robinsons have only sons and that, at the time, exploring and conquering new lands was considered the prerogative of the male. Wyss does, however, recognise the need for and contributions of the female helpmeets, without which no family of the time was complete, in the form of the boys' mother and, latterly, Jenny, the castaway discovered on a nearby island, who marries the eldest son and returns with him to England (or Europe or Switzerland, depending on the version) at the end of the book.

Significantly, while the original family is dispersed at the end of the novel, Mr and Mrs Robinson and two of their children stay behind to await the arrival of new colonists, with whose help they plan to build a new outpost of Switzerland. In this way the novel shows the family as central to the work of the nation or, as Robinson-pater writes, 'None takes a better place in the national family, none is happier or more beloved than he who goes forth from such a home to fulfil new duties, and to gather fresh interests around him.'[5]

Another influential family in children's literature whose adventures map the expansion of a nation is found in the Little House books (1932–43) of Laura Ingalls Wilder. As in Wyss' novel, these stories of pioneer life oscillate between dramatic – often life-threatening – events and mundane domestic details, given a charm for the reader through the way Wilder highlights both the family's ingenuity and the absence of the sense of alienation relating to work, material possessions and the necessaries of life characteristic of modernity. Though the Ingalls family regularly changes location and has to reposition itself in response to new and unsettled frontiers, new economic challenges, new neighbours and new opportunities, the family itself is presented as indivisible: it can be augmented through marriage but the notion of family is sacrosanct.[6]

Family sagas for children, such as Wilder's, have their roots in the nineteenth century in famous series such as Alcott's books about the March family, which chronicle the lives of four sisters, Meg, Jo, Beth and Amy, growing up at home with their mother, Marmee, while their father is serving as a chaplain to the troops fighting in the American Civil War. The success of *Little Women* led Alcott to write three sequels, *Good Wives* (1869), *Little Men* (1871) and *Jo's Boys* (1886). Ever since Alcott shifted the focus of her novels to the March sisters, family-based series have tended to focus more on sibling relationships than on interactions between parents and children. For instance, E. Nesbit's fantasy stories featuring the adventures of Robert, Anthea, Jane, Cyril and 'the Lamb' (*Five Children and It*, 1902; *The Phoenix and the Carpet*, 1904; *The Story of the Amulet*, 1906) revolve around the children's games and needs while the parents are absent for a variety of reasons. Similarly, Arthur Ransome's Swallows and Amazons books about the Walker, Blackett and Callum children (1930–47) keep the parents very much at a distance, for the most part supplying provisions and monitoring the children's adventures from the shore. In Noel Streatfeild's family books, such as *Apple Bough* (1962), the adults are often artists preoccupied by financial worries and servicing the demands of their professions, while in Madeline L'Engle's stories about the Murrays, O'Keefes and Austins it is always the children who undertake quests and solve problems while their parents are left as spectators, and sometimes need to be rescued themselves as in the case of Mr Murray in *A Wrinkle in Time* (1962).

During the 1980s and 1990s few new series about families appeared for reasons that are explained below; however, since the turn of the twenty-first century, there has been a revival of the family saga typified by Hilary McKay's books about the Casson family, beginning with *Saffy's Angel* (2002). In some ways, McKay looks back to the eccentric, artistic families of Noel Streatfeild – both parents in *Saffy's Angel* are painters and they name their children after paint colours – but in others these are books that are new in the way they present family dynamics and their focus on the emotional needs of the children in the family rather than the events that befall them. This child-centred, psychological approach to writing about families needs to be understood as the product of a major shift in attitudes to the family that occurred in the middle years of the twentieth century. These will be discussed in the next section, but before considering the way hostile views of the family affected writing for children, it is important to look at an area of family fiction which retains its interest in whole families who, like the Robinsons and Ingalls, undertake difficult journeys.

The family adventure story survives in books that feature refugee families. What is significant about the many children's books in which families risk their lives, spend their fortunes and endure considerable hardships to leave countries where they have no future – usually because of war and its consequences – is that many do not focus on the strength of the biological family unit but look instead at the strains on families relocated to places with an unfamiliar language and complex and deep-rooted cultural differences.

Ian Strachan's *Journey of 1,000 Miles* (1984) details the hardships – as distinct from adventures – of refugees' journeys as Lee and his family become 'boat people' when they leave Vietnam for what they hope will be a safer and more secure future. Picture books too recount the experiences undergone by boat people, among them Michele Maria Surat and Vo-Dinh Mai's *Angel Child, Dragon Child* (1983), Sherry Garland's *The Lotus Seed* (1993) and Rosemary Breckler's *Sweet Dried Apples* (1996), though each of these books is primarily concerned with responses to separation from the home country and family members.

Linda Crew's *Children of the River* (1989) looks at the pressures on Sundara, a teenage girl living in Oregon with relatives with whom she fled from the Khmer Rouge. The novel begins with their hazardous journey, during which the baby cousin left in Sundara's care dies, before concentrating on Sundara's struggle to please her aunt and uncle by conforming to their expectations of how a good Cambodian girl should behave, while also trying to succeed academically and socially in the USA. Until the concluding pages of the book, the family is shown as divided and dysfunctional, with Sundara feeling that she belongs nowhere and her relatives resenting – but depending on – her superior ability to negotiate the language and customs of their new country. Resolution is achieved with the arrival of her grandmother from Cambodia. She helps fill in the gaps in the family's past, heal their wounds, and allow them to find an acceptable accommodation between assimilating and retaining key elements of their original culture.

A variation on the refugee family-under-stress narrative is provided by Beverley Naidoo in *The Other Side of Truth* (2000). When their mother is killed outside the family home, Sade and Femi are put in the care of a stranger who is paid to take them from Nigeria to London, where she abandons them. The book tracks their efforts both to survive and to make a new life in London and, in the absence of relatives and others from their former lives, to remember their culture and their parents. *The Other Side of Truth* is unusual in showing a refugee family in which it is the mother who is absent; more common is the story of the family in which the father has been killed, incarcerated or 'disappeared' during war or under harsh regimes, as in *Sweet Dried Apples* and *The Lotus Seed*.

Most stories that blend the family and adventure genres – including many refugee stories – tend to focus on children who have been separated from their families and who are either seeking to be reunited with parents and siblings or contriving to survive until they are rescued and restored to family life. Either way, these stories' roots in the tradition of *Goody Two-Shoes* are evident in the way they highlight the capacity of children who have no families to triumph over adversity. More common than tales about uprooted families are stories about families in more everyday situations; however, in the middle of the twentieth century, the nature of family-centred fiction underwent significant changes, the most important of which was that threats to child characters' well-being were portrayed as coming from within the family rather than from sources beyond it. The suspicions surrounding the family had their roots in fundamental social changes, leading to a new phase in the way childhood and families were viewed and believed to function.

Families under fire

For the first half of the twentieth century, families were seen as central to the smooth running of society. Increased prosperity meant that childhood was expected to last longer than it had for previous generations; the school leaving age was raised and children remained economically dependent on their parents well into, and even through, their teenage years. Images of stable nuclear families with white, straightforwardly heterosexual parents who conformed to traditional gender roles abounded in books for children well into the 1950s (many contemporary books also feature the same kind of families, though white, heterosexual couples are no longer held up as the norm). For the young, these often took the form of highly domestic tales which focused on daily routines and family relationships, typified by Dorothy Edwards' Naughty Little Sister stories (from 1952) in the UK, and those about the Quimby family in the USA (beginning with *Beezus and Ramona*, 1955). However, just as the eighteenth century saw the emergence of conflicting discourses about childhood and the family, so the middle years of the last century saw children's books simultaneously setting up the traditional nuclear family as an ideal and encouraging readers to see it as inadequate or even pernicious.

Hostility to and mistrust of the family were driven by figures such as the anthropologist Edmund Leach, and the psychiatrist R. D. Laing. From their different perspectives, both were highly critical of the nuclear family, seeing it as inward-looking, emotionally stressful, alienated from community, and hence damaging to its members. Leach blamed the family for many of the ills of society, including increases in violent behaviour, while Laing suggested that families prevented individuals from using their talents and being fulfilled, sometimes leading to mental illness. By the 1960s these new ways of thinking about the family were beginning to take shape in children's literature. For instance, S. E. Hinton's novels about teenage gangs, *The Outsiders* (1967) and *Rumblefish* (1975), feature protagonists who come from dysfunctional families, with parents who are living apart, drink too much, and who are apparently indifferent to the fate of their offspring. The novels of Robert Cormier are littered with families in which parents and children fail to communicate or to trust each other, leading to precisely the kinds of problems at home and in society highlighted by Laing and Leach. Katherine Paterson's highly praised *Bridge to Terabithia* (1977) uses the model familiar from eighteenth-century children's books of contrasting one ideal family with one that is struggling, and showing how the young respond to caring interventions. In *The Friends* (1973) and following novels, Rosa Guy shows black families sinking under the pressures to succeed in urban America, while two decades later, Melvin Burgess' *Junk* (1996) traces the way two British runaways (one from a neglectful and abusive family) are caught up in cycles of addiction, criminality and degradation.

During the final years of the last century, much Young Adult fiction centred on intergenerational conflict and emotional struggles within families: all too often the problems of these 'problem novels' begin with the family. In keeping with the development of a youth culture that rejected the bourgeois, materialistic and damaging nature of middle-class life, fiction for young people increasingly focused on protagonists who ultimately reject their families and the lifestyles in which they have been raised. Far from preparing their children to take up the kinds of values and careers that would reproduce the existing Anglo-American culture, families in juvenile fiction were often shown to be turning out misfits and rebels. As Jameson's economic wheel turned to the most recent phase of capitalism, then, substantial areas of children's literature were radiating discontent with traditional family life. In the current late phase of capitalism, literary visions for the future frequently try to by-pass the family in favour of other social organisations, from group marriage through single-sex or even optional kinship systems. As has been true throughout history, children's literature today is engaging in interrogations of the family to suit new conditions, though arguably the alternatives it is proposing are more radical than any that have gone before.

Post-family futures?

Young people today are growing up in an era of 'consumer capitalism', which Jameson sees as determined by information technologies, service industries, multinationalism and marketing, and characterised by postmodernity. There is a variety of evidence that this economic climate has put the nuclear family under considerable strain. For instance, in 1995, controversial British writer and broadcaster Melanie Phillips argued that 'the disintegration of the nuclear family is the most serious problem facing British society' resulting in a 'generation of dysfunctional and underachieving children'.[7] Since then there has been a spate of television programmes in both the UK and the USA about families who need to call on the services of 'supernannies' or send their children to 'brat camps'. Sociologist Juliet Schor's *Born to Buy* (2004) claims we are living through an epoch in which children are contemptuous of adults and families, identifying primarily with their roles as consumers. The current generation of children, she suggests, has little desire to become adult.

Critics associated with children's literature are voicing similar concerns. In *Sticks and Stones* (2001), Jack Zipes argues that, as a direct consequence of the incessant urge to consume and to develop brand loyalties, many young people feel a stronger sense of belonging to corporate culture – say, to groups of consumers of Nike products, or Coca-Cola – than to their families. It is this epoch that is experimenting with dismantling the family story altogether and replacing the nuclear family with the 'family of choice', comprised of young people of roughly the same age and perhaps most familiar through popular television programmes such as *Friends* (1994–2004) and *Buffy the Vampire Slayer* (1997–2003). In these serial narratives, biological families are incidental: what counts are your friends, and the lifestyle you can create together.

In fact, the phenomenon of groups of children functioning as families in children's literature is not itself new, but the way they function has changed in significant ways. It is a commonplace of children's literature criticism that adventure fiction tends to begin by removing any parents or other responsible adults, and when this happens in early twentieth-century books for children – for instance, those by Arthur Ransome and Enid Blyton – the older children generally take on the traditional, gendered, roles of parents, providing food, establishing routines and taking responsibility in difficult situations. They do this consciously and often willingly, in the knowledge that the circumstances are temporary; their relatively unsupervised interludes act as rehearsals for adult life.

Ian Serraillier's *The Silver Sword* (1956) is typical of this subgenre – which often takes war-time settings. It tells the story of the three Balicki children, who are separated by force from their parents towards the end of the Second World War, during the Nazi occupation of Poland. They cope well, with the older two children (a boy and a girl) parenting the youngest and Jan, an orphan they gather into their 'family' as they travel towards Switzerland where they are eventually reunited with their parents. Eleanor Graham's *The Children Who Lived in a Barn* (1938) rings the changes on the sibling-family convention in that the five Dunnett children (ranging in age from seven to thirteen) believe their parents have been killed in a plane crash, so when they set up home in a local barn in an attempt to stay together rather than be taken into care, they do not expect their parents to return and their previous family life to be resumed. When it transpires that their parents have not been killed, and despite the fact that the children have succeeded remarkably well in looking after themselves, they are more than ready to become children in a family again. In fact, they never revel in their success and independence, and relinquish autonomy readily. Both novels are typical of earlier examples of children's texts in which children end up living as a family unit without parents: the children do not choose to live without adults; the new families consist of siblings rather than friends; and the return of the parents and traditional family life is idealised, longed for and finally attained.

While the phenomenon of same-generation 'family' groups may not be new, its current iteration is. For more than a decade, the challenges to the family associated with living in an epoch of consumer capitalism have been addressed in writing for the young through narratives that experiment with, and pilot, new definitions of what is meant by the term 'family', and with the family story itself. One way they do this is by reflecting the alternative family structures typical of what the influential British sociologist Anthony Giddens terms our post-traditional society.[8] Works by Jacqueline Wilson, Anne Fine, Margaret Mahy, and a large number of picture books, feature single-parent families; blended, adoptive and step-families; families parented by gay and lesbian couples; and the many cross-household families that are the products of remarriage. Another way in which children's books are offering new ways of thinking about the family takes the form of narratives based on families created through choice rather than biology. Such narratives differ from the earlier stories of children living together in the way they seek to develop an ethos of interdependence based on equality, rather than deriving from the power dynamics based on sex and age associated with traditional nuclear families.

Two novels that reflect this change in the role and nature of the family and offer alternative families composed of peers are Francesca Lia Block's *Weetzie Bat*, published in America in 1989, and Meg Rossof's first novel, *How I Live Now*, published in the UK in 2004. Both show young people coming together to create unconventional 'family' groups in response to inadequate biological families. Both also critique the cultures that gave rise to the original families, using the elective families metaphorically to call into question long-standing ideas about intimacy and belonging. In their diversity and lack of concern with blood-ties, the new peer families in these books reflect changes in the idea of the family; they also challenge some of the age and gender power dynamics of conventional families – perhaps especially the residual influences of patriarchal autocracy associated with the days when father was always credited with knowing best – and so have the potential to break some entrenched patterns of behaviour and ways of relating.

Block's novel places value on relationships that are emotionally satisfying rather than bolted together through external forces such as religion or the law. It revolves around Weetzie Bat and her friend Dirk, who live in Los Angeles, hate school and have a highly developed aesthetic life: everything they do, from the food they eat to the people they love and the performances they give on the street and screen, seems to be experienced and evaluated by a shared aesthetic code, though one based entirely on consumer capitalism since most of what they do also involves shopping or eating in fast-food restaurants. In a series of magical realist twists they acquire a house, financial independence and a pair of perfect lovers (Dirk is gay so Weetzie lives with three men).

Weetzie's parents have divorced, her mother is an alcoholic and her father eventually dies of a drug overdose. While she cares about them, Weetzie lives a life in which her parents are largely incidental, and styles herself as a new-fashioned, unjudgmental, fulfilled matriarch in opposition to their self-obsessed, self-destructive and rootless existences. The replacement family she and Dirk and their lovers set up becomes a haven in a chaotic world. They make mistakes in their relationships, and Dirk and Duck live in the shadow of AIDS, but Block imbues each member of this new-style family with an intuitive emotional literacy which makes it possible for them to deal with the consequences of their mistakes and experiences. Unlike their parents' generation, this family of friends consciously fashion their lives as they want them to be, free from the complications of oppressive family structures and supported by the new family model they have invented, symbolised by the household baby, Cherokee. Cherokee is a 'three-dad' baby, probably the product of a night when Weetzie, Dirk and Duck set out to make a baby because Weetzie's lover doesn't want to bring a baby into the world. Eventually he changes his mind and, when Cherokee is born, they agree that she looks like all of them, thus creating a notional blood bond between all the members of this elective family.

Such a family can, of course, only be imagined in the most affluent circumstances where mundane cares about survival don't impinge; nevertheless, Block's new-style family is notable for the way it challenges many forms of social control and the drive towards ideological replication associated with the traditional nuclear family. *Weetzie Bat* not only caught the mood of a generation (as evidenced by internet fan activity and sales), but reflected a latent radicalism in new activity around the idea of the family in culture.

How I Live Now is set sometime in the not-too-distant future when Daisy, an anorexic teenager from Manhattan whose father has recently remarried, is sent to stay with cousins in England while the baby he and his new wife are expecting is born. The cousins have become remarkably self-sufficient because their mother, their only parent, is completely absorbed in campaigning for world peace. Shortly after Daisy arrives, her aunt leaves for a peace rally, and terrorists attack England, which has so many troops in other countries 'keeping the peace' that there aren't enough at home to defend the country. For a time the children exist happily on their own in the country; as war breaks out, they are separated; and eventually Daisy is returned to her father, no longer anorexic. There is much here that is familiar and parallels the indictment of late twentieth-century parenting in *Weetzie Bat* and a myriad of other books, including influential, bestselling books such as J. K. Rowling's *Harry Potter* novels with its damaging Dursleys. A twist in this story is that Daisy's return to her father, which traditionally would have signalled reconciliation and reward, is forced and unwelcome. She has to wait until she is twenty-one and England has started accepting visitors again before she can be reunited with her cousins.

This is a text that confronts many areas of anxiety about the world we live in – fears of war, terrorism and invasion; worries about our inability to be self-sufficient in cultures based on supermarkets and service industries; and some young people's sense that their parents care more about their work and the world outside the family than for the family itself. At its heart is the sense that families at all levels in society are under strain, with many failing to work, and that this is both a symptom and a cause of the greater national and international cultural failures to which Rossoff gestures. The response in *How I Live Now* is not a return to basics and a call for conventional families to be reasserted and strengthened (this is what Daisy's father does when he carries her off to his home with its mother, father and sibling set-up). Instead, it suggests that strength will come from groups bound together by mutual empathy, identification, interests and accumulated experience: in other words, self-selected.

It seems then, that, from *Goody Two-Shoes* to *How I Live Now*, children's literature has contained a strand that not only explores the extent to which children benefit from living outside traditional family structures and celebrates their strength, resilience and creative energy, but, more importantly, participates in reshaping the idea of the family to suit the social, economic and emotional needs of the times. This does not mean that the traditional family will disappear from either society or writing for children, or that the alternative/elective family is being presented as the only legitimate social unit for today's world. Indeed, it could be argued that, precisely by questioning the traditional family and showing it as under threat, books such as these are working to preserve it by reminding readers why they think it is important. Nevertheless, with new world orders taking shape and a new series of threats to the future, from global warming through terrorist activities to a revival of the nuclear arms race, the times are changing again, and children's literature is playing its part in opening up thinking and offering young people opportunities to revision relationships, culture and power structures.

NOTES

1. Maria Edgeworth, *The Parent's Assistant; or, Stories for Children, Part I*, 2nd edn (3 vols., London: J. Johnson, 1796), p. iv.
2. See Andrew O'Malley, *The Making of the Modern Child: Children's Literature and Childhood in the Late Eighteenth Century* (London: Routledge, 2003).
3. Brenda, *Froggy's Little Brother* (1875; London: John F. Shaw, n.d.), p. 199.

4. Johann Wyss, *The Swiss Family Robinson*, ed. William H. G. Kingston (1814; London: MacDonald, 1949), p. 320.
5. Wyss, *The Swiss Family Robinson*, p. 321.
6. Biographical studies of the real-life Ingalls family can present a rather different picture: see, for instance, Anita Clair Fellman, 'Laura Ingalls Wilder and Rose Wilder Lane: The Politics of a Mother–Daughter Relationship', *Signs: Journal of Women in Culture and Society*, 15 (1990), 535–61.
7. Michael Peplar, *Family Matters: A History of Ideas About the Family Since 1945* (London: Pearson, 2002), p. 3.
8. Anthony Giddens, *The Transformation of Intimacy: Sexuality, Love and Eroticism in Modern Society* (Cambridge: Polity Press, 1994).

13

MAVIS REIMER

Traditions of the school story

Since the very definition of childhood is often entwined with social norms for schooling, it is unsurprising to find the beginnings of a body of literature that might be identified as specially for children in the ancient and medieval schoolbooks designed to teach young people the manners and the linguistic skills they needed to be successful in their societies, schoolbooks that often took the form of lively dialogues and included diverting accounts of extracurricular episodes of schoolboy life.[1] The traditions of modern English-language children's literature, with which this volume is principally concerned, are also rooted in the school story, with Sarah Fielding's story of the nine pupils of Mrs Teachum's 'little female academy', *The Governess* (1749), frequently identified as the first continuous narrative for children in English. Fielding's narrative stages the binary organising principle of children's literature: the attempt to fuse instruction and delight. Taking as its setting the school, the scene of instruction itself, the story also works to engage readers' interests, by recounting the girls' confessions of the moral struggles they faced in their lives before they entered school, detailing their meetings with the people of Mrs Teachum's neighbourhood during their rambles, tracing the growth of their friendships and sense of common purpose, and, not least, by interpolating the tales the girls read to one another into the narrative of their school life together. These tales are interpreted by the girls in terms of their application to their own lives, in accordance with their governess' wish that they 'make the best Use of even the most trifling Things', and so, in turn, become part of the teaching Fielding's text directs to its readers.[2]

In linking reading and interpretation to moral development, Fielding not only inaugurates a recurrent theme in the genre of the school story, but also points to the older tradition of allegory that stands behind the school story. Allegories such as John Bunyan's *The Pilgrim's Progress* (1678) were understood to show the way to a heavenly home beyond the vicissitudes of the earthly world; the school story redirects the allegory into a narrative of the progress of the child through the 'little world' of the school towards the achievement of successful adulthood in the 'wide world' of modern life. Although the school story substitutes a secular destination for a spiritual one, many of the best examples of the genre retain some of the resonance of allegory, an 'other speaking' that invites interpretation and holds out the promise of meaning. Fielding's narrative, for example, begins with the girls fighting over who should have the biggest apple from a basket left in the garden for distribution by Jenny Peace, the oldest of the students. Surprised by the return of their governess, they face Mrs Teachum with dismay, each with evidence of the fray – locks of hair, bits of torn clothing – clenched in their hands. This opening scene can be read through conventional allegorical tropes as a version of the biblical story of the Fall of Man in the Garden of Eden, the guilty girls, like the disobedient Adam and Eve, ashamed before the eyes of judgment. While the rest of Fielding's narrative does not correspond in any particular details to the biblical story that has been evoked, the recreation of a harmonious society in Mrs Teachum's garden nevertheless reverberates with significance, as the girls repent their folly and remake themselves over the course of nine days, through their confessions and conversations teaching one another the self-control, benevolence and ability to interpret others expected of young ladies in their society.

Like Fielding, Mary Wollstonecraft's story of girls' schooling, *Original Stories from Real Life* (1788), presents disciplined reading not only as an important way to gain self-knowledge, but also as a model for approaching 'real life' itself. In this high valuation of reading, Fielding and Wollstonecraft are at odds with the influential programme of education set out by Jean-Jacques Rousseau in *Émile* (1762), for he had restricted Émile's reading to one book, *Robinson Crusoe*. Early English school stories for the most part follow Fielding's lead in representing their fictions as intended for the high purpose of shaping the minds of child-readers as they prepare to enter the world of school, a world understood to be a place of struggle. Lady Ellenor Fenn in *School Dialogues for Boys* (1783), for example, hopes that her book will 'fortify' the young boy for whom she writes 'against the contagion of bad example' and 'the poison of pernicious counsel', and will put him on his guard by showing him 'what characters he may expect to meet with'.[3]

The end of education is self-discipline in the view of these early school-story writers and, in their narratives, the achievement of this objective is asserted as a happy ending. Fielding's story, for example, concludes with the notice that Mrs Teachum's school becomes an example throughout the country of what young people, 'properly employed on their own Improvement', can attain: every young lady leaving the school has learned 'always to pay to her Governors the most exact Obedience, and to exert towards her Companions all the good

Effects of a Mind filled with Benevolence and Love'.[4] The yoking of exact obedience and a mind filled with love suggests that these school stories might usefully be read in the context of the disciplinary society which Michel Foucault argues is forming in the seventeenth and eighteenth centuries. Such a society is one in which capitalism can thrive, since the extension of disciplinary power is 'economically' effective, not only in terms of involving little expenditure, but also in being politically discreet and so attracting little resistance. A primary product of the disciplinary society is the subject who takes responsibility for constraining himself, who participates in his own subjection. For Foucault, this subject is produced through panoptic surveillance, which he understands not as a state in which one is constantly observed, but rather as a state of 'conscious and permanent visibility' in which one is sure one might be seen at any time.[5] The school, among other social institutions, is an important site for the exercise of such surveillance. Indeed, many school stories, from Fielding's narrative to contemporary television series set in schools, include scenes in which students recognise that they could be, or are being, watched by school authorities, often by a distant head or principal who generally remains absent or unseen. In Fenn's *School Dialogues for Boys*, a teacher, Mr Sage, explains to visitors how the school implements its principle of visible but unverifiable surveillance:

> VISITOR. Does Mr. *Aweful* keep much in the school?
>
> SAGE. His breakfast-room ... communicates with the school; when he enters, and seats himself behind a screen, no one knows of his entrance; so that he should never be supposed to be absent. Yet he is not known to be present, but when he pleases.
>
> LADY. A proper restraint.
>
> SAGE. To the *good*. – but the greater part never think of him, any more than we do of a superior witness.[6]

In having Sage draw a parallel between the eye of the headmaster and the eye of God, Fenn claims a divine model for the practice of surveillance in the quotidian world of school.

The metaphor of the world of school, which Fenn references in the address to the reader that prefaces her dialogues, is also a rhetorical figure borrowed from allegory. While the repeated use of the metaphor sometimes makes it appear to be little more than a commonplace, there is a residual power in the figure. It is a figure that asserts that a school is a complete and circumscribed system, but at the same time a figure that implies the correspondence of the school system to 'world' systems on other scales and levels. The metaphor is not only used in school stories, but also embedded in the traditions of actual schools, particularly British public schools (that is to say, old-established, fee-paying boarding schools), and the discourses about them. For example, in a sermon preached in the school chapel on Ash Wednesday in 1844, Rugby's most famous headmaster, Thomas Arnold, took as his theme the complexities of the idea of the 'world': the boys, he assumed, had already learned in their lives before coming to school 'how apt the world is to tempt you' and they needed to remember during the years of their education that to them, for the present, 'school is the world'.[7] Arnold's peroration invokes the idea of the 'world' as the realm of the material as opposed to the spiritual, and simultaneously warns the boys – in language reminiscent of such writers as Fenn – that school life will have its temptations and reassures them that, in the restricted sphere of school, they can win such a challenge. In *Tom Brown's Schooldays* (1857), the novel Thomas Hughes wrote about school life at Rugby under Arnold, Tom registers the lesson being taught by the doctor, 'a man whom we felt to be, with all his heart and soul and strength, striving against whatever was mean and unmanly and unrighteous in our little world'.[8] It is this form of the metaphor, the school as a 'little world' preparing its students for other, larger spheres of action, that is most common in the school stories. Such analogies between microcosm and macrocosm are often motivated by a need for order and comprehension, an expression of the desire to master the environment by placing what is outside inside, where it can be contained or managed.

'An expression of the desire for mastery' is a useful gloss on the boys' school stories that proliferated in Britain from the mid nineteenth century. In fact, one of the important early books in the field, F. W. Farrar's *Eric, or Little by Little* (1858), has been widely scorned by critics of school stories from the time of its first publication exactly because its schoolboy hero fails to master the rules of the little world of school. Eric triumphs only when he has left school, repenting of his errors after going to sea. Farrar's fault might be said to be his failure to conform to generic expectations. Not only is the school story a secular allegory, but also, in the mainstream of the boys' school-story tradition exemplified by such popularisers as Talbot Baines Reed and Harold Avery, the world of the school is enclosed and self-sufficient, with conflicts resolved within the terms of that world. In this, the school story is characteristic of children's narratives in general: they build pictures of concentrated worlds by explicitly mapping their geographies and boundaries; they demonstrate the principles by which power is exercised and distributed; they enact rules that assign morality and immorality to conduct; they institute the marks of belonging and exclusion. In Hugh's first day at Crofton in Harriet Martineau's *The Crofton Boys* (1841), for example, he learns that 'there were such things as bounds' and that the way to be left in peace is to 'show that you are up to play'.[9] The early experiences of Louis in E. J. May's *Louis's*

Schooldays (1850) and Tom in *Tom Brown's Schooldays* teach them that a haircut or a hat can signal their status and their aspirations to their school-fellows. In all of these novels, the boys also learn more consequential rules: to understand the conditions under which cribbing to prepare your lessons is and is not thought to be cheating by boys; to naturalise the narrow line between the 'low' sin of bearing tales to adults and the courageous act of telling the whole truth when confronted by a rightful authority; and to navigate the complicated distributions of power among prefects, captains, monitors and older boys.

The basic plot of a school story, focusing as it does on the initiation, conflicts and eventual successes of a new student, supports the narrative presentation of the school as a world just discovered and open to exploration. Indeed, an early review of Hughes' novel observes that the 'great success' of the novel is in its telling a familiar story as if it were a tale of colonial adventure: 'It is no mean triumph to have been the Columbus of the world of schoolboy romance. It lay within easy reach, indeed, but was practically undiscovered.'[10] The transference of the newness of the child subject to the world which that subject meets is a common technique in children's literature, and, as the reviewer suggests, an effective strategy for defamiliarising and dramatising the ordinary. In the case of the boys' school story, however, it also points to the specific historical circumstances of British colonial expansion in which these books were produced.

The main narrative of Hughes' novel clearly is a 'little world' narrative, an account of Tom's progress from what Arnold called the 'natural imperfect state of boyhood' towards the state of being a 'brave, helpful, truth-telling Englishman, ... gentleman, and ... Christian', the goal Tom's father had identified for his son's schooling.[11] Like Fielding's *The Governess*, then, Hughes' novel shows its links to allegory. Indeed, Tom himself is often read by critics as the contested middle ground in the moral struggle of the story, with the pious Arthur the representative of his better, spiritual nature and the bully Flashman the representative of his lower, material nature (fig. 13). More complicatedly allegorical is the way in which the text repeatedly reads Tom's moral struggle as an analogue of struggles in the wider world of nation and empire, reversing the conventional movement of allegory from the literal and historical instance to the moral and spiritual meaning. Here, the moral struggle leads to a clearer sense of the 'higher' historical and political meanings, a movement assumed, for example, in the narrator's commentary about the meaning of fights:

> After all, what would life be without fighting, I should like to know? From the cradle to the grave, fighting, rightly understood, is the business, the real, highest, honestest business of every son of man. Every one who is worth his salt has his

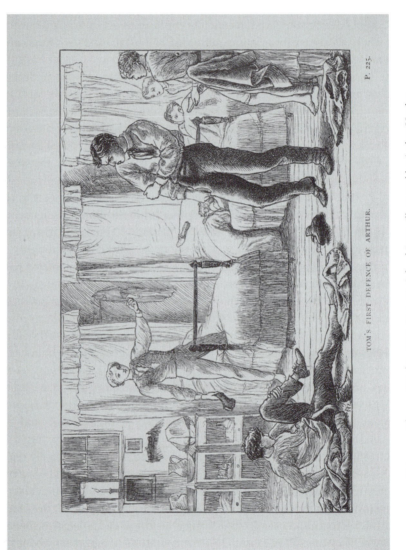

TOM'S FIRST DEFENCE OF ARTHUR.

P. 225.

Figure 13. Thomas Hughes, *Tom Brown's School Days*. Illustrated by Arthur Hughes. London: Macmillan, 1867, facing p. 255. 'Tom's first defence of Arthur'.

enemies, who must be beaten, be they evil thoughts and habits in himself or spiritual wickednesses in high places, or Russians, or Border-ruffians, or Bill, Tom, or Harry, who will not let him live his life in quiet till he has thrashed them.[12]

Public schools functioned, proudly and explicitly, as 'the chief nurseries' for the empire in the nineteenth century.[13] Hughes' novel was, and continues to be, understood to show schoolboys the values, attitudes and strength of character needed by the future leaders of what was at the time the world's most powerful nation. Not surprisingly, then, *Tom Brown's Schooldays* ends with a series of references to imperial concerns: as Tom searches for direction on what his 'work in the world' might be, he notes that East, his first friend at school, has already joined a regiment in India; and the unnamed 'young Master' with whom Tom has his final conversation at Rugby apparently refers to the Indian 'Mutiny' breaking out at the time of the novel's publication, when he muses that the school seems to be 'the only little corner of the British Empire which is thoroughly, wisely, and strongly ruled just now'.[14]

In its strong and explicit linkage between the text and its historical situation, Hughes' novel exhibits the quality of 'worldliness' Edward Said attributes to texts in which 'the circumstantiality' and 'historical contingency' of the writing are 'incorporated in the text, an infrangible part of its capacity for conveying and producing meaning'. Such texts, Said suggests, place restraints upon interpreter and interpretation, because their interpretation – 'by virtue of the exactness of their situation in the world – *has already commenced*'.[15] *Tom Brown's Schooldays* was an important source for character types, plot incidents and motifs for school stories for at least a century following its publication and, arguably, left an indelible mark on the generic form itself. One might speculate, then, that the capacity of school stories in general for 'conveying and producing meaning' is tied to ideologies of the nation. Indeed, many important school stories are set against the backdrop of wars, which are often occasions for the blatant performance of national identities and sometimes occasions for searching inquiries into such ideological formations. *A Separate Peace* (1959) by American writer John Knowles, for example, is set in a New England boarding school during the school year of 1942–3, shortly after the belated entry of the United States into the Second World War, and is a meditation on the promises made to boys about the meanings of manhood in times of military conflict and the ways in which such meanings are betrayed. William Golding's *Lord of the Flies* (1954), a school story turned inside-out, with a school of boys marooned on an island after their aeroplane is shot down during an unnamed war, the boys unlearning (or, possibly, revealing the deep structure of) the practices of civilisation, demands to be read in the context of Cold War tensions. Robert Cormier's *The*

Chocolate War (1974), with its bleak indictment of school life as a thin layer of virtue concealing the violence by which the consent of the governed is secured, was published in the United States as the decades-long Vietnam War was coming to its inglorious end. Even Charles Hamilton's Greyfriars stories, published under the pseudonym of 'Frank Richards' in various forms between 1908 and 1965, might profitably be read against the backdrop of the slow decline of the British empire from the Boer War (1899–1902) to the Suez Canal crisis (1956), and the reassessments of the national self-image entailed by such a declension. Undisciplined, untruthful, conniving and obtuse as he is, the eponymous hero of *Billy Bunter of Greyfriars* (1947) nevertheless can summon a bit of 'genuine old British pluck' to save the day when he needs to do so.[16]

The precursor to all of these ironic, knowing revisions of the school story is undoubtedly Rudyard Kipling's *Stalky & Co.* (1899), a series of stories loosely based on Kipling's own schooldays at United Services College, a boarding school established by ex-Army officers for boys destined for military training. When the book was first published, one reviewer declared that Kipling's great achievement was to write from inside the point of view of the boy, 'unscrupulously glorifying the boy's ideals'.[17] It is true that the narrative voice of the experienced guide is largely absent from the stories, which are full of detailed accounts of Stalky, Beetle and M'Turk's exuberant escapades out of bounds and transcriptions of their slangy conversations. Even their punishments, when they come, are bracing rather than subduing to the trio; for Kipling's boys know that there are two sets of incompatible attributes required of successful administrators and soldiers of the British empire – virtue and violence, obedience and defiance, discipline and transgression – and that they are expected to learn both of them. The Head of the school several times signals his appreciation of the ingenuity and dexterity with which the little band of boys outwits the lower masters and the neighbouring farmers, but he never says anything that could be so construed. Indeed, the terms of this code are clear: you can break the rules, but you must not be caught; you can know, but you must not tell. The final chapter, in which the 'boys', now grown men, gleefully recount Stalky's exploits in India, documents just how effectively the double imperative produces military men who thrive in the service of their country.

After *Tom Brown's Schooldays*, the main tradition of boys' school stories clearly functioned to create the gendered masculine subject, a subject closely connected to national and imperial imaginaries. It is entirely predictable, then, that girls' school stories of the period are significantly different in their plots and styles, since what was wanted of girls was quite different from what was wanted of boys. The female subject, however, was also an imperial subject. In her school story, *A Little Princess* (1905), Frances Hodgson Burnett directly addressed the question of what an empire girl should be. The short story on which *A Little Princess* was based, *Sara Crewe; or, What Happened at Miss Minchin's* (1887), suggests two different imperial events as contexts for Sara's experiences: the Indian 'Mutiny' of 1857 during which Ram Dass, the Indian servant of Sara's neighbour, has saved the life of his master, Mr Carrisford, and the discovery and exploitation, beginning in 1867, of the rich deposits of diamonds and gold in South Africa, an adventure given in Burnett's novel to Ralph Crewe and his school friend Carrisford. However confused the history, the point of the references is clear. Both Crewe and Carrisford are damaged by their participation in overseas adventures, Crewe dying of 'jungle fever' and Carrisford ill and despondent after the untimely death of his friend. Sara's role as a daughter of the empire is to transform the brutal and brutalised male friend of her father into a healthy and benevolent surrogate father. Sara succeeds in fixing her 'Indian gentleman' through her remarkable ability to tell stories; in particular, to construct the narrative of a family in which he wishes to participate. In Burnett's novel, then, the happy ending of the school story is the retreat of the girl from school – a school that is run by a hard and mean mistress – into a family home. Mary Molesworth's *The Carved Lions* (1895) similarly details Geraldine Le Marchant's attempts to find a way to return to the enclosure of home rather than bear her unhappy existence at school. Like Sara Crewe, Geraldine is an orphan of empire, her father being given the opportunity to recoup his financial losses by taking a post in South America. Unlike Sara, Geraldine initially looks forward to school, but finds that the structure of school life allows her neither physical or intellectual privacy nor emotional intimacy with the headmistress. The happy ending of her story comes after she runs away from school, when she is adopted by an elderly couple to await her parents' return to London.

Fielding had ended *The Governess* with Jenny Peace leaving Mrs Teachum's school, having received a letter from her aunt summoning her home; Wollstonecraft had ended hers with Caroline and Mary's father removing them from the tutelage of Mrs Mason; Burnett and Molesworth end theirs with Sara and Geraldine recreating homes they have lost. In Susan Coolidge's *What Katy Did at School* (1873), Katy attends school only briefly, knowing from the beginning of her year away that her widowed father cannot spare her from her home duties for long. Anne, in L. M. Montgomery's series of six novels about her, spends four years, but only one novel, away from home attending college in *Anne of the Island* (1915). In the final scene of the novel, Anne finally accepts Gilbert Blythe's proposal of marriage and looks forward to the home they will build together. The most valued girls' school stories in the English-language tradition across several centuries, it seems, are those that firmly bracket school life with domestic spaces towards which the girls inevitably move.

But, if such a summary accurately encapsulates the canon, it accounts for only a small fraction of the girls' school stories produced between the 1880s and the 1950s. This other tradition might be said to have begun in earnest with L.T. Meade's publication in 1886 of *A World of Girls*, which Meade wrote after reading Talbot Baines Reed's *The Fifth Form at St Dominic's* (serialised in *The Boy's Own Paper*, 1881–2). Meade eventually wrote some forty school stories, the last six published after her death in 1914. While each story was set in a new school and had a different cast of characters, they can be grouped into four general types: boarding-school stories, private-school stories, day-school stories and college stories. The stories set in boarding schools and colleges, in particular, demonstrate Meade's interest in the new, intellectual education for girls and women being theorised by first-wave feminists and put in place by such reforming headmistresses as Dorothea Beale and the principals of the new women's colleges at Oxford and Cambridge. The headmistresses of Meade's fictional establishments can be identified as members of the new generation of educationalists by their allowance for privacy in the arrangements of girls' bedrooms and studies, by their attitudes to the need for systematic training and by their establishment of behavioural codes focusing on ideals of honour and the good of the group.

The plots of Meade's boarding-school stories all describe a similar trajectory. An adolescent girl is sent to school when her family home is disrupted. Her arrival at the beginning of the story causes a disturbance of established routines and loyalties within the school body. She soon finds herself in an untenable situation, her better self prompting her to declare allegiance to one girl or group of girls while she is simultaneously under the secret influence of another more dangerous girl or group. The resolution of the conflict always involves public disclosure of what she has borne in silence for much of the story and, finally, her full integration into the school. Unlike more canonical girls' school stories, L.T. Meade's boarding-school stories do not end with girls leaving school. Indeed, the only girls who return home are the girls banished from the school community in disgrace. The ending of Meade's first school story, *A World of Girls*, is typical in this respect. Annie Forest, who has been wrongly accused of the vandalism that is bedevilling the school, finds and returns the abducted little girl Nan to school. A complicated story of honour and dishonourable conduct among the girls unravels in the final chapters of the novel, as various members of the school community freely tell the secrets they know. Susan Drummond, the miscreant who only admits to her transgressions when she is directly questioned, is removed from the school at night, a scene not shown in the narrative. The final chapter does not turn towards the outer world and replace the girls in domestic spaces, but turns back to the text itself. In the last episode, an account of a prize-giving ceremony, Meade introduces a group of characters she identifies only as 'companions' of Annie Forest. Acting as empty characters, a blank space into which readers may project themselves, this group of unnamed girls asks Annie to 'tell us' about her award-winning essay. The story ends here, with Meade in this gesture attempting to include both the girls inside the text and the girl readers outside the text in her celebration of the world of girls.

A residue of allegory is evident in Meade's stories. But, rather than being 'little world' stories, they are examples of narratives of 'worlds apart'. The larger world does figure in the stories, but only as an intrusion. In the subplots of her novels, girls are abducted, assaulted and robbed of their purses by rough and dirty men. In representing the dangers of the wider world for girls in these symbolic scenes, Meade alludes to contemporary panics about how young women taking up the paid employment for which their education was preparing them and entering public space unescorted can be distinguished from prostitutes or working-class women. Meade's use of the 'world apart' narrative structure, then, does not suggest her ignorance of, or her disso-ciation from, the determinate conditions of her time and place. Indeed, the tensions enacted in Meade's school stories – between the patriarchal home and the world of girls, between the exhilaration of leaving home and the fear of the world – were central contradictions in the ideological formation of femininity in late-Victorian England. Meade does not propose a narrative solution to these contradictions. The only answer she gives is to hold open the imaginative space she has created for her readers in the stories by refusing to return her scholars to an outside world.

Like Fielding and Wollstonecraft, Meade is preoccupied with telling, rea-ding, writing, interpretation – with textuality itself – as the enabling condition of a female community apart from the wider world. Evelyn Sharp, who was an avid reader of the girls' magazine *Atalanta* at the end of the nineteenth century when Meade edited it, challenges the celebration of such worlds of girls in her school story, *The Making of a Schoolgirl* (1897), but does so exactly by foregrounding questions of reading, writing and interpretation. Sharp's main character, Becky, has woven her expectations and hopes about school from her reading of girls' school stories. She believes, for example, that she can expect to suffer before she is fully accepted into the school, that the headmistress will dislike her very much at first, and that there will be one teacher who will take her part. As it turns out, school is not very much like this. But elsewhere in Sharp's novel misreadings reveal rather than obscure meanings. When the girls stage Lord Tennyson's narrative poem *Enoch Arden*, for example, they read selectively, leaving out 'all the meaning ... and all the long words, and the stuffiness, and all that' and playing only the 'lively' and 'jolly' parts of the domestic drama; the resulting spectacle clearly shows marriage to be a proprietary contest between men for the ownership of a woman, an interpretation that is hidden by the sentiment and mystifications of Tennyson's language.[18]

Sharp, unlike Meade, locates the world of girls within the wider world of which it is a part. A significant part of the novel is taken up with the exchange of letters between Becky and her brother and playmate, Jack. Part of Becky's task is to learn to read the world of the school in light of her own experiences of it, despite her brother's constant denigration of all things female. By the end of the novel, when Jack and Becky re-unite at home for a school holiday, Becky is well on her way to recognising the limitations of his descriptions and judgments.

The girls' school story flourished between the late nineteenth and the mid twentieth century. Most authors followed Meade's solution of establishing female communities as worlds apart. Some, like Elinor Brent-Dyer in the Chalet School series, set their schools in remote locations, so that the school world literally is separated from its context by language and custom. Writers like Angela Brazil documented the minutiae of school life and shut out the claims of the larger world, as suggested by the common motif in Brazil's stories of letters forgotten in coat pockets or lost before being opened. For many of the popular writers, the series form allowed the creation and maintenance of complete world systems that existed only textually. There are seven books in Dorita Fairlie Bruce's popular Dimsie series, for example, and fifty-nine books in Brent-Dyer's Chalet School series. Elsie Oxenham not only published thirty-seven books in her Abbey series, but also had characters from various of her series meet and make connections with one another. The sheer volume of reading, to say nothing of the complicated storylines of such series, required engaged and committed readers. Indeed, fan clubs for some of the most popular of the writers were established, so that readers created female worlds of their own outside the texts, enabled by their common reading and interpretation of the textual worlds of girls. For many of these readers, Rosemary Auchmuty speculates, the appeal of the books is as 'an escape for girls and women from the worst pressures of patriarchal life', allowing them to explore 'all-female worlds with strong role models, friendships between and among women, and a range of ways of being which went far beyond conventional prescriptions of femininity'.[19] Such unofficial extensions of the narrative worlds of school stories have proliferated with the general availability of the internet, and especially following the enormous success of J. K. Rowling's *Harry Potter* novels (1997–2007).

Rowling's novels are the great exception to a general migration in recent times of the most popular school stories from books to television. In the UK, *Grange Hill* lasted thirty years from its first broadcast in 1978; in Australia, the *Glenview High* series appeared in 1977 and 1978; in Canada, *Degrassi Junior High* was first produced in 1987, various offshoot series later being developed to capitalise on the success of the original shows; in the USA, since the early 1990s, school-story series have regularly been scheduled on network channels during the prime hours of young people's television viewing. One of the longest-running of these is *Beverly Hills 90210*, first broadcast in 1990 and produced for ten years before moving into re-run schedules. In addition, popular series from the past, such as Richards' Greyfriars series, have been re-made for television. The comfortable fit of the school story into the TV format is the result in part of the formal features of the genre, which include, as Jeffrey Richards has observed, a 'multiplot structure, a large cast of characters, [and] the intermingling of comedy and drama', as well as recurrent patterns of action.[20]

However familiar these features might be to readers of school stories, the series set in schools were innovations in the 1970s in television programming for young people, which was dominated at the time by family comedies and focused on intergenerational conflicts. The school stories, by contrast, emphasised peer dynamics and depicted the school as a relatively autonomous space of teen culture. In the North American series in particular, the conflicts between students and school authorities so much a part of the nineteenth-century British school stories were relegated to the background. In the first season of *Degrassi Junior High*, for example, the principal of the school is never seen, his presence indicated only by his voice on the public address system. Students solve their problems primarily through interactions with one another, although the relation of the concerns of their 'little world' to the larger world is often indicated by signs and posters caught by the camera as it tracks characters' movements down hallways or streets. In *Beverly Hills 90210*, the school clearly functions as a 'world apart', a fantasy space in which young people can explore and express themselves, with teachers generally ineffective in enforcing desirable behaviour in the school and powerless in the world of wealth and influence that surrounds the students outside of school. The only obvious adult moral authorities are the parents of the twin brother and sister who are the central characters of the series, the highly unusual involvement of parents in their lives attributed to the fact that the Walshes have recently moved to Los Angeles from Minnesota and have not yet learned the rules of the new world.

Both series, nevertheless, have been praised as 'realistic' depictions of contemporary adolescence, a reference to the willingness of the producers to include in the storylines such problems as differences in class status, racism, shoplifting, family breakdown, drug use and, most notoriously, gender stereotypes, teen sex, pregnancy and abortion. The critical attribution of realism to school stories has been a recurrent marker of value since at least the publication of *Tom Brown's Schooldays*; now, as then, such a descriptor seems principally to indicate that a narrative has made visible the particular tasks the society of the day has assigned to childhood and adolescence. School stories of the late twentieth century make it apparent that the creation of successful gendered and sexual identities has recently been understood to be a primary task for young people. Gene Kemp's *The Turbulent Term of Tyke Tiler* (1977), for example, is a conventional story of the little world of school, but for the startling revelation in the postscript that Tyke is a girl, a fact that sends readers back to re-read the narrative to discover why they assumed she was a boy and how the new information changes their response to Tyke's story. Adèle Geras uses three of the fairy tales commonly read as stories of young girls' sexual awakening – Rapunzel, Sleeping Beauty and Snow White – as the basis for the school stories of her Egerton Hall trilogy (beginning with *The Tower Room* in 1998). A number of writers have explored the possibility of sexual readings of the close, passionate friendships between girls that have been central to the girls' school story at least since the novels of L.T. Meade. In American Deborah Hautzig's *Hey, Dollface* (1979), Australian Jenny Pausacker's *What Are Ya?* (1987) and Canadian Catherine Brett's *S. P. Likes A. D.* (1989), the central girl characters recognise that their intense feelings for a best friend are sexual as well as emotional, and contemplate the implications of taking up a lesbian identity in the homophobic 'real world' outside school. Melvin Burgess' *Doing It* (2003) assumes a heteronormative society inside and outside school, but exploits the conventions of the school story to tell the stories of the first sexual experiences of three high-school boys. Not only does Burgess use the common techniques of focalising the stories through the teenagers themselves and allowing them to tell their stories in the vocabulary of schoolyard slang, but also he structures his story around a secret that threatens the solidarity of the little band of friends. The secret in this case is that one of them is in a coerced sexual relationship with a teacher.

There is a dearth of contemporary school stories for young people with positive depictions of gay male relationships. This may be, ironically, a result of the long and perplexed history of the representation of homosexual relations between boys in the school story. Thomas Hughes insisted that a footnote he had written about the 'little friend' system at Rugby be allowed to stand in the published version of *Tom Brown's Schooldays* despite the protests of some of his early readers, and Alec Waugh's *The Loom of Youth*

(1917) is notorious for its autobiographical description of the sexual relationships of schoolboys. A number of boys' school stories in the late nineteenth
and early twentieth centuries, including H. O. Sturgis' *Tim* (1891) and
H. A. Vachell's *The Hill* (1905), featured physically and emotionally effusive
relationships between boys, although these loves were not depicted explicitly
as sexual. As Eric Tribunella has demonstrated in his reading of *A Separate
Peace*, however, narrative prohibitions staged to enforce gender conformity
can function perversely to eroticise 'the forbidden object', so that locating the
'queer potential' of a school story might be as much a chosen reading strategy
as an element of the text.[21]

The schools in which most contemporary stories are set are comprehensive,
mixed schools, rather than the single-sex, private boarding schools that
provided the most common setting until the middle of the twentieth century.
Whether comprehensive or private, however, schools continue to provide
the 'enclosed world[s], narrow and intense, close-knit and passionately
experienced' spaces that Isabel Quigly maintains are an ideal framework for
any fiction and central to the success of the school story.[22] Among the most
provocative of the contemporary stories are those that explicitly investigate
the closed and narrow boundaries of school, and interrogate the disciplinary
structures of these worlds. In Gillian Cross' *The Demon Headmaster* (1982),
for example, the Headmaster is so successful in using hypnosis and the
prefectural system to control the student body that he believes he can use
his comprehensive school as the site from which to launch a bid to impose
order on the entire nation. It is the task of a small group of resisting students
to fight for freedom by creating disorder. Cross' series of novels was the basis
of a successful television series in the UK. Diana Wynne Jones' *Witch Week*
(1982) is a fantasy about a boarding school set in a 'world apart' in which
witches are regularly burned in 'bone-fires'. Attempts by school authorities to
ensure that the witch-orphans who have been placed in the school restrain
their powers and conform to the expectations of the 'normal' world are
entirely unsuccessful. It is the world itself that is reconstructed, literally and
dramatically, in the final scene. The conclusion of Julian Houston's autobiographical *New Boy* (2005) is less spectacular but also optimistic about
the possibility of change. The first African-American boy to attend an elite
boarding school in Connecticut in the 1960s, Rob Garrett recognises that he
will never become fully integrated into the school community. But he chooses
to stay at school nevertheless, in the hope that the movement towards inclusion in the 'little world' of school will prompt corresponding changes in the
wider world of the nation. Bebe Faas Rice in *The Place at the Edge of the
Earth* (2002) and Sylvia Olsen in *No Time to Say Goodbye* (2001) also look
back in history, to write the stories of Native American and Aboriginal

Canadian children compelled by governments to attend residential schools, with the expectation that such schooling will work to assimilate them into dominant white cultures. There is no triumphant ending either to Rice's 'world apart' or to Olsen's 'little world' stories. For both writers, the most important achievement is the telling of tales that have been hidden for too long, a telling that rewrites the history of 'the civilising mission' in North America.

Criticism of schools as places of injustice, unhappiness and coercion have featured in narratives from the beginning of the genre, but such critiques have been a comparatively thin thread through the tradition. More typical is the story in which the new scholar learns first to understand, then to accept, and finally to excel at, the ways of the strange world he or she is entering. Writing about ideological analysis in literary and cultural studies, James Kavanagh proposes that ideology be understood as 'designat[ing] a rich "system of representations," worked up in specific material practices, which helps form individuals into social subjects who "freely" internalize an appropriate "picture" of their social world and their place in it'.[23] The system of children's literature clearly is one such material practice and Kavanagh's definition seems an apt description of the work of the school story. Giving young readers pictures of complete, self-sufficient and contained systems, the school story seeks to persuade them that they, too, have a place in the world before them.

NOTES

1. See Gillian Adams, 'Ancient and Medieval Children's Texts', in *International Companion Encyclopedia of Children's Literature*, 2nd edn, ed. Peter Hunt (2 vols., New York: Routledge, 2004), vol. I, pp. 225–38.
2. Sarah Fielding, *The Governess; or, The Little Female Academy*, ed. Candace Ward (1749; Peterborough, ON: Broadview Press, 2005), p. 84.
3. [Ellenor Fenn], *School Dialogues for Boys* (2 vols., London: John Marshall, 1783), vol. I, p. x.
4. Fielding, *Governess*, p. 176.
5. Michel Foucault, *Discipline and Punish: The Birth of the Prison*, trans. Alan Sheridan (New York: Vintage, 1979), p. 201.
6. [Fenn], *School Dialogues*, vol. II, p. 136.
7. Thomas Arnold, *Sermons* (3 vols., London: Rivington, 1830), vol. II, p. 44.
8. Thomas Hughes, *Tom Brown's Schooldays* (1857; London: Macmillan, 1979), p. 115.
9. Harriet Martineau, *The Crofton Boys* (1842; London: Routledge, n.d.), pp. 65 and 70.
10. 'School and College Life: Its Romance and Reality', *Blackwood's Edinburgh Magazine*, 89 (February 1861), 132.
11. Arnold in a letter written in March 1828, quoted in J. J. Findlay, *Arnold of Rugby: His School Life and Contributions to Education* (Cambridge: Cambridge University Press, 1925), p. 30; Hughes, *Tom Brown's Schooldays*, p. 61.

12. Hughes, *Tom Brown's Schooldays*, p. 282.
13. Public School Commission, Report, *Parliamentary Papers*, vol. xx, session 1864, vol. i, p. 56.
14. Hughes, *Tom Brown's Schooldays*, pp. 362, 351 and 355.
15. Edward W. Said, *The World, the Text, and the Critic* (Cambridge, MA: Harvard University Press, 1983), p. 39.
16. Frank Richards, *Billy Bunter of Greyfriars* (1947; London: Hawk Books, 1991), p. 222.
17. 'Boy, Only Boy', *The Academy*, 57 (21 October 1899), 457.
18. Evelyn Sharp, *The Making of a Schoolgirl*, ed. Beverly Lyon Clark (1897; New York: Oxford University Press, 1989), p. 62.
19. Rosemary Auchmuty, 'The Critical Response', in *The Encyclopaedia of Girls' School Stories*, ed. Sue Sims and Hilary Clare (Aldershot: Ashgate, 2000), pp. 19–20.
20. Jeffrey Richards, 'From Greyfriars to Grange Hill', in *School Stories From Bunter to Buckeridge*, ed. Nicholas Tucker (Lichfield: Pied Piper, 2003), pp. 25–39 (p. 37).
21. Eric Tribunella, 'Refusing the Queer Potential: John Knowles's *A Separate Peace*', *Children's Literature*, 30 (2002), 81–95 (p. 93).
22. Isabel Quigly, 'The School Story as Adult Novel', in *School Stories From Bunter to Buckeridge*, ed. Tucker pp. 4–8 (p. 6).
23. James Kavanagh, 'Ideology', in *Critical Terms for Literary Study*, ed. Frank Lentricchia and Thomas McLaughlin, 2nd edn (Chicago and London: University of Chicago Press, 1995), p. 310.

14

ANDREA IMMEL, U. C. KNOEPFLMACHER AND JULIA BRIGGS*

Fantasy's alternative geography for children

In *The Impulse of Fantasy Literature* (1983), Colin Manlove arranged fantasies according to their divided topographies. Whereas some fantastic narratives may describe a journey from our world to a supernatural one, he wrote, others, like William Morris' romances, Tolkien's *The Hobbit* and Ursula Le Guin's *Earthsea* trilogy, immediately plunge us into a wholly fantastic world with little reference to our own reality. Still others, Manlove noted, may try to harmonise orders that are considered to be separate only in the minds of their readers, or, quite to the contrary, hint that magic and miracle are so rare that they can only become manifest to 'certain types of people'.[1] Though helpful, this topography overlooks the persistent presence of the child as a special 'type' in fantastic landscapes. Indeed, with their special perspective, where neither innocence and experience nor the real and imaginary have drifted into opposition, children are prime players as characters in, and creators and readers of, fantasy texts.

In its focus on the figure of the child, this chapter will offer a parallel perspective on Manlove's taxonomy. In 'Dubious binaries', we question the pervasive opposition between fantasy and reason, as well as a concomitant tendency to designate fantasy texts as being exclusively for either children or adults. We then examine the roles played by children in three very different kinds of fantastic narratives, none of which strictly follows the conventions based on medieval romance, Welsh legend or Northern European mythology that still operate in works of 'high' fantasy, such as C. S. Lewis' *Chronicles of Narnia*, Susan Cooper's *The Dark Is Rising* or Lloyd Alexander's *Chronicles of Prydain*. The texts we next consider in 'Domestic disturbances' feature young protagonists whose encounters with exotic intruders from different realms or times create awkward conflicts with the everyday routine of parents or guardians. Still, since any disruptions created by a clash between such conflicting realities are short-lived and without lasting consequences, they can ultimately be laughed away or even forgotten. The narratives we take up in 'Worlds upside down', however, are more prone to enlisting the child's own magical thinking to create alternative worlds as an antidote to the convention-bound notions of his or her elders' reality. Here, too, such conflicts may be temporary, since the maturing child must eventually relinquish the empowering immersion in these early imaginings. But the prospect of retaining some of that potency can also ensure the fantasy's preservation. Last, in 'Wayfarers in strange lands', we highlight texts in which child-men or children are thrust into parallel worlds to overcome treachery or evil. Such texts, which can appeal as much to grown-up as to juvenile readers, are potentially tragic and theologically inflected, and hence fundamentally different from the comic or nostalgic fanta-sies taken up in the second and third sections of this chapter. Since a soul, a world or an entire universe may now hang in the balance, much depends upon the heroic but inexperienced protagonist's ability to acquire the self-knowledge and wisdom needed to surmount the challenges she or he must meet.

Dubious binaries

In the preface to her highly influential collection of children's stories, *The Parent's Assistant* (1796), the British novelist and educator Maria Edgeworth boldly challenged the 'authority' of Dr Samuel Johnson. It was incorrect, she held, for him to assert that 'Babies do not like to hear stories of babies like themselves' and hence prefer 'to have their imaginations raised by tales of giants and fairies'. Even if Dr Johnson's assertion were to be true, something which Edgeworth greatly doubted, why should children be 'indulged', she asked, in their preference for escapist narratives? Exposure of young readers to narratives about 'fairies, giants, and enchanters' might only delay their needed ability to confront the verities of everyday life: 'Why should the mind be filled with fantastic visions, instead of useful knowledge? Why should so much valuable time be lost?'[2]

Edgeworth's attack on fantastic narratives was derided by post-Romantic critics who questioned her position that such texts taught nothing profound and hence could never serve worthy ends. These critics even went beyond Dr Johnson by endorsing all writings that valued the child's construction of alternative realities. British Romantics such as Blake and Wordsworth, and Victorians such as the fantasists of the pivotal 1860s (Charles Kingsley, George MacDonald, Lewis Carroll and Jean Ingelow), thus were upheld as foils to the utilitarian and supposedly dry educational ideology espoused by Edgeworth and her followers. Well after Mitzi Myers vindicated the artistic sophistication of Edgeworth and her fellow-Georgian 'mentorias' and exposed the over-simplifications of literary historians such as Geoffrey Summerfield, the opposition between fantasy and reason still stands mostly intact, although more in principle than in practice.[3]

Yet that division remains highly arbitrary. Children, after all, learn to identify different levels of reality quite early in their mental development. And they soon recognise different systems of representation as part of the same process that enables them to acquire language. Moreover, their awareness that representation is a mode distinct from reality soon allows them to find a vicarious pleasure in safely acting out situations that can be probable or 'realistic' as well as improbable or 'fantastic' (the humorous 'nonsense' of nursery rhymes is, of course, predicated on just this principle). The child's sophisticated way of responding to representations thus parallels the operation of language itself, which, like fiction, functions as a coherent and elaborated system of analogies to the material world.

Thus 'wonder', a word all too often deliberately deployed to encourage young readers to plunge into imaginary landscapes (*Alice's Adventures in Wonderland*, *A Wonder-Book for Girls and Boys*, *Granny's Wonderful Chair*, *The Wonderful Wizard of Oz*) can just as easily be applied to any youthful discovery of startlingly new, yet real experiences. Edgeworth herself vividly captures the 'distinctive' excitement of her alter ego Rosamond, the little girl whose 'bewildered immersion in London's plethora of sights and sounds' becomes a necessary prolegomenon for mastering the art of discrimination in 'The Purple Jar'.[4] And Edgeworth fully endorses the allure of a natural or practical magic in 'Wonders', a story in which Rosamond discovers that an ordinary insect like the flea is, when magnified under a microscope, as extraordinary as the most fantastic of imaginary creatures. Rosamond's wonder at the microscope's marvellous capability to transform the flea's appearance also awakens her curiosity and sparks her desire to learn more about the true nature of things. Her wonder is hardly uncritical, but rather stems from a laudable passion for the transformative powers of knowledge.

Conversely, texts considered to be fantastic quite frequently offer highly useful, 'didactic' information. Far from being dry, the scientific facts disseminated in Kingsley's *The Water-Babies* (1863), the retellings of British history in Kipling's *Puck of Pook's Hill* (1906) or the mathematical problems that must be solved to break the spells in Nesbit's 'The Island of the Nine Whirlpools' (1899) and 'Melisande; or Long and Short Division' (1901) are certainly wondrous in their own right. Technology, too, is hardly incompatible with the fantastic. The eponymous 'Old Thing' in Susan Cooper's 1993 *The Boggart* indulges his love of mischief by wreaking havoc with the electricity running through a television set, a theatre's light board, and the wires controlling the signals of a busy Toronto intersection. The intricate operations of all those 'reassembled and specially modified' devices that dethrone Manny Rat in Russell Hoban's 1967 fantasy about two wind-up toy mice who hope to become self-winding have been lovingly worked out by an author who clearly relishes such mechanical contraptions.[5] Although the balloon designed by the Wizard of Oz may be of questionable use in a world ruled by powerful witches, it allows him to return to Kansas without having to resort to the magical slippers on which Dorothy must rely. And in Diana Wynne Jones' *The Dark Lord of Derkholm* (1998), the griffin-children of Wizard Derk and the sorceress Mara are the miraculous results of their father's experiments in genetic engineering.

But in the 1790s Edgeworth's preference of 'useful knowledge' over the kind of learning that can be imparted through 'fantastic visions' may have been directed as much at the seventeenth-century religious allegory that would continue to loom as large as fairy tales in children's reading through the end of the Victorian period. In 1684, when John Bunyan published the second part of *The Pilgrim's Progress from this World to That Which Is to Come, Delivered under the Similitude of a Dream*, he proudly noted that his 'holy Pilgrim' had already become as popular with children as with adults. In 'The Author's Way of Sending Forth His Second Part of the "Pilgrim"', Bunyan adduced the enthusiastic testimonials of juvenile readers to overcome the lingering resistance of educated adults. His young audience had transcended their elders' divisions of class. For not only had 'Young Ladies, and young Gentlewomen' eagerly taken his pilgrim to 'Their Cabinets, their Bosoms, and their Hearts', but so had their less affluent counterparts:

> The very Children that do walk the street,
> If they do but my holy *Pilgrim* meet,
> Salute him will, will wish him well, and say,
> He is the only *Stripling* of the Day.[6]

Bunyan here welcomes the approval of children as a testimonial that disarms all those who may still protest that his fantasy's metaphoric texture is too removed from the 'Solidity' of their surroundings. If children find his narrative accessible and his allegory easy to decode, how then can any adult claim to be baffled? ('Some say his Words and Stories are so dark, / They know not how by them to find his mark.') Whereas in Part 1 of *The Pilgrim's Progress*, Christian was compelled to forsake his children, in Part 2, they and the offspring of others can join their parents in a pilgrimage towards a higher reality. Not only does Christiana now travel with her sons, but Mr Dispondency is also accompanied by a young daughter who, at the end, joyously goes 'through the River singing', although 'none could understand what she says'. If a child's ability to discern veiled truths makes it a better reader than a sceptical grown-up 'Carper' who professes to be impeded by Bunyan's 'darker lines', that same credulity can also empower the story's child pilgrims.

Thought difficult to translate into words, intuited truths are themselves fresh, ever-young, preserved in their own 'Swaddling-clouts'.[7]

Bunyan's sketch of a daughter whose song her elders cannot 'understand' curiously resembles George MacDonald's fuller portrait of his own cryptic river-crosser, little Diamond in *At the Back of the North Wind* (1868–9). Diamond's mother, bound by the sequential logic of her everyday world, cannot appreciate the illogic of an endless poem about a river that fascinates Diamond after his brief return from the other-worldly realm to which he had been taken by the gigantic North Wind. Puzzled by 200 lines 'of euphonious, unpunctuated, repetitive yet ever-varying combinations of a limited number of words', the boy's mother offers to find him a better poem.[8] But he identifies the rhymed verses with the 'tune' sung by the river he watched in a realm in which he and his fellow-pilgrims had silently communicated and automatically understood 'everything'.

When major Victorian fantasists such as MacDonald and Charles Kingsley chose to write for children, they were as deeply indebted to Bunyan's allegorical seventeenth-century text as C. S. Lewis (MacDonald's self-avowed disciple) would become in the twentieth century. Although the theologies behind MacDonald's and Kingsley's book-length and socially conscious fantasies are certainly far more idiosyncratic and unorthodox than the Puritan allegory promoted by *The Pilgrim's Progress*, the child pilgrims featured in *The Water-Babies* and *At the Back of the North Wind* are, like Bunyan's salvation-seekers, souls in search of a higher order of reality. Preceded not only by Kingsley's 1860 preface to a new edition of Bunyan's book but also by his own study of marine biology in the 1857 *Glaucus, or, the Wonders of the Shore*, Kingsley's 1863 *The Water-Babies* can be read as a curious amalgam of these separate incursions into 'real' and unreal realms. MacDonald's own first book-length work for children also is an amalgam of sorts, since *At the Back of the North Wind* not only harks back to his 1858 *Phantastes: A Faerie Romance for Men and Women*, a novel about a young dreamer who wants to 'translate' his visionary adventures among symbolic landscapes into the ordinary life of humans, but also reflects his own deep investment in *Pilgrim's Progress*, a book held in such high esteem in the MacDonald household that this former clergyman and his family repeatedly acted out its plot in private and public theatricals.

Kingsley's orphaned chimney-sweep, little Tom, and MacDonald's little Diamond, a coachman's son, will not reach adulthood: Tom sheds his soiled and undernourished body when he drowns, but instantly acquires a new form as an amphibious, immortal water-baby who is joined in his piscatory adventures by Ellie, an upper-class, yet similarly transformed, girl. Diamond, on the other hand, grows up sheltered in the warm, manger-like, stable where he is soon visited as an elect by the apparition of a female North Wind. Though nurtured by his working-class family, lionised by his genteel admirers, and tutored by North Wind, the boy spends most of his short life facing the hardships of his Dickensian present. His constant awareness of a higher reality, however, is re-inforced by his sojourn in the limbo to which North Wind takes him and by his vivid dreams about a pre-natal world of fellow-angels. Diamond thus acts as an inarticulate witness of events that MacDonald's self-conscious narrator finds difficult to translate. Like Tom, Diamond is given a girl partner. But unlike Tom's alliance with Ellie, Diamond's investment in 'poor' Nanny the street-sweeper, a Tom-like waif, is one-sided. Nanny regards her benefactor with the same scepticism that led Bunyan's worldly wise Pliable to distrust Christian's holy zeal.

Still, despite their indebtedness to Bunyan, both Kingsley and MacDonald markedly differ from his precedent by persistently interrogating his single-minded, unitary point of view. Fantasy, as Rosemary Jackson points out, became increasingly dialogical, 'with the result that the "real" is a notion which [came] under constant interrogation'.[9] Whereas, for Bunyan, the trappings of the everyday world were a falsifying delusion that his pilgrim souls could willingly shed, the 'solidity' of Diamond's London and even the workings of Tom's fluid marine world retain weightier ballasts. The concrete and highly particularised realities that both of these boy pilgrims must process cannot be easily dissolved by sheer metaphor or allegory. Both Diamond and Tom must therefore be instructed by symbolic agents who, unlike Bunyan's Evangelist, are cast as limited mediators who are themselves involved in a dialogic tug-of-war between contrary realities.

Edgeworth did not live to read texts which, like *The Water-Babies* and *At the Back of the North Wind*, aspire to harmonise the laws of the natural world with the higher metaphysical laws of a world adumbrated by the imagination. But one suspects that she might have noticed that friction and juxtaposition seem far more dominant than reconciliation in ambitious constructs that enlist the child as seeker and seer, and yet remain profoundly didactic. It seems significant, in this respect, that towards the end of his career, in an essay called 'The Fantastic Imagination' (1893), George MacDonald should confirm the importance of children as readers and protagonists of fantastic narratives. Assuming the persona of an elliptical expositor, MacDonald casts his essay as a dialogue in which he addresses a parent who wants to know how to decode the elusive 'meanings' of such enigmatic texts. Children, MacDonald assures his worried interlocutor, 'are not likely to trouble you about meaning. They find what they are capable of finding, and more would be too much. For my part, I do not write for children, but for the childlike, whether of five, or fifty, or seventy-five.'[10] MacDonald here updates

Bunyan's own privileging of the child as an ideal interpreter of visionary fantasies.

Domestic disturbances

In a chapter exclusively devoted to her work, Manlove rightly highlights E. Nesbit's exploitation of 'comic incongruities'.[11] Nesbit's delight in creating frictions between incongruous realities even extends to her deformation of earlier fantasy-texts. That intertextual playfulness is evident in *The Phoenix and the Carpet* (1904), which features the five children who also appear in *Five Children and It* (1902) and *The Story of the Amulet* (1906). Given tickets to a musical play at the Garrick Theatre, the children are informed by their mother 'that you're going to see "The Water-Babies" all by your happy selves'. She does not know, of course, that her children will share this performance with another spectator, namely, the ancient Phoenix whom they have secretly hatched. Since this resurrected golden bird possesses a full memory of its previous life-cycles, it pedantically inquires about the nature of the spectacle to which he will be taken: 'What is the show at the theatre to-night? Wrestlers? Gladiators? A combat of cameleopards and unicorns?'[12]

This visitor from a mythological past is disappointed to hear that it will be introduced to a musical adaptation of a book about 'chimney-sweeps and professors, and a lobster and an otter and a salmon, and children living in the water'. The fire-bird shivers at such a 'chilly' prospect, but is reassured when told that theatres are 'warm and pretty, with a lot of gold and lamps'. Once there, the egotistical Phoenix mistakes the theatre for a shrine devoted to its exclusive worship: '"This is indeed my temple," it said again and again. "What radiant rites! And all to do honour to me!"' But when it flaps its wings and addresses the actors as its 'servants' and complains about the lack of a fiery 'altar' and drops sparks that become little flames that 'opened like flower-buds', the Phoenix does not only shatter the stage-illusion created by the acting of Little Tom and of the lobster whose 'gem of a song' it has so rudely interrupted, but actually sets the theatre on fire. The chapter ends with the children whispering to each other, 'We must get rid of that Phoenix.'[13]

The Phoenix creates anarchic disruptions in the everyday world of his youthful hosts. Concealed from parents and servants, he and the Psammead of *The Five Children and It* may well stimulate the imagination of their excited child partners. But the troubles these visitors cause also become increasingly dangerous. If the Phoenix merely sets fire to a theatre, the wish-granting Psammead, who places the children in search of the intact Amulet on a vast historical stage, exposes them to the perils posed by aggressive armies, suicidal sailors and cataclysmic tsunamis. As a result, the exit of such secret guests always makes the return to domesticity a decided relief. After the exorcism of the sorcerer's troublesome spirit in Penelope Lively's *The Ghost of Thomas Kempe* (1973), James quietly walks home, marvelling at the stillness of the beautiful summer evening, 'his head full of confused but agreeable thoughts, hungry and a little tired, but content'.[14]

Relief can also come in the form of an agreement to obliterate the child's memory of its chance contact with representatives of fantastic 'otherness'. In Kipling's *Puck of Pook's Hill*, the fairy who introduces Una and Dan to resuscitated visitors from England's past prevents the two children from telling adults about their various encounters. Puck gives them three leaves to chew – one of Oak, one of Ash and one of Thorn: '"Bite these," said he. "Otherwise you might be talking at home of what you've seen and heard, and – if I know human beings – they'd send for the doctor. Bite!"' When her father asks Una why she is 'chewing leaves' just for 'fun', the little girl only knows that it was 'for something' she no longer can 'azactly remember'.[15]

Even a work like Jean Ingelow's 1869 *Mopsa the Fairy*, a novel in which the boy Jack agrees to take some tiny English fairies to their own fantastic homeland, ends on a regressive note of domestic oblivion. When he returns home, Jack forgets the fairy queen who has surpassed him in her growth. Asked 'no questions' by the parents he dutifully kisses before he is sent to bed, the little boy is delighted 'to find all the house just as usual', says his prayers, and 'comfortably' falls asleep in his 'little white bed'.[16] Will he, on waking up, remember the wonders that had marked his journey? Or will the white bed-sheets blank out what may, after all, have been as much of a daydream as that of Lewis Carroll's Alice? *Wonderland*'s child-dreamer at least left her older sister to process adventures she had relinquished. But when Ingelow's book ends with a laconic 'That's all', that two-word sentence dismisses the reader, along with Jack, to run off to play now that the story is over. It is as if the teller expects that the memory of those fantastic encounters, delightful as they were, will simply vanish without leaving a trace.

Worlds upside down

If Nesbit's Amulet children or Lively's James forgo – and gladly forget – the notoriety briefly conferred on them through their chance acquaintance with unpredictable and powerful magical creatures, other fictional children – or child-like adults – relish the unexpected acquisition of a pre-eminence denied to them in real life. Charles Dickens created a perky child author, 'Miss Nettie Ashford', aged 'half-past six' in *A Holiday Romance* (1868), who sets her story of 'Mrs. Orange and Mrs. Lemon' in a utopia for children that turns into a dystopia for the subjugated parents under their total control. Nettie begins by describing this fantasy-land: 'There is a country which I will show you when I get into maps, where the children have everything their own way. It is a most delightful country to live in. The grown-up people are obliged to obey the children, and are never allowed to sit up to supper except on their birth-days.'[17] Written for what would now be called a 'cross-over' audience, Dickens intended *A Holiday Romance* to amuse both parents and children: it first appeared in *Our Young Folks* in America and *All the Year Round* in Britain, both family magazines meant to be read aloud and enjoyed by all generations.

Nettie's story not only feeds a child's fantasy of what it may be like to be an adult but also invites adults to indulge a yearning for departed childhood freedoms. This double inversion operates in comic fantasies such as F. Anstey's *Vice Versa, or, A Lesson to Fathers* (1882) and Mary Rodgers' twentieth-century updating, *Freaky Friday* (1972). Though published nearly ninety years apart, these narratives with body-swapping plots, in which Anstey's boy thrives as a prosperous businessman while his father goes back to school and Rodgers' girl runs the household while her mother becomes an irresponsible teenager, hold an identical appeal for their young and grown-up readers.

The popularity of texts such as A. A. Milne's *The House at Pooh Corner* (1928), however, suggests that no such transpositions are needed to give fantasies of child-power a cross-generational appeal. Christopher Robin recognises his imminent loss of agency when he tells Pooh, 'What I like *doing* best is Nothing', before reluctantly announcing, 'I'm not going to do Nothing any more.' When the perplexed Pooh demands, 'Never again?', the boy responds: 'well, not so much. They don't let you.' Milne's suggestion that Christopher's world is about to be sundered is somewhat softened by the consolatory hint that childhood enchantments are renewable. Christopher's final exchanges with the bear he has animated remain tentative and incon-clusive until the voice of an adult author intervenes with a wishful closure:

> 'Pooh,' said Christopher Robin earnestly, 'if I – if I'm not quite –' he stopped and tried again – 'Pooh, *whatever* happens, you *will* understand, won't you?'
> 'Understand what?'
> 'Oh, nothing.' He laughed and jumped to his feet. 'Come on!'
> So they went off together. But wherever they go, and whatever happens to them on the way, in that enchanted place on top of the Forest a little boy and his Bear will always be playing.[18]

Milne's closure is elegiac, yet it involves less of a rupture than the ending of Kenneth Grahame's *The Golden Age* (1895), a book originally intended for adults that also acquired a younger readership. When Edward, the oldest of the children who have shared a fantasy world, leaves for boarding school, his undisturbed siblings continue their games of make-believe; armed with bows and arrows, they remain convinced that their 'Ulysses' will return intact. But the narrator predicts that, once back from 'Troy', their former leader will 'scornfully condemn their clumsy but laborious armory as rot and humbug and only fit for kids'.[19] By way of contrast, Milne allows Christopher to remain almost as ignorant as the toys he leaves behind. The site he had animated through magical thinking need not be violated.

Still, Grahame shares Milne's desire to prolong the habit of magical thinking. If young readers must eventually surrender one way of seeing the world, they may also recover or rediscover its contours between the covers of a book. The wistful annals of ideal boyhoods are not so much turned upside down as rejected in fantastic meta-fictions authored by girl characters who gleefully subvert adult and textual authority. In Eleanor Estes' *The Witch Family* (1960), seven-year-old Amy (modelled upon Estes' daughter Hannah) imperiously 'banquishes' mean Old Witch to a glass hill until she can learn to be good. Although an extremely wicked, powerful and important witch, she is nevertheless subject to the moral dictates and narrative whims of Amy and her friend Clarissa, who gradually create for her 'a bad good witch's paradise' where the boundary between reality and fantasy is delightfully and unambiguously porous.[20] The characters that Amy and Clarissa draw, inspired by ones that were the subject of running stories told by Amy's mother, can move from the glass hill into the girls' world where they all participate in nocturnal hurly-burlies, just as the girls apparently become the alter egos of their favourite witchy characters.

Wayfarers in strange lands

In *Practical Education* (1798), a volume published two years after her *Parent's Assistant*, Maria Edgeworth acknowledged the pleasure children took in travellers' tales, which allowed them to venture into unknown territories without leaving their chairs. But the consumption of adventure stories, where thrilling description might overwhelm thoughtful reflection, Edgeworth observed, could aggravate a restless desire to wander around the world. Here then, supposedly, was another kind of quasi-fantastic narrative that provoked a kind of wonder without offering lasting benefits for the reader. By Edgeworth's time, not only Defoe's *Robinson Crusoe* (1719), but also the first two books of Jonathan Swift's *Gulliver's Travels* (1726), had become canonical works with a peculiar cross-over status. That Defoe's dogged and endlessly resourceful castaway would serve as a model for the protagonist of children's adventure fiction would not have surprised her. But she probably could not have imagined Gulliver, that surprisingly wide-eyed ship's surgeon stranded four times on the strangest of shores, as a forerunner of the girl heroine who travels across worlds in modern fantasy. All travellers passing through regions yet to be described are more or less naïve like Gulliver. Since their temporary ignorance can level the differences between adult and child, their unfamiliarity with the physical and social laws that govern newly discovered worlds also creates a kinship between the innocent traveller feeling his way and his readers, for whom it is as pleasurable as exciting to observe how the protagonist changes through encounters with the other. But where Gulliver's ability to move out of himself is compromised by his peculiar child-man status, the girl traveller typically attains a kind of wise grace.

Provided with maps such as those which Dickens' Nettie proposed to draw up, *Gulliver's Travels* certainly promulgated the 'taste for adventure' that Edgeworth did not condone. Young readers could readily identify with the naïf Gulliver as a power-hungry fellow-child and exult in his acts of prowess among the Lilliputians, whether Swift's satire hit home or went over their heads. Gulliver's capture of the entire Blefuscan fleet is in keeping with the wildest imaginings of a boy who longs to animate his toy ships and toy soldiers. But Gulliver instead regards himself as the inferior of his royal patrons, deferring like a gigantic child to the manikins he could crush at will. He meekly tries to vindicate his character 'in Point of Cleanliness to the World' when he soils his prison floor at night. He likewise fails to impress his tiny masters when he voids prodigious amounts of urine to suppress the fire that had threatened the Empress' palace. Although such scatological episodes were often omitted in juvenile abridgments, they are entirely in keeping with Gulliver's boyish attempts to earn the respect he covets from his minuscule royal benefactors by placing his enormous body in their service. This child-man's empowerment comes to as abrupt an end as that of a Christopher Robin, but it is debatable who takes away more from his experiences – the benign ruler of the Hundred-Acre Wood or the Man-Mountain.

Children could likewise empathise with Gulliver's humiliating reversal of status when he finds himself a Lilliputian in the Land of Brobdingnag. He is persistently rankled by his reduction in size and the corresponding diminution of respect. Instead of capturing enemy fleets, Gulliver must now content himself with killing a rat with his rapier. He is a marvel to be gawked at, first, before the boorish spectators gathered by his greedy master; thereafter, he provides a more refined amusement for the philosopher-king who gently mocks his adult pretensions. Worst of all, a monkey mistakes him 'for a young of his own Species, by his often stroaking my Face very gently' and by 'holding me like a Baby in one of his Fore-Paws, and feeding me with the other, by cramming into my Mouth some victuals'. Heroism inevitably eludes the tiny traveller in the land of giants. Indeed, it is a fitting irony that Gulliver's best friend and protector there should be a child, the forty-foot girl, 'my dear Glumdalclitch', who cares for him more tenderly than her dolls and mourns bitterly the loss of her playfellow.[21]

The gigantic figure of Glumdalclitch caring for her 'grildrig' would seem the antithesis of the adventurous heroines of later fantasies. Yet it is not unusual for those girls, like her, to be capable of a selfless devotion to the boys or men that they are so willing to protect. But whereas Swift does not allow Glumdalclitch to do more than ward off threats that might endanger any miniature man in domestic circumstances, a modern fantasy writer could quite easily adopt the little giantess' point of view and send her out into an alternative world where she would overcome apparently insuperable obstacles to rescue the beloved man-boy.

Little Gerda in Hans Christian Andersen's *The Snow Queen* (1843) never asks how she will find Little Kai or what she will have to do to wrest him from her seductive elemental adversary. Gerda sets out, armed with only her faith and innocence, unaware that the latter will be the source of a mysterious power over the people and animals who gladly assist her on the journey north. As the Finnish Woman explains, if Gerda were to be told of this power, it would dissipate and void all chance of rescuing Little Kai. Immune to the Snow Queen's terrifying advance troops of living snowflakes by virtue of her prayers, Gerda passes into the vast hall, where she finds Kai alone, her rival having dashed out to dust Etna and Vesuvius with snow. Kai is diverting himself with the Game of Reason, having been promised by the Snow Queen that he will become his own master if he can form the word 'eternity' with the geometric shapes of his ice tangram. When Gerda is reunited with him, she weeps on his breast, the hot tears dissolving the lump of ice in his heart. Now that he can cry again, his joyful tears wash the shard of the devil's mirror out of his eye. For the first time he shivers in the desolate cold of the Queen's palace and wonders at the arid intellectualism of his pastimes. Animated by the children's loving display of affection, the puzzle pieces form themselves into the word that will restore Kai to his true nature and set him free to return home with his girl-saviour.

The puzzle pieces that Meg Murry must reassemble in Madeleine L'Engle's *A Wrinkle in Time* (1962) demand that she journey to an alternative reality controlled by It, from which she will wrest not one, but two, beloved male figures, her physicist father and her younger brother Charles Wallace. Unlike Gerda, Meg must actually face down her adversary in a mental contest where her rational mind is of little assistance. Meg's greatest test comes when she resists the appeal of a boy who looks and dresses like Charles Wallace yet is a delusive substitute, a doll foisted on her by the antagonists of the unearthly figures who have been her steadfast allies. It is when this false brother asks her to hate these allies, however, that Meg summons the overpowering love that now restores 'the baby who was so much more to her than she was, and yet was so utterly vulnerable'. When 'the real Charles Wallace, the child for whom she had come back' to a dangerous world, embraces her, Meg feels an 'icy cold blast' and hears an 'angry, resentful howl', before she and her father are reunited in the family's vegetable garden on a 'sweet smelling autumnal earth'.[22] And unlike Gerda, Meg will be called upon again in *A Wind in the Door* (1973) to develop psychic and spiritual powers of which she was unaware, to combat the spirits called the Echthroi, demonic un-namers that threaten the life of her precious Charles Wallace.

A determined innocence is sufficient to safeguard Gerda on her journey. The profound capacity for love is Meg's greatest weapon against It and the Echthroi. But in Philip Pullman's *His Dark Materials* (1995–2000), Lyra Belaqua will be set against enemies more duplicitous, ambitious and powerful than Lilliputian courtiers, the Snow Queen or It. But the question of the heroine's education is central to the first book in the trilogy, *Northern Lights* or (in America) *The Golden Compass* (1995), in a way it is not in the other two fantasies. The prophecy about Lyra is quite clear that, in fulfilling a destiny as cosmic in magnitude as that of Meg, she 'must do it all without realizing what she's doing'.[23] In other words, she must be kept ignorant of the prophecy and left free to decide for herself what must be done. She therefore goes north to rescue Roger, who is among the children kidnapped by the Oblation Board for experimental purposes, but also to set her father free from Svalbard by restoring the alethiometer to him. She has little true notion of what hangs in the balance.

The question of Lyra's education weighs oppressively on her guardian, the Master of Jordan College, when he sends her off with Mrs Coulter to London on the first stage of her travels, apparently as unprepared as Gerda upon her departure. But by having allowed the young aristocrat in his charge to run like a 'half-wild cat' with the town urchins and college servants' children, the Master provided Lyra with the best education she could have received in the great university centre of Oxford. Like explorers of uncharted territories, Lyra and her companion Roger, the kitchen boy, have scrambled over 'the irregular Alps of the college roofs' or braved the 'netherworld' of Jordan's crypts and catacombs.[24] Proud of calling the historically rich and powerful Jordan College her home, Lyra also senses that, through that community of scholars, she is connected to politics at the highest levels, even before learning that Lord Asriel and Mrs Coulter are her parents. While apparently doing 'nothing', Lyra learned the arts of war and politics of forming alliances in its streets and clay beds, as well as developing her considerable powers of leadership, all without sacrificing her innate sense of loyalty and of justice. She learns to lie convincingly in tight spots, unaware that she is the child of god-like liars. Only Lyra the barbarian, armed with the alethiometer, could have rallied Roger and the other dispirited, frightened children kidnapped by the Oblation Board, to execute her plan for breaking out of Bolvangar.

In Svalbard, however, the nature of the challenges she faces are more demanding. To overcome her enemies, Lyra depends upon her intuitive ability to synthesise her interpretations of the alethiometer, her readings of character and her knowledge about the nature of dust, the connection between humans and their dæmons. This is a tall order for a twelve-year-old girl, even one with the potential to become a scholar-adventurer like her parents or John Parry, all of whom are expert at grasping the implications of an apparently haphazard collection of data in order to devise a plan for action. She devises a brilliant plan to engineer the downfall of the usurper Iokur Rakinson by exploiting his fatal flaw, the desire to be human, by pretending to be the dæmon of the deposed bear king Iorek Byrnison. But her father Lord Asriel is a much more difficult subject to read than the foolish bear king. Blinded by her pride in being the daughter of such a man, but with the vaguest of conceptions of his dream for the rebellion to end all rebellions, she hopes that the presentation of the alethiometer will establish her worthiness to walk beside him across the bridge between worlds. Instead, she unwittingly delivers Roger to Lord Asriel, who coolly sacrifices the boy to breach universes. In spite of her innocent but catastrophic betrayal of Roger, the rueful Lyra refuses to abandon the journey. 'I reckon we've got to do it, Pan', she muses; 'We'll go up there and we'll search for Dust, and when we've found it we'll know what to do.'[25] As she walks into the sky undeterred by the possible consequences of Roger's death or by fears of her parents' future machinations, she has achieved a formidable grandeur that belies her filthy furs and substandard English. Instead, little by little, the new Eve is learning how to transcend the contrarieties of innocence and experience, of intuition and education, of the material and spiritual, and of good and evil.

Fantasy needs the child as mediator. Given the child's ability to move between contradictory realities and mental states, its prominence in texts that appeal to both young and mature readers calls for a refinement of the topographical models that we questioned at the outset of this chapter. Whether strange or familiar, the landscapes in which fantasy operates are most fully realised by the perceptive eye of innocence. The suspension of disbelief brought about by our earlier, more fluid, negotiations between the real and fantastic provides the foundation for mastery of reality that Maria Edgeworth wanted child-readers to acquire. Madeleine L'Engle suggested that such a continuity between our child and adult perspectives exists, when she stated in 1982 that 'A child denied imaginative literature is likely to have more difficulty understanding cellular biology or post-Newtonian physics than the child whose imagination has been stretched by fantasy and science fiction.'[26] More than twenty years later, Philip Pullman makes a similar case for a unitary self in the hints about Lyra's future beyond the three volumes of *His Dark Materials*. Early in *The Golden Compass*, the narrator confides that Lyra would eventually 'know more about Dust than anyone in the world'.[27] This aside suggests that, even after reaching puberty at the end of *The Amber Spyglass*, Lyra's maturation will continue. It is significant that the letters following the narrative of Pullman's prequel *Once Upon a Time in the North* (2008) should come from the pen of Lyra Silvertongue, M. Phil. candidate in history at St Sophia's College, Oxford.

NOTES

* Professor Briggs expanded ideas she had set out at the 'Sharpening the Subtle Knife' conference at Princeton University in November 2006, but, tragically, died in August of 2007 before she could develop them any further. As it now stands, this chapter is by Andrea Immel and U. C. Knoepflmacher, but Julia's notes, which Robin Briggs generously allowed them to consult, greatly helped them in formulating their approach to this topic.

1. C. N. Manlove, *The Impulse of Fantasy Literature* (Kent, OH: Kent State University Press, 1983), p. 45.

2. Maria Edgeworth, *The Parent's Assistant: or Stories for Children*, 2nd edn (London: J. Johnson, 1796), p. xi.

3. Mitzi Myers, 'Wise Child, Wise Peasant, Wise Guy: Geoffrey Summerfield's Case Against the Eighteenth Century', *Children's Literature Association Quarterly*, 12 (1987), 107–11.

4. Mitzi Myers, 'Socializing Rosamond: Educational Ideology and Fictional Form', *Children's Literature Association Quarterly*, 14 (1989), 52–8 (p. 55).

5. Russell Hoban, *The Mouse and His Child* (1967; New York: Avon Books, 1974), p. 143.

6. John Bunyan, *The Pilgrim's Progress from this World to That Which Is to Come, Delivered under the Similitude of a Dream*, Part 2 (London: Nathaniel Ponder, 1684), pp. [vi–vii].

7. Bunyan, *The Pilgrim's Progress from this World to That Which Is to Come, Delivered under the Similitude of a Dream* [Part 1] (London: Nathaniel Ponder, 1678), pp. [vi], [vii] and 219; p. [viii].

8. U. C. Knoepflmacher, 'Erasing Borders', in *Ventures into Childland: Victorians, Fairy Tales, and Femininity* (Chicago and London: University of Chicago Press, 1998), p. 251.

9. Rosemary Jackson, *Fantasy: The Literature of Subversion* (London: Methuen, 1981), p. 36.

10. George MacDonald, 'The Fantastic Imagination', in *The Complete Fairy Tales*, ed. U. C. Knoepflmacher (London: Penguin Books, 1999), p. 7.

11. Manlove, *Impulse of Fantasy Literature*, p. 57.

12. E. Nesbit, *The Phoenix and the Carpet* (1904; London: Puffin Books, 1978), pp. 221 and 223.
13. Nesbit, *Phoenix and the Carpet*, pp. 223, 225 and 232.
14. Penelope Lively, *The Ghost of Thomas Kempe* (1973; New York: Puffin Books, 1995), p. 186.
15. Rudyard Kipling, *Puck of Pook's Hill*, ed. Sarah Winkle (1906; London: Penguin Books, 1987), p. 58.
16. Jean Ingelow, *Mopsa the Fairy*, in *Forbidden Journeys: Fairy Tales and Fantasies by Victorian Women Writers*, ed. Nina Auerbach and U. C. Knoepflmacher (Chicago: University of Chicago Press, 1992), p. 316.
17. Charles Dickens, *A Holiday Romance*, in *Holiday Romance and Other Writings for Children*, ed. Gillian Avery (London: Everyman, 1995), pp. 428–9.
18. A. A. Milne, *The House at Pooh Corner* (1928; London: Egmont, 2004), pp. 169, 175, 159 and 176.
19. Kenneth Grahame, *The Golden Age* (1895; London: Wordsworth, 1995), p. 195.
20. Eleanor Estes, *The Witch Family* (1960; San Diego: Harcourt, Brace, Jovanovich, 1990), p. 220.
21. Jonathan Swift, *Gulliver's Travels*, ed. Claude Rawson, Oxford World's Classics (1726; Oxford: Oxford University Press, 2005), pp. 111 and 130.
22. Madeleine L'Engle, *A Wrinkle in Time* (1962; New York: Dell, 1987), pp. 122, 187 and 188.
23. Philip Pullman, *The Golden Compass* (New York: Ballantine, 1995), p. 28.
24. Pullman, *Golden Compass*, pp. 33 and 43.
25. Pullman, *Golden Compass*, p. 350.
26. Madeleine L'Engle, 'Childlike Wonder and the Truths of Science Fiction', *Children's Literature*, 10 (1982), 102–10 (p. 105).
27. Pullman, *Golden Compass*, p. 35.

15

DAVID RUDD

Animal and object stories

The association of animal and child in children's books is so common that it is easy to forget the figurative nature of this alliance – the way we have penned the animals in – whether it be Kermit the Frog, Rupert Bear, Bugs Bunny, the Cat in the Hat, Peter Rabbit or Toad of Toad Hall. In this chapter I want to explore this relationship, showing how it has been used in children's literature both to support the dominant order, and also to subvert it. There are wider issues to explore too, for the word 'animal' has its etymological roots in 'breath' and 'soul', which link it to that which is 'animate', and this is exactly the transformation that writers and illustrators so readily perform, making animals live in all manner of anthropomorphic ways. And not only animals, for other 'things' are just as easily animated: from puppets and dolls (Pinocchio, Winnie-the-Pooh, Woody in *Toy Story*) to more everyday objects such as coins, peg-tops and looking-glasses.

So, first of all, we need to ask why there is such a close association between animals and children in narratives for children. Perry Nodelman suggests that, in terms of 'humanized animals', the association happened 'more or less by accident', in so far as Aesop's fables provided a suitable early example of didactic literature for children, which was then emulated by others.[1] Karín Lesnik-Oberstein, on the other hand, sees the key association being forged by the Romantics, where the child is linked to nature, existing outside culture and language in some Edenic space.[2] But the association is surely far older. Aristotle, for example, in the fourth century BCE, claimed that a child differed little from an animal. Clearly, there is no innate connection, but the persistence of the link seems to arise from the fact that those at the top of the human ladder wish to see themselves as most distant from animals, as civilised, with 'lesser' beings automatically coded as closer to nature. Hence it is not only children to whom animals are linked: they are also linked to women, slaves, peasants, the working class, the mad, ethnic minorities, migrants – in fact, to anyone seen as 'other'. For example, in the nineteenth century the Irish were regularly represented as simian: in Charles Kingsley's *The Water-Babies*

(1863) we are informed that the 'wild Irish' who did not listen to St Brandan were 'changed into gorillas, and gorillas they are until this day'.[3]

Associating 'lesser' beings with animals, however, is fraught with problems, which can be traced back to two of the earliest forms of animal story: the fable and the folktale. Very broadly, the former tends to be associated with teaching moral lessons, which make far more palatable reading when mediated via animal figures. The folktale, on the other hand, is anything but a didactic form, often undermining traditional figures of authority (as demonstrated in the many animal-hybrid tricksters, such as Anansi the spider or Joel Chandler Harris' Br'er Rabbit).

One might, then, trace a line of development from the fable, and later the bestiary, to more modern anthropomorphic animal stories, all of which exhibit an impulse to control behaviour, both human (through the edifying example of animals) and animal (by seeing beasts in human terms, as ours to command). Although this impulse can be traced back to the Old Testament, where God has Adam name the animals, it is most famously consolidated in the philosophy of René Descartes (1596–1650). Here 'man', with his sovereign ego, dependent on his rationality, is seen as superior to all other species; not only that, but animals are viewed simply as machines ('things', in fact). However, this attempt by man to distance himself from the rest of creation is always open to challenge. For, in that children are so regularly associated with animals ('kids', 'little beasts'), one can argue that they are thereby given licence to behave so (as not properly human); yet, if this is the case, adult humans are themselves compromised, especially when they seek to use animals as exemplary figures. William Rankin commented on this predicament in *A Mirrour of Monsters* (1587): 'A shame it is ... to humanitie, that brutish beasts, wanting reason, should instruct men'. Its significance, Erica Fudge argues, lies in the implication that 'it is through the animal that human-ness can be found. This lays bear [sic] the problem. There is no human without an animal present, but the presence of the animal can itself disrupt the status of the human.'[4] The unintended ursine interloper amusingly demonstrates, almost like a Freudian slip, just how disruptive animals can be. Penning in the animals is therefore never a simple, straightforward process; rather, it points to the anxieties of writers and illustrators who try to contain and distance them – and, by implication, those with whom the animal is linked: in this case, children.

Kenneth Grahame's *The Wind in the Willows* (1908) provides one of the most famous examples. To create his rural, riverbank, English idyll, he turns away from humans to animals, for, Clayton Hamilton reported him to have said,

> Every animal, by instinct, lives according to his nature. Thereby he lives wisely, and betters the tradition of mankind. No animal is ever tempted to deny his

nature. No animal knows how to tell a lie. Every animal is honest. Every animal is true – and is, therefore, according to his nature, both beautiful and good.[5]

However, in effect, Grahame does no such thing. Rather than the nature of animals, we learn instead about the anxieties of the middle-class Edwardian male: specifically, Grahame's fear of the 'other' in the shape of women and the working-class (or even worse, both together!) – anxieties that are wittily reworked and exposed in Jan Needle's *Wild Wood* (1981), giving us the others' perspective, for example the animals whose labour makes Toad's life of privilege possible.

Precisely because of the ease with which we can anthropomorphise animals, some authors have tried to represent them more realistically – albeit suggesting an underlying, anthropocentric commonality of feeling and suffering. Anna Sewell's *Black Beauty* (1877), selling a million copies in its first two years and reputedly the most popular children's animal story ever written, provides a rich example.[6] At the literal level, Sewell attacks the then-current cruel treatment of horses, especially the use of the bearing rein, which kept horses' heads high, making breathing hard, and shortening their lives. However, as Moira Ferguson has demonstrated, Sewell also invokes the discourse of slavery and misogyny. Aside from the protagonist's name (and elsewhere Black Beauty is referred to as 'Darkie'), he is born on a 'plantation' by 'our master's home', separated from the rest of his family, and broken in. In the hunt scene, runaway slaves could easily be substituted for the pursued hares: 'One of the huntsmen rode up and whipped off the dogs, who would soon have torn her to pieces. He held her up by the leg, torn and bleeding, and all the gentlemen seemed well pleased.' Likewise women might find their situation reflected in passages in the book, particularly exhibited in the way that the spirited mare Ginger is treated:

> 'Several men came to catch me, and when at last they closed me in … then another took my underjaw in his hard hand and wrenched my mouth open, and so by force they got on the halter and the bar into my mouth; then one dragged me along by the halter, another flogging behind, and this was the first experience I had of men's kindness.'[7]

The attack sounds very much like gang rape, a sexual molestation.

So, in Sewell's novel protesting about the treatment of horses, other marginal groups find their situations voiced. As I said above, it is easy to see how those who are oppressed can here find common ground, including children, with whom the book has been perennially popular. There are (again) obvious parallels between their respective treatments: children, like horses, were also 'broken in'. And the child's bridling involves, besides harnessing, swaddling and withholding of food, the infamous non-sparing of the rod, lest one spoil the child. Furthermore, children suffered as badly as cab horses in their employment, and often in their schooling too.

Sewell's book is also a good example of the animal autobiography genre (the title-page declares that it is 'translated from the original equine'), which had originated in the eighteenth century, along with the life stories of other objects, like pincushions and hackney coaches (which have their own view of horses!). Finally, Sewell is an early writer in what would now be known as 'animal rights' literature – which also originates in the eighteenth century, one of the most famous examples being Sarah Trimmer's *Fabulous Histories* (1786), later known as *The History of the Robins* and subtitled 'for the instruction of children on their treatment of animals'.

One would have thought that pictorial illustration would have increased the impact of Trimmer's message, but she forbade this for, although she strove to create a realistic picture, she was also aware that, in having her birds speak, she was dangerously close to the kind of fantasy she strongly disapproved of (talking animals were most commonly found in fairy tales, which Trimmer decried vociferously). Again, the ambivalent nature of anthropomorphism, mentioned earlier, is ineluctably present: hearing the conversations of Robin, Dicky, Flapsy and Pecksy might help readers understand and identify with the little birds, but it thereby compromises their difference, their otherness; moreover, in suggesting affinities, we thereby query our own species' (or specious) claim to distinction. So while Trimmer's book clearly underwrites the class and gender inequalities of her time, she cannot help but destabilise that very order in her fictional natural history. On the one hand, then, the robins' behaviour celebrates family values, but on the other, we learn that each parent had a previous mate and earlier broods of children, effectively undermining the nuclear family.

While it would be easy to be critical of Trimmer's *Fabulous Histories* nowadays, its animal rights message is little different from contemporary examples such as Anne Fine's *The Chicken Gave It to Me* (1992). In Trimmer's work it is an adult, Mrs Benson, who champions the animals' cause, holding that some creatures 'have been expressly destined by the Supreme Governor as food for mankind', but she maintains that we should still make 'their short lives as comfortable as we can', and elsewhere a farmer even speaks of his animals being 'entitled to wages', which rather undermines their divinely ordained position![8] In Fine's work, it is aliens – little green men who liberate the Earth's chickens and cage the humans for food instead – who draw attention to our lack of humanity: 'If it doesn't smile a lot / Then it won't go in my pot', as a radio slogan has it. The anonymous chicken narrator (whose written memoir the child protagonists, Gemma and Andrew, have discovered) is content with this outcome: 'they were caring; they were sensitive; they were humane'. In other words, eating other species is not in itself an issue.

However, one key difference between *The Chicken Gave It to Me* and *Fabulous Histories* is that, in Trimmer, it is a knowing adult who instructs potentially cruel children, whereas in Fine it is the children who rail against a cruel adult establishment. They tellingly speculate on what would be the adult reaction if they were to dress up and chase animals to their death, or to start 'poking about at an animal as if it were just a toy', wanting 'to look at the clockwork inside'. Moreover, it is not *personal* cruelty in *The Chicken Gave It to Me*, but an anonymous, institutionalised one, a fact reinforced by the children discussing these issues clandestinely, in school – where they tellingly contrast the chicken's story with a more stereotypical picture book about animals. Gemma explodes: 'Why do they try and trick us into thinking everything's fine and hunky-dory? This book is as bad as a lie!'[9] It is a comment that brings to mind the noble horses, the Houyhnhnms, of Jonathan Swift's *Gulliver's Travels* (1726), who are amazed how humans can speak of 'the thing that was not'. It is also worth noting that Fine's story, in having humans become the caged food, draws on the tradition of the 'world-turned-upside-down', where the animals take up arms against humans and treat their former masters as subject beasts; for instance Ann and Jane Taylor's *Signor Topsy-Turvy's Wonderful Magic Lantern* (1810) and Roald Dahl's *The Magic Finger* (1966) are both animated by this trope.

All these works are successful in drawing attention to the plight of animals, and calling for their better treatment, but none is radical in modern animal rights terms (that is to say, concerned with the sanctity of all life). Even in works that do move closer to this position, the focalised creature tends to be treated as an exception – as, for instance, is Wilbur in E. B. White's *Charlotte's Web* (1952), in which Fern protests on behalf of the runt while the bacon sizzles unheeded. Nick Park's 2000 animated film *Chicken Run*, although it addresses similar issues to Fine's book, also seems to fall short in this respect, for the chickens are pictured as being kept under concentration camp conditions simply because of Mrs Tweedy's regime rather than this being seen as the lot of chickens everywhere. Hence the 'great escape' the film depicts cannot be to some 'normal' farm, for this would necessitate an acknowledgement of the near-universal cruel treatment of chickens, but must be to an island on a lake; effectively a utopia, a no-place.

The situation is no different in 'realistic animal stories', where the animals are not given the power of speech. In Enid Bagnold's *National Velvet* (1935), for instance, where the horse Pi is very much loved, the girl protagonist Velvet Brown's father is a butcher, blithely processing all manner of other animal flesh. So although these texts might be considered 'a form of protest literature', Kathleen R. Johnson's analysis shows how this is compromised by the pet status of most of the animals.[10] Pets, of course, are by definition property, required to be submissive to the 'owners' for whom they exist, like the hound that patiently waits years for his master's return in William H. Armstrong's *Sounder* (1969). The expendable nature of the animal is then consolidated, often, by having its death mark a rite of passage into adulthood for the human protagonist, as in Fred Gipson's *Old Yeller* (1956).

But the issue of realism – that is to say, trying to avoid the anthropomorphism that Johnson makes central – seems less certain to me. Although there are undoubtedly degrees of anthropomorphism (from the animalised humans in Richard Scarry's *Busy, Busy World* in the 1960s to attempts to represent creatures in their natural habitats, such as Ernest Thompson Seton's 1898 *Wild Animals I Have Known* and Henry Williamson's 1927 *Tarka the Otter*), we need to question what, exactly, characterises this 'anthropos' (man) that morphs. For while it might be a fantasy to imagine we can capture the essence of any animal, this fantasy extends to humans, too. So, when 'man' is referred to, it is generally a very specific version that is implied: a modern, Western, adult male – not a woman, not a child and not a Native American (the latter, indeed, being renowned for refusing to separate the human from the landscape and its fauna in the West European manner).

Rather than anthropocentrism, then, it is actually what Jacques Derrida called 'logocentrism', the rule of the Word, that is at issue. Words – what Jacques Lacan termed 'the Symbolic' – create our reality; but, as he added, they do so by the murder of the thing itself (what he termed 'the Real'). One of the most famous examples of this is of Freud's grandson playing in his cot, throwing away a cotton reel and then retrieving it, saying 'Gone' and 'There', showing the child finding a symbolic substitute for his absent mother: the Real is thus replaced by the reel, an object. However, as Slavoj Žižek emphasises, the Real still obtrudes, as demonstrated in Werner Holzwarth and Wolf Erlbruch's *The Story of the Little Mole Who Knew it was None of his Business* (1989) when the mole pokes his head out of his hole, secure in his Symbolic universe, only to have another animal defecate on him. Language, then, creates the very categories through which we experience the world, and, to a certain extent, we are forced to genuflect before these. The 'bad news' is that, though we are free of alien cages, we are nevertheless trapped in the alienating prison-house of language, so can never capture the real animal (any more than our real selves). The Symbolic is thus, in many ways, associated with death (we murder the thing itself). Somewhat paradoxically though, the Symbolic also seems to confer life (the 'good news'), allowing us, imaginatively, to animate any 'thing': animals, certainly, but also vegetables, flowers, dolls, clocks, wooden peg-tops, pincushions – even Dr Seuss's Things One and Two. So, although the Symbolic frequently reduces marginal people to things – hence children and animals are frequently described using the neuter pronoun, 'it', as, indeed, were slaves (Harriet Beecher Stowe's *Uncle Tom's Cabin,* for instance, was originally to be subtitled 'The Man Who Was a Thing') – the process of signification cannot preclude disruption and sub-version, producing an anti-Cartesian world where animism rules, where all things are democratically, anarchically even, given voice. In fact, a tacit awareness of this vital, excessive power of language is often epitomised in alphabet books, where individual letters, even punctuation-marks, exhibit signs of life.

This paradox of signification, hovering between life and death, haunting us, can be traced back to earliest times, when we represented animals using their own blood as paint, their pelts as brushes; and it was to continue in the very materiality of book production, from the sheet of horn that protects the printed text in the hornbook to the animal hide that is made into vellum pages and leather binding, to animal glue, quill pens and so on. Death and the Symbolic are thus ineluctably tied, pointing finally to what Freud saw as the strange appeal of the uncanny, where the inanimate suddenly comes to life, or vice versa.

In the eighteenth century there was a particular vogue for such 'it-narratives', which told the life histories of both animate and inanimate things, as though ultimately there were no difference. Mary Ann Kilner wrote *The Adventures of a Whipping-Top* (1784) about a boy's toy which deteriorates from new, as many of these objects do, first becoming a dog's plaything before ending its days in a river, there to compose the very memoirs that are to be magically dispatched, via the river's current, to a publisher. Most of the personified objects are also commodities (rather than found objects), as one might expect at a time when property was first being produced in quantity (including children's books, toys and games). And, indeed, many of the animals described were also property, the popularity of pet-keeping then increasing. So, at the very time that capitalism was expanding, the children's book market was working hard to define and gender the 'proper' and 'propertied' child, showing children not only how to deport themselves, but how to play, and what to play with. Publishing sought to separate out a proper children's reading matter, too – moving away from the lower-class chapbooks, and the more distinctly adult-oriented it-narratives – and, finally, to gender the books more overtly.

But having things define us has a double edge. Not only do these objects suggest a more pagan universe, raising problems for orthodox religion, but, by having objects and animals talk, they also seem to undermine the very rationality of the Enlightenment. And while seeking to establish the sovereignty of the individual (objects being separated out and given voices), these works simultaneously undermine it; for not only is individualism parodied (it is seen as excessive if *everything* has it: 'It thinks, therefore it is'), but, in the process, the owners of the objects also become more replaceable, expendable and, as 'propertied classes', dependent on property for their being. Commodity fetishism rules, in Karl Marx's terms, with objects concealing human labour and agency within them. Interestingly Marx sometimes uses fairy tale terms in *Das Kapital* to depict this very process: 'Mister Capital and Mistress Land carry on their goblin tricks as social characters and at the same time as mere things', creating 'an *enchanted*, perverted, topsy-turvy world'.[11] And it is precisely these topsy-turvy novels, where the objects write back, that often 'spill the beans' about their origins. If people are defined by their possessions, small wonder that these objects seem possessed.

A modern work in this tradition is John Lasseter's computer-generated animated film *Toy Story* (2000), its very title suggesting that it is about the toy equivalent of Everyman. It captures the central contradiction of capitalism: that consumption must be never-ending, with the new displacing the old, until such time as the old becomes 'retro', and can again be repackaged as the new. In this case, it is the cowboy, Woody, whose very name suggests a more folksy, pioneering spirit, threatened by new technology in the metallic-plastic form of the astronaut Buzz Lightyear. Apart from Buzz, the toys are aware – just like the it-narrators – that they are mass-produced. Moreover, being retro toys partly justifies their stereotyping as predominantly male, 'white' and with clear gender demarcation. The only person who threatens this world is Sid, a child who dismembers and makes mutant, Hieronymus Bosch-like assemblages from his toys. Clearly, he represents a threat – not just to the toys, but to the whole American dream. He is less defined by his toys than the other children, actually 'playing with' them – that is, imaginatively reworking them, rather than accepting the manufacturers' orthodoxy – and is thus less dependent on their products (although Sid's mutant toys were, inevitably, themselves made into merchandise). But as a result, Sid is presented as less child-like (indeed, like Fine's adults, he wants 'to look at the clockwork inside') – until, that is, he is turned back into a child by those very toys telling him how to behave.

In achieving this, the toys explicitly contravene the convention that they should not speak when humans are around, suggesting that the toys are animated only when children are *not* playing with them. In *Winnie-the-Pooh* (1926) this notion is explicit, Christopher Robin having to be inducted into the imaginative world of his toys. Being told about Pooh's first adventure, and of how 'the first person he thought of was Christopher Robin',

Christopher Robin interrupts to ask '"*Was that me?*" ... *hardly daring to believe it.*' '"*That was you*"', he is told.[12] Outside the stories, Pooh is simply something to be bumped up and down stairs on his head. Of course, this is yet another example of adults seeking to control children's literature, to have children play in particular ways, and providing them with suitable scripts. Sid, too, is an adult creation but, while his behaviour is shown as unacceptable, it unavoidably opens a space of contention.

To recap: we have seen the double-edged nature of language. In many ways we are imprisoned by it, made to see the world in certain ways: humans as superior to animals, for instance, with the latter divided into such categories as 'pets', 'vermin' and 'food' – distinctions which often necessitate re-labellings: 'pork' not 'pig', 'sardine' not 'brisling'. But perhaps the most invisible term of all is 'animal' itself. Despite the fact that we are included in this term, we tend to forget it. This chapter should really have been referring to 'nonhuman animals' throughout. Yet most books about animals – children's or adults' – do not feature humans, even though they belong to the primate section. Not all of us are Creationists, but much of the time we act as though Darwin had never existed.

That the Symbolic order operates in favour of a particular version of 'man' – white, middle-class and, almost 'naturally', male – is also crucial. Those further from this norm are more likely to be seen as less than human and, thereby, as linked with animals in some way – children being a prime example. But as we have also seen, this creates problems, in that the more marginalised a group, the less transparent the world's categories become. It has been argued that meat-eating is particularly associated with patriarchy, being championed foremost by the ruling class (who, at one time in England, protected their meat on pain of death or transportation). It is therefore of note that many of the more heterodox texts I have discussed have been by women (Trimmer, the Taylors, Kilner, Sewell, Fine) – and that it is women who were particularly active in pushing for the more humane treatment of animals. So, although animals will never be able to fight their own cause (as with children too), the way we represent them in children's books warrants attention – especially the way that some authors and illustrators have deliberately sought to derail our standard and, perhaps, unthinking responses.

The first way involves challenging traditional Cartesian notions of a separate, sovereign ego. It recognises that no-one really has such autonomy, initiating actions *ex nihilo*, which then have their desired effects. Rather, we are all seen to be locked into a variety of networks and institutions that either help to empower or hinder us. Agency is therefore dispersed. We have to work together – as recognised by the welded-together wind-up toy protagonists in Russell Hoban's classic *The Mouse and His Child* (1967). Disability Studies provides a useful model here, where, rather than seeing an individual as disabled, it is the whole community or society that is ultimately responsible, either enabling or disabling (ramps and lifts versus steps and stairs and so on).

The ideas behind this notion of an inveterate connectedness come from various sources. Donna Haraway, for example, is a primatologist who credits her primates with co-authoring her work. Bruno Latour similarly claims that 'things do not exist without being full of people', a remark that echoes Erica Fudge's claim that 'There is no human without an animal present.' For Latour, modernity has artificially separated out the inanimate from the animate.[13]

In terms of children's literature, recognising such connectedness would entail looking at animal books from a new perspective; for example, by asking what circumstances made possible the adventures of Laura Ingalls Wilder's pioneering family in the Little House books (1932–43): their links with the Native Americans, with the environment, with developments in technology. It would also involve trying to create new narratives which, in the terms of Chaos Theory, seek to show what happens in Tokyo when a butterfly flaps its wings in New York. Jeremy Rifkin provides an informative template, writing about 'How the West was Lost': 'Behind the facade of frontier heroism and cowboy bravado, of civilizing forces and homespun values, lies a quite different tale: a saga of ecocide and genocide, of forced enclosures of land and people, and the expropriation of an entire subcontinent for the exclusive benefit of a privileged few.'[14] Here he is speaking about the cattle industry, imposing its monoculture in the beginnings of what we might now term 'McDonaldisation'.

One book that does strike me as achieving this enlarged perspective, in a totally novel way, is Chris Raschka's *Arlene Sardine* (1998), a picture book about 'a happy little brisling', 'born in a fjord', that wants to be part of the food industry: to become a sardine, or dead fish. In the second half of the book, having been caught by fishermen, she 'swam around in the net for three days and three nights and did not eat anything, so her stomach would be empty. There is a word for this. The word is thronging.' Raschka's quiet emphasis on the shift in meaning of this term, from the original 'crowded together' to 'starving', exposes the ways in which humans attempt to disguise the processes by which they turn animals into food. But Raschka is relentlessly candid: 'Here', his story continues, 'on the deck of the fishing boat, Arlene died'. From then on her eyes are closed, as she is sorted, salted, smoked, canned in oil, sealed hermetically ('with no air inside') and cooked. Arlene's dream – and the subject of the whole book – is the very nightmare that is usually erased from children's stories. Anthropomorphism is given a subtle shift here: clearly the notion of Arlene having an ambition, a quest, is common in humanised animal stories, but the nature of her ambition then alienates us – although, on reflection, this is *exactly* our anthropocentric desire: that there be tins of sardines on supermarket shelves. Yet again, in making this desire so blatant, and so readily ascribing it to a fish, we become aware of the limits of our anthropocentrism, and Arlene remains inscrutable, and 'other'. In animating Arlene, then, there is no attempt to escape the fact that she is also de-animated, the Word inescapably involving the murder of the Thing in that a sardine, by definition, always is and always was a dead fish.[15]

Although I have chosen *Arlene* because it shows this sense of connectedness and dispersed agency (how an individual fish is connected to the food industry), it also works by shifting our perspective. Arlene, then, has a precursor in the leg of mutton in Lewis Carroll's *Through the Looking-Glass* (1871) to which Alice is introduced. After it 'got up in the dish and made a little bow', Alice finds it impossible to eat, because, the Red Queen says, 'it isn't etiquette to cut any one you've been introduced to' (wittily punning on 'cut').[16]

This second tactic is 'defamiliarisation', derailing our more predictable (Symbolic) responses and thus helping us experience a sense of otherness – just what we find when the Real of an animal intrudes (through its sound, smell, touch, bite or look). Often this confounding of categories occurs only fleetingly in a text, when the anthropomorphism is suddenly undercut. Beatrix Potter is adept at this, although her work is sometimes dismissed for its simple anthropomorphism. However, it is precisely the switch from a cosy anthropomorphism to a more brutal, Darwinian universe that makes it so effective. In *The Tale of Mr Jeremy Fisher* (1906), for instance, it occurs with the sudden appearance of the predatory trout; or in *The Tale of Peter Rabbit* (1901) the threat presented by Mr McGregor shifts our perspective from Peter as civilised boy to Peter as garden pest or food source. In Pierre Macherey's terms, these scenes exhibit moments where the ideology of a text does not quite cohere. Even in a work as anthropomorphic as Kenneth Grahame's *The Wind in the Willows* there are instances. For example, in the very first chapter, when Otter has just appeared, we read the following:

'Did I ever tell you that good story about Toad and the lock-keeper? It happened this way. Toad...'
An errant May-fly swerved unsteadily athwart the current in the intoxicated fashion affected by young bloods of May-flies seeing life. A swirl of water and a 'cloop!' and the May-fly was visible no more.
Neither was the Otter.
The Mole looked down. The voice was still in his ears, but the turf whereon he had sprawled was clearly vacant. Not an Otter to be seen, as far as the distant horizon.

But again there was a streak of bubbles on the surface of the river.

The Rat hummed a tune, and the Mole recollected that animal-etiquette forbade any sort of comment on the sudden disappearance of one's friends at any moment, for any reason or no reason whatever.

This reminder of the reality of animal life (contrasted with their own luncheon-basket of 'coldtonguecoldhamcoldbeefpickledgherkinssaladfrenchrollscresssandwichespottedmeatgingerbeerlemonadesodawater') is particularly poignant as Mole has himself been described as just such an errant, intoxicated young blood seeing life, bursting out of his burrow 'in the joy of living and the delight of spring'.[17]

A more powerful and disarming example is provided by Anthony Browne's *Gorilla* (1983), a story in which a gorilla is deliberately anthropomorphised (or a human 'zoomorphised', we might say) to show, metaphorically, what is lacking in Hannah's cold, workaholic father. But Browne then sets up some barriers to any would-be cosiness with the caged beasts he depicts deliberately separated from the rest of the book in a single page opening, I think, in order that readers might not be distracted by the animal-human (or animal-landscape, animal-artwork) hybrids elsewhere. Hannah, we are told, 'thought they were beautiful. But sad.'[18] And they are profoundly moving. The orangutan (fig. 15), being so small, is less likely to hold our attention at first. Instead, we are drawn to another cage (fig. 14), mesmerised by the chimpanzee's huge, liquid eyes, looking directly at us (the whites looking almost like tears forming). It seems not only to hold our gaze but to solicit it – though, as was said before, it is a gaze that is not quite human, despite the fact that it fixes us. Akira Mizuta Lippit quotes Walter Benjamin's famous statement about a successful work of art having an 'aura', our 'investing it with the capacity to return our gaze'. As Lippit says elsewhere:

> The look that [animals] reflect back to us reminds us that in them we encounter something alien ... though it may be difficult to see past the layers of apparent familiarity. Animals may not participate in the world of human speech, but the muteness that shrouds their senses always accompanies us in the realm of our language ... unless we refuse to look at all, the muteness of an animal also imposes a moment of muteness on us.[19]

In the picture of the chimp, this notion is abetted by the thumb (that important, evolutionary, opposable thumb) over its mouth, showing that it is speechless, and with that pun intact; in other words, it is speechless because it is unable to comprehend its plight. However, the position of the hand also alludes to statues like Rodin's *Le Penseur*: it appears to be a thoughtful beast, as though it might just have something to say – to us, who are, after all, fellow anthropoids.

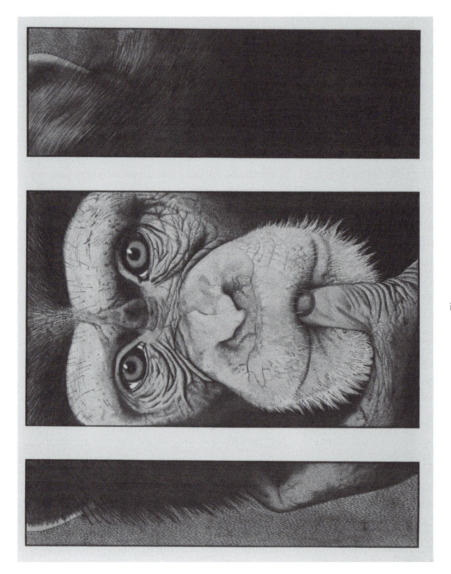

Figure 14

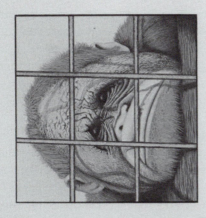

The gorilla took Hannah to see the orang-utan, and a chimpanzee. She thought they were beautiful. But sad.

Figure 15. Anthony Browne, *Gorilla*. London: Julia MacRae, 1983. (Double-page spread with fig.14.)

We might then return to the orang-utan, and give it more attention. After the relatively generous space given to the chimp, it appears to be even more confined, especially as the bars of its cage segment it into nine pieces, and the shadows of these bars also seem to mark its face, suggesting scarification perhaps, or the tracks of dried-up tears. The long downturn of the mouth is emphasised by being juxtaposed with those all-too-uniform bars, as though its whole face were collapsing. But most mysterious are the eyes, looking out at us from what seems an immense depth. Interestingly, the eyeline of the animals matches, so that, when the book is shut, the two caged beasts can contemplate each other, which might also make us see a parallel. For, from the beasts' point of view, we too are only seen through bars, and might be caged in ways we don't realise – caged in by a speciesist ideology, by the prison-house of language. The fact that the bars of the chimp's cage are represented by white space seems to be linked to this. We might at first think it a shame that these break up this picture, but this is what I think Browne wants: for us to *know* we are at a zoo. Also, representing the bars in this blank way draws more attention to the fact that we don't actually see the animal clearly; the white gaps make it explicit that this is just a *representation* of an animal: something that is not actually there; that does, indeed, haunt us, oscillating between presence and absence as it fades to white. Finally, the gaps suggest that this is something more than mere spectacle: 'beautiful', as Hannah's first thought is, but sad.

So, penning in the animal might be all that we can do, but we should try to do it with an awareness of the inveterately phallic power of that instrument. The pen is undoubtedly mightier than the sword, determining which animals are to be revered, which to be feared and which to be cut up, whether as food or for other purposes (we should remember that it is Descartes' philosophy that licenses vivisection). And this power carries over into children's books, where there has been a tendency to underwrite the accepted order of things. However, as we have also seen, children comprise a group seen as 'other' by those who determine what is orderly. Children, having been aligned with animals as not quite human, are, therefore, perhaps less likely to see the world from an orthodox perspective – especially as the whole process of anthro-pomorphising animals, and other 'things', has been shown to be unstable, unsettling the very hierarchy it seeks to underwrite. Finally, we have looked at some more explicit techniques whereby our tendency to pen in animals, unthinkingly, can be disrupted. This is perhaps the most important point to make: that although books can only ever represent animals textually, animals are not thereby only textual. If we lose sight of this, we might lose sight of them altogether, apart from as dodos. The Houyhnhnms and Kenneth Grahame might be appalled at the human animal's ability to lie, to say the thing that is not, but that is precisely the essence of fiction: its ability to go beyond the Real into the realms of possibility, to worlds where, potentially, anything can have a voice.

NOTES

1. Perry Nodelman, 'Something Fishy Going On: Child Readers and Narrative Literacy', in *Crossing the Boundaries*, ed. Geoff Bull and Michele Anstey (Frenchs Forest: Prentice Hall, 2002), pp. 3–16 (p. 7).
2. Karín Lesnik-Oberstein, 'Children's Literature and the Environment', in *Writing the Environment: Ecocriticism and Literature*, ed. Richard Kerridge and Neil Sammells (London: Zed Books, 1998), pp. 208–17.
3. Charles Kingsley, *The Water-Babies: A Fairy Tale for a Land-Baby* (London: Macmillan, 1863), pp. 193–4.
4. Erica Fudge, *Perceiving Animals: Humans and Beasts in Early Modern English Culture* (Basingstoke: Macmillan, 2000), pp. 65 and 90.
5. Alison Prince, *Kenneth Grahame: An Innocent in the Wild Wood* (London: Allison & Busby, 1994), p. 255.
6. Moira Ferguson, 'Breaking in Englishness: *Black Beauty* and the Politics of Gender, Race and Class', *Women: A Cultural Review*, 15 (1994), 34–52 (p. 35).
7. Anna Sewell, *Black Beauty: His Grooms and Companions. The Autobiography of a Horse* (London: Jarrold, 1877), pp. 13 and 33.
8. Sarah Trimmer, *Fabulous Histories: The History of the Robins* (1786; London: Grant and Griffith, 1848), pp. 122, 123 and 105.
9. Anne Fine, *The Chicken Gave It to Me* (London: Egmont, 1992), pp. 87–8, 46 and 15.
10. Kathleen R. Johnson, *Understanding Children's Animal Stories* (New York: Mellen Press, 2000), p. 125. Intriguingly, J. H. Plumb notes the way that eighteenth-century children were themselves seen as 'superior pets': 'The New World of Children in Eighteenth-Century England', *Past and Present*, 67 (1975), 64–95 (p. 90).
11. Quoted in *Marx on Economics*, ed. Robert Freedman (New York: Harcourt, Brace and World, 1961), p. 65.
12. A. A. Milne, *Winnie-the-Pooh* (1926; London: Egmont, 2004), p. 7.
13. Bruno Latour, 'The Berlin Key or How to Do Words with Things', in *Matter, Materiality and Modern Culture*, ed. P. M. Graves-Brown (London: Routledge, 2000), pp. 10–21 (p. 10).
14. Jeremy Rifkin, *Beyond Beef: The Rise and Fall of the Cattle Culture* (New York: Dutton, 1992), p. 107.
15. Chris Raschka, *Arlene Sardine* (London: Scholastic, 1998), unpaginated.
16. Lewis Carroll, *The Annotated Alice*, ed. Martin Gardner (Harmondsworth: Penguin, 1970), p. 331.
17. Kenneth Grahame, *The Wind in the Willows* (1908; London: Puffin, 1994), pp. 13–14, 7 and 2.
18. Anthony Browne, *Gorilla* (London: Julia MacRae, 1983), unpaginated.
19. Akira Mizuta Lippit, '...from Wild Technology to Electric Animal', in *Representing Animals*, ed. Nigel Rothfels (Bloomington: Indiana University Press, 2002), pp. 99–118 (pp. 101 and 99).

16

RODERICK McGILLIS

Humour and the body in children's literature

Children's humour depends largely on the body. Not entirely, but largely. Slapstick, caricature, parody, the grotesque, ridicule and the improbable in human predicaments concern the body, and so too does nonsense. A glance over Edward Lear's limericks or Lewis Carroll's *Alice* books will illustrate how often nonsense is associated with the body (long noses, wild hair, elongated bodies, collapsed bodies and so on). Reversals often deal with the matter of size: big and little, as we see in a number of recent films for children, like *Big* (1988), *The Kid* (2000) and *13 Going on 30* (2004). Even verbal humour may derive its effect from the body. Remember when we were kids, we often chanted 'Sticks and stones will break my bones, but names [or words] can never hurt me.' We were, of course, wrong. Words do relate to and register on the body. Just take names, for example. Funny names are often a reflection of the body, by implication if not by denotation: Leonard Neeble, Norman Bleistift, Mr Gutzman, Fat Albert, Freckles, Bonnie McSmithers, Gertrude McFuzz, Nicholas Knock, Margery Meanwell – these names are metonymic of the kind of person who carries the name. And we do not need to look farther than the Harry Potter books to see that words, other than names, can have dramatic effects on the body, as when Dudley got a pig's tail when Hagrid recited a spell of transfiguration.

From the beginning of children's literature, the body has been a source of humour. Hugh Rhodes' *Book of Nurture and School of Manners* (c. 1550) instructs children in proper behaviour, table manners, deportment in front of adults and so on. When the author cautions children not to eat with their fingers, not to spit over the table, or not to blow their noses in their napkins, it instructs and delights at the same time. Just the mention of a child picking his nose or burping in someone else's face teases the young reader with descriptions of defiant behaviour. Since Rhodes, we have moved through the entire alimentary canal. We now have instructive books such as Taro Gomi's *Everyone Poops* (1993) and practical books such as Sylvia Branzei's *Grossology: The Science of Really Gross Things* (1995) and its sequels and website. These books safely flirt with subversion, and teach with more than a dash of humour. But, as Rhodes' *Book of Manners* still raises a laugh today, earnestness too may amuse.

Whenever we have earnest instruction, as in Heinrich Hoffmann's *Struwwelpeter* (1845), we remind children of forbidden behaviour, and more often than not such behaviour has to do with the body – not washing or not trimming the nails or sucking one's thumbs or setting fire to oneself or not eating until the body wastes away or whipping a dog and receiving like treatment in return. Whatever the type of humour for children, the body plays its part. Often the body finds itself incorporated (as it were) in language itself. And so let's scan the history of humour in children's literature with a view to seeing just how insistent the body is, and a starting place is the size of the body. For children, size matters.

Religious writers for children in the seventeenth and early eighteenth centuries knew about the importance of size in the child's world. I'll begin with James Janeway, whose *A Token for Children* (1671–2) seems an unlikely work to include in a survey of children's humour. Laughter, as we know from John Bunyan's *Grace Abounding to the Chief of Sinners* (1666), was not something the Puritans took lightly. Laughter signalled frivolity and openness to wayward behaviour. And yet Janeway meant to entertain children even as he instructed them. What's so funny about four- and five-year-old children spending their time praying and then dying before they reach their fifth or sixth year? What's so funny about fire and brimstone? Perhaps not much. But Janeway did mean to give child readers pleasure by setting before them accounts of the '*joyful*' deaths of young children. He humoured children with these short factual narratives, and he did so by showing the heroism of small children in the face of a reaper less grim than welcome. They may have been little and weak, but their behaviour was larger than life. The humour here speaks to the body through the bodily humours and to the mind through its instinct for survival beyond this world. Humour here manifests itself in a spiritually healthy mind that steadies a sickly body.

Isaac Watts also knew something about the importance of size and the pleasure children might experience contemplating things big and small. His *Divine Songs* (1715) shows that he understood that children would find interest and pleasure in small things, busy bees, flowers, puppies who fight and scratch, and a boy too lazy to get out of bed. Watts knew very well the importance of the body in 'The Ant, or Emmet'. The child narrators take pleasure in treading ants to death by the 'troop' because they are so gigantic in comparison and because such little things are expendable.[1] But Watts also believed that his young readers would find delight in contemplating the big and small bodies and good and bad humours. In 'Against Pride in Clothes', he finds pleasure in contemplating raiment finer than the clothes we wear: 'Knowledge and virtue, truth and grace' are 'the robes of richest dress'. We might think that Watts argues for an inward transcending of the body, but when he remarks that 'The Son of God, when here below, / Put on this blest apparel too', he reminds us of the word made flesh.[2] The body informed by knowledge, virtue, truth and grace is the unfallen body. The clothes metaphor and the focus on creatures of nature argue for a balance of humours, because the greatest pleasure will be found in good humour.

At least one later writer for children saw the potential for laughter in the humour of Watts, and took this humour in a more modern direction. Lewis Carroll used Watts' poetry as an opportunity for the humour of displacement, substituting a lobster for a sluggard and a little crocodile for a little busy bee. Whatever else these displacements signify, they substitute either a little thing for a big thing or a big thing for a little thing, even though the big thing carries the qualifier 'little'. And so big things and little things inform much of children's literature. We have Big-endians and Little-endians, great big enormous turnips and little engines that could, Big Sarah and Little Tim, Big Bad Wolf and Little Princess, Big Anthony and Little Pony, and just plain Big or Little. Carroll's play with big and little bodies inaugurates the spirit of parody in children's literature, and we continue to have books that turn on size, as demonstrated by Florence Parry Heide's *The Shrinking of Treehorn* (1971) or Terry Pratchett's *Truckers* trilogy (1989–90) or his tiny Nac Mac Feegle people in *The Wee Free Men* (2003). Size and the changing of size interest children because children understand their own powerlessness and they enjoy contemplating the possibilities of power.

As early as *Gulliver's Travels* (1726), Swift has a big guy raising a guffaw by secreting his gigantic evacuations in the corner of his Lilliputian dwelling or by putting out a fire in the miniature royal palace in a manner unappreciated by the Lilliputians. Gulliver's means of fire suppression by urination only works because of his size. Later we have Alice growing large and crying not just a river, but a veritable sea. The humour here derives from the large body's effluence. Bigness is brash and we might even say juvenile. Take, for example, Dav Pilkey's *Kat Kong* (1993), an obvious parody of *King Kong*. Here the bigness takes a linguistic turn, relying on our preparation for and delight in pun and parody and platitude. Note, for example, that Kat Kong's captors wrap him in a giant burlap bag, and on their way to the city of Mouseopolis, they are careful 'not to let the cat out of the bag'.[3] On the other hand, in the delicate lives of the small, as in Mary Norton's *Borrowers* series, we have gentle rather than brash humour, and the books' linguistic comedy depends upon clever turns not groaners; in *The Borrowers Afield* (1955), Pod does not understand the word 'ethics', and he remarks that the word 'Sounds to me like something you pick up in the long grass.'[4] Pod mistakes an abstraction for an object, thereby enforcing the prominence of the material in books for the young. Words can become things, as in Andrew Clements' *Frindle* (1996).

Humour that derives from big bodies often results in not-so-subtle fun. As Susan Stewart suggests, the big body may serve as 'a metaphor for the abstract authority of the state and the collective, public life'.[5] Sometimes such authority is benign as is the case with the giant Hagrid in the Harry Potter stories or the helpful bigness of adult or child characters in *Winnie-the-Pooh* (1926); sometimes such authority is fearsome as in the many threatening giants from those that Jack slays to the civilised ones we have in Narnia at Harfanger. Big may be funny or fearsome, but it is always readily available for observation. Take, for example, the eponymous character John Henry in Julius Lester's 1994 version of this American folktale. While still a 'brand-new baby', John Henry jumped from his mother's arms and started growing. We read that John Henry 'grew and grew and grew. He grew until his head and shoulders busted through the roof which was over the porch.' This made John Henry laugh so loud that he scared the sun, and it 'scurried from behind the moon's skirts and went to bed'.[6] John Henry is a force of nature as well as a representative of a people. Here is bigness to be proud of. On the other hand, we can have the bigness of Jack Prelutsky's 'The Dragon of Death', in *Nightmares: Poems to Trouble Your Sleep* (1976). As its name suggests, this dragon signifies something terrible. Here is enormity big enough to make the mountaintops tremble. This dragon has seven tails, seven mouths and seven heads. It is timeless. And so we have the sublime, always an aspect of large-scale objects and creatures. The sublime, like bigness itself, is both terrifying and exhilarating, and always on the edge of humour. Largeness that scales the sublime may teeter into the grotesque.

As far back as Rabelais' Gargantua (1534), we have examples of the big body as the grotesque body. And often the grotesque is a feature of how that body functions. Consumption and evacuation, ingress and egress, the comings and the goings, the processes of the body, its kinetic activity are the stuff of play and humour. Eating can provide opportunity for fun, as the description of Gulliver's dining in Lilliput illustrates: he has 300 cooks and 120 waiters. Eating still provides occasion for humour as Robert Munsch's *More Pies* (2002), or the old lady who swallowed a fly, indicates. And so the alimentary canal is a source of humour based on bigness. Humour associated with the alimentary canal is attractive to the young partly because adults often discourage discussion of what goes in and what comes out of our bodies. Talk of eating and evacuating is serious business. Eating and evacuating have to do with matters of desire in that we eat what we think will satisfy us (cravings come to mind), and we evacuate at the call of signals from within that may be uncomfortable, but nonetheless pleasurable. Pleasure performs its peristalsis. Food and waste are intimately connected, as are life and death. This may be one reason why food, so often in children's literature, is life itself. We have many instances of cannibalism or the suggestion of cannibalism in stories for the young – think of the witch in 'Hansel and Gretel' or Sendak's Wild Things cheerfully saying they will eat Max up, and in turn Max's similar offer to his Mother. Humour of this rather excessive kind serves to remind us that Eros and Thanatos occupy both ends of the same canal.

Evacuations of one kind or another provide an opportunity for humour, and the bigger the evacuations, the greater the risible effect. Perhaps a nice example is the story of Tom Thumb, the little guy swallowed accidentally by a cow. Tom escapes harm when the cow emits a gaseous explosion sending Tom flying into the outside air (or in a cowpat, depending on the version). The fun in poop appears to have staying power as a variety of recent books will show; the most egregious must be the Danish picture book, *Pigen der Ikke Ville Pa Potten* by Henrik Hohle Hansen and Charlotte Pardi (2000). The protagonist of this book is as anally retentive as they come and her willed constipation ultimately results in a prodigious evacuation. Perhaps Naja's eventual evacuation can best be characterised by mentioning another title, *Jurassic Poop* (2006) by Jacob Berkowitz. Books for children have had, and continue to offer their readers, an excremental vision.

We have big bodies supplying humour throughout books for children. Take Giant Snap-em-up, for example, a character in 'Uncle David's Ridiculous Story', the ninth chapter of Catherine Sinclair's *Holiday House* (1839). He engages in the funny business of snapping up little boys, the chubbier the better, and eating them as a 'side dish' with his dinner. Like his buddy, Gargantua, Snap-em-up has a prodigious appetite; he is all-consuming. And like Gargantua, he is funny precisely because he is so large. In a famous joke, the story's narrator tells us that Snap-em-up 'was obliged to climb up a ladder to comb his own hair'.[7] The nonsense here is an important container for a humour that is fundamentally violent (the same principle is at work in both Lear and Carroll). The humour in 'Uncle David's Ridiculous Story' reminds us that unpleasant and painful experiences may also be humorous; the humour offers relief from the unpleasantness. The cannibal Snap-em-up can't even comb his own hair without a support. After such nonsense as preparation, we are primed to enter his home and find the dead bodies of six boys, see an 'enormous cook' 'brandishing' a large knife, and hear the giant talking of whipping children to death and of having 'a good large dish of scalloped children at dinner'.[8] We laugh.

Such excess in the aid of humour is apparent throughout much eighteenth- and nineteenth-century literature for the young. Take, for example, the ostensibly innocuous *Life and Perambulations of a Mouse* (1783) by Dorothy Kilner. Here we have an example of humour that delights in the gruesome and the excruciating. Our mouse narrator delivers a visceral description of the crunched bones and flattened body of his brother, the unfortunate mouse named Softdown. Softdown and his world may be small, but the description of his death is big. Caught in a trap, Softdown finds himself removed from the trap by the footman John. John ties a thread to Softdown's tail, and then allows the mouse to swing from the thread. To the mouse narrator, John is a pitiless monster. Watching the brutal treatment of his brother, our narrating mouse wishes he were big so that he could thrash the tormentor. But he is small and must stand and watch as John crushes Softdown with his foot, and then kicks him into the ashes as a leaving for the cat. But the narrative does not leave the incident here. The mouse narrator informs us that his blood ran cold as he recollects the spurt of his brother's blood and the crunch as his bones break. Is this passage funny? I think it is, to a certain extent. It moves in the direction of humour in its excess. There are surely affinities with the Hanna and Barbera *Tom and Jerry* cartoons. True, the Softdown incident reminds us of the body's fragility, and of the power of bigness. A certain nostalgia lurks in the desire of the narrating mouse either to restore his brother (to rescue him) or to deliver just punishment to the inhuman monster who crushes him. The narrative quickly moves on to turn the incident into a learning experience. We understand that Softdown's death serves a purpose; it returns the mouse and his remaining brothers to their duty. And so if we felt humour in the viscerally described death scene, we can realise that the humour provides us with a necessary distancing from the death so that we can take in the lesson this death delivers.

My point is not that violent excess of this kind is not horrendous, but that in this instance we can smile because a mouse is expendable. Okay, we might argue that no creature is expendable, but, relatively speaking, we can say that little Softdown occupies a place somewhere near 'the dead bodies of six other boys' in the story of Giant Snap-em-up or Watts' troop of ants. The dead body and the body in pieces are recurring features of children's stories and fantasies, and it is quite possible to find humour in the body in pieces, as many cartoons – say those by Tex Avery – will suggest. This is especially the case when the dead or dismembered body is not the body of a human, as in the Grimms' fairy tale 'The Goose Girl'.

The fairy tales we know may be somewhat less bloody than what we see in the death of Softdown, but they nonetheless take delight in burned bodies, pecked-out eyes, sliced-off toes, lopped-off heads, and gruel made with the body of a small boy. In the story by the Brothers Grimm known in English as 'The Juniper (or Almond) Tree', a step-mother slams a trunk lid down on her young step-son's head, sending it flying off among the apples in the trunk. The effect is comic rather than tragic, and accordingly the young boy returns hale and hearty at the end of the most familiar versions. There are examples galore, but the point is that humour is often broad and focused on that which is potentially subversive, unacceptable, against the grain, less than decorous and difficult to miss. It functions in the way carnival functions: either as a safety valve for the rambunctious or as a reminder that convention is artificial and always susceptible to change.

We can see the potentially subversive aspect of humour most clearly in its scatological and violent manifestations, its obsession with the body and all its discernible parts. This is a kind of humour that relates back to Gargantua and his prodigious capacity for taking in and releasing out. We can see such humour in something as melodic as one of Edward Lear's limericks:

> There was a young person of Janina,
> Whose uncle was always fanning her;
> When he fanned off her head, she smiled sweetly, and said,
> 'You propitious old person of Janina.'[9]

Here's a 'head's off' rhyme that concerns the body detachable. Lear noted that writing for children should be 'incapable of any meaning but one of sheer nonsense', and by 'sheer nonsense' I suspect he meant such obvious body humour as huge noses, hair big enough for birds to build nests in, prodigious feats of eating, large animals and the like.[10] But he also means large linguistic turns: Gromboolian plains, Quangle Wangles, Mr and Mrs Discobbolos, runcible spoons and a borascible person of Bangor. In Lear, language itself provides broad humour. Sometime the bigness is uncontainable, as in Gromboolian, and sometimes its bigness moves in the direction of language's capacity for innuendo. The young person of Janina, remember, smiles sweetly at her 'uncle' even as he fans off her head; she slyly refers to him as 'propitious'. Why is a person who fans off another person's head propitious? 'Propitious' suggests something positive, downright favourable and sweet. According to the young woman, her uncle is pleasing; she appreciates his fanning. His fanning is, she implies, a propitiation, an offering. The pleasure she receives from this fanning is profane.

The illustration Lear provides for this limerick communicates its own humour, some of which is obvious and some subtle. The obvious humour here is the detached head of the young person, her smile and her gesture of pleasure. But the uncle's clothes and fan are also noteworthy. The large fan (it takes two hands to manipulate it), pantaloons, pointed slippers and headpiece might remind us of a person from the east rather than the west, despite the fact that Janina is a city in Greece. In other words, Lear's limerick with its illustration just might reflect the coloniser's association of the 'other' with pleasure of a bodily kind. Lear's work participates in a familiar orientalism. The humour here is a way of managing something, most likely fear of the other and fear of sexuality. We have masculine images associated with the young woman (her hair with its topknot and feather, looking like an ink bottle and quill pen), and feminine images associated with the male (the fan and distinctive dress). The colonial implications suggest a fear of women, sexuality and the foreign.

We might think of Lear's menagerie and his eccentric characters as grotesques. The grotesque is funny when it reaches beyond pathos and fear. And the humourous grotesque is more often than not reflected in caricature. Many of the characters in William Makepeace Thackeray's *The Rose and the Ring* (1855) are caricatures, their grotesque appearance manifesting itself both in literary onomastics (the study of proper names) and in illustrations that owe something to the Punch and Judy tradition. We have Gruffanuff, Glumboso, Doctor Pildrafto, Baron Sleibootz, the princes Bulbo and Giglio, King Padella and King Valoroso. The names work in various ways, some of which carry earthy suggestions, and some of which direct our attention to the gallery of grotesques Thackeray delivers in his drawings. In *The Rose and the Ring*, we have a character turned into a door-knocker, an example of the human turned into object that we can see in many books for children – some of William Steig's books, for example. The grotesque appears in both dismembering and transforming into object; it is also a feature of bigness. Children's literature offers many examples of the grotesque associated with bigness, from the impossibly large Alice who fills a house to Raymond Briggs' Tin-Pot Generals and Iron Ladies to the various grotesqueries Harry Potter meets.

But I mean bigness in an expansive sense. We have big humour when we have grotesque moments such as the one in George MacDonald's *The Light Princess* (1864) when the Princess Makemnoit arouses one of the White Snakes of Darkness. Into a tub of water, Makemnoit tosses what appears to be a piece of dried seaweed, along with some powder. Then she grasps a 'huge bunch of a hundred rusty keys'. She sits down and begins to 'oil' each key. As she eagerly oils, behind her from the tub of water, rise 'the head and half the body of a huge grey snake':

> It grew out of the tub, waving itself backwards and forwards with a slow horizontal motion, till it reached the princess, when it laid its head upon her shoulder, and gave a low hiss in her ear. She started – but with joy; and seeing the head resting on her shoulder, drew it towards her and kissed it. Then she drew it all out of the tub, and wound it round her body.[11]

With the snake coiled round her body, Makemnoit marches off to the cellar muttering to herself: 'This *is* worth living for!' We might recall that John Ruskin fretted over an earlier passage in the story in which talk of uplift, fall and elevation struck him as too suggestive of a certain kind of bodily pleasure not to be spoken of in front of children.[12] His silence on the passage before us may just indicate that MacDonald here rendered him speechless. And MacDonald does not finish here; less than a page later we read of the snake moving its head back and forth 'with a slow oscillating motion', until it suddenly darts to the roof and clings to it 'with its mouth'. The snake hangs there, 'like a huge leech, sucking at the stone', for seven days and seven nights. The snake's capacity for sucking is prodigious, perhaps even sublime. The seven days and nights are either a parodic touch or an indication of something creative (or procreative) going on.[13]

The humour here might have some connection with the humour we are supposed to find in the cavorting of seventeen-year-old Sandra Francy in Melvin Burgess' *Lady: My Life as a Bitch* (2001). The humour in this book, in carnivalesque manner, derives from the connection of the human animal with the non-human animal. Sandra finds herself transformed into a dog and Burgess tries to have fun with the freely expressive animal body. Sandra at one point plops herself down in the middle of the street and proceeds to lick her genitals. Late in the book, in a rather improbable scene, Sandra, in her dog form, awkwardly and laboriously dresses herself and applies lipstick in order to communicate to her family that, despite appearances to the contrary, she really is her parents' loving daughter. Clearly, the comedy in this book serves to remind us of just how important the body is to the human condition. What is less clear is how we are to take carnival in this book. Laughter is big when it is King, and in *Lady: My Life as a Bitch*, laughter is King.

I refer here to a central passage in Bram Stoker's *Dracula* (1897). In this novel, a young innocent woman, Lucy Westenra, apparently dies after a strange wasting away. Only one person in the novel, Dr Van Helsing, understands just exactly what has happened to Lucy – that she is, in fact, not truly dead, but more accurately 'undead', a vampire. At Lucy's funeral, Van Helsing begins to laugh, and he laughs loudly and uncontrollably. His friend, Dr Seward, is outraged at such behaviour, and asks for an explanation for the offensive outburst. In reply, Van Helsing launches into a long speech concerning what he calls 'King Laugh'. He goes on for a page or two before he comes directly to the point in his final short sentence. He laughs, he says, 'Because I know'.[14]

The humour that King Laugh produces is neither the humour of carnival, nor the playful humour we associate with children. What I mean to say is that the humour prompting King Laugh may serve both official and unofficial ends. In either case, it is brash and its brashness at least pretends to subversion. A book such as Henrik Drescher's *Pat the Beastie: A Pull-and-Poke Book* (1993) has fun with Dorothy Kunhardt's *Pat the Bunny: A Touch-and-Feel Book* (1940), but I'm not sure that pulling and poking are any more fun or funny than touching and feeling. But we are supposed to find *Pat the Beastie* parodic; it challenges our sense of decorum. Lots of books for children present themselves as indecorous; they wish to appeal to the pirate instinct in the child-reader. Kerry Mallan notes that 'humorous literature' invites the young reader 'to view people and their actions in ways which tend to reveal discrepancies between expectations and reality'. She goes on to say that children will find in humorous literature 'the accepted order frequently turned upside down', and consequently 'humorous literature can be seen as quite subversive, demanding critical readers who do not passively accept what they read'.[15] I would like to believe this. I suspect, however, that ostensibly subversive humour serves to satisfy the urge to question and resist. How can anyone resist Jon Scieszka and Lane Smith's *The Stinky Cheese Man* (1992) or Dav Pilkey's *Captain Underpants* (1997) or Roald Dahl's *Revolting Rhymes* (1982)? These ostensibly outrageous works just may serve to satisfy the rebellious spirit rather than activate it.

The point is that much humour for children is exaggerated, fantasy writ large, a reminder of the monstrous and the freakish. The freakish serves, as Susan Stewart asserts, to normalise the person reading about or looking at the freak, 'as much as it marks the freak as an aberration'. The freak is, she adds, 'tied to the cultural other', and she might have added to the psychic other as well.[16] The freak is, arguably, precisely the character the reader wishes to be. The freak is the reader's fantasy, in both a positive and a negative sense. The freak is often, although not always, freakish because of scale, especially large scale. When the giant or monster fascinates, it does so because it beckons from the territory of what Jacques Lacan calls 'the Real'. The Real is that which beckons us and frightens us; it both gives us identity and subverts identity. The Real is sublime in that it both attracts and repels.

While we are in Lacanian territory, I note that Lacan, unlike Freud, suggests that human cognition 'aims at not knowing certain things'. Robert Pfaller expands on this:

> A large number of thought experiments in literature and film, therefore, deal not with the principles of an unfamiliar world ... that enriches our previous knowledge, but with our present world in a recognizably distorted, parodic way: That is why the preamble 'How would it be if ...' is simply a charming disguise for the statement: 'That is how it is here and now.'[17]

I might return to Sandra Francy for a moment to scamper across this Lacanian territory. *Lady: My Life as a Bitch* ends with Sandra, in the form of a dog, facing rejection from her family. She cowers in her second-floor bedroom, both accepting of what she is (a young person with the desire to act outside convention) and unable to be the person she might truly wish to be (human and yet with the freedom of the bitch). Out of the window she can hear the two dogs (former humans) Fella and Mitch, encouraging her to jump and run with them. She goes to the window and it is open a crack, just enough for her to nudge her canine nose under the opening and raise it high enough so that she can pass through it. And she does. The book ends with her posterior disappearing out the window. What are we to make of this? Inside we have the human family; outside we have the dogs and the hunt and the animal delight in a life lived for the moment. Inside we have the law of the father; outside we have, perhaps, *jouissance* of some kind. But what kind? Outside the window what waits for Sandra is the Real, a world of swirling and running and energetic chaos. Outside the window she may defecate wherever she likes, but she will also lose her memory and her capability to rationalise. She may have fun, but she will not understand why she is having fun. In other words, outside the window is a world akin to death from a human point of view. In her freakish state, Sandra can have what she desires – *jouissance* – but at what price? This is the world as it is: we can have what we want, but at what price?

Burgess is clever enough not to follow Sandra out of the window. He leaves us at the sill, silly with wonder, and inside the symbolic arena where language must substitute for what Sandra appears to have. And where reason occupies the front row. Humour reminds us of the appeal of imaginative exuberance, but as nonsense and fantasy it contains its exuberance in a rational structure. We do not so much learn anything from the story of Sandra Francy, as recognise in this story the world as it is – a dog's life. Faced with this view of the world, we can only laugh, like Van Helsing.

We have, however, another kind of humour: gentle humour. Gentle humour allows us to laugh at a Bear of very little brain or find amusement in the frolic of a little boy and a Snowman. Just look at Raymond Briggs' *The Man* (1992). Here's the story of a little person who speaks in bold letters, sometimes in upper-case bold letters, and who threatens to burn down a house. The interaction between the boy and the little man in Briggs' book gives us a humorous treatment of familiar themes: tolerance, manners and stock assumptions. This humour deals mainly with the private rather than the public. The small man represents interior space; he is the common person. In *The Man*, as always, Briggs concerns himself with familiar things made recognisable. Humour has a deeply humanistic function. And the small size of characters such as the Man or Winnie-the-Pooh remind us that the body need not be large to have large desires or hopes or ambitions. The body need not always be large or frenetic in expending its energy.

We find gentle humour in work by the likes of Dorothy Kilner, Sarah Trimmer, Mary Wollstonecraft and Maria Edgeworth. Take, for example, Edgeworth's story 'The Most Unfortunate Day of My Life'. Young Robert can never stick to one task; he is continuously changing his mind and leaving off one thing to take up another. Of course, his business creates minor havoc. He leaves feathers and string on the carpet in the drawing room, and when 'two remarkably neat, nice elderly ladies' come to visit, their feet are entangled in the string and their dresses are covered in bits of feathers. Edgeworth treats Robert's difficulties with good humour rather than blunt disapproval. Edgeworth's stories of Rosamond, the best known of which is 'The Purple Jar' (1796), turn on conversations, often the conversations between Rosamond and her mother. What good is, after all, a book without conversations? The conversations in Edgeworth's stories point forward to the conversations we have between 'adult' characters such as the Duchess or the Mad Hatter and Alice. They turn on particular reasoning, and the humour derives from the twists and turns of this reasoning as young Rosamond tries to come to decisions on whether to plant this seed or that, to choose this plum or that, or to choose a purple jar instead of a pair of shoes.

A different kind of gentle humour relates to what we have already seen as brash humour. Note, for example, the fun in Sir Roger L'Estrange's 1692 translation of Aesop. Much of the fun of L'Estrange's translation derives from language, as we might expect, but situations too have their humour. My favourite of the fables is the short one entitled 'Apples and Horse-Turds':

> Upon a very great Fall of Rain, the Current carry'd Away a Huge Heap of *Apples*, together with a Dunghill that lay in the Water-Course. They Floated a good while together like Brethren and Companions; and as they went thus Dancing down the stream, the *Horse-Turds* would be every foot crying out still, Alack a day! How wee *Apples Swim*![18]

The fable's expected lesson – here the horse-turds pretend to be what they are not – finds expression in a pleasurable dip into scatology. L'Estrange's version of Aesop is instructive because it combines a number of elements relating to humour that we can identify in children's literature across history. I have mentioned scatology, and, as we have seen, scatology continues to inform much humour for children as pleasurable instruction. The verbal ingenuity of this fable is also a feature we continue to see in children's books, as the work of William Steig makes abundantly clear. Simple inflations such as 'water-course' for 'stream', the pun inherent in the 'dancing' turds crying out 'every foot', and the energetic colloquialism of 'Alack a day' contribute to the linguistic bounce of this short fable. Limited though it may be in this fable, verbal humour continues to entertain young readers, as a glance at the verbal play in a book such as Daniel Pinkwater's *Slaves of Spiegel* (1982) will illustrate.

The dancing turds also remind us of energy emanating from kinetic bodies. Much fun for children derives from active rather than passive behaviour. Here the dancing turds are a satire of false pretence and bodies performing duplicity. They may float and cavort among the apples, but like the emperor in his new clothes they cannot hide their true nature. Although parody is more prominent in children's literature (and we might almost see 'Apples and Horse-Turds' as a parody of the fable), true satire does occur. Take, for example, Dr Seuss' *Yertle the Turtle* (1950), a story that is both a parody of the Brothers Grimm story 'The Fisherman and His Wife' and also a satire of political ambition and unjust desire for power. Satire and parody deserve separate scrutiny. Here, however, it will be sufficient for me to point out that much humour for young readers finds expression in satire and parody. Examples abound, but I might just note the work of John Scieszka and Lane Smith (*The Stinky Cheese Man and Other Fairly Stupid Tales*) because of its clear intertextuality. Satire and parody thrive on the interconnectedness of literature, and much of the fun young readers have in reading satiric and parodic books derives from the game of spotting the intertextual connection. 'Spot the reference' has always been a feature of children's books, but the game has virtually taken over much contemporary literature for children. And now intertextual connections are made not only to literature, but to the full range of cultural production. Two examples will suffice: the picture book *Willy's Pictures* (2003) by Anthony Browne takes art history for its parodic subject, and Brian Selznick's *The Invention of Hugo Cabret* (2007) depends upon the reader's knowledge of literature, art, film and film history.

Humour in children's literature comes in a variety of forms, both verbal and visual. A taxonomy is useful, but perhaps we can collapse the various forms into their ultimate destination: the body. Just as the body is the source of so much humour for children, so too is the body the destination for this humour; it is subject and object. The question is: just what is the body supposed to do when it receives humorous communication from books? My question might well initiate an investigation into the politics of laughter. Without embarking on such an investigation, I note here that the various forms of humour from nonsense to parody, from reversal to exaggeration, ostensibly have both a participatory and a liberatory function. I say 'ostensibly' because the various forms of humour also may function to put quietness on the reader. The appeal of humour is its call to bodily pleasure, a pleasure that serves either quietness or thunder.

NOTES

1. Patricia Demers (ed.), *From Instruction to Delight. An Anthology of Children's Literature to 1815*, 2nd edn (Don Mills, ON: Oxford University Press, 2004), p. 84.
2. Demers (ed.), *From Instruction to Delight*, p. 83.
3. Dav Pilkey, *Kat Kong* (New York: Harcourt, 1993), unpaginated.
4. Mary Norton, *The Complete Adventures of the Borrowers* (New York: Harcourt, Brace and World, 1967), p. 291.
5. Susan Stewart, *On Longing: Narratives of the Miniature, the Gigantic, the Souvenir, the Collection* (Durham, NC: Duke University Press, 1993), p. xii.
6. Julius Lester, *John Henry*, pictures by Jerry Pinkney (New York: Dial, 1994), unpaginated.
7. Catherine Sinclair, *Holiday House: A Book for the Young* (1839; London: Hamish Hamilton, 1972), p. 127.
8. Sinclair, *Holiday House*, pp. 128–30.
9. Edward Lear, *The Complete Nonsense of Edward Lear* (New York: Dover, 1951), p. 186.
10. Quoted in John Rieder, 'Edward Lear's Limericks: The Function of Children's Nonsense Poetry', *Children's Literature*, 26 (1998), 47–60 (p. 47).
11. George MacDonald, *The Light Princess*, ill. Maurice Sendak (1864; New York: Farrar, Straus, and Giroux, 1969), p. 74.
12. See William Raeper, *George MacDonald* (Tring: Lion Publishing, 1987), pp. 222–3.
13. MacDonald, *Light Princess*, pp. 74–6.
14. Bram Stoker, *Dracula* (London: Archibald Constable and Company, 1897), pp. 177–80.
15. Kerry Mallan, *Laugh Lines: Exploring Humour in Children's Literature* (Newtown, NSW: Primary English Teaching Association, 1993), p. 18.
16. Stewart, *On Longing*, p. 109.
17. Robert Pfaller, 'The Familiar Unknown, the Uncanny, the Comic: The Aesthetic Effects of the Thought Experiment', in *Lacan: The Silent Partners*, ed. Slavoj Žižek (London: Verso, 2006), pp. 198–216 (p. 201).
18. Sir Roger L'Estrange, *Fables of Æsop and Other Eminent Mythologists with Morals and Reflexions* (London: R. Sare et al., 1692), p. 124.

FURTHER READING

General studies

Avery, Gillian, *Behold the Child: American Children and Their Books 1621–1922*, Baltimore: Johns Hopkins University Press, 1994

Avery, Gillian, and Julia Briggs (eds.), *Children and their Books: A Celebration of the Work of Iona and Peter Opie*, Oxford: Clarendon, 1989

Carpenter, Humphrey, *Secret Gardens: A Study of the Golden Age of Children's Literature*, London: Unwin, 1985

Darton, F. J. Harvey, *Children's Books in England: Five Centuries of Social Life*, 3rd edn, rev. Brian Alderson, London: British Library, 1999

Dusinberre, Juliet, *Alice to the Lighthouse: Children's Books and Radical Experiments in Art*, London: Macmillan, 1987

Grenby, M. O., *Children's Literature*, Edinburgh: Edinburgh University Press, 2008

Hunt, Peter, *An Introduction to Children's Literature*, Oxford: Oxford University Press, 1994

Immel, Andrea, and Michael Witmore (eds.), *Childhood and Children's Books in Early Modern Europe, 1550–1800*, New York: Routledge, 2006

Lerer, Seth, *Children's Literature: A Reader's History from Aesop to Harry Potter*, Chicago: University of Chicago Press, 2008

Lurie, Alison, *Not in Front of the Grown-Ups: The Subversive Power of Children's Literature*, London: Bloomsbury, 1990

McGavran, James (ed.), *Romanticism and Children's Literature in the Nineteenth Century*, Athens, GA: University of Georgia Press, 1991

Marcus, Leonard S., *Minders of Make-believe: Idealists, Entrepreneurs and the Shaping of American Children's Literature*, Boston: Houghton Mifflin, 2008

O'Malley, Andrew, *The Making of the Modern Child: Children's Literature and Childhood in the Late Eighteenth Century*, New York: Routledge, 2003

Pickering, Samuel F., Jr, *John Locke and Children's Books in Eighteenth-Century England*, Knoxville: University of Tennessee Press, 1981

Reynolds, Kimberley, *Radical Children's Literature: Future Visions and Aesthetic Transformations in Juvenile Fiction*, Basingstoke: Palgrave, 2007

Richardson, Alan, *Literature, Education, and Romanticism: Reading as Social Practice, 1780–1832*, Cambridge: Cambridge University Press, 1994

Stephens, John, *Language and Ideology in Children's Fiction*, London: Longman, 1992

Chapter 1 (The origins of children's literature)

Adams, Gillian, 'Ancient and Medieval Children's Texts', in Peter Hunt (ed.), *International Companion Encyclopedia of Children's Literature*, 2nd edn, 2 vols., London: Routledge, 2004, vol. I, pp. 225–38

Alderson, Brian, 'New Playthings and Gigantick Histories: The Nonage of English Children's Books', *Princeton University Library Chronicle*, 60 (1999), 178–95

Arizpe, Evelyn, and Morag Styles, with Shirley Brice Heath, *Reading Lessons from the Eighteenth Century: Mothers, Children and Texts*, Lichfield: Pied Piper, 2006

Grenby, M. O., 'Chapbooks, Children, and Children's Literature', *The Library*, 8 (2007), 277–303

Hunt, Peter, 'Passing on the Past: The Problem of Books that Are for Children and that Were for Children', *Children's Literature Association Quarterly*, 21 (1996–7), 200–2

King, Margaret L. 'Concepts of Childhood: What We Know and Where We Might Go', *Renaissance Quarterly*, 60 (2007), 371–407

Lerer, Seth, *Chaucer and his Readers: Imagining the Author in Late-Medieval England*, Princeton: Princeton University Press, 1993

Morgenstern, John, 'The Rise of Children's Literature Reconsidered', *Children's Literature Association Quarterly*, 26 (2001), 64–73

Plumb, J. H., 'The New World of Children in Eighteenth-Century England', *Past and Present*, 67 (1975), 64–95

Shaner, Mary E., 'Instruction and Delight: Medieval Romances as Children's Literature', *Poetics Today*, 13 (1992), 5–15

Shefrin, Jill, '"Governesses to their Children": Royal and Aristocratic Mothers Educating Daughters in the Reign of George III', in Andrea Immel and Michael Witmore (eds.), *Childhood and Children's Books in Early Modern Europe, 1550–1800*, New York: Routledge, 2006, pp. 181–211

Sommerville, C. John, *The Discovery of Childhood in Puritan England*, Athens, GA: University of Georgia Press, 1992

Wooden, Warren W., *Children's Literature and the English Renaissance*, ed. Jeanie Watson, Lexington: University Press of Kentucky, 1986

Chapter 2 (Children's books and constructions of childhood)

Fass, Paula S. (ed.), *Encyclopedia of Children and Childhood in History and Society*, New York: Macmillan Reference, 2004

Gupta, Suman, 'Sociological Speculations on the Professions of Children's Literature', *The Lion and the Unicorn*, 29 (2005), 299–323

Hollindale, Peter, *Signs of Childness in Children's Books*, Stroud: Thimble Press, 1997

Lesnik-Oberstein, Karín, *Children's Literature: Criticism and the Fictional Child*, Oxford: Clarendon Press, 1994

Matthews, Gareth B., *The Philosophy of Childhood*, Cambridge, MA: Harvard University Press, 1994

Pennac, Daniel, *The Rights of the Reader*, trans. Sarah Adams, London: Walker Books, 2006

Rose, Jacqueline, *The Case of Peter Pan or the Impossibility of Children's Fiction*, London: Macmillan, 1984

Spufford, Francis, *The Child that Books Built: A Life in Reading*, New York: Metropolitan Books, 2002

Turner, Susan M., and Gareth B. Matthews, *The Philosopher's Child: Critical Essays in the Western Tradition*, New York: University of Rochester Press, 1998

Zelizer, Viviana, *The Priceless Child: The Changing Social Value of Children*, Princeton, NJ: Princeton University Press, 1994

Zipes, Jack, *Sticks and Stones: The Troublesome Success of Children's Literature from Slovenly Peter to Harry Potter*, New York: Routledge, 2001

Chapter 3 *(The making of children's books)*

Alderson, Brian. 'Novelty Books and Movables: Questions of Terminology', *Children's Books History Society Newsletter*, 61 (1998), 14–22

Alderson, Brian, and Felix de Marez Oyens, *Be Merry and Wise: The Origins of Children's Book Publishing in England, 1650–1850*, New Castle, DE: Oak Knoll Press, 2006

Gaskell, Philip, *A New Introduction to Bibliography*, Oxford: Clarendon Press, 1972

Glaister, Geoffrey Ashall, *Encyclopedia of the Book*, 2nd edn with a new introduction by Donald Farren, New Castle, DE: Oak Knoll Press, 2001

Jennet, Seán, *The Making of Books*, 5th edn, London: Faber & Faber, 1973

McLean, Ruari, *Victorian Book Design and Colour Printing*, 2nd edn, London: Faber, 1972

Chapter 4 *(Picture-book worlds and ways of seeing)*

Alderson, Brian, *Sing a Song of Sixpence: The English Picture-Book Tradition and Randolph Caldecott*, Cambridge: Cambridge University Press, 1986

Bader, Barbara, *American Picturebooks: From Noah's Ark to the Beast Within*, New York: Macmillan, 1976

Nikolajeva, Maria, and Carole Scott, *How Picturebooks Work*, New York: Routledge, 2006

Nodelman, Perry, *Words About Pictures: The Narrative Art of Children's Picture Books*, Athens, GA: University of Georgia Press, 1988

Spitz, Ellen Handler, *Inside Picture Books*, New Haven, CT: Yale University Press, 1999

Steiner, Evgeny, *Stories for Little Comrades: Revolutionary Artists and the Making of Early Soviet Children's Books*, trans. Jane Ann Miller, Seattle: University of Washington Press, 1999

Trumpener, Katie, 'City Scenes: Commerce, Modernity, and the Birth of the Picture Book', in Richard Maxwell (ed.), *The Victorian Illustrated Book: New Explorations*, Charlottesville, VA: University of Virginia Press, 2002, pp. 332–84

Whalley, Joyce Irene, and Tessa Rose Chester, *The History of Children's Book Illustration*, London: John Murray with the Victoria and Albert Museum, 1988

Chapter 5 *(The fear of poetry)*

Flynn, Richard, 'Consolation Prize', *Signal*, 100 (2003), 66–83

Rubin, Joan Sherley, *Songs of Ourselves: The Uses of Poetry in America*, Cambridge, MA: Harvard University Press, 2007

Rukeyser, Muriel, *The Life of Poetry*, Ashfield, MA: Paris Press, 1996

Sloan, Glenna, 'But Is It Poetry?' *Children's Literature in Education*, 32 (2001), 45–56

Sorby, Angela, *Schoolroom Poets: Childhood and the Place of American Poetry, 1865–1917*, Durham, NH: University of New Hampshire Press, 2005

Styles, Morag, *From the Garden to the Street: Three Hundred Years of Poetry for Children*, London: Cassell, 1998

Thomas, Joseph T., Jr, *Poetry's Playground: The Culture of Contemporary American Children's Poetry*, Detroit, MI: Wayne State University Press, 2007

Chapter 6: (Retelling stories across time and cultures)

Beckett, Sandra L., *Recycling Red Riding Hood*, New York: Routledge, 2002

Chaston, Joel D., 'Baum, Bakhtin, and Broadway: A Centennial Look at the Carnival of Oz', *The Lion and the Unicorn*, 25 (2001), 128–49

Gates, Geoffrey, '"Always the Outlaw": The Potential for Subversion of the Metanarrative in Retellings of Robin Hood', *Children's Literature in Education*, 37 (2006), 69–79

McCallum, Robyn, 'Film Adaptations of Children's and Young Adult Literature', in *The Oxford Encyclopedia of Children's Literature*, 4 vols., New York: Oxford University Press, 2006, vol. II, pp. 73–7

Stephens, John, and Robyn McCallum, *Retelling Stories, Framing Culture: Traditional Story and Metanarratives in Children's Literature*, New York: Garland Publishing Inc., 1998

Wagner, Geoffrey, *The Novel and the Cinema*, Rutherford, NJ: Fairleigh Dickinson University Press, 1975

Chapter 7: (Classics and canons)

Cai, Mingshui, *Multicultural Literature for Children and Young Adults: Reflections on Critical Issues*, Westport, CT: Greenwood, 2002

Clark, Beverly Lyon, *Kiddie Lit: The Cultural Construction of Children's Literature in America*, Baltimore: Johns Hopkins University Press, 2003

Gorak, Jan (ed.), *Canon vs. Culture: Reflections on the Current Debate*, New York: Garland, 2001

Lundin, Anne, *Constructing the Canon of Children's Literature: Beyond Library Walls and Ivory Towers*, New York: Routledge, 2004

Morrissey, Lee, *Debating the Canon: A Reader from Addison to Nafisi*, New York: Palgrave Macmillan, 2005

Stevenson, Deborah, 'Sentiment and Significance: The Impossibility of Recovery in the Children's Literature Canon; or, the Drowning of *The Water-Babies*', *The Lion and the Unicorn*, 21 (1997), 112–30

Stimpson, Catharine R., 'Reading for Love: Canons, Paracanons, and Whistling Jo March', *New Literary History*, 21 (1990), 957–76

Chapter 8 (Learning to be literate)

Fischer, Steven Roger, *History of Reading*, London: Reaktion Books, 2003

Meek, Margaret, *On Being Literate*, London: Bodley Head, 1991

Monaghan, E. Jennifer, *Learning to Read and Write in Colonial America*, Amherst and Boston: University of Massachusetts Press, 2005

Nel, Philip, *Dr. Seuss: American Icon*, New York: Continuum, 2004

Salmon, David, *The Practical Parts of Lancaster's Improvements and Bell's Experiment*, Cambridge: Cambridge University Press, 1932

Spufford, Margaret, *Small Books and Pleasant Histories*, London: Methuen, 1981

Waterland, Liz, *Read with Me*, Stroud: Thimble Press, 1985

Chapter 9 (Gender roles in children's fiction)

Clark, Beverly Lyon, and Margaret R. Higonnet (eds.), *Girls, Boys, Books, Toys: Gender in Children's Literature and Culture*, Baltimore: Johns Hopkins University Press, 1999

Kidd, Kenneth B., *Making American Boys: Boyology and the Feral Tale*, Minneapolis: University of Minnesota Press, 2004

Knoepflmacher, U. C., *Ventures into Childland: Victorians, Fairy Tales, and Femininity*, Chicago and London: University of Chicago Press, 1998

Lehr, Susan (ed.), *Beauty, Brains, and Brawn: The Construction of Gender in Children's Literature*, Portsmouth, NH: Heinemann, 2001

Levstik, Linda S. '"I am no lady!": The Tomboy in Children's Fiction', *Children's Literature in Education*, 14 (1983), 14–20

Mitchell, Sally, *The New Girl: Girls' Culture in England, 1880–1915*, New York: Columbia University Press, 1995

Nelson, Claudia, *Boys Will Be Girls: The Feminine Ethic and British Children's Fiction, 1857–1917*, New Brunswick: Rutgers University Press, 1991

Paul, Lissa, 'Enigma Variations: What Feminist Criticism Knows about Children's Literature', *Signal*, 54 (1987), 186–202

Reynolds, Kim, *Girls Only? Gender and Popular Children's Fiction in Britain, 1880–1910*, Hemel Hempstead: Harvester Wheatsheaf, 1990

Richardson, Alan, 'Reluctant Lords and Lame Princes: Engendering the Male Child in Nineteenth-Century Juvenile Fiction', *Children's Literature in Education*, 21 (1993), 3–19

Stephens, John, 'Gender, Genre and Children's Literature', *Signal*, 79 (1996), 17–30

Vallone, Lynne, *Disciplines of Virtue: Girls' Culture in the Eighteenth and Nineteenth Centuries*, New Haven, CT: Yale University Press, 1995

Chapter 10 (Children's texts and the grown-up reader)

Beckett, Sandra (ed.), *Transcending Boundaries: Writing For A Dual Audience of Children and Adults*, New York: Garland, 1999

Gubar, Marah, *Artful Dodgers: Reconceiving the Golden Age of Children's Literature*, Oxford: Oxford University Press, 2008

Knoepflmacher, U. C., 'Kipling's "Just-So" Partner: The Dead Child as Collaborator and Muse', *Children's Literature*, 25 (1997), 24–49

Kuznets, Lois R., 'Permutations of Frame in Mary Norton's Borrowers Series', *Studies in the Literary Imagination*, 18 (1985), 65–78

Chapter 11 (Ideas of difference in children's literature)

Keith, Lois, *Take Up Thy Bed and Walk: Death, Disability and Cure in Classic Fiction for Girls*, New York: Routledge, 2001

McGillis, Roderick (ed.), *Voices of the Other: Children's Literature and the Postcolonial Context*, New York: Garland, 1999

Pace, Patricia, 'The Body-in-Writing: Miniatures in Mary Norton's *The Borrowers*', *Text and Performance Quarterly*, 11 (1991), 279–90

Sands-O'Connor, Karen, 'Why are People Different? Multiracial Families in Picture Books and the Dialogue of Difference', *The Lion and the Unicorn*, 25 (2001), 337–426

Swartz, Patti Capel, 'Bridging Multicultural Education: Bringing Sexual Orientation into the Children's and Young Adult Literature Classrooms', *Radical Teaching: A Socialist, Feminist, and Anti-Racist Journal on the Theory and Practice of Teaching*, 66 (2003), 11–16

Chapter 12 (Changing families in children's fiction)

Coontz, Stephanie, *The Way We Never Were: American Families and the Nostalgia Trap*, New York: Basic Books, 1992

Davin, Anna, 'Waif Stories in Late Nineteenth-Century England', *History Workshop Journal*, 52 (2001), 67–98

Gamble, Nikki, and Nicholas Tucker, *Family Fictions*, London: Continuum, 2001

Hareven, Tamara K., *Families, History, and Social Change: Life-Course and Cross-Cultural Perspectives*, Boulder, CO: Perseus Books, 2000

Humble, Nicola, 'Eccentric Families in the Fiction of Adolescence from the 1920s to the 1940s', in K. Reynolds (ed.), *Childhood Remembered*, Lichfield: Pied Piper Publishing, 2003

Schor, Juliet B., *Born to Buy: The Commercialized Child and the New Consumer Culture*, New York: Scribner, 2004

Thiel, Elizabeth, *The Fantasy of Family: Nineteenth-Century Children's Literature and the Myth of the Domestic Ideal*, London: Routledge, 2007

Chapter 13 (Traditions of the school story)

Auchmuty, Rosemary, and Joy Wotton (eds.), *The Encyclopaedia of School Stories*, 2 vols., Aldershot: Ashgate, 2000

Briggs, Julia, '"Delightful Task!" Women, Children, and Reading in the Mid-Eighteenth Century', in Donelle Ruwe (ed.), *Culturing the Child 1690–1914: Essays in Memory of Mitzi Myers*, Lanham, MD: Scarecrow Press, 2005, pp. 67–85

Cadogan, Mary, and Patricia Craig, *You're a Brick, Angela!: The Girls' School Story 1839–1985*, London: Gollancz, 1986

Grenby, M. O., *Children's Literature*, Edinburgh: Edinburgh University Press, 2008

Pickering, Samuel F., Jr, 'Allegory and the First School Stories', in Joseph H. Smith and William Kerrigan (eds.), *Opening Texts: Psychoanalysis and the Culture of the Child*, Baltimore: Johns Hopkins University Press, 1985, pp. 42–68.

Quigly, Isabel, *The Heirs of Tom Brown: The English School Story*, London: Chatto and Windus, 1982
Richards, Jeffrey, *Happiest Days: The Public Schools in English Fiction*, Manchester: Manchester University Press, 1988

Chapter 14 *(Fantasy's alternative geography for children)*

Attebury, Brian, *Strategies of Fantasy*, Bloomington: Indiana University Press, 1992
Jones, Raymond E. (ed.), *E. Nesbit's Psammead Trilogy: A Children's Classic at 100*, Lanham, MD: Scarecrow Press, 2006
Lenz, Millicent, and Carole Scott (eds.), *His Dark Materials Illuminated: Critical Essays on Philip Pullman's Trilogy*, Detroit, MI: Wayne State University Press, 2005
Mendlesohn, Farah, *Rhetorics of Fantasy*, Middletown, CT: Wesleyan University Press, 2008
Nikolajeva, Maria, 'Fairy Tale and Fantasy: From Archaic to Postmodern', *Marvels & Tales*, 17 (2003), 138–56
Sammons, Martha C., *'A better country': The Worlds of Religious Fantasy and Science Fiction*, New York: Greenwood Press, 1988

Chapter 15 *(Animal and object stories)*

Baker, Steve, *Picturing the Beast: Animals, Identity and Representation*, Manchester: Manchester University Press, 1993
Blackwell, Mark (ed.), *The Secret Life of Things: Animals, Objects, and It-Narratives in Eighteenth-Century England*, Lewisburg: Bucknell University Press, 2007
Cosslet, Tess, *Talking Animals in British Children's Fiction, 1786–1914*, Aldershot: Ashgate, 2006
Fudge, Erica, *Animal*, London: Reaktion Books, 2002
Kuznets, Lois R., *When Toys Come Alive: Narratives of Animation, Metamorphosis and Development*, London: Yale University Press, 1994
Ritvo, Harriet, *The Animal Estate: The English and Other Creatures in the Victorian Period*, Cambridge, MA: Harvard University Press, 1987

Chapter 16 *(Humour and the body in children's literature)*

Lypp, Maria, 'The Origin and Function of Laughter in Children's Literature', in Maria Nikolajeva (ed.), *Aspects and Issues in the History of Children's Literature*, Westport, CT: Greenwood, 1995, pp. 183–9
McGillis, Roderick, 'Coprophilia for Kids: The Culture of Grossness', in Kerry Mallan and Sharyn Pearce (eds.), *Youth Cultures: Texts, Images, and Identities*, London: Praeger, 2003, 183–96
Mallan, Kerry, *Laugh Lines: Exploring Humour in Children's Literature*, Newtown, NSW: Primary English Teaching Association, 1993
Wolfenstein, Martha, *Children's Humour: A Psychological Analysis*, Bloomington, IN: Indiana University Press, 1978

INDEX

Cambridge Companions To...

AUTHORS

Edward Albee *edited by Stephen J. Bottoms*

Margaret Atwood *edited by Coral Ann Howells*

W. H. Auden *edited by Stan Smith*

Jane Austen *edited by Edward Copeland and Juliet McMaster*

Beckett *edited by John Pilling*

Aphra Behn *edited by Derek Hughes and Janet Todd*

Walter Benjamin *edited by David S. Ferris*

William Blake *edited by Morris Eaves*

Brecht *edited by Peter Thomson and Glendyr Sacks* (second edition)

The Brontës *edited by Heather Glen*

Frances Burney *edited by Peter Sabor*

Byron *edited by Drummond Bone*

Albert Camus *edited by Edward J. Hughes*

Willa Cather *edited by Marilee Lindemann*

Cervantes *edited by Anthony J. Cascardi*

Chaucer, *second edition edited by Piero Boitani and Jill Mann*

Chekhov *edited by Vera Gottlieb and Paul Allain*

Kate Chopin *edited by Janet Beer*

Coleridge *edited by Lucy Newlyn*

Wilkie Collins *edited by Jenny Bourne Taylor*

Joseph Conrad *edited by J. H. Stape*

Dante *edited by Rachel Jacoff* (second edition)

Daniel Defoe *edited by John Richetti*

Don DeLillo *edited by John N. Duvall*

Charles Dickens *edited by John O. Jordan*

Emily Dickinson *edited by Wendy Martin*

John Donne *edited by Achsah Guibbory*

Dostoevskii *edited by W. J. Leatherbarrow*

Theodore Dreiser *edited by Leonard Cassuto and Claire Virginia Eby*

John Dryden *edited by Steven N. Zwicker*

W. E. B. Du Bois *edited by Shamoon Zamir*

George Eliot *edited by George Levine*

T. S. Eliot *edited by A. David Moody*

Ralph Ellison *edited by Ross Posnock*

Ralph Waldo Emerson *edited by Joel Porte and Saundra Morris*

William Faulkner *edited by Philip M. Weinstein*

Henry Fielding *edited by Claude Rawson*

F. Scott Fitzgerald *edited by Ruth Prigozy*

Flaubert *edited by Timothy Unwin*

E. M. Forster *edited by David Bradshaw*

Benjamin Franklin *edited by Carla Mulford*

Brian Friel *edited by Anthony Roche*

Robert Frost *edited by Robert Faggen*

Elizabeth Gaskell *edited by Jill L. Matus*

Goethe *edited by Lesley Sharpe*

Günter Grass *edited by Stuart Taberner*

Thomas Hardy *edited by Dale Kramer*

David Hare *edited by Richard Boon*

Nathaniel Hawthorne *edited by Richard Millington*

Seamus Heaney *edited by Bernard O'Donoghue*

Ernest Hemingway *edited by Scott Donaldson*

Homer *edited by Robert Fowler*

Ibsen *edited by James McFarlane*

Henry James *edited by Jonathan Freedman*

Samuel Johnson *edited by Greg Clingham*

Ben Jonson *edited by Richard Harp and Stanley Stewart*

James Joyce *edited by Derek Attridge* (second edition)

Kafka *edited by Julian Preece*

Keats *edited by Susan J. Wolfson*

Lacan *edited by Jean-Michel Rabaté*

D. H. Lawrence *edited by Anne Fernihough*

Primo Levi *edited by Robert Gordon*

Lucretius *edited by Stuart Gillespie and Philip Hardie*

David Mamet *edited by Christopher Bigsby*

Thomas Mann *edited by Ritchie Robertson*

Christopher Marlowe *edited by Patrick Cheney*

Herman Melville *edited by Robert S. Levine*

Arthur Miller *edited by Christopher Bigsby*

Milton *edited by Dennis Danielson* (second edition)

Molière *edited by David Bradby and Andrew Calder*

Toni Morrison *edited by Justine Tally*

Nabokov *edited by Julian W. Connolly*

Eugene O'Neill *edited by Michael Manheim*

George Orwell *edited by John Rodden*

TOPICS

The Classic Russian Novel *edited by Malcolm V. Jones and Robin Feuer Miller*

Contemporary Irish Poetry *edited by Matthew Campbell*

Crime Fiction *edited by Martin Priestman*

Early Modern Women's Writing *edited by Laura Lunger Knoppers*

The Eighteenth-Century Novel *edited by John Richetti*

Eighteenth-Century Poetry *edited by John Sitter*

English Literature, 1500–1600 *edited by Arthur F. Kinney*

English Literature, 1650–1740 *edited by Steven N. Zwicker*

English Literature, 1740–1830 *edited by Thomas Keymer and Jon Mee*

English Novelists *edited by Adrian Poole*

English Poetry, Donne to Marvell *edited by Thomas N. Corns*

English Poets *edited by Claude Rawson*

English Renaissance Drama, second edition *edited by A. R. Braunmuller and Michael Hattaway*

English Restoration Theatre *edited by Deborah C. Payne Fisk*

Feminist Literary Theory *edited by Ellen Rooney*

Fiction in the Romantic Period *edited by Richard Maxwell and Katie Trumpener*

The Fin de Siècle *edited by Gail Marshall*

The French Novel: from 1800 to the Present *edited by Timothy Unwin*

German Romanticism *edited by Nicholas Saul*

Gothic Fiction *edited by Jerrold E. Hogle*

The Greek and Roman Novel *edited by Tim Whitmarsh*

Greek and Roman Theatre *edited by Marianne McDonald and J. Michael Walton*

Greek Tragedy *edited by P. E. Easterling*

The Harlem Renaissance *edited by George Hutchinson*

The Irish Novel *edited by John Wilson Foster*

The Italian Novel *edited by Peter Bondanella and Andrea Ciccarelli*

Jewish American Literature *edited by Hana Wirth-Nesher and Michael P. Kramer*

The Latin American Novel *edited by Efraín Kristal*

The Literature of the First World War *edited by Vincent Sherry*

The Literature of World War II *edited by Marina MacKay*

Literature on Screen *edited by Deborah Cartmell and Imelda Whelehan*

Medieval English Literature *edited by Larry Scanlon*

Medieval English Theatre *edited by Richard Beadle and Alan J. Fletcher* (second edition)

Medieval French Literature *edited by Simon Gaunt and Sarah Kay*

Medieval Romance *edited by Roberta L. Krueger*

Medieval Women's Writing *edited by Carolyn Dinshaw and David Wallace*

Modern American Culture *edited by Christopher Bigsby*

Modern British Women Playwrights *edited by Elaine Aston and Janelle Reinelt*

Modern French Culture *edited by Nicholas Hewitt*

Modern German Culture *edited by Eva Kolinsky and Wilfried van der Will*

The Modern German Novel *edited by Graham Bartram*

Modern Irish Culture *edited by Joe Cleary and Claire Connolly*

Modernism *edited by Michael Levenson*

The Modernist Novel *edited by Morag Shiach*

Modernist Poetry *edited by Alex Davis and Lee M. Jenkins*

Modern Italian Culture *edited by Zygmunt G. Baranski and Rebecca J. West*

Modern Latin American Culture *edited by John King*

Modern Russian Culture *edited by Nicholas Rzhevsky*

Modern Spanish Culture *edited by David T. Gies*

Narrative *edited by David Herman*

Native American Literature *edited by Joy Porter and Kenneth M. Roemer*

Nineteenth-Century American Women's Writing *edited by Dale M. Bauer and Philip Gould*

Old English Literature *edited by Malcolm Godden and Michael Lapidge*

Performance Studies *edited by Tracy C. Davis*

Postcolonial Literary Studies *edited by Neil Lazarus*

Postmodernism *edited by Steven Connor*

Renaissance Humanism *edited by Jill Kraye*

Roman Satire *edited by Kirk Freudenburg*

The Spanish Novel: from 1600 to the Present *edited by Harriet Turner and Adelaida López de Martínez*